ASIAN LAW SERIES
School of Law
University of Washington
Number 15

ASIAN LAW SERIES

School of Law
University of Washington

The Asian Law Series was initiated in 1969, with the cooperation of the University of Washington Press and the Institute for Comparative and Foreign Area Studies (now the Henry M. Jackson School of International Studies), in order to publish the results of several projects under way in Japanese, Chinese, and Korean law. The members of the editorial committee are Jere L. Bacharach, Donald C. Clarke, Daniel H. Foote, John O. Haley (chairman), and Toshiko Takenaka.

1. *The Constitution of Japan: Its First Twenty Years, 1947–67,* edited by Dan Fenno Henderson
2. *Village "Contracts" in Tokugawa Japan,* by Dan Fenno Henderson
3. *Chinese Family Law and Social Change in Historic and Comparative Perspective,* edited by David C. Buxbaum
4. *Law and Politics in China's Foreign Trade,* edited by Victor H. Li
5. *Patent and Know-how Licensing in Japan and the United States,* edited by Teruo Doi and Warren L. Shattuck
6. *The Constitutional Case Law of Japan: Selected Supreme Court Decisions, 1961 to,* by Hiroshi Itoh and Lawrence Ward Beer
7. *Japan's Commission on the Constitution: The Final Report,* translated and edited by John M. Maki
8. *Securities Regulations in Korea: Problems and Recommendations for Feasible Reforms,* by Young Moo Shin
9. *Order and Discipline in China: The Shanghai Mixed Court 1911–27,* by Thomas B. Stephens
10. *The Economic Contract Law of China: Legitimation and Contract Autonomy in the PRC,* by Pitman B. Potter
11. *Japanese Labor Law,* by Kazuo Sugeno, translated by Leo Kanowitz
12. *Constitutional Systems in Late Twentieth Century Asia,* edited by Lawrence W. Beer
13. *Constitutional Case Law of Japan, 1970 through 1990,* edited by Lawrence W. Beer and Hiroshi Itoh
14. *The Limits of the Rule of Law in China,* edited by Karen Turner, James V. Feinerman, and R. Kent Guy
15. *Legal Reform in Tawan under Japanese Colonial Rule, 1895–1945: The Reception of Western Law,* by Tay-sheng Wang

Legal Reform in Taiwan under Japanese Colonial Rule, 1895–1945

The Reception of Western Law

TAY-SHENG WANG

UNIVERSITY OF WASHINGTON PRESS

Seattle and London

Copyright © 2000 by the University of Washington Press
First paperback edition published 2015 by the University of Washington Press
Printed and bound in the United States of America
18 17 16 15   5 4 3 2 1

All rights reserved. No part of this publication may be reproduced or transmitted in any form or by any means, electronic or mechanical, including photocopy, recording, or any information storage or retrieval system, without permission in writing from the publisher.

University of Washington Press
www.washington.edu/uwpress

Library of Congress Cataloging-in-Publication Data

Wang, T'ai-sheng
Legal reform in Taiwan under Japanese colonial rule, 1895–1945
: the reception of western law / Tay-sheng Wang
    p.   cm. — (Asian law series ; no. 15)
Includes bibliographical references and index.
ISBN 978-0-295-99447-5 (pbk. : alk. paper)
1. Law reform—Taiwan—History.
I. Title.
II. Series.
KNP46.8.W36   1999   99-26277
340'.3'0951249—dc21   CIP

The paper used in this publication is acid-free and meets the minimum requirements of American National Standard for Information Sciences—Permanence of Paper for Printed Library Materials, ANSI Z39.48–1984. ∞

Contents

Preface *vi*

Introduction *3*

1 / Background of Legal Reform *12*

2 / Reception of Western Law in Colonial Legislation *36*

3 / Modern Judiciary in the Colony *63*

4 / Criminal Justice and Changing Society *105*

5 / Westernization of Civil Justice *140*

6 / Appraisal and Legacy *170*

Conclusion *184*

Appendix A / Development of Taiwanese Law *189*

Appendix B / The Law Relating to Laws and Ordinances to Be Enforced in Taiwan *192*

Appendix C / The Civil, Commercial, and Criminal Law *195*

Appendix D / The Bandit Punishment Law *196*

Glossary *199*

Abbreviations *205*

Notes *207*

Bibliography *259*

Index *277*

Preface

The legal development of Taiwan is a topic worthy of reexamination. During the period of cold war between the West and the People's Republic of China (PRC; "Communist China"), Taiwan was distorted as "Free China"; under this republic, Taiwan's uniqueness was neglected. After the reconciliation between the United States and the PRC in the late 1970s, however, Taiwan gradually took off the mask of "China" and began to display its original characteristics. Recently, Taiwan has played an important role in the Pacific Rim as a result of its economic strength. More people are therefore interested in understanding Taiwan's story, including its legal development. It is not difficult for an observer to discover that Taiwan has a remarkably modern legal system far different from that of traditional and contemporary China. Legal modernization on Taiwan in fact has proceeded for a hundred years, beginning from the advent of Japanese rule in 1895. We cannot understand all of the factors that have shaped today's Taiwan if we continue to use the traditional China-centered viewpoint.

This study thus focuses on the Taiwanese reception of Western law under Japanese rule. It will attempt to demonstrate the extent to which Taiwanese legal concepts diverged from those of the Chinese legal tradition and moved toward those of modern Western law during the fifty-year (1895–1945) Japanese colonial period. Although I also discuss the legacy of Japanese rule facing the Chinese Nationalist (Kuomintang; KMT) regime on Taiwan after 1945, the legal modernization in Taiwan under the KMT's rule is not the main concern of this research.

The Japanese legal reform certainly allowed the Taiwanese people to become familiar with the form of many Western-style legal institutions, but the fundamental spirit of modern Western law was not yet generally known. Before the early 1920s, only a few Japanese Westernized laws were enforced in colonial Taiwan; for the most part, Taiwanese customary law was followed. During the latter period of Japanese rule, however, as a result of the colonial

PREFACE

policy of the extension of Japanese law to Taiwan, most Western-style Japanese laws were put into effect in Taiwan. Those Westernized laws in colonial legislation were effectively implemented by the modern judiciary in Taiwan and gradually penetrated into Taiwanese society, although some colonial special institutions obstructed the spread of Western law. In criminal justice, Japanese colonialists established modern state authority by ruthless suppression of Taiwanese resistance, but their actions also resolved the social disorder prevalent in Ch'ing Taiwan. The general population accepted the Western-style criminal institutions because they represented state authority, not because they were presumed just. In Taiwanese civil justice, property law was largely transformed into modern Western law. On the other hand, status law was modified by Western legal ideas only to a minor extent. Indeed, the Japanese regime was a competent reformer in Taiwan's legal modernization. However, those benefits gained from the Japanese-led legal reform came at a very high cost to the Taiwanese.

This book could not have been completed without the valuable advice and suggestions of several scholars. I am deeply indebted to Professor John O. Haley for his encouragement, intellectual stimulation, and guidance. Professors Donald C. Clarke, Dan H. Foote, Stevan Harrell, Dan F. Henderson, and Clark W. Sorensen generously gave me valuable comments at various stages. Several readers and commentators, especially Professor William C. Jones, helped me refine my argument. I wish to express my sincere appreciation to them. The mistakes that remain are my own.

I am very grateful to a number of people and institutions for their assistance in the preparation of this study as well. The Taiwan Provincial Historical Commission kindly allowed me to read the unique archives of the Japanese colonial government on Taiwan, and the Taiwan Branch of the ROC Central Library allowed me access to its abundant materials. My research received much help from able and cordial librarians, particularly the staff in the libraries of the University of Washington. Special thanks are due Wang Shih-ch'ing, a pioneer of Taiwan studies, as well as Chang Yu-chung Esq. and Judge Hung Shou-nan, two Taiwanese who served as judges during the Japanese colonial period, for their providing precious data. Meanwhile, a scholarship under the student-exchange program of the University of Washington and National Taiwan University considerably lessened my financial burden while conducting this research at Seattle. Finally, Joanne Sandstrom skillfully edited the manuscript, and University of Washington Press editor Lorri Hagman shepherded it to publication.

PREFACE

I must express my greatest gratitude to my family. My wife, Hui-lin, has firmly supported my study of Taiwanese legal history. The financial assistance of my parents assisted me during my research for the doctoral dissertation. My father unfortunately died in April of 1996 and never had an opportunity to see its publication. To the memory of my father, I dedicate this book.

Legal Reform in Taiwan under Japanese Colonial Rule, 1895–1945

INTRODUCTION

Legal Reform as an Emerging Issue in Taiwan Studies

L aw and justice in Taiwan under Japanese colonial rule have not received the attention one might expect. In the United States, the study of Taiwan's history initially began largely for the sake of Chinese studies in general.[1] Since early historians in the West regarded Taiwan's history as local Chinese history, they tended to concentrate their research on the history of Taiwan under the Ch'ing empire (1683–1895), neglecting the history of Taiwan under Japanese rule (1895–1945).[2] At that time, many American social scientists interested in the economic development or social change in postwar Taiwan ignored the history of prewar Taiwan; for the most part, they confined their research to the period after 1945, when political authority changed, and did not deal in depth with the continuity of Taiwanese society itself.[3] Studies by American anthropologists further enforced this tendency.

Taiwan became an ideal place for field research in China studies, not only because the People's Republic of China (PRC) was inaccessible, but also because there was abundant, accessible data concerning traditional Han Chinese society in Taiwan.[4] Although scholars conducting field research in Taiwan knew that Taiwanese society had been ruled by an efficient non-Chinese regime for half a century, most did not pay much attention to the period of Japanese rule inasmuch as they wished to confirm a proposition that was a prerequisite of their field research: that traditional Chinese society could be found in Taiwan. These anthropologists presumed that Japanese rule had not transformed rural Taiwan from traditional patterns of Chinese social life, although they recognized that Japanese rule had brought a higher standard of living in material terms for the Taiwanese people.[5] Not surprisingly, the influence of Japanese colonial law was often thought to be considerably limited by some scholars who focused on the legal development of Chinese society in Taiwan.[6]

When the object of study is not traditional Chinese society but Taiwanese society, however, previous approaches have to be modified. Like the English in North America, Han Chinese formed a settler society in the colony of Taiwan, a society that was somewhat different from traditional Han Chinese society in mainland China. Not until late Ch'ing, about the 1860s, did the Han Chinese on Taiwan gradually develop a traditional Chinese community, the characteristics of which will be defined in the first section of chapter 1.[7] Because the situation in Taiwan in the late Ch'ing period before 1895 was representive of traditional Chinese society, scholars have extensively employed the materials recording the law and practice in late Ch'ing Taiwan to explore Chinese legal traditions.[8] The question is whether the fifty years of Japanese rule thereafter left a physical legacy only: railroads, electricity, and so on. Those scholars who regarded the Japanese effect upon Taiwanese traditional society as slight generally restricted their research to traditional family institutions such as marriage, adoption, kinship, lineage, worship, and the like in rural Taiwan.[9] It was generally thought that the Japanese authorities did not want to reorganize rural society in Taiwan because traditional agrarian institutions were advantageous to Japanese colonialism.[10] The fact is, however, that the colonial courts had already changed some Taiwanese customs concerning family relations through their decisions.[11] Even supposing that the traditional Chinese family system on Taiwan was largely free of the courts' influence, one should not conclude that other aspects of Taiwanese social life still reflected Chinese traditional patterns. That Taiwanese civil customs were in general transformed by modern Western law during the Japanese period will be examined in detail in chapter 5. In addition, as the island became more urbanized during the 1930s and 1940s, differences between city and country grew.[12] Thus, observations concerning Taiwanese society on the basis of data from only rural areas are inadequate.

Since the late 1960s or early 1970s, the unique development of Taiwanese society has gradually come to the attention of some American scholars (although, as before, Taiwan's legal development has continued to be ignored as a specific topic), and the unique aspects of Taiwanese society have begun to be reevaluated.[13] Today, whether the shaping of Taiwanese society is linked to Chinese traditions or is moved by foreign forces that have no necessary connection with traditional China remains a controversial question.[14] In response to this controversy a suggested approach is to give greater attention to the critical Japanese period because "[t]o those who stress [Chinese] cultural continuity, the Japanese period is the bridge to the past; to those who suspect that the Japanese period changed Taiwan significantly, these decades must be shown to have produced major transformations."[15] In the United States, a few articles have specifically discussed the development of Taiwan under Japanese rule. However, they are mainly concerned with politics, society, economy, and education.[16] The legal development of Taiwan during the Japanese period is only touched upon as an incidental aspect of the study of colonial Taiwan.

Once we broaden our view to cover universal legal development, rather than merely that of China, we will discover that the Taiwan case, in which the prewar Japanese empire gradually imposed its Westernized law, is worth examining. In the eyes of extreme Chinese nationalists, the legal system in Taiwan under Japanese rule is nothing but "Japanese" law. To the objective observer, however, the legal system that the Japanese brought to the island was "Japanized and colonialized" Western-style law. In the late nineteenth century, Western powers directly imposed their law or legal conceptions on their Asian or African colonies and indirectly induced a few Asian independent states to adopt Western law.[17] In 1895, Japan acquired Taiwan as its first colony. In Taiwan, Japan gradually enforced the laws that it had just received from the West. Taiwan's experience (and that of Korea) is therefore unique among countries receiving modern Western law in that Western law was imposed to replace traditional Chinese law by an Asian colonialist power. The uniqueness of the Taiwan case, however, seems to go unnoticed in most studies concerning the reception of Western law.[18]

Some may raise an embarrassing question: why have no Taiwanese ever studied these issues, which are an integral part of their own society? One important reason is that in the past decades, the study of Taiwan's history was regarded as "unwelcome" by the government of the Republic of China (ROC) on Taiwan unless undertaken from the official perspective, namely, that Taiwan is a part of China and therefore all social phenomena on the island must be aspects of local Chinese history, not Taiwanese history.[19] The significance of the fifty-year history of Japanese rule is by official reckoning summarized as "suffering Japanese colonial exploitation, Taiwan's Chinese strongly resisted the Japanese government."[20] Not until the loosening of the government's control of Taiwan's society in the 1980s was a new approach tolerated, one that examined Taiwan from the viewpoint of the Taiwanese, meaning only the people who live on the island of Taiwan. At present, many new-generation scholars in Taiwan consider that when we study Taiwan's history, we must rid ourselves of the Han-centered or China-centered attitude taken in the past and should further extend our attention to aborigines and Taiwan's relations to the global environment, not merely the Chinese environment.²¹ Based on this new approach, the fifty years of Japanese rule is certainly a crucial period to be explored. As some recent research papers have pointed out, Japanese rule brought about dramatic changes in Taiwanese society and continued to influence the later development of Taiwan after the Japanese left in 1945.²² The same is true of legal studies in Taiwan. For a long time, the "legal history" of the people on Taiwan almost excluded Japanese colonial law. Very few legal studies of thirty or more years ago discussed the Japanese legal system, and most merely emphasized the oppressive nature of Japanese colonial laws in Taiwan.²³ Nonetheless, in 1986, one year before the lifting of martial law, two legal scholars in Taiwan remarked that Japanese colonial rule had made some contributions to the Taiwanese reception of Western-style codes.²⁴ This comment was not the main topic of their lectures, but it is testimony to the recognition of these contributions. In fact, the issue of Taiwan's reception of Western law was typically discussed in the context of the reception of Western law by late Ch'ing China and later the Republic of China. But Taiwan was not governed by these two Chinese regimes from 1895 to 1945.²⁵ For Taiwanese society before 1945, the Westernization of law in mainland China was the experience of a foreign nation. Admittedly, the experience in China before 1945 influenced the settlers who came to Taiwan from the Chinese mainland after 1945 and especially in 1949, when the central government of the ROC retreated to the island. It should be kept in mind, however, that the majority of Taiwan's present population is an extension of the Taiwanese society prior to 1945, which had come into contact with Western legal concepts for the first time under Japanese rule at the end of the nineteenth century, as will be examined in later chapters (see also table A.1 in appendix A).²⁶

As one of the parties involved, the Japanese might be expected to have their own comments on Japanese colonial law in Taiwan.²⁷ Initially, after World War II, Japan had little interest in the independent study of Taiwan, partly because they regarded Taiwan as a part of China.²⁸ However, since colonial Taiwan was an important chapter in the development of prewar Japanese colonialism, a major theme in modern Japanese history,²⁹ the Taiwanese political struggle against the colonial authorities and the Japanese economic exploitation in Taiwan became main concerns of research for scholars in Japan, especially those who had been a part of Japanese colonial rule in Taiwan.³⁰ Only a few scholars in postwar Japan have discussed Japanese colonial law in Taiwan for the purpose of researching Japanese legal history.³¹ It is noteworthy, however, that a Japanese institute has begun to study the relations

INTRODUCTION

between governing policies and the colonial legal system in Taiwan.[32] In the future, perhaps we will gain some insight into how the Japanese view their former colonial legal system.

ABOUT THIS BOOK

From the perspective of Taiwan studies, one of the most significant characteristics of Japanese colonial rule in Taiwan's legal development is that the Japanese introduced Western-style law. The study in this book will focus on the Taiwanese reception of Western law under the Japanese legal reform, especially emphasizing criminal and civil law. It will examine the extent to which the Taiwanese under Japanese rule replaced traditional Chinese concepts with the new Western legal concepts. For the student of comparative law, this study will at the same time show how and to what extent a non-Western power was able to implement Westernized law in its colony.

Indeed, it is difficult to generalize all cases of the reception of law into a single theory because every instance is inevitably influenced by particular conditions and surrounding circumstances. But in general, anyone seeking to formulate such a theory must look at (1) background and causation, (2) the process of reception, and (3) the effects of the new law, usually focusing on particular areas of law, such as criminal or civil codes.[33] The studies of the reception of modern Western law by East Asian countries that were originally influenced by Chinese legal traditions therefore frequently concentrate on the incentive for modernization (Westernization) of law; the adaptation of Western-style codes, especially criminal and civil codes; and finally the actual implementation of the codes. These approaches, with certain modifications, can be adopted in exploring the extent to which Western legal concepts were received by the Taiwanese through Japanese imposition of Western-style laws in the colony inasmuch as Taiwanese society is also an East Asian society influenced by imperial Chinese law.[34] On the other hand, the uniqueness of the Taiwan case must be taken fully into account in this study as well. First, unlike Japan or China, but like Korea, Taiwan had Western law imposed by a foreign colonialist power rather than promulgated by an indigenous government. Second, unlike Western powers, the imposing state itself was still influenced by its own traditional, sinicized legal culture. Third, unlike the Koreans under Japanese rule, in the late nineteenth century the subjected Taiwanese retained some characteristics derived from their frontier settler society and initially were imbued with traditional ethnic consciousness rather than modern nationalism.[35]

INTRODUCTION

Accordingly, chapter 1 of this book will survey the Taiwanese settler society, which had been governed by three substantially different regimes by the late nineteenth century, and the Japanese regime, with its rudimentary experience in receiving Western law in its homeland.

Chapter 2 will examine the question of who had power to make the law in Taiwan during the Japanese period and then survey the number of Western-style laws adopted in colonial legislation and Taiwanese attitudes toward adopting Western law. As with other countries in East Asia, in Taiwan modern Western law was introduced primarily through legislative reception, that is, political authority actively legislating Western-style law.

Meanwhile, Western-style judicial administration is indispensable in implementing legislatively received Western law. Such features as judicial institutions and physical facilities, a qualified legal profession, and easy access to court undoubtedly influence the societal reception of Western law, so that Westernized law penetrates into the social life of the people. Hence, I will discuss the modern judiciary in the colony in chapter 3 and then explore the causes and degree of social reception by the Taiwanese of criminal justice and civil justice in chapters 4 and 5, respectively. The last chapter will appraise the entire Japan-led legal reform in Taiwan and discuss its legacy in Taiwan's later legal development.

For this study, I have referred to some primary sources, in addition to existing essays related to the topic. The archives of the Government-General of Taiwan (Taiwan Sōtokufu, hereafter abbreviated as GGT) are a collection of documents filed by the headquarters of the Japanese colonial government in Taiwan (called Taiwan Sōtokufu kōbun ruisan, hereafter abbreviated as GGT Ac.).[36] The judicial section of the archives holds the records of the GGT's enacting laws in Taiwan and their actual enforcement. The judicial section of GGT Ac. from 1895 to 1905 (hereafter abbreviated as J. Ac.) has been translated into Chinese and published.[37] The rest, however, have not yet been published and thus are cited here according to a general catalog for GGT Ac.[38] Another important source in understanding colonial law is the collection of reported decisions of the courts in Taiwan.[39] These published decisions include some selected cases from the years between 1896 and 1940, but only the court's holding and some rationale, without the entire set of facts, was extracted from the 1896–1919 decisions. In addition, Japanese jurists or judicial officials wrote many legal commentaries on the colonial law in Taiwan. Those were largely published by the Japanese authorities in a series of books entitled *Taiwan shihō* (Taiwanese private law) and two journals: *Taiwan kanshū kiji* (Records of Taiwanese customs, January 1901–August 1907) and *Taihō geppō* (Monthly report of Taiwan's law, June 1907–November 1943; called *Hōin geppō* before

8

Jan. 1911).⁴⁰ Moreover, abundant statistics about judicial affairs in colonial Taiwan were published by the Japanese government.⁴¹ Some Taiwanese jurists published their views, which present a radically different perspective on colonial administration, in an anti-GGT journal, *Taiwan seinen* (Taiwanese youth, 1920–24; called *Taiwan* after April 1922).⁴² Literature (such as novels and autobiographies) written by the Taiwanese who experienced Japanese rule also reflects the legal consciousness of the general public under Japan's imposition of Western-style law.

Regarding terminology, as used in this book, "Taiwanese" is roughly equivalent to the Japanese *hontōjin* (people in this island) as used during the period of Japanese rule. It includes the Han Chinese (Southern Fukienese [*min-nan-jen*] and Hakka [*k'e-chia-jen*]) who had immigrated from Fukien or Kwangtung before 1895 and the plains aborigines who lived in the plains areas of Taiwan and received the culture of Han Chinese, as well as the descendants of these two groups.⁴³ I will use "Chinese" to refer to those who were Han Chinese immigrants in Taiwan before 1895 but selected Ch'ing nationality after 1897 as well as any Han Chinese who came to Taiwan after 1895, although they were called *shinkokujin* (Ch'ing nationals) or *chūkaminkokujin* (nationals of the Republic of China) in Japanese law and *kakyō* (overseas Chinese) in general usage.⁴⁴ The term "aborigines" (*yüan-chu-min*) from the Japanese *banjin* (barbarians) or *takasagozoku* (Formosan aborigines), refers to those people who generally lived in the mountain areas of the island, preserving their original culture, and were administratively isolated in the *banchi* (barbarian areas) where the legal system was much different from the rest of Taiwan. The term "Japanese" refers to *naichijin* (people in the mainland), including those who initially lived in Japan but then came to Taiwan for short- or long-term stays, as well as their descendants.⁴⁵ Accordingly, "Taiwanese" in this book means the "original Taiwanese" within the group now classified as Taiwanese, which also includes the aborigines and "Chinese-mainlanders."⁴⁶

This study concentrates on Taiwanese (*hontōjin*) justice on the grounds that the number of Chinese as defined above was very small during this period, that the colonial laws governing the aborigines were different from those governing the Taiwanese, and that the Japanese were only a minority and then left Taiwan after 1945 (see table 1.1).

The usage of languages in this book has to be mentioned as well. Because Taiwan has been ruled by different regimes with different languages and legal systems, I have decided to use the official language of each period. The institutions and agencies of the Ch'ing period will be romanized from Mandarin Chinese; those of the Japanese period, from Japanese.⁴⁷ For example, the *pao-chia* system in Ch'ing Taiwan is called *hokō* in Japan's Taiwan, although the

TABLE I.1 Population of Taiwan under Japanese Rule

Year	Taiwanese	Japanese	Aborigines	Chinese	Total
1896	2,577,104	10,584	NA	NA	2,587,688
1900	2,707,322	37,954	95,597	5,160	2,846,108[a]
(%)	95.1	1.3	3.4	0.2	100.0
1905	2,942,266	59,618	113,195	8,223	3,123,302
(%)	94.2	1.9	3.6	0.3	100.0
1910	3,064,499	98,048	122,106	14,840	3,299,493
(%)	92.9	3.0	3.7	0.4	100.0
1920	3,436,071	166,621	130,310	24,836	3,757,838
(%)	91.4	4.4	3.5	0.7	100.0
1930	4,259,523	232,299	140,553	46,691	4,679,066
(%)	91.0	5.0	3.0	1.0	100.0
1940	5,523,912	346,663	158,321	46,190	6,077,478
(%)	90.9	5.7	2.6	0.8	100.0
1942	5,827,857	384,847	162,031	50,429	6,427,932
(%)	90.7	6.0	2.5	0.8	100.0

SOURCE: Ch'en Shao-hsiang, *T'ai-wan te jen-k'ou pien-ch'ien*, pp. 96–97.
[a] Totals for 1900, 1940, and 1942 include non-Chinese foreigners, who are excluded in other years.

characters are the same. For easy reading, Mandarin Chinese romanization, as used in present Taiwan, will be used for the names of places and Taiwanese people, however. Mandarin Chinese is romanized in the Wade-Giles system rather than the pinyin system used extensively in the People's Republic of China, with the exception of certain well-established place names, for example, Taipei for T'ai-pei. The Chinese and Japanese terms used can be found in the glossary.

Like Taiwan's short but complex history, scholarly works on Taiwan are not voluminous but are nevertheless full of controversy. As Thomas Gold has pointed out, the emotional and political nature of many studies of Taiwan—pro-Nationalist, anti-Nationalist, pro-reunification, pro-independence (left, right, nonaligned)—has forced readers to take such studies with so many grains of salt as to render them nearly indigestible.[48] Still, facts may be disclosed through the discussion. Facing the same facts, however, writers probably will make different comments on the basis of different beliefs. Therefore, commentators should express their own subjective values by which any value judgment upon facts is made. As for myself, I take the interests of the Taiwanese people who live on the island (in whatever period) as the basis for evaluating all facts and regimes throughout Taiwan's history, regardless of the ethnic origin of the ruling class. Certainly there is no absolute answer about what are the best interests of the people. Most rulers, like the Japanese colonialists in Taiwan, argue that they pursued "the welfare of the people."[49] I believe, however, that there are conflicts of interest between the ruler and the ruled and therefore "the best interests" should be determined by the will of the people themselves through democratic process.

1 / Background of Legal Reform

To determine the legal and social context in which modern Western law was implemented in Taiwan at the end of the nineteenth century, I will first briefly describe the development of Taiwan's society under various outside rulers before the advent of Japanese authorities in 1895. This exposition is necessary not only to understand the later modernization (Westernization) of law by the Japanese regime but also to appraise the colonial Japanese achievement in Taiwan.

TAIWAN SOCIETY AND OLD RULERS (PRE-1895)

Taiwan comprises the main island of Taiwan (Formosa; hereafter referred to as Taiwan Island) and its adjacent islands, mainly the Pescadores (P'eng-hu). Taiwan Island lies a hundred miles east of China, some seven hundred miles south of Japan, and two hundred miles north of the Philippine Islands. It is surrounded by the Pacific Ocean, which for sometime isolated it from the neighboring imperial Chinese as well as from the Hindu and Buddhist civilizations of East and Southeast Asia. The maritime expansion of Europe in Asia in the sixteenth and seventeenth centuries, however, brought Taiwan into the mainstream of global development. Aborigines, Han Chinese, Japanese, and Europeans have all helped to shape the history of Taiwan.[1]

With an area of 13,807 square miles, Taiwan Island is a little larger than the Netherlands, a trifle smaller than Switzerland.[2] The Pescadores encompass only 48 square miles but are important for Taiwan because of their strategic location, slightly east of the midway point of the Taiwan Strait, which separates Taiwan from the East Asian continent.[3] At one-sixth the size of Korea, another important Japanese colony, Taiwan was a mere 5.34 percent of the total size of the prewar Japanese empire.[4] Needless to say, compared to mainland China, Taiwan is nothing more than a tiny island.

Early History of Taiwan (Pre-1624)

Exactly how long Taiwan has been inhabited is not known, but Taiwan "aborigines" are probably the earliest inhabitants of the historical period.[5] Racially they belong to the Proto-Malay group and are different from the Han Chinese (*Han-jen*). Linguistically and culturally, the aborigines are akin to the Malayo-Polynesian peoples of the Philippines and other parts of Southeastern Asia.[6] Before contacting other civilizations, they generally practiced primitive subsistence farming, which was supplemented by hunting and fishing.[7]

The second major group to contact Taiwan, at this point inhabited by these aborigines, undoubtedly were the Han Chinese, although when this contact began has yet to be conclusively determined.[8] At least some Han Chinese from southern Fukien province of China (Ch'üan-chou) migrated to the Pescadores in the twelfth century. The Pescadores then became a part of Fukien in Southern Sung China (1127–1279). The Mongol empire in China (1280–1368) later installed a local administrative official on the Pescadores. At that time, Han Chinese were aware of Taiwan Island, but only a few fishers and traders occasionally visited the island. Continuous migration of the Han Chinese to Taiwan was hindered by the maritime prohibition policy of Ming China (1368–1644), under which the administrative office in the Pescadores was abolished and the Han people were moved back to the Chinese mainland. Beyond the jurisdiction of the Ming government from this point on, Taiwan was thus an ideal shelter for Chinese and Japanese pirate-traders who often attacked the coastal areas of China. Ming forces were sent to the Pescadores and Taiwan Island to annihilate those pirates, but Ming contact with Taiwan was limited to this occasional policing of the area.[9] One of the pirate-trade groups operating in the Taiwan Strait at this time developed into the Cheng band; in 1662 they became the Cheng regime on Taiwan, which will be discussed later.[10]

The first Japanese who had contact with Taiwan were pirate-traders. By about 1560 they already regarded Taiwan as their base for invading Fukien. Merchants from Nagasaki, having obtained special government licenses, opened offices in northern Taiwan Island (Keelung) in 1592. In the next year, Toyotomi Hideyoshi tried to send a letter to order Takasago (or Takayamakuni; namely, Taiwan) to submit tribute to Japan, but there was no government on the island to receive the order. Then, after an unsuccessful attempt at contact in 1609, the Tokugawa shogunate sent a fleet to conquer Taiwan in 1615, but this attempt failed because the fleet encountered a typhoon. Japanese pirate-traders, however, continued to use Taiwan as a trading base until the bakufu ordered the closing of Japan (*sakoku*) in 1639.[11]

European explorers, missionaries, and traders composed the fourth group of arrivals to Taiwan. In the 1550s, Taiwan was "discovered" and named Ilha Formosa (beautiful island) by the Portuguese.[12] Because of Taiwan's strategic location regarding trade with China and Japan, it became one of the important targets for control by the European maritime powers. In the late sixteenth century, the Spanish based in Manila tried to conquer Taiwan Island but, like the Japanese, failed because their ships were sunk by a typhoon.[13]

The Dutch came next to the Taiwan Strait in search of a base for trade with China. In 1622, the Dutch occupied the Pescadores. After initial conflict and negotiation, the Dutch and Ming China finally reached an agreement in 1624 that required the Dutch to abandon the Pescadores but allowed them to occupy Taiwan Island; accompanying the agreement was a mutual understanding that the Dutch were permitted to trade with China. Thus the Dutch, the latest arrivals, with some assistance from Ming China, moved to occupy Taiwan Island.[14]

Dutch and Spanish Colonial Rule (1624–62)

The Dutch Republic established its authority on Taiwan Island in 1624, the first alien, colonial regime on the island.[15] The Dutch constructed forts at present-day Tainan (a city in southern Taiwan) as their headquarters.[16] The task of governing the island was undertaken by a trading organization, the Dutch East India Company. Since the company was entrusted with diplomatic, administrative, judicial, and other functions of sovereignty by the Dutch government, the Dutch Republic legally exercised its authority on Taiwan Island.[17] The Spanish had established another regime in northern Taiwan Island (1626–42), and the Pescadores remained under the jurisdiction of Ming China. Thus, Taiwan, as defined today, was simultaneously subjected to three sovereigns.[18]

The Dutch occupation of Taiwan Island was chiefly motivated by the prospect of mercantile profits, not by a desire to extend territorial power.[19] As a business organization, the Dutch authorities in the island were organized as efficiently as possible. With a small number of personnel, the company's governor of Taiwan and his council exercised all administrative and judicial functions under the supervision of the East Indian Government (the central government) in Batavia (in Jakarta). To cut costs, the Dutch allowed the aborigines and Han Chinese to elect their own chiefs with the approval of the colonial authorities. Receiving instructions from the company, the chiefs were for all practical purposes in charge of the administrative and judicial affairs of their people. Dutch justice in fact applied only to cases involving Europeans.[20] The Dutch colonialists adopted the principle of legal dualism for colonized peoples and merely brought a premodern pattern of Western government to the island.

During the late period of Dutch rule, as Dutch trade with China became difficult because of problems in acquiring needed merchandise from wartime China, Dutch interest in the island gradually declined.[21] The Dutch finally were ousted from Taiwan Island in 1662 by the Cheng band, another maritime power in the Taiwan Strait, ending their thirty-eight-year rule in Taiwan.

The Dutch, no doubt, did profit through their exploitation of both the Han Chinese and the aborigines, but they also left something behind for Taiwan.

Because, beginning in the 1630s, the Dutch East India Company in Taiwan, as in Java, recruited farmers from China to develop colonial agriculture, many Han Chinese peasants living in southern Fukien were attracted to Taiwan Island and settled there for the first time. Because of famine, war, and overpopulation in China, this movement continued through the late period of Dutch rule.[22] The population of Han Chinese settlers during the Dutch period is estimated at fifty thousand. Although the Han Chinese effectively colonized Taiwan Island, these settlers did not establish their own government, but were governed by the Dutch colonial regime. The 1652 Kuo Huai-i Incident, in which Han Chinese rebelled against the government in response to heavy tax burdens, reflects the inherent conflict between Han Chinese settlers and Dutch colonialists during this time.[23]

Dutch colonialism deeply affected the agricultural development of the island. To increase production for export, the company improved cultivation and encouraged the development of commercial crops such as sugarcane. Han Chinese settlers therefore were introduced to mercantilist production, which was different from their original self-sufficiency production on the Chinese mainland.[24]

Dutch "civilizing" effects had considerable influence upon the aborigines. Although some aborigines rejected Dutch rule and moved to mountain areas beyond Dutch control, many aborigines accepted Dutch rule and settled in plains areas and were later referred to as "plains aborigines" during the Ch'ing and Japanese periods. In Ch'ing Taiwan, the aborigines who had been governed by the Dutch continued to use roman script for transliterating their local dialects in contracts with Han Chinese.[25]

A few important Dutch legal measures were followed up by later Chinese regimes on Taiwan. The Dutch crown fields and taxation system continued to be enforced on the island by the Cheng regime. The system of local chiefs was also maintained by the immigrant society of Taiwan.[26]

The Spanish colonial rule in northern Taiwan Island did not succeed.

BACKGROUND OF LEGAL REFORM

Concerned about Dutch threats to the safety of their trading establishment in Manila, the Spanish constructed forts at Keelung and Tanshui (in northern Taiwan Island) in 1626 and 1629, respectively. They used these forts for commercial and religious purposes as well; however, an inhospitable natural environment and lack of funds made it difficult for the Spanish to achieve their goals. Gradually their holdings on the island were no longer considered an asset for which it was worth fighting. In 1642, the Dutch in the south ousted the Spanish from the island. The Spanish therefore had little influence on northern Taiwan Island.[27]

Military Rule of the Cheng Regime (1662–83)

As the Dutch had defeated the Spanish, in 1662 a band of pirate-traders led by Cheng Ch'eng-kung (known as Koxinga in the West) defeated the Dutch on the island and imposed their authority over Taiwan Island as well as the Pescadores. Koxinga organized the Cheng band into a government at Amoy (a port of Fukien) in 1655 under the nominal jurisdiction of the Southern Ming government. Four years later the Southern Ming government was extinguished by the Manchu forces, who had established the Ch'ing dynasty in most of China in 1644. When Koxinga led his men to attack the Dutch on Taiwan Island in 1661, there was no Ming government in China. Therefore, after 1662 the Cheng government became, de facto, the supreme authority on the island. Subsequently, Taiwan was recognized as an independent state by Europeans.[28] However, from the viewpoint of the aborigines and those Han Chinese who had settled on the island during the Dutch period, the Cheng government was an alien, Han Chinese regime.[29]

In fact, the Cheng rulers were unwilling to reside on the island; they regarded Taiwan as a temporary base for war against the Ch'ing to restore Ming rule in China.[30] Taking advantage of an unrelated insurrection against the Ch'ing empire in 1673, the second ruler of the Cheng regime, Cheng Ching, mounted a military counterattack against mainland China. However, a shortage of supplies by 1679 brought failure, and he returned to Taiwan in the next year.[31]

The Ch'ing government was concerned with the Cheng regime's threats to Ch'ing authority on mainland China rather than the acquisition of Taiwan. In the peace talks of 1679 the Ch'ing negotiators expressed their willingness to treat Taiwan as an independent state like Korea or Japan since Taiwan originally was not included in the territory of China but was simply exploited by the Cheng family; however, the Cheng forces in return had to withdraw from and stop attacking Ch'ing China.³² When the Cheng regime insisted on keeping a port on China's coast, the peace talks broke down, and the Ch'ing government decided to invade Taiwan. In 1683, Shih Lang, a former Cheng commander, led a Ch'ing fleet to attack Taiwan. By this time, six years of continuous fighting in China had exhausted the Cheng regime. The Cheng government soon surrendered, and their twenty-one-year rule on Taiwan came to an end.³³ Within a period of less than sixty years, sovereignty over Taiwan had changed three times.

One of the most stimulating effects of the Cheng regime on Taiwan's society was the legacy of the legal and political system of imperial China and the Confucian educational institutions it bequeathed.³⁴ Under Cheng rule, Taiwan basically changed from a Dutch plantation colony into a Han Chinese settlement colony.³⁵

The sinicization of Taiwan under the Cheng rule should not be overemphasized, however.³⁶ The Han Chinese on Taiwan, unlike those in China, maintained a practical and pragmatic relationship with the European powers.³⁷ The Confucian literati made up only a very small portion of the whole population in Taiwan society.³⁸ With prosperous international trade, many people on Taiwan, unlike those in the inland areas of China, conducted or were influenced by mercantile activities. Moreover, because of the hostility between the Ch'ing and the Cheng, the Han Chinese on Taiwan were separated from those in mainland China politically, socially, and economically.³⁹

The Cheng regime, although established by Han Chinese, did not give unlimited advantages to the Han Chinese settlers. In the beginning, the settlers welcomed the advent of Koxinga's government.⁴⁰ To feed a large number of soldiers, the Cheng government reclaimed vast tracts of land for agriculture through a military colony system, under which soldiers were required to engage in farming in their garrisons. To the detriment of the aborigines, Han Chinese settlers thus acquired more land to cultivate, and their population increased to a hundred thousand at least, almost double that during the Dutch period.⁴¹ Nevertheless, the rulers of this dynasty, pursuing their own political ambitions, refused to make peace with Ch'ing China and continued to fight for restoration of Ming rule in China at the expense of the settlers. The Han Chinese settlers on Taiwan therefore were ruled by a militarized government under martial law. The settlers also had to pay onerous taxes—as heavy as the Dutch had levied—to support Cheng's expensive military actions, especially those in mainland China from 1674 to 1679.⁴² But it is doubtful whether the political aims of the Cheng regime were shared by the settlers, who had left the Chinese mainland because of famine and war.

Imperial Rule of Ch'ing China (1683–1895)

Ruling Policies and Ch'ing Laws. In 1684, for the first time, the regime on mainland China decided, somewhat reluctantly, to govern Taiwan Island. Having invaded Taiwan merely to eliminate the last threat to Ch'ing rule in China, the Ch'ing empire initially intended to govern only the Pescadores, excluding Taiwan Island as had Ming China. Influenced by advice that unless the Ch'ing retained the island, it would inevitably be occupied by rebels or foreign powers and then used to threaten southeast China, the Ch'ing emperor finally decided to establish a local government on Taiwan in the next year after defeating the Cheng regime.[43] In fact, the Manchu emperors appeared to be more interested in conquering Central Asia than in controlling a faraway island.

Unfortunately, neither the Ch'ing nor any other empires in China had experience governing a large overseas island like Taiwan.[44] Nor could the Ch'ing adopt the trading policy of the Cheng regime on Taiwan inasmuch as the Ch'ing dynasty was a land power not accustomed to maritime activities. The Ch'ing empire could only govern the island according to its real concern in retaining Taiwan, that is, to prevent Taiwan from developing into a base against the empire.[45] Therefore, in the first 190 years of Ch'ing rule on Taiwan, government policy toward this island was always negative and prohibitive. That was reflected in the statutes of Ch'ing relating to Taiwan, although they were ordinarily ignored by the people, as will be discussed later on.

First, from 1684 to 1875, the Ch'ing court restricted migration to Taiwan. According to the rules on Registration of Immigrants in Taiwan enacted in 1684,[46] only those people who had family and property in Taiwan and had not committed a crime punishable by penal servitude or more severe punishment were allowed to stay in Taiwan, but they were not permitted to bring their families from the Chinese mainland. Only married men with an official permit could migrate to Taiwan, but their families had to live on the mainland. The purpose of these rules was to discourage Han Chinese immigrants from settling in Taiwan. From this point on, the Ch'ing government was forced to change the immigration regulations several times. After 1760 immigrants were finally allowed to bring their families to Taiwan, but single men and those people who had no relatives in Taiwan were still banned from immigrating to the island. These restrictions were not totally eliminated until 1875.[47]

During the period from 1684 to 1875, Han Chinese were prohibited from crossing the border into aborigine reservations or marrying aborigine women.[48] Han Chinese immigrants in Taiwan therefore could reclaim very little uncultivated land on Taiwan because at this time the majority of the land was classified as "aboriginal land."[49] The Ch'ing court adopted these regulations for two purposes. One was to prevent Han Chinese from occupying aboriginal land, for such occupation would probably result in rebellion among the aborigines; the other was to prevent Han Chinese rebels from entering aboriginal areas and becoming a force that might threaten Ch'ing authority. Not surprisingly, although some officials in Taiwan suggested opening the border to settle unemployed people, the Ch'ing central government rejected doing so until Ch'ing ruling policy toward Taiwan changed in 1875.[50]

The Ch'ing government's attempts to prevent rebellion in Taiwan were reflected in two special provisions for Taiwan's people. The Ch'ing code gave officials in Taiwan the authority to execute criminals who committed robbery or treason.[51] In addition, Taiwan people were forbidden to manufacture guns or extract sulphur because these could be used for military purposes. Only twenty-seven blacksmith shops were authorized to manufacture hardware and farm implements, and all iron had to be purchased from the mainland.[52]

Preventive measures also applied to officials in Taiwan. Officials who were assigned to Taiwan received high salaries and could be promoted after a short term. They had to leave their families "hostage" on the mainland, however, a provision that remained in effect until 1824, when it was rescinded.[53] Furthermore, all soldiers garrisoned in Taiwan had to be recruited from mainland China because, in the words of a Ch'ing official, "employing Taiwan people to defend Taiwan amounts to giving Taiwan to the Taiwan people."[54]

Unlike Japanese rulers, Ch'ing rulers did not enact a special legal structure to govern Taiwan. Since the Ch'ing government was not willing to develop Taiwan, no special laws were promulgated in response to particular economic or social conditions of Taiwan. The Ch'ing's general official code (that is, the Great Ch'ing Code), which incorporated those negative regulations mentioned above, was applied to Taiwanese people. Local customs, unofficial sources of law in imperial China, therefore played an important role in meeting the particular needs of the settler society in Taiwan.[55]

Only after Japan and the European powers showed interest in Taiwan did Ch'ing China change its policy toward this island. Influenced by Japan's military campaign in "the aboriginal areas" of Taiwan in 1874, the Ch'ing government strengthened its defending forces on the island and began to conquer the aborigines so that "the aboriginal areas," namely, eastern Taiwan Island, could be included in the territory of the Ch'ing empire. Thus, the restrictive measures noted above were repealed in 1875. Not until 1887, however, 204 years after Taiwan was incorporated into Ch'ing China, was the island established as a province and governed by an active policy. The reason for this change was that Ch'ing China wanted to fortify Taiwan to shield its southeastern provinces from invasion by the Western powers.[56]

But the Ch'ing government's change of policy toward Taiwan was too late. In 1895, after Japan defeated Ch'ing China in Korea and southern Manchuria, Taiwan was ceded to Japan without consideration of the views of Taiwan's people. Thus, 212 years of Ch'ing rule on Taiwan ended.

In conclusion, the Ch'ing court only pursued its own imperial interests in governing Taiwan, and those did not include the well-being of the people, whether in Taiwan or in mainland China. From the viewpoint of an imperial ruler, Taiwan was too small to merit attention. The Ch'ing government was therefore not willing or able to adopt special measures, different from those enacted for the mainland, to develop Taiwan according to its unique conditions. In contrast, the Cheng regime also pursued the rulers' interests, as mentioned before, but Cheng's policy, such as encouraging reclamation and international trading, was based on Taiwan's circumstances. While furthering the rulers' interests, such policies could at the same time bring some benefits to the Han Chinese settlers on Taiwan.

Popular Disrespect for Law. The fact that Ch'ing law in Taiwan was enacted neither for the people nor in response to the particular economic or social conditions of Taiwan to a large extent resulted in the popular disrespect for official law during the Ch'ing period. First, the legal prohibition of migration to Taiwan proved to be an empty gesture from the start. Numerous poor men from Fukien and Kwangtung immigrated to Taiwan where it was said that "money flowed around residents' ankles." The migration from Ch'üan-chou and Chang-chou of Fukien began in the late seventeenth century. Later, many Hakka from Kwangtung also came to Taiwan. Despite the laws to the contrary, many also tried to bring their families to the island. During the eighteenth century, the Han Chinese population on Taiwan grew rapidly, from about 100,000 in 1680 to 1,945,500 by 1811, a nearly twentyfold increase within 130 years. These immigrants constituted the majority of Han Chinese settlers in Taiwan. Because of the legal prohibition against immigration, most of those who came were smuggled in or were able to come more openly by bribing local officials. They were technically illegal immigrants.[57]

Since these settlers had migrated to Taiwan illegally, they had no compunctions about not observing the law prohibiting them from crossing the border of aborigine reservations to acquire land from the aborigines. In fact, land-hungry immigrants cultivated whatever arable land they found. They acquired the aborigines' land both by force and by "peaceful" means, including fraud. Use of force or fraud was of course illegal. Even some peaceful means, such as purchases or leases from the aborigines, were sometimes prohibited by official law during the early period of Ch'ing rule.[58] But local officials generally turned a blind eye to Han Chinese reclamation of aboriginal land. Later, the government often regarded those Han Chinese who occupied the once aboriginal land as the owners.[59]

Similarly, the proscriptions against intermarriage and manufacture of weapons were not enforced. Because there were so few Han Chinese women on the island, many unmarried Han Chinese men, who by law were not allowed to stay in Taiwan, wanted to marry aborigine women. For a Han Chinese immigrant, intermarriage with an aborigine woman also meant that he could acquire her land. In addition, because the settlers frequently needed weapons to fight rival ethnic groups (including the aborigines) or to defend themselves against bandits, they disregarded the official prohibition and armed themselves with a large number of swords, spears, muskets, bamboo guns, and even cannons.[60]

Meanwhile, Taiwan's people circumvented imperial law in traditional ways. For example, according to the official rate of taxation, taxes levied in Taiwan were several times higher than those on the Chinese mainland, and taxes could not be reduced even under special circumstances such as crop failure resulting from natural disasters or other calamities.[61] As on the mainland, Han Chinese immigrants in Taiwan concealed some of their fields when reporting to the government so that they could decrease the total amount of taxes paid.[62] The officials knew that "every household has concealed fields." Yet officials in Taiwan were reluctant to correct the reported number of fields because they feared that the increase in the taxes that would result might further result in a popular uprising.[63]

Another major cause of the general disrespect for law was the corruption and incompetence of the officials who were supposed to maintain law. As Hsu Tsung-kan, Taiwan intendant (1848–54) said, "In the empire, the Fukien government is the worst; within Fukien Province, the Taiwan government is the worst." Few officials on Taiwan were capable and honest.[64] The majority only hoped that nothing out of the ordinary occurred during their terms of office so that they could be smoothly promoted. Moreover, like magistrates throughout imperial China, the magistrates in Taiwan, who could not speak the settlers' dialects, inevitably assigned their administrative and judicial tasks to clerks and runners.[65] Labeled by local residents as "tiger sires" for their ferocity, these clerks and runners mistreated ordinary people via the "law." When they were asked to deal with crimes committed against settlers, however, their "law" proved useless. It was said that the officials often refused to handle criminal cases with the excuse that the accused was too mean to detain. If the accused was detained, the officials usually released him upon receiving bribes. Wrongdoers thus believed they would be freed if they paid big enough bribes.[66]

Disturbance of Public Order. Given the prevalent disrespect for law, the lack of public order in Ch'ing Taiwan was only natural. The main sources of disturbance in the Han Chinese community were banditry, communal strife (*fen-lei-hsieh-tou,* largely interethnic rivalry),[67] and popular uprisings.

One of the origins of these disturbances was the social problem of vagrants (*lo-han-chiao*).[68] After the late eighteenth century, it was difficult for newcomers to find arable land on the west coast. Some unemployed men roamed the streets and caused trouble. They often burglarized and robbed, and they organized themselves through sworn brotherhoods and secret societies. These vagrants frequently agitated communal strife and were ready to be participants in any community disturbance or popular uprising. In fact, what these vagrants needed was employment, but the Ch'ing officials could not resolve this problem.[69]

Over time, banditry in Ch'ing Taiwan became even more violent and rampant. Ch'ing criminal law harshly punished banditry, but the law was not enforced. During the last quarter of the nineteenth century, a single brigand band could comprise as many as a hundred men. In 1894, when both communal strife and popular uprisings had decreased, banditry remained Taiwan's worst problem. A few bandits, Chinese Robin Hoods, invaded the houses of local gentry and officials, relieving the poor with the money they looted.[70]

The principal community disturbances occurred among the three main ethnic groups in the settler society during the Ch'ing period, that is, the Ch'üan-chou people, the Chang-chou people, and the Hakka. The first two came from southern Fukien and, in almost equal numbers, made up 80 percent of the Han Chinese population on Taiwan. The Hakka made up the remainder of the population and were ordinarily poorer than the other two; their dialects and customs also differed from those of the Southern Fukienese. The Ch'üan-chou people and Chang-chou people, on the other hand, spoke variations of the same dialect with somewhat different accents. Immigrants from the same native locale generally settled in the same areas in Taiwan. Also, the three ethnic groups often worshiped different patron deities.[71]

Community conflict was frequently caused by the struggle for land or for irrigation or commercial facilities. The key problem, however, was that corrupt and inefficient officials failed to resolve fairly and rapidly disputes between parties not belonging to the same group or village that could not be settled by local headmen.[72] Because of appeals by the disputing parties to the sympathy of their own friends and relatives, these disputes then might develop into disputes between two communities, and the local leaders were expected to "protect" their own members. To consolidate their own position, the local leaders thus mobilized their followers through ethnic ties to fight with other communities. Consequently, communal strife occurred.[73] After antagonism between these ethnic groups had deepened as a consequence of repeated conflicts, even a trifling matter was enough to ignite another outbreak.[74]

Although large-scale communal strife between the three ethnic groups gradually decreased after the 1860s,[75] original ethnic sentiments remained prevalent into the late nineteenth century, when the Japanese arrived in Taiwan. Under such circumstances, the three ethnic groups did not share a common identity much less, needless to say, modern Taiwanese or Chinese nationalism.[76]

The third source of social disorder was popular uprisings. Antigovernment attitudes became a part of the political culture of Ch'ing Taiwan. When dissatisfaction with the government reached a certain degree, a popular uprising would break out. A well-known saying was "a minor revolt every three years and a major one every five years." The rebels were usually *lo-han-chiao* vagrants or tenant peasants, but the rebel leaders came from all three ethnic groups and from every social strata except literati degree-holders.[77]

Nevertheless, the Ch'ing government on Taiwan was never overthrown by these popular uprisings, although scholars have estimated that there were at least sixty eight and perhaps as many as eighty-five uprisings during the 212 years of Ch'ing rule.[78] The reason for this lack of success was that the Ch'ing government always used and encouraged "righteous volunteers" from the rival ethnic groups to suppress the revolts. These "righteous volunteers" did not fight out of allegiance to the Ch'ing but for revenge on their rivals. The people living in Taiwan therefore could not unite themselves against the authority of the central government.[79]

On the other hand, those involved in these revolts were probably motivated by their awareness of being oppressed rather than by any concepts of revolution or of class. Beyond the "extermination of venal officials," they rarely if ever offered any specific program for redistribution of political power, nor did they express demands for social and economic reform in their slogans.[80] For ordinary people, "if the rebels win a battle, the villagers become their followers, but if the government troops are victorious, the villagers become law-abiding people." The nature of popular uprisings was neither "opposing the Ch'ing and restoring the Ming" nor a struggle for the peasant class.[81]

Settler Society in the Late Ch'ing. Because Ch'ing rule on Taiwan was weak, Ch'ing policies and statutes, although influential, were not able to channel the development of Taiwan's settler society. By the late nineteenth century, the settler society in Taiwan developed on its own into a traditional Chinese society with some variations, especially in the economy.

Han Chinese settlers in Taiwan had gradually formed their own traditional Chinese society by the late nineteenth century. Most settlers had arrived in Taiwan during or before the eighteenth century. After one or two hundred years, their descendants regarded Taiwan as their permanent home. It was natural that local lifestyles from the Chinese mainland were transplanted into the new society in Taiwan.[82]

Han Chinese settlers shaped the legal relations to land on Taiwan in accordance with the customs of their native regions in China. Taiwan's settlers developed a "three-tiered system of multiple ownership" patterned on the prevalent practice in Fukien.[83] There were three kinds of fields: private fields, aboriginal fields, and official fields, of which the first were the majority. In private fields, persons who were granted official permits to reclaim land were proprietors and had to pay land taxes to the government. Most of these proprietors then recruited farmers to do the actual labor under a "permanent lease" contract, under which the lessee would pay about 10 percent of the gross produce of the land to the lessor-proprietor. In turn, the lessee often subleased the fields to tenant peasants and received as rent about 50 percent of the gross produce of the land. Accordingly, the lessor-proprietor, who had power to collect rents from the original lease, customarily was called the large-lease holder (*ta-tsu hu*), and the original lessee, who had power to collect rents from the sublessee, was called the small-lease holder (*hsiao-tsu hu*). Gradually the small-lease holder was able to dispose of the land freely and independently, becoming owner of the fields. Similar land relationships occurred for aboriginal and official fields, although the large-lease holders thereunder were the aborigines or the government respectively.[84]

Dispute resolution in the settler society was basically in line with Chinese legal tradition. In Ch'ing Taiwan, perhaps as everywhere, unofficial resolution for civil disputes was socially preferable to official adjudication. The common people ordinarily attempted to settle their disputes through conciliation, frequently presided over by their relatives or local notables. Even in cases where private conciliation had failed or had seemed impossible and thus official settlement had been required, the Ch'ing magistrate in Taiwan, like his colleagues in imperial China, often directed the parties to solicit mediation from relatives or local notables or mediated the disputes personally or through his representatives. When various forms of mediation failed, the magistrate, as a judge, of course had to formally try the disputes.[85] It is noteworthy that those disputes resolved by conciliation or mediation were actually settled in accordance with local customs, which originated from the region where the settlers came from, Fukien or Kwangtung, as well as on Taiwan (for example, commercial customs to reflect the high risk of transporting goods through the Taiwan Strait).[86]

The leading class in the settler society, however, was not entirely like the gentry class in tradition China. In the early period of Ch'ing rule, much land on Taiwan was occupied by those Ch'ing officials who had defeated the Cheng regime and those who had good relations with the Ch'ing. These landlords possessed the large-leases, becoming a powerful new class in Taiwan. However, they were ordinarily absentee landlords living in town or even on the Chinese mainland. After the mid-eighteenth century, resident small-lease holders gradually took actual power in the settler society; some small-lease holders even purchased or appropriated the rights of absentee large-lease holders.[87] Meanwhile, resident large-lease holders and these small-lease holders who actually managed the land ordinarily invested in constructing public facilities, such as irrigation works, dikes, roads, and bridges, and controlled a large number of tenant peasants on their land. In addition, they also built temples and ran the committees that maintained them. Consequently, these resident landlords became local leaders through their land holdings, followers, and prestige in public affairs.[88] Unlike the gentry class in the mainland, however, these local leaders in the island did not acquire their political powers through the government examination.[89] In fact, they often led popular uprisings against the government. In the late nineteenth century, however, some of these local leaders became less like frontier local notables and more like the conventional literati of imperial China, passing the official examination and serving as agents of the government; at the same time, urban-based merchants emerged in the settler society.[90]

Moreover, the economic development of Taiwan was quite distinct from that of much of mainland China.[91] Because Taiwan's external trade had existed since the Dutch rule, the peasants on Taiwan were allowed to develop commercial crops according to their comparative advantages. During the Ch'ing period, some trading lines—largely controlled by Chinese merchants in Fukien or Kwangtung—still remained between Taiwan and the Chinese mainland. In the 1860s, about 180 years after the British ceased trade with Taiwan because of the collapse of the Cheng regime, four treaty ports on Taiwan were opened to foreigners. Some British and American merchants, through Chinese merchants in Fukien or Kwangtung, took over the foreign trade of Taiwan, lending money to Taiwan's peasants to encourage the peasants to produce cash crops.[92] At this time, Taiwan's international trade was far more prosperous than that of any Chinese mainland province. Taiwan's commoditized economy thus led the people to adopt a market-oriented attitude and produced a few wealthy local merchants in late Ch'ing Taiwan. Meanwhile, Taiwan's people became aware of conditions throughout the entire world, not merely in China.[93]

During this development of Taiwan's society, the Ch'ing government did not provide competent rule. It contributed next to nothing in terms of building an infrastructure to increase economic exchange and trade or to promote agricultural expansion.[94] Only during the last ten years of Ch'ing rule, under Governor Liu Ming-ch'uan (1886–91), were some modernization plans carried out in Taiwan. Some of Liu's achievements in Taiwan were the result not only of his personal influence in the central government but also of the remoteness of Taiwan; because the island was far away, it attracted less attention of officialdom, thereby allowing Liu to make unorthodox changes.[95]

The Ch'ing government could not be expected to reform Taiwan's legal system. In the late nineteenth century, many Asian societies faced strong pressure from the West to accept modern Western law.[96] This wave of legal Westernization would influence Taiwan's society sooner or later. Since the Ch'ing regime was not even able to implement existing laws, it obviously could not introduce alien Western law. For example, partly because he lacked an honest and efficient administrative system, Liu was unable to completely clarify the complicated relations of land ownership; consequently, there was a popular uprising during his rule. Moreover, until 1895, the year in which Ch'ing China lost Taiwan, no influential high-ranking officials of Ch'ing China, not even the most advanced Governor Liu, had proposed modernizing the traditional Chinese legal system. The modernization (Westernization) of Taiwan's legal system was thus left to the new Japanese regime, which had adopted Western codes to modernize its own legal system by the end of the nineteenth century.

Some Appraisals

Two points have to be noted concerning the history of Taiwan prior to 1895 before discussing the Japanese implementation of modern Western law in Taiwan. First, in the case of Taiwan, Westernized Japanese codes and statutes would be enforced in a society that was culturally a traditional Han Chinese society and, on the other hand, an untamed and vigorous frontier settler society. Second, the Han Chinese authorities, whether the local government of the Chinese empire or an independent government on the island, did not necessarily do everything for the benefit of Han Chinese settlers. Nevertheless, the colonial authorities, like the Dutch government, did not have only a negative effect on Taiwan. The rulers of Taiwan generally pursued their own interests rather than those of the ruled. Sometimes, however, the measures they introduced also benefited the ruled at that time or subsequently, albeit incidentally since such results were indeed not the initial or primary purpose of the rulers. Such understanding, I believe, is imperative in evaluating fairly the Japanese administration in Taiwan, which is often blamed merely because it was not a Chinese regime and whose beneficial legacy is frequently denied merely because the measures adopted were those of a colonial regime.

REFORM EXPERIENCES OF THE NEW JAPANESE RULERS

In the latter part of this chapter, the focus will shift to the Japanese Meiji government, which began to Westernize its legal system two and a half decades before it conquered Taiwan in 1895. First I wish to make clear why and how the Meiji statesmen reformed Japan's legal system and the extent to which the Japanese themselves adopted Western legal ideas and institutions, especially before 1895.

Intention of Modernization of Law

Japan's Western-style legal system was not adopted immediately after the Meiji government was established in 1868. Facing the threat of Western colonialists, the Meiji statesmen were eager to create a strong, centralized state to give Japan equal status with the European powers.[97] As a first step, the decentralized feudal system under the Tokugawa shogunate had to be replaced by a unifying political force. Under the political slogan "Revive imperial rule" (*ōsei fukko*), the emperor (*tennō*), who had prestige without power in the Tokugawa era, was designated to lead a centralized government.[98] It is not surprising, therefore, that the Meiji leaders initially revived the ancient *ritsuryō* code, which a previous emperor had adopted from the imperial T'ang code (of China) in the seventh century for the purpose of establishing a unified central government.[99] The Meiji government clearly adopted Chinese legal traditions of the Ming and Ch'ing in enacting the 1870 Outline of the New Criminal Code and the 1873 Amended Criminal Regulations.[100]

Soon, however, the Meiji leaders acknowledged that Westernization of law was not only desirable but also inevitable if they were to achieve their ultimate goal of becoming an independent state equal to the Western powers. To "enrich the country, strengthen the army" (*fukoku-kyohei*), they decided to modernize their state by adopting Western capitalism. A Western-style legal system was thus indispensable for nurturing various capitalistic relationships.[101] Further, the deprivation of customs autonomy and the extraterritoriality provided in the unequal treaties between Japan and Western powers had an extremely grave influence on the Japanese political and economic system. The best resolution of this problem was of course the revision of the treaties. Because the Western powers argued, at least superficially, that they had to maintain the extraterritoriality to protect their nationals and investments in Japan from "uncivilized" Japanese justice, the Meiji government realized by at least 1872 that the best means for Japan to end extraterritoriality and to achieve equality was to compile modern codes based upon Western law.[102] In sum, Meiji Japan's Westernization of law was pursued for the sake of promoting capitalism and abolishing extraterritoriality.

Characteristics of Japan's Reception of Law

Gradual Transformation. The political need for treaty revision accelerated Japan's Westernization of law. In fact, one of the reasons for directly imitating European codes instead of adopting Anglo-American common law or Japanese common law was to meet urgent diplomatic or systematization problems.[103] The rate at which the Japanese drafted and enforced modern codes always corresponded to the effects these codes had on treaty revision.[104]

Nevertheless, the Meiji government did not summarily enact and enforce their Western-style codes but instead worked carefully at this task step by step. First, Japanese specialists in modern Western law, which was far different from indigenous Japanese law influenced by Chinese legal traditions, were essential for Japan to successfully adopt Western legal concepts and further implement Western-style codes. From 1869, the government was engaged in the translation of the French codes. Foreign legal scholars were then invited to teach in Japan and to assist in drafting Japan's codes. In 1871 the first law school with instruction in modern Western law was established in the Ministry of Justice. Along with other newly established government law schools, it produced a corps of superior judicial officials. New private law schools also began to train many practicing lawyers. A system allowing students to study abroad was promoted. As a result, thirty years after the Meiji Restoration, Japan already had enough legal experts to compile a civil code based on Western legal concepts.[105]

Another requirement for reception was Western-style judicial institutions. The organization of a modern judiciary was closely related to the completion of Japan's modern political and administrative structure and depended on access to sufficient fiscal support from the government.[106] In Japan, the authority of the Meiji government gradually was stablized and strengthened after some initial unrest. The desire to abolish extraterritoriality also motivated the government to invest in establishing judicial organs. Meanwhile, the policy of "increasing production and raising industries" (*shokusan kōgyō*) in practice promoted Japanese capitalistic society, although it was still in its infancy, and resulted in some disputes that had to be resolved by modern courts.[107]

It took time for the Japanese to adopt the Western idea of judicial independence. In 1872 the first modern court was established in Tokyo, but lawsuits within each prefecture continued to be adjudicated by the judicial section of each prefectural office because there were not yet sufficient legal personnel and facilities to operate modern courts nationwide. The 1872 Official Regulations for the Justice Department introduced a conception that was previously unknown by the Japanese, that the judiciary was to be independent from executive power, although such independence was not complete at that time.[108] The judicial reform of 1875 formally established the modern court system in accordance with the French model of a Great Court of Cassation (Daishin' in) at the apex under which were courts of appeal (*kōsoin*) and prefectural courts, but the majority of prefectures still lacked courts, and therefore provincial administrative officials continued to serve as judges. Moreover, under the 1875 regulation for courts, the president of a court could interfere with individual trials, and judges did not have secure tenure. Not until 1877, with a few exceptions, was the right of the local administrative officials to act concurrently as judges abolished in law. More than ten years later, the Meiji Constitution and the 1890 Court Organization Law finally recognized the principle of judicial independence.[109] That principle was further confirmed by the *Otsu* case of 1891, in which the Great Court of Cassation refused to follow the instructions from the cabinet, making a judgment based on its own legal interpretation.[110]

It was not easy for the Japanese to become acquainted with Western-style court proceedings. Tokugawa traditions with respect to criminal procedure were continued in the beginning of the Meiji era. The 1872 regulations brought about a sharp change, providing a primitive structure for the use of Western-style criminal procedure. Because of a deficiency in judicial finances and personnel, these procedures were not actually implemented, but this shortcoming did not alter the direction of the reform. Japan continued to move toward adopting Western models of criminal procedure. In 1876 and 1879 respectively the government declared that, contrary to Chinese legal traditions, the testimony of the accused was not a part of evidence required for conviction, and torture was absolutely forbidden. Finally, the 1880 Code of Criminal Instruction, which was modeled on French law and free from

Chinese influence, became effective in 1882.[111] Again there were problems in enforcing this comprehensive set of Western-style procedures partly because of the lack of judicial organs and qualified judicial officials. In 1883, the year after the code took effect, a contemporary legislative organization proposed that it be repealed and the old law restored. Some of the code's provisions were thus suspended or amended; these actions severely altered the code's original structure. In fact, actual implementation of the portions that were not modified was not ensured. The prohibition against torture, for instance, was reconfirmed in the 1880 Code of Criminal Instruction but was publicly violated in the suppression of political dissidents in the 1880s.[112] This situation is not surprising considering that there had been no independent judiciary before this and that there were only a few legal professionals who were familiar with the new Western-style law. Improvement in the actual implementation of the 1880 code was only achieved under the judicial reform of 1890.

Japan's first code of civil procedure was not enacted until 1890. Like criminal procedure, civil procedure in the early Meiji era largely followed Tokugawa traditions, in which civil cases were not distinguished from criminal cases. However, unlike criminal procedure, the paper reform of 1872 did not introduce Western civil procedure into Japan. In fact, until 1879, officials could treat the party to a civil suit as a criminal and place him in jail or subject him to torture. Moreover, as in the Tokugawa period, conciliation was encouraged in the newly established modern courts. In 1884 the office of mediator, undertaken by a judge, was thus created for each Peace Court and given the exclusive task of mediating civil suits. Before 1877, judges could even reject civil petitions at will. One of the few changes was to allow civil appeals after 1874. On the other hand, the compilation of a code of civil procedure in accordance with Western legal ideas had begun in 1876. Fourteen years later, the 1890 Code of Civil Procedure was finally promulgated and became effective in 1891.[113] However, the related codes, such as the Law of Procedure in Personal Matters or the Law of Procedure in Non-Contentious Litigation, were not put into effect until 1898.[114]

As stated before, criminal law at the beginning of the Meiji era was influenced by Chinese imperial law. However, the 1873 Amended Criminal Regulation, although still basically consistent with Chinese law, for the first time adopted Western-style criminal penalties instead of traditional ones. From 1872 to 1880 the Meiji government had been engaged in compiling a criminal code modeled on Western law. In 1880 Japan adopted its first Western-style criminal code, based on a draft made by the French adviser-jurist Gustave Boissonade.[115] The code became effective in 1882. It included many fundamental criminal principles adopted from the West; for example, no punishments could be meted out except when expressly provided for by law; penalties were to be decided upon with no regard to the social class of the accused; and guilt was to be limited to the accused himself—his family members were not attainted. The official justification given for enacting this code was to end extraterritoriality. In 1883, proposals were made to repeal the 1880 Criminal Code and the 1880 Code of Criminal Instruction. However, this new Criminal Code had to be maintained at least as window dressing for negotiating treaty revision with the West. In fact, the Meiji government continued to enforce both but enacted some special criminal statutes to meet internal needs.[116]

A Western-style civil code was certainly strange to the Japanese, who had not had any civil code before. As with other codes, the Meiji government had employed foreign experts since 1871 to help in compiling a civil code. Meanwhile, through a few special statutes, several feudal restraints were abolished to recognize the right of land ownership and the freedom of alienation.[117] Based on these developments as well as several drafts of the Civil Code, the government promulgated a Civil Code in 1890, but the Diet of 1892 decided to postpone its enactment, which actually never occurred. A new drafting committee was formed and a new code was written. The first three books (General Provisions, Rights over Things, Obligations) were enacted in 1896; the last two books (Family and Succession) were enacted in 1898.[118] That year, the first modern Civil Code of Japan became fully effective. The new code incorporated the nineteenth-century European concept of individualism with its three basic principles of absolute ownership, freedom of contract, and responsibility for fault.[119]

In conclusion, the Meiji government spent nearly thirty years in shifting its positive law from traditional Chinese law to modern Western law by means of gradually codifying Western-style law and laying the institutional foundations for its enforcement.

Progovernment Selection in Reception. The question which legal system was suitable for adoption was answered in accordance with political considerations rather than theory. Attracted by the military and economic power of the West, Japan decided to adopt modern Western law. The Meiji leaders would further select what Western legal rules were to be received and what indigenous legal rules were to be preserved.[120]

It is naive to think that the Meiji leaders, who originated from lower-ranking warriors (*samurai*) of the feudal era, wanted to establish a democratic state.¹²¹ In the beginning, natural law was employed as an ideological premise for the reception of Western law. The governing statesmen interpreted natural law in terms of its unifying and technically universal character in order to abolish feudal restraints, to achieve political unity, and to nurture capitalistic relationships. However, they never espoused a theory of "heaven-given" human rights, which was fundamentally disadvantageous to them.¹²² The more stable the Meiji government became, the more its absolutist nature was disclosed. In 1880 a liberal movement for civil rights (*jiyu minken undō*) started to demand the creation of a parliament. The government on the one hand in form agreed to this request and corrupted many leaders of this movement, while on the other hand it severely suppressed any popular antigovernment movements.¹²³

The Meiji Constitution thus implemented Western law in a highly selective manner.¹²⁴ In 1881 the Meiji leaders had secretly decided to draw up a constitution following the Prussian model to create a parliament. They envisioned a new constitution granted by the emperor to his subjects. For this reason the absolutist character of the Prussian empire was more attractive to them than the government of France or England, where democratic liberalism prevailed.¹²⁵ This political selection further influenced the later development of Japan's various codes and legal theories. Accordingly, after the 1880s, the main source from which the Japanese received Western law gradually changed from French law to German law. Numerous Japanese students went to Germany because "there was no law except German law."¹²⁶

Under the 1889 Meiji Constitution, executive supremacy somewhat restricted the function of Japan's new judicial system. Jurisdiction over cases against officials did not belong to ordinary courts but rather to the administrative court. The jurisdiction of the administrative court, however, was limited to those cases related to official misapplication of law that were enumerated by statute. As a result, not only were many kinds of official actions free from administrative court review, but any matters involving official discretion, which were commonplace, could not be adjudicated by this court.¹²⁷

Like their counterparts in the Tokugawa, Japan's new criminal law and numerous special criminal statutes served as useful vehicles for authoritarian control of popular agitators and the liberal movement for civil rights. In the 1880 Criminal Code, the provisions authorizing harsh punishment in dealing with riots were included to dispose of peasant uprisings, and the more abstract provisions concerning disrespectful acts committed against the members of the imperial family were considered to be a trump card against the civil rights movement.¹²⁸ At the same time, many special police laws were promulgated in the 1880s and 1890s for similar purposes, such as the Police

Regulation on Public Meetings, the Press Law, Libel Law, Book Censorship Law, and Peace Preservation Law.[129]

In contrast to the reliance on Western notions in drafting new legal rules on property and obligations, Western concepts of family law were excluded from the new Civil Code. From the beginning of the drafting process in 1871, the Meiji statesmen had already insisted that the Japanese patriarchal family system be maintained. Although features of Western law in the draft gave way one by one to elements of the Japanese traditional family system, the Civil Code of 1890 was criticized for its inconsistency with traditional values. In the words of one commentator, "The Civil Code appears and loyalty and filial piety die."[130] The Meiji leaders did not welcome Western family law because it threatened the traditional hierarchical structure of Japanese society, a structure integrally related to the power of the leaders themselves. Japan's prewar household (*ie*) system denied the principle of equality. Family members were distinguished in terms of sex, age, and relationship with males, elders, and parents; and all were subject to the control of the head of household. Family law thus related to Japan's family state ideology of the tennō system, under which the emperor was the head of all Japanese families.[131]

The modern codes of Japan, although in principle modeled on European law, thus still incorporated some traditional Japanese practices and rules. Such an "autonomous" adoption of law (*hō no sesshu*) was helpful in maintaining the cultural identity of the Japanese people.[132] Further, Japan's reception of Western law was selective in that the Meiji government selectively enforced only those aspects of the codes that served its own ends.[133]

Enforcement by Traditional Obedience. The establishment of Japan's modern legal system was a response to internal and external needs of the state rather than to social necessity. The Meiji government did not have time for Western-style codes to arise spontaneously in response to the needs resulting from the gradual transformation of the social structure from a feudal to a capitalist society. A gulf thus existed between the social structure presupposed by the ideological foundations of the received legal system and that which operated in Japan.[134] Because Japanese social structure in large degree, either purposely or out of necessity, was left intact, a hierarchical order of a feudal nature remained in many aspects of Japanese life.[135] Thus the Meiji government used indigenous tradition to enforce Western-style codes in Japanese society. Because of their respect for and submission to superiors (authority) in the traditional hierarchical society, the people would abide by state law, although it had been Westernized.[136] What people obeyed was more the authority of officials than the legitimacy of the new Westernized law.

Legal Concepts of Japanese Imperialists

Though the legal reform was undertaken in the name of "Westernization," traditional legal concepts borrowed from imperial China still deeply influenced the Meiji leaders. Adopting a foreign legal system was not novel for the Japanese in the Meiji era. Early in the seventh century, the Japanese for the first time learned a sinicized version of law from the T'ang dynasty of China (618–906), under which law was an instrument of government control upon society, serving the interests of those who exercised paramount political authority.[137] The Meiji leaders favored these traditional legal ideas over the Western liberal version of law. Although Meiji statesmen eagerly pushed to Westernize law in Japan, they continued to be influenced by traditional legal concepts, which contradicted modern Western law under which law was employed to check the powers of government. For example, Etō Shimpei, an initiator of the 1872 reform that adopted the Western judicial system, was an admirer of Chinese Legalism.[138] According to Chinese Legalism, the king had complete power to enact laws, which all officials and subjects should obey.[139] Accordingly, Japan's pro-government selectivity when adopting Western law was a natural phenomenon.

Furthermore, modern Japanese imperialism was also influenced by the legacy of imperial China. Long ago the ancient idea of a "Central Kingdom" and a "tributary" world had been advanced by the Chinese empire, and the Meiji leaders thought that now, in the late nineteenth century, modern Japan had succeeded in absorbing the advances of Western civilization and was the power center of all Asian nations, which should now be arranged under Japan's leadership.[140] Early in 1887, Japan's foreign minister Inoue Kaoru already advocated the establishment of "a new, European-style empire on the edge of Asia."[141] This emerging Asian imperialist state would employ newly learned Western skills to invade its neighbors, with a traditional spirit of imperial rule.

SUMMARY

Taiwan's geographic position as an isolated island near China and Japan, the ethnic diversity of its inhabitants, and its three quite distinct political regimes all contributed to the uniqueness of old Taiwan's society. The first three alien rulers, who came from outside of Taiwan's society, produced benefits for the people on Taiwan only insofar as such benefits accorded with their own ruling interests. Taiwan's Han Chinese community, however, continued to develop, by itself, into a new settler society that possessed not only the legacy of traditional China but also the vitality of a frontier society in the late nineteenth century. Under the contemporaneous global tendency of legal Westernization, the Han Chinese settler society on Taiwan was led to proceed on this course by another alien ruler, the Japanese regime. What kind of legal reform would this regime bring to them?

To answer this question, we need to note how the Japanese conducted the Westernization of law in their own land. To establish an independent, authoritarian state, Meiji leaders began to modernize Japan's legal system according to Western law. Step by step, Japan took nearly three decades to transform its system of law into a fully codified Western-style system. But the Meiji leaders selected only the parts of Western law that met their needs of governance and were successful in carrying them out largely because of the traditional obedience of the people. In fact, Meiji leaders still maintained traditional legal concepts based on the imperial Chinese system, which regarded law as an instrument of government serving the interests of the rulers. Finally Japan, this "wealthy and strong" state unified under imperial Western-style law, would begin to forge an overseas empire.

2 / Reception of Western Law in Colonial Legislation

The main concern of this chapter is the extent to which Western law was received into the colonial legislation under Japanese legal reform in Taiwan. First, I will introduce the special legislative institutions in colonial Taiwan. Then I will discuss the content of colonial legislation and its relationship to Western law during the former and latter periods of Japanese rule. Finally, I will explain what kinds of laws the colonized Taiwanese wanted to enact in the legal reform.

LEGISLATIVE INSTITUTIONS IN COLONIAL TAIWAN

The Japanese Search for Governing Principles

The Japanese government began its rule on Taiwan with little preparation for the task of ruling a colony. By 1895, the Japanese considered Taiwan as a prospective area to conquer because they thought that the island was an individual territory not belonging to China proper and because the Japanese had briefly ruled the island (in Keelung) before, but Japan did not have a long-range plan for the annexation of Taiwan.[1] As a result of Japan's overwhelming victory in the Sino-Japanese War (1894–95), Japan's leaders decided to demand some areas of Chinese territory to demonstrate that Japan had become sufficiently advanced to duplicate what the Western powers had done to other countries and therefore should be considered their equal. On the other hand, Japan could not acquire territory from China without the risk of provoking Western intervention. Taiwan was thus selected since Japanese possession of this island was less likely to antagonize the Western powers.[2] Hence the Japanese government had neither detailed information about Taiwan nor a clear governing policy toward its new territory when it occupied the island in 1895. In fact, Japan had no experience in governing a colony.[3]

For Japan, the fundamental question in governing Taiwan was whether this newly acquired territory should be regarded as a prefecture under the central government, like Okinawa since 1879, or a colony under a resident government. Two foreign advisers were consulted about this problem, one from France, the other from England, the two strongest colonial powers with distinct governing policies at that time. On April 22, 1895, the French adviser, Michel Joseph Revon, proposed that Taiwan should be regarded, although not immediately, as a prefecture of the Japanese empire following the French example in Algeria. A week later, however, on April 30, 1895, the British adviser, William Montague Hammett Kirkwood, suggested that Taiwan should be a colony governed outside the purview of the Meiji Constitution; hence, the emperor would delegate his legislative prerogative for the colony to a resident legislative council composed of the governor-general, officials, and natives.[4]

The differences in these opinions reflected the differences in legal thought in France and England at the time. On the one hand, assimilation was the dominating principle of French colonial rule in the nineteenth century. Deriving their belief from the concept of universal law in Roman law and the 1789 Revolution, the French held that reason was the most widely shared human characteristic throughout the world. Hence law based on human universality was everywhere applicable. Less developed peoples subjected to colonial regimes would thus finally understand and receive law through "enlightenment." In contrast, the British thought that all legislation should vary with the circumstances and that each country should adopt only those laws that were appropriate to its own needs.[5]

At the beginning, the Japanese government seemed to prefer the French proposal, though these two different approaches to governance confused them. The Treaty of Shimonoseki, by which China ceded Taiwan to Japan, was ratified by the two nations on May 8, 1895. Japan had to take control of the island as soon as possible to prevent any possible change. Consequently, two days after the ratification, Premier Itō Hirobumi issued an instruction to the newly appointed governor-general of Taiwan for occupation of the island. This instruction was the result of practical, not doctrinal, concerns. The governor-general was granted broad and arbitrary power to cope with the changeable situation on Taiwan.[6]

Just before the Japanese army occupied Taipei and inaugurated colonial rule on June 17, 1895, a hastily organized Taiwan Affairs Bureau met and discussed the conflicting proposals of the two foreign advisers. Hara Kei (Takashi), a member of this bureau and later a premier (1918–21), emphasized the relative proximity of Taiwan and Japan and the ethnic and cultural similarity between the two peoples, advocating the French style. To avoid the unfavorable connotation of the British view of "colony," which implied white people exploiting the black and yellow peoples in the remote lands of Africa and Asia, most members of the bureau tended to accept Hara's opinion.[7] In fact, influenced by the Chinese idea of leadership of the "Central Kingdom," these Meiji leaders considered Japan to have become the new civilized "Central Kingdom" in East Asia, responsible for "enlightening" neighboring peoples, including the Taiwanese.

But unexpected Taiwanese armed resistance changed the initial plans for colonial legislation. The cession of Taiwan by the Ch'ing empire was not sufficient to make Japan the master of the island.[8] Japan's army first had to conquer Taiwan by force. The Taiwanese people desperately resisted this invader. Even though the Japanese authorities declared on November 18, 1895, that all of the island was pacified, Taiwanese guerrilla resistance continued.[9] In fact, the civilian government originally designed to govern the island could not function except in the Taipei area. After August 6, 1895, Taiwan was directly governed by Japanese military authorities. Military orders (*nichirei*) thus became the initial source of law on Taiwan.[10]

Fundamental Law of the Colony

This first resistance led the Japanese government to be hostile to the Taiwanese and deeply influenced the legislative institutions on Taiwan. The Japanese central government initially preferred that legislative matters in Taiwan be regulated by Japanese statutes (*hōritsu;* Diet-enacted laws) and, where necessary, by imperial ordinance, as Hara had suggested.[11] However, Taiwanese armed resistance throughout the island forced the central government and the Imperial Diet to agree with the arguments of the GGT that the responsible officials on Taiwan, not in Tokyo, should have broad powers to enact laws for Taiwan to govern effectively the nearly three million natives whose customs and traditions were vastly different from those of the Japanese and whose loyalty to the Japanese was very uncertain.[12] In March 1896 the Diet enacted the Law Relating to Laws and Ordinances to Be Enforced in Taiwan under Title 63 (hereafter called Title 63; see appendix B).[13]

The key element of Title 63 was that the Diet delegated its legislative prerogatives for Taiwan to the chief executive officer of the Taiwan administration. The governor-general of Taiwan was charged with the duty of governing Taiwan. He had power to issue ordinances, called *ritsurei*, that had the same effect within his governing jurisdiction as Japanese statutes made by the Diet. Those portions of Japanese statutes that were to be applied to Taiwan should be provided by ordinance, called "an ordinance for application" (*shikō chokurei*).¹⁴ Meanwhile, under the Organic Regulations of the GGT, the governor-general possessed executive authority, military authority, and authority over judicial administration.¹⁵ Consequently, within the jurisdiction of Taiwan, a special legal zone of the Japanese empire, the governor-general of Taiwan had the legislative authority, under the supervision of the central government, to make law and enforce it without interference of the Imperial Diet or the legislative council in the colony.¹⁶

Controversies in Constitutional Law

Debate soon ensued over the validity of this fundamental law for colonial legislation under the Japanese Meiji Constitution, ordinarily called the issue of Title 63. Since no provision in the 1889 Meiji Constitution regulated colonies and their legislation, Japanese scholars versed in constitutional law presented varying interpretations on the issue.¹⁷ Because the effective duration of Title 63 was three years, the question of the constitutionality of Title 63 became an issue in the Imperial Diet every three years when the Diet was called upon to extend the law and thus drew politicians into the dispute.¹⁸ The threshold question of the constitutionality of Title 63 was whether the Meiji Constitution applied to Taiwan. Many scholars supported the argument that Taiwan was under the jurisdiction of the Constitution.¹⁹ In contrast, several influential legal scholars excluded Taiwan from the jurisdiction of the Meiji Constitution.²⁰ At the outset of the debate, the Japanese government initially did not recognize the application of the Constitution to Taiwan but very soon modified its position, asserting that although chapter 2 on the Rights and Duties of Subjects was not enforced in practice, the Constitution was partially applicable to Taiwan. The government then expressly agreed that the Constitution did apply to Taiwan inasmuch as Title 63 of 1896 was enacted through the legislative process provided by the Constitution.²¹ Such official interpretation appeared in Japan's propaganda to the West.²² A Japanese legal scholar in his publication in the United States also argued that the Constitution indeed applied to the colonies, although the character of certain constitutional provisions, like those relating to the rights and duties of subjects, allowed necessary special treatment in the colonies.²³ In addition, the GGT incessantly emphasized that the Constitution applied to Taiwan for various reasons.²⁴ It should also be noted that in 1905 a provision in a draft colonial procedural statute was deleted by the GGT on the ground that it contradicted the open-trial principle in the Constitution.²⁵

Insisting that the Constitution applied in Taiwan, the Japanese government inevitably encountered further challenges to the constitutionality of the idea of delegated legislation in Title 63. According to the interpretation of most Japanese legal scholars, the Imperial Diet could delegate only specific powers to the executive; otherwise, it would not actually perform its duties under the Constitution. The general and broad scope of the delegation of legislative power of Title 63 was thus argued to be unconstitutional.[26] It was not surprising that some scholars advocated the government's position, asserting that because the Constitution did not restrict the manner of exercising legislative power, the Imperial Diet was free to adopt a broad scope of delegation.[27] The government, however, avoided discussing the theoretical foundation of the delegated legislation in Title 63 but emphasized that the law had already been passed by the Diet in 1896 and had thus become a precedent, which in practice must be maintained.[28]

This attitude of the government revealed the real nature of the reason for issuing Title 63, which was a question of political choice in policy for governance of the newly acquired territory. In fact some legal scholars argued that the question about which law should be enforced in the newly acquired territory should be determined by the policy of the government rather than by a legal interpretation of the Constitution.[29] Most Western colonialist powers also considered the application of a constitution in a colony to be a matter of colonial policy rather than a legal issue.[30] The Japanese government was unwilling to recognize Taiwan as a colony in Western terms and therefore could only apply parts of the Constitution to Taiwan, but it tried to employ "legal interpretation" to resolve an essentially political question. In any event, the argument whether or not a law was constitutional had little meaning in positive law in prewar Japan because a so-called unconstitutional law could not be rescinded by the court and remained valid until it was repealed by another law.

The Imperial Japanese Diet in fact discussed the issue of Title 63 as a political question. Some argued that the broad legislative power of the governor-general was only an emergency measure and thus should be terminated when governance in Taiwan was stable. Others considered that such power of the governor-general was necessary to govern the rebellious Taiwanese and deal rapidly with the changeable situation in Taiwan.[31] Their primary consideration, however, was how to govern Taiwan effectively rather than which choice was more advantageous to the Taiwanese. Moreover, the issue of Title 63 served as the focus of a power struggle in Japanese political circles between the Diet and the government or between the civilian political parties and the army, which in fact controlled Taiwan.[32] For instance, this issue was used by the political party in power to bargain with the government to establish Tōhoku University (Sendai) in Japan.[33]

Although the core of the issue of Title 63 was who had power to legislate law in Taiwan, the Taiwanese had no voice in this argument. Obviously, the Taiwanese were "the object of governance," meaning a group who were governed by the empire but who had no political rights.[34]

Revision of the Colonial Fundamental Law

The duration of Title 63 was in fact extended again and again until 1906, when the Law Relating to Laws and Ordinances to Be Enforced in Taiwan was revised under Title 31 (hereafter referred to as Title 31; see appendix B). One of the amendments in Title 31 adopted the principle of the supremacy of Japanese law—that is, the *ritsurei* of the governor-general should not be in conflict with those Japanese statutes and ordinances that were enforced in the colony. This theoretically restricted the scope of the legislative power of the GGT. But since Japanese statutes and ordinances were seldom enforced in Taiwan after Title 31 was promulgated, as will be discussed later, this new restriction had little effect. Accordingly, Title 31 was virtually a continuation of Title 63 and later was followed in governing colonial Korea.[35] The five-year effective duration of Title 31 was also repeatedly extended until another revision emerged in 1921.[36] Therefore, the colonial legislative institutions formulated by Title 63 lasted for virtually twenty-five years in Taiwan.

Not until the entire colonial policy was changed did the fundamental law of the colony undergo a substantive change. After 1919 Japanese colonial policy turned to assimilation, and the Law Relating to Laws and Ordinances to Be Enforced in Taiwan was thus revised in 1921 under Title 3 (hereafter referred to as Title 3; see appendix B) to respond to the new policy. To further extend the Japanese mainland law to colonial Taiwan,[37] Title 3 moved the provision concerning the ordinance for application from the fifth (Title 63) or the fourth (Title 31) article to the first article of this fundamental law and, more important, created "the ordinance for exception" (*tokurei chokurei*) in the first article. Thereafter, newly created ordinances could contain special provisions that altered provisions in Japanese statutes that were extended to Taiwan to meet the special needs of the colony. With the ordinance for exception, it became easy to apply Japanese (mainland) statutes in colonial Taiwan. When a Japanese law was extended to Taiwan, the ordinance for exception allowed not only technical changes involving different legal terminology or agencies between the two distinct legal systems, but also more substantive changes for dealing with different societies.[38] Most special provisions for application of Japanese statutes in Taiwan were promulgated in the form of an ordinance for exception; only a few were stipulated in the Japanese statute itself.[39] Lacking such a provision in Korea, where the counterpart of Title 31 was maintained, the Japanese government was compelled to request the Diet to pass supplemental provisions for Korea every time it wanted to extend a Japanese statute to Korea. That was one reason why Japanese (mainland) statutes were less frequently extended to colonial Korea than to colonial Taiwan.[40]

Meanwhile, the delegated legislative power of the governor-general, although still preserved, was restricted by Title 3. Accompanying the existing principle of the supremacy of the Japanese law which was applied to the colony, Title 3 further provided that the authority for promulgating *ritsurei* was limited to the following circumstances: (1) there did not exist an appropriate Japanese statute, or the application of a Japanese statute accompanied by certain exceptions by ordinance was difficult, and (2) it was necessary to respond to the special conditions of Taiwan.[41]

However, Taiwan's status as a special legal zone was maintained. Japanese (mainland) statutes remained ineffective in colonial Taiwan without recognition under an ordinance for application. In the past, the *ritsurei* of the colonial government had the same effect as Diet-enacted statutes in Taiwan. Under Title 3, however, the effectiveness of the *ritsurei* was restricted, but ordinances for exceptions (which could alter provisions in Japanese statutes that applied in Taiwan) by the central government had the same effect as Diet-enacted statutes in Taiwan. The essence of Title 63, that an administrative agency had legislative power for Taiwan, was not changed, although the central government legally possessed more power in determining colonial law than before. In any event, once a Japanese statute had been applied to Taiwan via an ordinance for application, Taiwan would be no longer a special legal zone for matters governed by that statute.[42] Hence, if the number of Japanese statutes applied in Taiwan increased as a result of Title 3, Taiwan's affairs would increasingly be covered by the same system as Japan's.

Another important characteristic of Title 3 was its permanence; it had no fixed duration. This law seemed to be the final legal instrument for colonial legislation in Taiwan.

Practical Legislative Process

Whether the process for enacting colonial law changed because of the promulgation of Title 3 depended upon the process for enacting *ritsurei* under Title 63. According to Title 63, the GGT Consultative Council (Hyōgikai) had first to approve the enactment of *ritsurei*. *Ritsurei* then had to receive imperial approval through the prime minister (or another responsible minister) of the central government either before or, in case of emergency, after promulgation.[43] However, these rules were not so strictly adhered to as the provisions might suggest. The council comprised the governor-general and his high-ranking staff only, and the governor-general could reject the decision of the council, attaching his reasons to the decision.[44] The judicial archives of the GGT (1895–1905) show that the GGT Consultative Council was actually not a decision-making agency. Its decisions were only a formality for meeting the requirements of Title 63.[45] The archives also reveal that in some instances, the legal bureaucrats in the central government revised the wording of the proposed *ritsurei*, but they usually granted the imperial approval. Only in a few cases did the central government suspend a proposed *ritsurei*, by denying approval.[46] Under Title 63, through the enactment of *ritsurei*, the GGT was allowed to decide freely whether or not to follow Japanese law. The provisions of a *ritsurei* could be totally different from those of Japanese law. For instance, the GGT sometimes adopted Taiwan's old institutions, which did not exist on the Japanese mainland (Japan proper), by enacting *ritsurei*. On the other hand, the GGT could also adopt Japanese law through a *ritsurei*, with some modifications. Under the latter situation, the *ritsurei* would provide that certain matters should conform to (*yoru*) the Japanese statute named in the *ritsurei* (see, e.g., article 1 in appendix C).[47] The Japanese statutes named in the *ritsurei* thus became enforced indirectly in Taiwan, being put into effect through the *ritsurei*, rather than directly by an applicable statute.[48] Accordingly, the existence of a *ritsurei* did not necessarily always include special provisions for the colony. To apply a Japanese (mainland) statute to colonial Taiwan, the central government could also promulgate an ordinance for application under Title 63. But, unfamiliar with Taiwan's situation, the central government generally issued such an ordinance only upon the request of the GGT.[49] In practice, a Japanese statute was ordinarily not applied to Taiwan unless the GGT actively required its application.

Thus, under Title 63, the GGT itself virtually decided the number of Japanese statutes that were directly applied to Taiwan or indirectly enforced in Taiwan through *ritsurei* as well as the number of special laws for the colony.

Under Title 3, the power to issue *ritsurei* was restricted and the ordinance for exception was created. Therefore, the practice of employing *ritsurei* to indirectly enforce Japanese statutes with some special provisions for Taiwan was no longer absolutely necessary, although it still existed. Under Title 3, Japanese statutes could be applied directly to Taiwan under ordinances for application with special provisions enacted under ordinances for exception.[50] In theory, most colonial legislation was to be decided by the central government. Nevertheless, by cabinet resolution, ordinances of application or exception under Title 3 were, as a rule, to be issued "upon the report of the governor-general of Taiwan or after a request for his opinion" in order "to prevent conflict with the governing policy of the governor-general."[51] In practice, the process of promulgating ordinances for application and ordinances for exception was initiated by the department of judicial affairs of the GGT drafting a proposed ordinance with explanations. The governor-general of Taiwan would then approve the draft and send it to the prime minister (the minister of colonial affairs after 1929 or minister of home affairs after 1942) for approval by the cabinet.[52] This was the same as the process for enacting a *ritsurei*. The only difference was one of form in that an existing ordinance was required for ordinances of application or exception and imperial approval was required for *ritsurei*.[53]

In addition, because of the provision for supremacy of Japanese law under Title 3 (and Title 31), Japanese statutes that already applied directly to Taiwan took precedence over *ritsurei*. However, when the GGT wanted to enact a *ritsurei* that was in conflict with Japanese statutes effective in Taiwan, it would frequently request the Japanese central government to issue an ordinance for exception, by which the conflicting portions of the Japanese statutes would be amended. The GGT would then exercise its own legislative power to promulgate the desired *ritsurei*.[54]

In sum, the actual exercise of colonial legislative power under Title 3 was little different from that under Title 63 (and Title 31).[55] Within the special legal zone of Taiwan, the GGT in reality was, throughout the period of its rule of Taiwan, ordinarily able to decide the contents of colonial law.

Special Colonial Law and Mainland Law

Judging from the form of legislation, Title 3 was the watershed for two distinct periods. Title 3 was enacted in 1921 for the purpose of extending Japanese mainland statutes to Taiwan by ordinances as much as possible. The period from 1922, the year that Title 3 became effective, to 1945 was therefore called the period of "the ordinance as a main source of law"; in contrast, the period from 1896 to 1921 was called the period of "the *ritsurei* as a main source of law."[56] During the 1896–1921 period, 84 mainland statutes were applied to Taiwan by ordinances, but 203 *ritsurei* were promulgated; by the end of the 1922–45 period, 195 mainland statutes had been applied to Taiwan by ordinances, but only 67 *ritsurei* remained valid.[57]

We are concerned here, however, not with whether a law was effected by ordinance or *ritsurei* but with the extent to which the substance of colonial legislation adopted modern Western law. A *ritsurei* might either conform to Japanese mainland statutes that had received Western law or enact special colonial institutions irrelevant to Western law. That the *ritsurei* was a main source of law does not tell us much about the relationship between Taiwan's colonial law and Western law. Thus, it is necessary to divide colonial laws on Taiwan into two periods on the basis of their substantive contents rather than their legislative forms. Below, the 1895–1922 period is called "special colonial law as a principle," meaning that the majority of laws were enacted specifically for unique conditions in colonial Taiwan.[58] The latter period, 1923–45, is called "Japanese mainland law as a principle," meaning that provisions of Japanese metropolitan laws largely took effect on Taiwan through ordinances or *ritsurei*. The reasons for this periodization will be illustrated later.

SPECIAL COLONIAL LAW AS A PRINCIPLE

Experiment in Colonial Governance

Japanese Military Administration. During the initial pacifying period, the GGT first issued a series of penalty-related military orders to suppress Taiwanese guerrilla resistance. The Dispositions for Taiwanese Military Criminals punished various Taiwanese guerrilla activities, and the penalty was always death.[59] According to the 1895 Regulation regarding the Organization of the GGT Courts, a military tribunal was established to deal with Taiwanese criminal and civil matters.[60] Soon, the Penalty Order for Inhabitants of Taiwan was promulgated.[61] In addition to duplicating the provisions in the Dispositions for Taiwanese Military Criminals, this regulation also provided for the offenses of homicide, rape, theft, and robbery (as well as many others), stating that the provisions in the Japanese Army or Navy Criminal Code as well as the ordinary Criminal Code were applicable. The main concern remained penalties for guerrilla activities, which were even harsher than before.[62] Similarly, because of wartime needs, the Criminal Instruction Order for Inhabitants of Taiwan, under which the defendant was not allowed to appeal, did not follow Japanese modern criminal procedure.[63]

The GGT focused on criminal matters, paying little attention to Taiwanese civil affairs. The only provision concerning substantive civil law was the Civil Litigation Order for Inhabitants of Taiwan, which provided that civil lawsuits should be adjudicated in accordance with local customs and legal theory.[64] Again because of the "state of war," civil procedure was so simple that "the adjudicator could make whatever judgment he would according to the dictates of his own reasoning."[65] The decisions of the civil tribunal could not be appealed.[66]

Because the first phase of Japanese colonialism, like that of most European colonial empires, began with the initial disorder caused by colonial conquest, legislation during the period of military administration (June 17, 1895–March 31, 1896) emphasized suppression of rebellion.[67] In this situation legal reform was impossible.

Initial Period of Civil Administration. Although civilian government in Taiwan was instituted on April 1, 1896, the first three military governor-generals of Taiwan were still busy pacifying anti-Japanese guerrillas and managed the new colony by trial and error.[68] To maintain public order, colonial courts under the civil administration were hastily established under the 1896 GGT court Organization Law.[69] However, there was no substantive criminal law until a *ritsurei*, promulgated three months later, provided that the punishment for crimes on Taiwan was to conform to the Japanese Criminal Code except in cases in which the code's provisions were difficult to apply to Taiwanese.[70] Moreover, no civil law was enacted until July of 1898, but the courts in practice continued to apply local customs and legal theory to decide Taiwanese civil lawsuits as they had under the military administration.[71]

During this experimental period, the Japanese applied their experience with legal reform in the early Meiji era. Like the Meiji reformers,[72] the GGT, a centralized administrative authority, at first employed criminal law as an auxiliary tool, with a court hierarchy to support it. Many legal measures in this period imitated early Meiji counterparts. The GGT established a Temporary Court to adjudicate political crimes.[73] Judges and procurators in colonial courts were appointed by the governor-general without any system of security of tenure. Nor was there a complete separation of judicial functions from executive power. An administrator might be a judge in the district court and a police officer might be a procurator.[74] The chief of police and the captain of the Taiwan gendarmerie had the power to adjudicate immediately any offenses punishable by detention or a police fine.[75] Meanwhile, trial advocates (*soshō dainin*), for whom formal professional training as a lawyer was not required, were allowed on Taiwan.[76] All of these institutions were representative of early Meiji practice.[77] By 1890, however, those systems had been abolished in Japan, except for police adjudication of minor offenses. One possible reason for Japan's continuing to employ old institutions instead of new Western-style institutions on Taiwan was that on the one hand, the Japanese government was accustomed to resorting to old institutions to maintain public order and suppress political dissidents, and on the other hand, the Taiwanese people were entirely unfamilar with modern Western law. Moreover, under the pressure of the West, Japan had to enforce new Western-style codes in Japan proper. Since this Western demand did not extend to Taiwan, Japan had no urgent need to implement Western-style law in Taiwan.[78]

Special Colonial Law

Not until early 1898 did the fourth military governor-general, Kodama Gentarō, and his fully trusted civil administrator, Gotō Shimpei, shape a basic model for colonial legislation.[79] The first point Gotō clarified was that regardless of how Taiwan was referred to, it was a colony, and thus Japan had to borrow Western colonial legal institutions in governing the island.[80] He further asserted that Japan had to investigate old institutions in Taiwan and preserve only those advantageous to colonial rule.[81] In other words, he recognized that some legal institutions created by imperial China would be beneficial to Japan's rule on Taiwan.[82] Hence, in addition to Japan's own experience in law, Gotō wanted to employ both Western colonial law and Chinese imperial law to formulate a new legal system in Taiwan so that Taiwan could become a showcase of Japanese colonialism.[83] This new approach for legal reform in Taiwan was adopted by Kodama and several later governor-generals.

Thus many legal principles of Western colonial practice were adopted in establishing a legal system for Taiwan. If an indigenous Japanese law contributed to colonial governance, it would be enforced in Taiwan, even though it might have been abandoned in Japan. Meanwhile, traditional institutions in Taiwan were maintained to the extent that they were beneficial, or at least not harmful, to Japanese rule. This can be seen from the development of criminal and civil law after mid-1898, as discussed below.

Criminal Law. To maintain public order, Western colonialists consistently interfered with native criminal justice.[84] The Kodama administration, when enacting the 1898 Civil, Commercial, and Criminal Law (see appendix C), continued preexisting practice in enforcing the Japanese Criminal Code in Taiwan unless there were laws that provided otherwise.[85] As a result of the promulgation in 1907 of the Japanese Criminal Code, the GGT enacted an independent criminal law, that is, the 1908 Taiwan Criminal Law. It provided that criminal matters in Taiwan should conform to the new Japanese Criminal Code, but it also recognized the validity of certain special criminal laws.[86] Thus, Western-style Japanese criminal law was implemented in Taiwan from 1896.[87]

Special criminal law was commonplace in Western colonies, and Taiwan under Japanese colonial rule was no exception.[88] Some special criminal laws were enacted for criminal matters that occurred in Taiwan. The most famous was the 1898 Bandit Punishment Law (see appendix D).[89] Succeeding the Penalty Order for Inhabitants of Taiwan under the military administration, this law disregarded the principles of modern Western criminal law and adopted traditional terrorism.[90] Not surprisingly, in practice this law was applied only to the Taiwanese, although legally it also covered resident Japanese (Japanese mainlanders). Similarly, the 1897 Taiwan Opium Law was enacted for Taiwan as a whole but was primarily used to cope with opium smoking among Taiwanese.[91] In contrast, the 1900 Taiwan Press Law, which strictly controlled freedom of the press and legally applied to all people in Taiwan, was in fact enacted for the resident Japanese during the early days of Japanese rule.[92]

Certain special criminal laws were applied to the Japanese only. One example was the 1900 Taiwan Peace Preservation Regulation, under which those who misbehaved but had not committed crimes might be expelled from Taiwan.[93] This law partially imitated the Japanese 1887 Peace Preservation Law, which had been abolished in Japan in 1898.[94]

Other special criminal laws applied explicitly to the Taiwanese only, such as (1) the 1898 Hokō Law, under which an entire kō (a group of ten households) or ho (a group of ten kō) was liable for the conduct of individual members; for example, if a man in a kō committed a serious crime, all households within this kō could be punished by fines except those households whose head had previously reported the offense to the authority;[95] (2) the 1904 Fine and Flogging Law, by which fines or physical punishment could be imposed on the convicted;[96] and (3) the 1906 Taiwan Vagrant Discipline Regulation, which allowed the police to punish unemployed persons threatening public order.[97] The 1898 Hokō Law and the 1904 Fine and Flogging Law were adopted from imperial Chinese law, but they were not unfamiliar to the Japanese. The system of *goningumi* (literally, five-man groups) in Tokugawa Japan was similar to the Hokō system in colonial Taiwan.[98] The Japanese Outline of the New Criminal Code of 1870 also included the punishment of flogging.[99] Additionally, it seemed that the 1906 Taiwan Vagrant Discipline Regulation was modeled on the Japanese Preventive Prohibition Regulation of 1892.[100]

Under the 1898 Civil, Commercial, and Criminal Laws, the Japanese Code of Criminal Procedure was not enforced in trials of Taiwanese.[101] But the next year, in 1899, to remove the inconvenience resulting from nonunified procedures in various courts, Taiwanese trials were also conformed to the Japanese Code of Criminal Procedure.[102] This measure was confirmed in the 1908 Taiwan Criminal Law.[103] Thus, beginning in 1899, a Western-style criminal procedure was formally enforced in Taiwan as a consequence of the enforcement of Japanese law.

Western colonial policy taught that colonial criminal procedure should be simple and swift.[104] Soon after the Japanese procedural law was enforced in Taiwanese trials, the GGT promulgated a special law specifically for

Taiwanese only, providing that a procurator might directly institute public prosecution against any Taiwanese accused on the basis of very clear evidence without going through the process of preliminary examination in court.[105] To collect necessary evidence in such cases, the procurator and in certain circumstances the judicial police were given the authority to detain suspects or search places related to the crime, a power that originally belonged to the examining magistrate in the preliminary examination.[106] Absorbing these special laws, the 1905 Special Law for Criminal Litigation further extended the authority of judges, procurators, and judicial policemen so that criminal trials could be rapidly decided.[107] As a result, the protections for the accused in modern criminal procedure were gradually lessened, and the traditional inquisitorial system was strengthened step by step.

The GGT in fact never forgot the "merits" of the criminal procedure of imperial Chinese law. Under the 1904 Summary Judgment Law, the heads of local government, like Chinese magistrates, had the power to immediately adjudicate a broad range of criminal offenses; this power was more extensive than the similar system in Japan.[108] According to the 1905 Special Law for Criminal Litigation, the confession of the accused with which the procurator or victims did not express disagreement was sufficient for conviction in cases involving offenses punishable by less than one year of imprisonment.[109] Confession in traditional Chinese law had similar consequences. Because confession was frequently extracted with brutal torture, reliance upon confessions as the sole basis for conviction was legally abolished in Japan in the late 1870s; however, the GGT favored the use of confessions to end criminal trials quickly. The validity of the 1905 Special Law for Criminal Litigation was confirmed again by the 1908 Taiwan Criminal Law.[110]

Civil Law. Western colonial practice also showed that it was not prudent for the colonial government to interfere immediately with the private law of natives.[111] The 1898 Civil, Commercial, and Criminal Laws therefore explicitly provided that the civil and commercial matters involving Japanese were to conform to the Japanese Civil Code but those involving only Taiwanese or Chinese were to be decided in accordance with Taiwan's old customs unless there were laws that provided otherwise. The 1908 Taiwan Civil Law repeated such provisions and listed the special civil laws that were effective in Taiwan.[112] Therefore, with few exceptions, a modern Japanese civil code was not applicable for Taiwanese until the early 1920s.[113]

In the same way that Western colonial powers regulated the land system in their colonies, Japanese colonialists enacted many special civil laws relating to land on Taiwan.[114] These special land laws, which largely followed

Taiwanese customs in substance, applied to Taiwan territory and thus excluded related Japanese law.¹¹⁵ Based on Japanese experiences in Meiji legal reform, the GGT first investigated the legal relations regarding land and clarified the ownership of land according to the 1898 Taiwan Land Survey Regulations and the 1904 Arrangement for Large-lease.¹¹⁶ Later the 1910 Taiwan Forest Survey did the same for Taiwan's forests.¹¹⁷ In addition, under the 1905 Taiwan Land Registration Regulations, certain kinds of land transactions were invalid unless they were registered.¹¹⁸

As with criminal procedure, the simplification of colonial civil procedure was also suggested by Western experts.¹¹⁹ Based on the same reasons that governed their approach to criminal procedure, the colonial government ruled that Taiwanese civil lawsuits were to conform to the Japanese Code of Civil Procedure after 1899. However, not long after the code was enforced in Taiwan, the GGT simplified this Westernized civil procedure to expedite civil court proceedings. Under the 1905 Special Law for Civil Litigation, the authority of judges was strengthened and the rights of litigants relatively weakened.¹²⁰ The effectiveness of this Special Law was confirmed by the 1908 Taiwan Civil Law.¹²¹

Furthermore, didactic mediation by magistrates, a commonplace form of dispute resolution in imperial China, was restored. Under the Civil Disputes Mediation Law, local administrative officials could direct the disputants to reach a "compromise."¹²² The law was enacted to reduce the judicial expenditure of the colonial government.

Progovernment Legal Reform

Like the Japanese leaders who carried out the Meiji legal reforms, the Japanese colonial rulers also selected those laws that met the needs of colonial governance in their legal reforms in Taiwan. Past and present Japanese legal experience, Western colonial law, and Chinese imperial law became good references for such purpose. In addition, sometimes unprecedented "appropriate" measures were adopted for colonial governance.

The legislation for bandits is an example. During the period from 1898 to 1902, the greatest threat to Japanese rule was anti-Japanese guerrilla activity; the GGT therefore promulgated a series of substantive and procedural criminal *ritsurei* to suppress the "bandits." These legal measures included (1) reviving the imperial Chinese *pao-chia* system in 1898 (by the *Hokō Law*) to separate the members of anti-Japanese guerrilla groups from the general public,¹²³ (2) enacting a special criminal law with extremely harsh penalties (for example, the 1898 Bandit Punishment Law) in Taiwan, as was the practice in other

Western colonies,[124] (3) amending the law concerning the Temporary Court (an institution in metropolitan Japan before 1890) in 1898 to prohibit appeals and retrials for bandit cases,[125] (4) providing in 1899 that the procurator might institute a public prosecution against bandits without preliminary examination,[126] (5) providing in 1901 that defense counsel was not a requirement in trials of bandits as it was for other serious offenses.[127] In connection with the last two measures, the GGT modified existing Japanese criminal procedure in formulating its own law for the colony.

With respect to civil law, the GGT did not follow the Japanese Civil Code in deeming transactions involving rights in land that were not registered as valid between parties concerned (though invalid with respect to third parties), but provided that such unregistered transactions were absolutely invalid. The purpose of this law was to ensure that third parties could rely on the land registry and then complete a legally valid transaction, for rapid and secure land sales were important in promoting a capitalistic economy. For the development of a capitalistic economy, the GGT was willing to sacrifice the interests of (Taiwanese) landlords.[128] Similarly, the GGT decided to restrict high interest rates in Taiwan because high rates hindered economic development.[129] And until 1923, to protect Japanese capitalists on Taiwan, the GGT did not permit those enterprises organized by Taiwanese only to incorporate modern companies under the Japanese company law.[130]

The continuation of preexisting institutions in Taiwan was not the result of any concern for the interests of the Taiwanese. The maintenance or abolition of old Taiwanese customs in fact depended on whether they were considered advantageous or disadvantageous to the Japanese colonialists. Consequently, the GGT investigated old Taiwanese customs in detail.[131] Punishment by flogging and the right of administrators to adjudicate disputes reduced judicial expenditure and therefore were preserved, although they had been abolished in metropolitan Japan.[132] Allowing the Taiwanese to apply customary civil law lessened their hatred of the Japanese conquerors, but the diverse and unwritten customs made legal relations of commercial transactions unclear; therefore, old customs remained valid but needed to be clarified or further codified.[133] The traditional *hokō* system facilitated control by vicarious liability and served local administration, but formation of such groups also posed a potential threat to colonial rule; therefore, this system was maintained but tightly controlled by the local police. Although using opium and gambling were considered bad customs, it would have cost considerable government resources to eliminate them, and their elimination would contribute little to Japanese rule. Therefore, the government restricted them but established a system of licensed users to give people access to them.[134]

Finally, it is to be noted that "progovernment" frequently, but not always, meant "pro-Japanese" in colonial Taiwan. Judging from the example of the 1900 Taiwan Peace Preservation Regulation, the interests of the government were supreme in colonial legislation. Some people justified this law, arguing that it was useful in coping with numerous Japanese adventurers who came to Taiwan in the early days of Japanese rule.[135] But, as mentioned above, the counterpart of this regulation in Japan had already been rescinded by the end of the nineteenth century, and the colonial courts surely could have punished illegal actions of Japanese vagrants without this regulation.[136] The real intention for enacting this regulation was to expel resident Japanese who were undesirable in the eyes of the GGT. Under this regulation, some reporters from the press, lawyers, and even a former procurator were expelled.[137] In fact, some Japanese lawyers in Taiwan objected to the colonial law enacted by the GGT.[138] Nevertheless, this regulation was preserved as a last resort against anti-GGT Japanese mainlanders in colonial Taiwan throughout the period of Japanese rule. In addition, as mentioned above, the GGT also employed the Taiwan Press Law to oppress resident Japanese.

JAPANESE MAINLAND LAW AS A PRINCIPLE

Colonial Legislation under Assimilation Policy

Development of Japanese Colonialism. In the 1920s, Japanese democratic imperialists reshaped the colonial policy of Japan. The extent of Korean protest in the March First Movement of 1919 and the brutality of the Japanese colonial response evoked considerable criticism among the public in Japan proper, where people were allowed to more freely express their voices under Taishō liberalism. Most Japanese democrats who preferred Western-style liberalism argued strongly that colonial administration should be reformed on the basis of a colonial policy of assimilation.[139] Though such a policy might sound "liberal" or "modern," in essence, the policy of assimilation defines the colonized people and their social institutions as "inferior." Out of a sense of supremacy, Japanese democratic imperialists did not extend their respect for other individuals to respect for other ethnic groups. Only a few Japanese specialists in colonial governance supported home rule of the colonies; some of them even admitted the possibility of colonial independence.[140]

But after 1931, amid the growing sense of national crisis and militancy, the movement toward democratic assimilation also waned. The central concern of Japanese colonial policy shifted to the economic consolidation of the empire and the compulsory integration of the colonial economies to meet the requirements of the Japanese mainland. Finally, after 1936 the policy for the "imperialization of subject peoples" (*kōminka*) was put into effect in the colonies. This militarist assimilation policy, stripped of all considerations of accommodation or equal opportunity for colonizer and colonized, was intended solely to mobilize the people and resources of the colony for the Japanese war effort.[141]

The Extension of Mainland Law. In 1919, the first commoner premier of Japan, Hara Kei (Takashi), appointed the first civilian governor-general of Taiwan, Den Kenjirō, as the initial step for carrying out a new colonial policy. Japanese party leaders regarded the establishment of the same institutions in the colony as necessary for assimilating the colonized peoples and thus supported the extension of Japanese mainland law to the colonies. But considering that colonial societies with different conditions could not be changed immediately, they adopted a gradualist approach to carry out their program for extending mainland law. In practice, those politicians hoped to consolidate the colony and the empire and thereby suppress the newly emerging nationalism of the colonized people, who were inspired by ideas of self-determination spreading throughout the world after World War I. The 1921 Title 3 was just one aspect of this new colonial policy.[142]

As pointed out before, Title 3 did not greatly change the original legislative institutions for Taiwan. The GGT could still to a large extent decide colonial law. Although the Japanese government in Diet hearings promised to gradually extend Japanese law to Taiwan, Title 3 itself did not set up a timetable or a list of Japanese statutes to be extended because such extension, it was determined, had to be decided according to, in official terms, "the degree of culture of the island people."[143]

After Title 3 became effective in 1922, a large number of Japanese statutes were applied to Taiwan by ordinance. First, under the 1922 Application of Civil Statutes Order, several Japanese civil statutes were applied to Taiwan from January 1, 1923, including the Civil Code, the Civil Code Enforcement Order, the Commercial Code, the Commercial Code Enforcement Order, the Code of Civil Procedure, the Law of Procedure in Personal Matters, the Law of Procedure in Non-contentious Litigation, and so on.[144] At the same time, the 1922 Exceptions of Applied Statutes provided many special provisions for Taiwan, relating to civil law, commercial law, and registration law.[145] From then on, further application of Japanese civil statutes or enactment of exceptions for those applied statutes was frequently made by means of modifying these two ordinances.[146] Meanwhile, the GGT issued a new *ritsurei* rescinding prior *ritsurei* that were in contradiction with these applied Japanese statutes.¹⁴⁷ Additionally, the Japanese government also extended many Japanese administrative laws to Taiwan (a topic that is beyond the scope of this book).¹⁴⁸ In brief, after the 1922 reform the influence of Western colonial law and Chinese imperial law upon Taiwan's legal system was reduced, and Japanese mainland law dominated the law of colonial Taiwan.

The period from 1922 to 1945 is frequently referred to as the ordinance legislation period, in contrast to the former *ritsurei* legislation period. However, it should be noted that *ritsurei* still existed after Title 3 became effective in 1922 and that *ritsurei* could extend Japanese law to Taiwan insofar as their contents conformed to Japanese law. In fact, the GGT had already enacted some *ritsurei* to carry out the extension of mainland law before the 1921 Title 3 was promulgated.¹⁴⁹

The Road to Western Law

Generally speaking, the colonial legislation in Taiwan further introduced Western law into Taiwan by the enforcement of more Japanese law after the 1922 reform. Under Japanese colonial rule, Taiwan's legislation was inevitably influenced by the development of Japanese law. After the early 1920s, most of Japan's Western-style codes completed in the Meiji reform applied to Taiwan. But after 1931, Japanese militarism spread rapidly, until Japan's defeat in World War II. During this process, especially after 1938, Taiwan had no choice but to be gradually merged into the Japanese wartime legal system.¹⁵⁰

Criminal Law. Colonial criminal law on Taiwan was less influenced by modern Western law than any other colonial laws on Taiwan. After 1919, several measures influenced by Chinese legal tradition were amended as follows: (1) in 1921, punishment by flogging was abolished; (2) in 1929, opium smoking was prohibited except by persons with original licenses; (3) in 1945, the *hokō* system was abolished.¹⁵¹ Nevertheless, the Japanese Criminal Code still did not apply to Taiwan. Thus many *ritsurei* relating to criminal law, like the Bandit Punishment Law, remained in effect. The 1930 Japanese Burglary Prevention Law could not be directly applied to Taiwan because one of its provisions applied the Japan Criminal Code, but it was incorporated into the Taiwan Criminal Law (a *ritsurei* enacted in 1908) by a new *ritsurei*.¹⁵² In contrast, unlike the Criminal Code, many Japanese special criminal statutes were directly applied to Taiwan in the 1920s, such as the Public Order Police Law, the Peace Preservation Law, and the Violence Punishment Law, which were enacted for controlling political parties and their activities, suppressing the Communist movement, and preventing mass violence in labor disputes and tenancy disputes, respectively.¹⁵³

The GGT followed metropolitan Japan in enacting various authoritarian criminal statutes. In 1936, a *ritsurei* already imitated Japanese mainland law in regulating "inflammatory pamphlets" (*fuon-bunsho*).[154] After the Sino-Japanese War broke out in 1937, the GGT enacted a large number of *ritsurei* for economic regulations; these *ritsurei* basically followed Japanese mainland law.[155] Meanwhile, many Japanese statutes establishing coercive wartime controls also applied to Taiwan, such as the National Mobilization Law.[156] Finally, almost all Japanese wartime criminal law, which strictly restricted the freedom of people, was brought into effect in Taiwan either by statutes (applied by ordinance) or *ritsurei*.

Japan's modern criminal procedural law was also largely applied to colonial Taiwan. The 1922 Japanese Code of Criminal Procedure became effective in Taiwan on January 1, 1924, the same day as in metropolitan Japan.[157] The *ritsurei* relating to criminal procedure were thus repealed except for the Summary Judgment Law. But the contents of the repealed 1905 Special Law for Criminal Litigation were actually duplicated in 1923 in the revised Exceptions of Applied Statutes.[158] Because of the Summary Judgment Law and the Exceptions of Applied Statutes relating to criminal procedure, the criminal procedure implemented in Taiwan was less Westernized than that in Japan. When the war came, all Japanese Special Wartime Criminal Law gradually applied to Taiwan.[159]

Civil Law. In contrast, during this period the Taiwanese enjoyed the same Western-style civil law as the Japanese. On January 1, 1923, the Westernized Japanese civil and commercial laws, including those that had already applied to Taiwan in the former period, became applicable to the Taiwanese. Taiwanese family and succession, however, generally continued to be governed by Taiwanese custom;[160] because the provisions in the Civil Code were regarded as "legal theory," only a few of them were actually applied to the Taiwanese. Of course, as mentioned previously, the books of the Japanese Civil Code on Family and Succession only to a certain extent followed Western law. Finally, after 1938, numerous wartime economic regulations related to private law were enforced in Taiwan.[161]

After 1899, Japanese Western-style civil procedure was largely enforced in Taiwan under *ritsurei* legislation. The 1922 reform further repealed the 1905 Special Law for Civil Litigation and, unlike criminal procedure, was not duplicated by an ordinance for exception. But the Civil Disputes Mediation Law was kept intact, partly because after the 1920s the mediation system was emphasized in Japan as well. Finally, the Japanese Wartime Special Civil Law also applied to Taiwan except the provisions relating to mediation.[162]

Legal Reform for Colonial Rule

Colonial-style Reform. The model for legal reform formulated by the GGT was quite different from the pattern of the Meiji legal reform. In view of the results of legal reform in Taiwan, it might seem that the GGT had intended to pursue in Taiwan the gradualist approach of the Meiji reform in Japan. However, without the same incentives that inspired the Meiji reform,[163] the GGT had no intention of modernizing law in Taiwan by gradually implementing Western-style law. In fact, the GGT followed the Western colonialist approach of dualism in law to form a colonial legal system in Taiwan. As a consequence, during the early period of Japanese rule, imperial Chinese law was still prevalent in Taiwan's legislation. Because Japanese colonial policy made a hasty change in 1919, numerous Japanese mainland laws were extended to Taiwan. Under the name of "Japanese law," more modern Western law therefore was introduced into colonial Taiwan than before. This can explain why in 1914 the GGT intended to enact the Taiwan Civil Code based on Taiwanese customary law but in 1922 changed its policy to apply the Japanese Civil Code. While the overall goal of the Meiji reform was to adopt Western-style law, that was not the case in Taiwan's legal reform under Japanese rule.

Colonizer and Colonized. The requirements of Japanese colonialism remained the decisive fact in selecting the law in Taiwan during the latter period of Japanese rule. Under the policy of democratic assimilation, Japanese colonialists tried to improve the appearance of colonial rule. Hence, the GGT agreed that Japanese status law would not be applied to Taiwanese family and succession matters, as the majority of Taiwanese expected.[164] Such a "benefit," however, was only used to conceal the essence of authoritarian rule.[165] Then, under militarist assimilation, the slogan of "impartiality and equal favor" (*isshi dōjin*) seemed only to mean common obligations and restraints. Those Japanese laws that were helpful for governmental control were always applied to Taiwan by ordinances or were indirectly enforced on the island by *ritsurei*.[166] The peace preservation legislation and emergency legislation on the Japanese mainland were enforced in Taiwan, except that Taiwan had more "efficient" control measures like the Summary Judgment Law and the Civil Disputes Mediation Law.

In fact, the GGT never trusted the "rebellious" Taiwanese. The extremely harsh Bandit Punishment Law was continued in effect throughout the period of Japanese rule. Although there were many substitutes for this law and it actually was never applied to a concrete case after 1916, the law was kept as a means for terrifying the people.[167]

RECEPTION OF WESTERN LAW

STRUGGLE FOR AUTONOMOUS LAW

Call for a Colonial Legislature

The first generation of modern Taiwanese intellectuals tried to initiate a program of legal reforms for their society. Encountering Japan's self-interested legal reforms, the Taiwanese reacted at first only with negative hostility toward their rulers. But a Japanese-trained generation of Taiwanese intellectuals emerged in the 1920s. They challenged the colonial legal system's discrimination against the Taiwanese.[168] As a consequence of their modern education in Japan, most Taiwanese intellectuals identified themselves as a colonized people and were accustomed to considering the Taiwanese (*hontōjin*) as a single unit instead of as disparate groups—Ch'üan-chou, Chang-chou, and Hakka. Acknowledging that the Taiwanese were not treated the same as the Japanese, they used their fluent Japanese to express their dissatisfaction. At first, they attacked Title 63 as the legal basis for all colonial special laws. However, as Lin Ch'eng-lu, an influential Taiwanese legal expert,[169] pointed out, the issue of Title 63 was only related to who, the Diet or the GGT, would have legislative power over Taiwan. To protect Taiwanese interests, the Taiwanese should struggle for their own legislative power. He then proposed a popularly elected colonial legislature, which would have authority to enact laws for Taiwan.[170]

Between 1921 and 1934, petitions for the establishment of a Taiwan parliament were submitted to the Japanese Diet on fifteen different occasions. These petitions proposed that consent by a Taiwan parliament, composed of representatives elected by the inhabitants of Taiwan regardless of whether they were Taiwanese or Japanese, should be required for special legislative matters applying to Taiwan (enacted by *ritsurei* under Title 3) as well as the budget of Taiwan. All other legislative matters involving both Taiwan and the Japanese mainland were to be decided by statutes enacted by the Imperial Diet.[171] In brief, they advocated a policy of limited home rule within the jurisdiction of the Empire of Japan.

The leaders of this effort believed that the best choice for the Taiwanese was for Taiwan's status as a special legal zone to be kept intact (to preserve its delegated legislative power, the GGT also supported this aim) so that Taiwanese culture and identity would not be annihilated by Japanese assimilation. They maintained, however, that special colonial law should not be legislated merely at the will of the GGT, but instead that the consent of Taiwan's people should be required. From this perspective, their request represented not only a democratic movement but, more important, a movement of emerging Taiwanese nationalism, which sought rights and freedom for the Taiwanese people as a whole; in the words of their slogan, "Taiwan is Taiwanese Taiwan." On the other hand, these Taiwanese intellectuals did not completely object to the official policy of extending mainland law. As a second choice, they believed that the enforcement on Taiwan of Japanese mainland law would enhance the rights and freedom of individual Taiwanese, even though as a result the Taiwanese would gradually disappear within a "greater Japan."[172]

Attitudes toward Western Law

Pro-Western Tendency. The Taiwanese intellectuals who led the effort for democratic legal reforms in the 1920s in fact welcomed modern Western ideas. They objected to Japanese colonial rule but not the Western elements within the Japanese system. For this reason they were willing to accept the extension of mainland law as a compromise. In addition to their political movement, however, they were also engaged in spreading "new" culture (especially through the Taiwan Cultural Association). "New" culture meant the Western ideas of freedom and equality. While cherishing their indigenous Han Chinese culture and society, they strongly criticized what they viewed as the feudal heritage in traditional Han Chinese culture. Taiwan, in their view, should be an island "keeping abreast of Europe and America" as well as having its own "independent culture."[173] Influenced by modern jurisprudence in Japan, contemporary Taiwanese jurists also admired the Western liberal legal system.

Differences in Reformative Schemes. Although Taiwanese jurists as a whole shared a common sympathy toward Western legal ideas, they held among themselves differing views about whether or not foreign law should be introduced immediately as Taiwan's positive law. In discussing the application of the Japanese civil and commercial codes to Taiwan, for example, a Taiwanese lawyer, Cheng Sung-yü, argued in 1921 that with regard to legal reform, the codification of customary law was best for the interests of the people on the ground that different societies frequently had different values and attitudes toward the same behavior and that these differences were reflected in their laws. Because of the urgent need to abolish extraterritoriality, the Meiji reformers did not codify Japanese customary law, yet they still insisted that family relations and succession should conform to Japanese customary law. Therefore, Cheng asserted, all Taiwanese customary law that differed from Japanese civil and commercial law should be preserved unless it was contrary to public order or good morals because Taiwanese customary law was neither totally good nor totally bad.[174]

In contrast, Lin Ch'eng-lu, another Taiwanese jurist, argued that it was sometimes necessary to enact a legal rule or principle in anticipation of what should or might happen soon in the future. Western commercial law, which was followed by many countries all over the world, was a good example of this kind of legislation. Taiwan's capitalistic commerce could not progress if the traditional customary commercial law remained in place. Japanese Westernized commercial law thus should be introduced in anticipation of the emersion of modern capitalism in Taiwan. He therefore criticized the Japanese authorities for their delay in extending the Japanese commercial code to Taiwan. Similarly, he advocated applying the books on General Principles, Obligations, and Rights over Things of the Japanese Civil Code to Taiwan without exception. He exempted, however, family law and succession. He argued against applying to Taiwan the books on Family and Succession in the Japanese Civil Code because they differed from Taiwanese customary law at least with respect to persons qualified for inheritance. Moreover, in his view Taiwanese rules for equality among all sons in succession were better than Japanese primogeniture, at least in terms of the principle of equality in modern Western thought. However, he added that some old Taiwanese customs in status law should be abolished, such as the legality of concubinage and adopted daughters-in-law (*t'ung-yang-hsi*).[175]

The issue of what kinds of old customs should be abolished, however, remained unsettled. Even though the idea that modern (Western) property law and commercial law should be adopted and traditional status law should be maintained unless it was contrary to public order or good morals was generally accepted, controversies persisted about what was meant by "contrary to public order or good morals." In the 1920s, several articles written by modern Taiwanese intellectuals discussed the traditional marriage system, adopted daughters, women's rights, female servants, and so on.[176] Although their general tendency toward modern Western thought was the same, their comments on certain specific matters were often diverse. For example, Lin advocated the abolition of concubinage without exception, but Cheng had some sympathy for its function of continuing the family line by ensuring a male heir.[177] On the other hand, Lin supported the customary classification of relatives in Taiwan to take into account social stability, although he recognized the inequality in this system, which emphasized male prerogatives and placed women in an inferior status.[178] Some feminist intellectuals at that time may have rejected such views.

Taiwanese intellectuals also disagreed about the merits of liberalism and socialism. The arguments of the Taiwanese intellectuals mentioned above basically followed Western liberalism. Other Taiwanese intellectuals, however, tended toward socialism. Early in 1923, one Taiwanese socialist expressed his objection to the petition for a colonial parliament, asserting that only a proletarian movement could emancipate the Taiwanese as a whole.[179] This faction in the Taiwanese anti-Japanese political movement grew stronger after 1927, although the activities on the island of those who expressed such views were completely suppressed by the GGT in 1931. In any event, these two factions illustrate contending views espoused by Taiwanese intellectuals with regard to legal reform. In 1927, the Taiwan Popular Party, the first Taiwanese political party, adopted Western liberalism and thus demanded the establishment of a local autonomous government by popular election and the enforcement of judicial independence, a jury system, an administrative court system, and other reforms modeled after institutions in those Western countries where liberalism prevailed.[180] In 1928 the Taiwan Communist Party was established in Shanghai; the party emphasized the establishment of government under the dictatorship of the proletariat and the future abolition of private land ownership.[181]

An Unrealized Dream

Few if any rulers will give up power unless forced to do so by external pressure. Unfortunately, the Taiwanese did not rally enough strength to produce such pressure upon the Japanese colonialists. As Korean nationalists with diverse ideologies and tactics could not unify and thereby gain enough popular strength, so too Taiwanese nationalists were unable to unite.[182] Although the petition for a Taiwan parliament was supported by most influential Taiwanese associations at that time, only the liberal faction was active in pursuing such a petition. Living as they did under colonial authoritarian rule, the majority of Taiwanese did not wish to be involved in such a political movement, even though they approved its goal. Moreover, not surprisingly, several pro-GGT Taiwanese objected to the petition for a Taiwan parliament to show their loyalty to the GGT.[183]

The fatal attack upon the movement for a Taiwan parliament no doubt came from the GGT, whose power it directly challenged. The GGT first employed various forms of pressure to urge people not to sign the petition. In 1923, the colonial authorities resorted to the Public Order Police Law to punish the leaders of the petition movement. When such prosecution proved unsuccessful in suppressing the movement, the GGT adopted other strategies: (1) using the police to restrict the movement's activities, (2) encouraging the division of the leadership into radical and conservative factions, and (3) inducing the conservative faction to pursue political power in the process of extending mainland law to Taiwan.[184]

Under such circumstances, the failure of this attempt to acquire colonial legislative power under the existing legal framework was inevitable. As democratic assimilation became the prevailing policy in the Japanese Diet, the creation of a Taiwan parliament, which emphasized Taiwan's special status, was destined to be rejected. After the early 1930s, as democratic institutions faded in Japan, the Taiwanese request was doomed. In 1931, the majority of the leaders who had initiated the movement for a Taiwan parliament in 1921 organized the League for Attainment of Local Autonomy. Local autonomy in this context meant a local system of governance within the framework of metropolitan Japan, a system that could be permitted under the official policy of extending mainland law to Taiwan. In effect, these liberal intellectuals retreated to their original second choice, pursuing individual liberty rather than national liberty. The league was disbanded in 1937; by that time a lawful anti-GGT movement had become impossible.

The struggle of Taiwanese intellectuals to achieve legislative power for colonial legal reform failed, but the effect of the struggle was to spread modern Western legal ideas to Taiwanese society during the 1920s and early 1930s, a period when Taiwanese dissidents were allowed to express their opinions in public under Japanese rule.

SUMMARY

After initial disorder resulting from colonial conquest, Japan decided to regard Taiwan as a special legal zone in which under Title 63 the GGT in fact possessed nearly autonomous legislative authority. Although numerous scholars considered this fundamental law for colonial legislation unconstitutional, the Japanese government maintained it as necessary for colonial policy. Only after Japanese colonial policy changed were some modifications made to colonial legislative institutions under Title 3. In practice, however, throughout the period of Japanese rule, the GGT maintained extensive powers to direct legal reform in Taiwan.

During the first half of Japanese rule on Taiwan, except the initial experimental period, colonial legislation followed mostly Western colonial legal practice and Chinese imperial law, in addition to Japan's own legal experience. Thus, criminal law basically conformed to existing Japanese law, with the addition of harsh special criminal regulations for the colony. Like many Western colonial powers, Japan applied customary law in dealing with native civil matters but actively regulated land relations. For judicial convenience, Japanese procedural laws were simplified and then enforced in colonial Taiwan. Western law was therefore coincidentally introduced to Taiwan simply because mainland laws—which had recently been modeled on Western law—were to be enforced in the colony. This is not surprising because the purpose of legal reform in Taiwan was not to modernized or Westernize but to promote the interests of the colonial government.

Because of the colonial policy of extension of mainland law, Japanese modern civil and commercial codes were applied directly to Taiwan. Thus during the last half of Japanese rule, criminal and civil law in Taiwan was virtually the same as Japanese mainland law. As a consequence, Western law was gradually introduced into Taiwan through Japan's Westernized laws. Unlike the Meiji government in Japan, however, the GGT did not at first intend to legislate Western-style laws but adopted them only because of the change in Japanese colonial policy.

Facing Japan's self-interested legal reform, new-generation Taiwanese intellectuals sought to establish institutions by which the people on Taiwan could enact their own laws. These intellectuals tended to admire the Western legal system, but they could not agree on the approach to reform or on concrete legal provisions. In any event, they lacked sufficient political strength to attain legislative power for Taiwan.

3 / Modern Judiciary in the Colony

This chapter will briefly review the development of the court system in colonial Taiwan. Then it will explore the extent to which the Western principle of an independent judiciary was carried out in Taiwan. Since Western-style judicial institutions cannot operate without courts and personnel, the judicial facilities and the legal profession in Taiwan under Japanese rule will also be discussed. Finally, I will examine the accessibility of the courts to the people, which is closely related to the implementation of the Westernized positive law examined in the preceding chapter.

COURT SYSTEM IN TAIWAN

Experimental System

Before Japanese colonial rule, judicial institutions on the island basically followed imperial Chinese law. In Ch'ing Taiwan, judicial affairs were handled by the chief of the local government. There were no independent courts. The Ch'ing government in Taiwan was usually passive in dealing with criminal cases involving misdemeanors and civil cases. In fact, the Taiwanese people were ordinarily accustomed to resolving civil disputes and even criminal cases by themselves.[1]

In late 1895, the GGT court under the military administration was actually a military tribunal.[2] Not until May of 1896 was a Western-style court under civil administration created by a GGT *ritsurei*. As mentioned in the preceding chapter, from the beginning of the civil administration to early 1898, Taiwan's legal system was for the most part formed on the model of the institutions of the early Meiji. After Japan's Great Court of Cassation (Daishin'in) was created in 1875, there were three levels (later four levels) in the court hierarchy, in charge of the first instance, appeal (*kōso*, the second instance), and re-appeal (*jōkoku*, the third instance), respectively.[3] Similarly, the GGT established the District Court (Chihō hōin), the Court of Appeal (Fukushin hōin), and the Higher Court (Kōtō hōin) to serve respectively as the court of first instance, appeal, and re-appeal.[4] Thus, the court system of three instances found in continental Europe was established on Taiwan. Meanwhile, the Temporary Court was established to try political criminals without appeal.[5] Under the GGT Bureau of Civil Administration, the Department of Judicial Affairs (Hōmubu) was charged with judicial administration.[6]

1898 Reform

Under the Kodama administration (1898–1906), the GGT studied other Western colonial court systems with a view to reorganizing the court system in Taiwan. The Department of Judicial Affairs made extensive studies on how Western colonialists dealt with judicial affairs in their colonies,[7] and a Western-style court system was maintained for colonial governance. Probably to more easily administer the court system, however, the GGT did not set up a special tribunal for natives in Taiwan, as was done in some colonial judicial systems, but used the Japanese court system with necessary modifications.[8] One of the modifications was to abolish the GGT Higher Court, allowing for more efficiency, a primary goal in colonial justice.[9] Similarly, to reduce the caseload of colonial courts, the GGT prohibited civil lawsuits in which the claim arose before Japan acquired sovereignty over Taiwan on May 8, 1895, and required a high deposit for criminal appeals so that such appeals became very difficult.[10]

The court system in colonial Taiwan was entirely separate from the court system in metropolitan Japan. Another prevailing institution in Western colonialism, especially in British colonies, was the appeal against decisions of a colonial court to a supreme court in the mother country.[11] The GGT initially suggested letting the Daishin'in in Tokyo be the tribunal of re-appeal for the lawsuits in Taiwan's courts. Seeing this suggestion as an opportunity to increase its influence, the Ministry of Justice advocated that the Japanese Court Organization Law be applied to Taiwan. In this way, the ministry could supervise the judicial officials in Taiwan, and the court and procuracy in the Japanese mainland would be charged with the execution of those lawsuits that had been re-appealed to the Japanese Supreme Court. This counter-proposal reduced in practice the judicial authority of colonial government. It is no wonder that the GGT withdrew its original motion.[12] In the end, it was decided that the GGT Court in colonial Taiwan would be totally independent of the court in the Japanese mainland.[13] Because the original GGT Higher Court had been abolished, there was no higher-level court in Taiwan to act as court of re-appeal under Japanese procedural law. From 1898 to 1919, there were only two levels of courts (the District Court, the Court of

Appeal) and two instances for a lawsuit (first trial, appeal) in Taiwan. The model of an independent colonial court system was duplicated in Korea, where, however, there were three levels of courts and three instances for a lawsuit.[14]

1919 Reform

Because of the policy of extension of mainland law implemented in 1919, the court system in Taiwan saw a series of reforms, one of which was the restoration of the court of re-appeal in Taiwan. The GGT Higher Court was reestablished, but the Court of Appeal was abolished. The Re-appeal Division (Jōkoku-bu) in the Higher Court undertook the function of the court of re-appeal within Taiwan's court system. Since the legal interpretations of the Re-appeal Division in cases had to be followed by other courts in Taiwan, this division was undoubtedly the supreme court in Taiwan, similar to the Great Court of Cassation in metropolitan Japan. Another division in the Higher Court was the Appellate Division (Fukushin-bu). It undertook the function of a court of appeal within Taiwan's court system, similar to the Appellate Chamber in metropolitan Japan. The GGT District Court remained as the court of first instance.[15] Therefore, the three instances for a lawsuit (first trial, appeal, re-appeal) were revived in Taiwan, making the system the same as Korea's. But in form there were only two levels in the court hierarchy of Taiwan, the Higher Court and the District Court.

To bring Taiwan's judicial system into line with that of the Japanese mainland, the Temporary Court was abolished and its original jurisdiction given to the Re-appeal Division of the Higher Court.[16] Political criminals in colonial Taiwan therefore were not tried by a special court any more. Similarly, the special regulation relating to a high deposit for a criminal appeal in Taiwan was rescinded.[17] As in other fields, the court system in Taiwan adopted more elements of Western law because of Japan's policy of the extension of mainland law to Taiwan.

In Taiwan, however, the GGT District Court had to undertake the functions of the District Court and the Ward Court in the court hierarchy of Japan. Before 1919 all cases in the GGT District Court were presided over by a single judge. There was no question that the cases belonging to the jurisdiction of the Japanese Ward Court should be tried by a single judge in Taiwan according to the summary procedure in Japanese civil procedural law. However, the cases belonging to the jurisdiction of the Japanese District Court, which were tried by a collegiate bench of three judges in Japan, were also tried by only a single judge in Taiwan.[18] In 1919, to achieve the same system in Taiwan as in Japan, it was provided that a collegiate bench of three judges in the GGT District Court would be required to try most cases under the jurisdiction of the Japanese District Court. These consisted of (1) criminal cases involving felonies and those misdemeanors that had been tried by preliminary examination and (2) civil cases involving 1,000 yen or more (2,000 yen or more, after 1926) or objects not capable of monetary valuation (after 1929), cases concerning status in a family, and bankruptcy cases. The GGT District Court Branch in principle dealt with the cases tried by a single judge, but some of the branches were able to try cases by a collegiate bench. The Detached Office of the GGT District Court, on the other hand, was only in charge of the registry and notary public.[19]

The 1927 reform further made Taiwan's court system more similar to the Japanese court system. In 1927 the collegiate bench of three judges in Taiwan's district courts, which had been created in 1919, was designated as an independent division of the GGT District Court, to be called the Collegiate Division. Moreover, the judgments of the Single Division in the GGT District Court, in which only one judge presided, could be appealed to the Collegiate Division. The Collegiate Division therefore performed the duty of a court of appeal in these cases.[20] Thus in fact, the court system in Taiwan was divided into four levels: the Single Division of District Court, Collegiate Division of District Court, Appellate Division of Higher Court, and Re-appeal Division of Higher Court. There were three instances for a lawsuit (first trial, appeal, re-appeal), just as in Japan. In contrast, there was nothing similar to the 1927 court reform in Korea.[21]

From 1927 to the end of Japanese rule, the court system in Taiwan did not change, except that the functions of the court of appeal were abolished under the 1942 Wartime Exceptions of Court Organization Law (this law was applied to Taiwan after 1943).[22]

Although many Japanese statutes applied directly to Taiwan after 1919, the court system in Taiwan was regulated by *ritsurei* rather than by Japanese statutes (the only exception is the wartime law prohibiting appeals mentioned above), for the GGT wanted to maintain some special measures in Taiwan for colonial governance.[23] For example, the prewar Japanese administrative court system, under which people were entitled to sue officials, was never applied in colonial Taiwan, and therefore the people on Taiwan had no power to file administrative suits in court. Hence, the Western-style courts in colonial Taiwan neither completely followed Western law nor entirely adopted Japan's Westernized court system. Rather, the basic structure of the court system in Taiwan from 1898 to 1943 took the two principal forms shown in table 3.1.

MODERN JUDICIARY IN THE COLONY

TABLE 3.1 Court System in Taiwan, 1898–1943

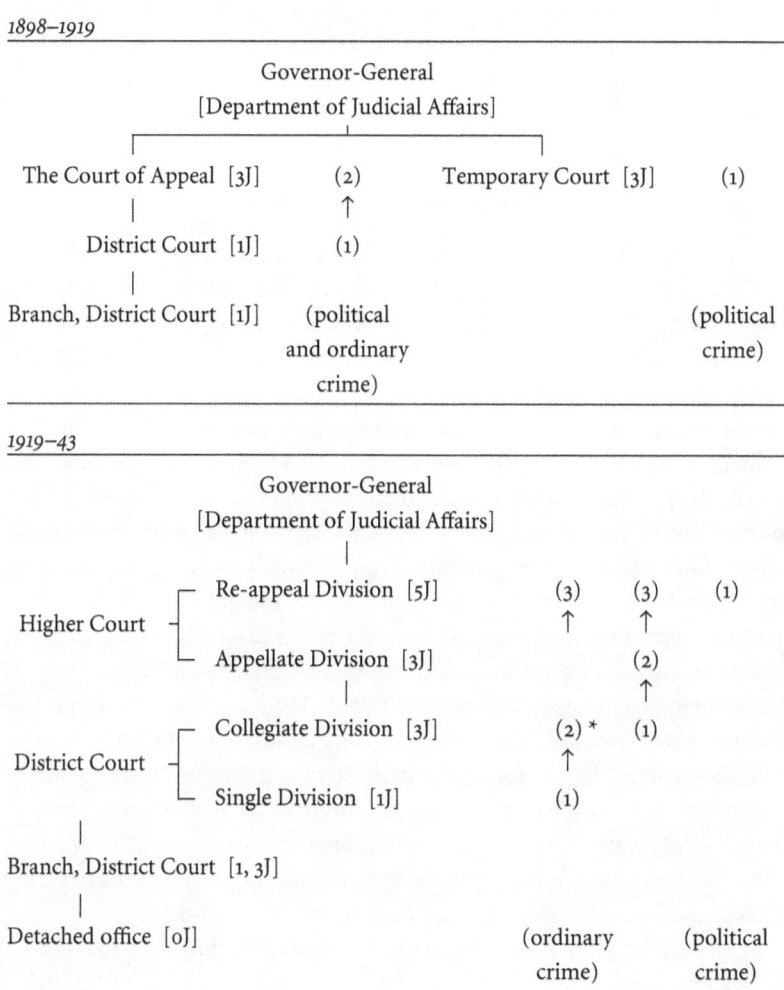

NOTE: J = Judge; (1) (2) (3) indicate respectively first trial, appeal, and re-appeal; * : after 1927.

INDEPENDENT JUDICIARY

The separation of judicial power from executive authority is a fundamental principle in modern Western law. In contrast, traditional Sino-Japanese political thought held that the administration of justice could not be separated from general administration and, further, that the former was necessarily contained in the latter.[24] The idea of an independent judiciary was certainly new to Taiwanese society, and Japanese rulers had only recently adopted it. Examining to what extent this principle was carried out in the Japanese-led legal reform in Taiwan is therefore a good means of exploring the influence of Western law upon Taiwan under Japanese rule.

Initial Experimental Period

The *Takano* case of 1897 demonstrates the lack of an independent judiciary in Taiwan during the initial period of Japanese civil administration before the Kodama administration (April 1896–February 1898).

Like the 1891 *Otsu* case in Japan, the *Takano* case was a test for judicial independence.[25] Takano Takenori was the first chief justice of the GGT Higher Court in Taiwan. In 1897, while dealing with cases involving suspected bribery of high-ranking officials of the GGT, he was suspended as chief justice by the Japanese government. Strongly arguing that pursuant to article 58 of the Meiji Constitution his post was secured, Takano rejected the order of suspension. The governor-general of Taiwan finally assigned policemen to oust him from his office in the court. Later, the Japanese government removed him from office on the grounds of his disobedience. Because of this case, fourteen judges in Taiwan voluntarily resigned or were forced to leave their positions. It was said that most judges in Taiwan supported Takano, except two judges in the Higher Court. Meanwhile, because the government defended its action on the basis that the tenure of Taiwan's judges was not secured by the Constitution, the application of the Constitution in Taiwan and the protection for tenure of judges became issues in the Imperial Diet.[26] As most people expected, Takano was never restored to the bench.[27] Unlike the *Otsu* case, in which executive authority was unable to influence judges' decisions, the executive power dominated the judiciary in colonial Taiwan.

From the *Takano* case, we can fully understand the importance of protection from interference by the executive branch to an independent judiciary. If the executive power is able to oust judges at will, as the colonial government ousted Judge Takano to keep him from trying suspected bribery cases, it is capable of interfering in the adjudication of a trial by ousting or threatening to oust the judges. The judiciary thus becomes subject to the executive power.

The insistence of Takano and his colleagues on an independent judiciary illustrates that Japanese judges trained in Western jurisprudence cherished this principle. After 1896, the judges in the GGT Court had to be qualified under the 1890 Japanese Court Organization Law, except those judges in district courts.[28] With their professional training by modern Western law, they could not accept the traditional practice that regarded judges as ordinary officials who should obey the orders of superior officials. The colonial authorities, however, did not consider this to be a question of executive interference with adjudication, arguing that the case was merely the result of the strife between two factions, executive officials and judicial officials in the colony.[29]

In fact, the Japanese government did treat qualified judges like ordinary officials.[30] One reason for the government's attitude was that during this period, a judicial official often also undertook the post of administrative official, and vice versa. For example, Takano himself was also the head of the Department of Judicial Affairs.[31] Therefore, the judiciary in Taiwan was not separated from the executive branch of government at this time.

The 1898 Judicial Reform

Because the Taiwanese judiciary was a colonial system, the 1898 judicial reform carried out by the Kodama administration did not establish a Japanese independent judiciary in Taiwan. Some Western colonialists, like the British and Dutch, extended the concept of an independent judiciary to their colonies; others, like the French, did not.[32] Japan's adoption of a Western independent judiciary was influenced by Tokyo's desire to get rid of extraterritoriality. Because there was no such outside pressure in the colony, Japan naturally selected a French-style colonial judiciary, which was more similar to its traditional institutions than the British or Dutch style.[33] At a secret hearing in the 1902 Imperial Diet, Kodama clearly expressed Japanese sinicized ideas about the role of the judiciary, saying that the most important detail in governing the people in its newly acquired territory was to wield absolute authority over them; if the administrative officials in Taiwan lacked judicial power, they would lose this indispensable absolute authority.[34] Not surprisingly, the 1890 Japanese Court Organization Law, which adopted a Western independent judiciary, was never extended to Taiwan or Korea.[35]

In fact, the independent judiciary in prewar Japan was not without its own problems. According to the 1890 Japanese Court Organization Law, a judge could not be transferred to another office, assigned to other courts, suspended, removed from office, or penalized by reduction in salary unless (1) he had been convicted of a criminal offense or punished by disciplinary measures, or (2) a panel of judges in the Great Court of Cassation or Appellate Chamber had determined him to be incapable of performing his duties because of mental or physical incompetence. Before serving as a judge, he was required to pass the professional examination and complete three years (one and a half years, after 1908) of training as a probationary legal official in the courts and the procurators' offices. A procurator was required to have the same qualifications as a judge, but was merely guaranteed not to be removed from office against his will unless he had been convicted of a criminal act or subjected to disciplinary measures.[36] However, the power of general administrative supervision over the judiciary remained in the hands of the minister of justice, although he had no authority over the judges in the exercise of their judicial functions. Consequently, Japanese judges and procurators on the one hand had a strong sense of professional integrity and advocated the concept of independent adjudication. On the other hand, personnel administration within the judiciary (for example, promotion in the court hierarchy), was inevitably influenced by the government through the "judicial administrative power" of the minister of justice.[37]

The special judicial system in the colony thus maintained the judicial administrative power of the executive branch over the judiciary but reduced the security of tenure of judicial officials. Both judges and procurators in Taiwan were appointed by the governor-general of Taiwan, and the GGT court and the Bureau of Procuracy in Taiwan were directly supervised by the governor-general.[38] After 1898 all judges in the GGT Court were required to be judges qualified under the Japanese Court Organization Law, but they were only guaranteed not to be removed from office or transferred to other offices against their will, without the other guarantees their counterparts in Japan enjoyed. Furthermore, the governor-general had power to suspend a judge and reduce his salary by three-fourths.[39] It was said that the power of suspension was often exercised and became a means of dismissing judges found undesirable by the executive branch; meanwhile, the process of disciplining judges was initiated upon the request of the governor-general and frequently was dominated by him.[40] Additionally, the procurator in Taiwan was not guaranteed tenure at all. Although after 1899 the procurator in Taiwan was also required to be qualified under Japanese law, the position of procurator in district courts could still be filled by a police officer.[41]

Moreover, in Taiwan, judges were required to associate with procurators, and the judicial officials (judges and procurators) were required to cooperate with executive officials. In Japan, judges were sometimes criticized for always supporting the arguments of procurators.[42] But in Taiwan, judges were regularly expected to hold conciliation meetings with procurators.[43] Probably influenced by the *Takano* case, the Kodama administration emphasized the cooperative relations between judicial officials and executive officials.[44] In 1908, the chief administrator under the Sakuma administration (1906–15) explicitly instructed judicial officials in Taiwan to depend on and cooperate with executive officials so that judicial power could be exercised efficiently.[45]

The executive authority in Taiwan interfered regularly with the exercise of judicial functions of procurators and sometimes even judges. In 1898, the chief administrator of the GGT issued an internal instruction to the heads of all courts and the procurators to require them to exercise their powers of suspending the detention of the accused as frequently as possible because prison facilities were overcrowded.[46] In 1915, one of the GGT's reasons for objecting to the extension of the Japanese court organization law was that the GGT had to rapidly direct procurators for prosecution in the colony.[47] Under the criminal procedural law in colonial Taiwan, the procurators had extensive judicial powers (for example, deciding whether or not to prosecute a suspect and the power to detain people or search houses). However, their exercise of those powers was subject to the direction of the administrative branch.

No subsequent case similar to the Takano affair occurred in Taiwan during the period from 1898 to 1919, probably because it was already made sufficiently clear that administrative officials would exercise their power to remove judicial officials on Taiwan, if necessary, thereby causing judicial officials to follow the directions of administrative officials.

The 1919 Judicial Reform

After the 1919 judicial reform under the policy of extension of mainland law, the first civilian governor-general of Taiwan declared in the 1921 Diet that Taiwan's judiciary was as independent as Japan's.[48] However, although the original power to suspend judges with a lowered salary had been abrogated, the other elements of security of tenure—such as the guarantee against being assigned to other courts, being suspended, or having one's salary cut— did not exist as before.[49] Therefore, judges in colonial Taiwan still were not guaranteed the same tenure as judges in metropolitan Japan, though their tenure was more secure than that of judges in colonial Korea.[50] Moreover, the tenure of Japanese procurators was never given to the procurators in Taiwan.

The *Taiwan Parliament* case of 1923 can give us some clues regarding the question of whether adjudication in Taiwan was in practice independent of administrative authority after the 1919 reform. Considering that the 1920s was a relatively democratic period during Japanese rule, the circumstances of this case were favorable for demonstrating an independent judiciary. As discussed in the preceding chapter, a group of Taiwanese intellectuals led a movement for the creation of a Taiwan parliament in 1921. In accordance with the Public Order Police Law, they reported in 1923 to the GGT for permission to organize an association to promote this movement. Soon it was prohibited on the grounds of "impeding peaceful order." But they employed a tricky legal argument derived from the fact that Taiwan was a special legal zone separate from the Japanese mainland. The application to form the organization was made in Tokyo, where such an organization was not prohibited. The procurators in the GGT Court, however, still accused the group of breaching the prohibitive order under the Public Order Police Law. It is clear from the proceedings of the court that this case was regarded as a de facto political case. In the court of first instance, the procurator paid more attention to attacking the defendants' objection to the GGT's policies than to their violation of law; in turn, the defending counsel and defendants themselves also advanced arguments more political in nature than legal. It is surprising that the collegiate bench of three judges in the Taihoku (Taipei) District Court acquitted all the defendants. They admitted that the defendants used a legal trick, but decided that, according to law, they were not guilty. The procurator appealed. Similar political arguments were conducted in the court of appeal, and the procurator even explicitly stated that there was no other way to stop the defendants' spreading dangerous antigovernment ideas, except by using the Public Order Police Law to prohibit their activities. The Appellate Division of the GGT Higher Court found thirteen defendants guilty; they were punished by a maximum of four months' imprisonment. Five defendants were acquitted. Finally, the re-appeal of the defendants was dismissed by the Re-appeal Division of the GGT Higher Court on the ground that their behavior in Tokyo was an extension of acts that had been prohibited in Taiwan and therefore the defendants in fact continued to conduct acts prohibited under the Public Order Police Law.[51]

Three points can be inferred from this case. First, the abolition of the governor-general's power to suspend judges encouraged Japanese judges who were inspired by the Western principle of independence from political influence to decide this case against the will of the colonial government at the district court level. Second, colonial procurators had close relations with the government and tended to maintain the governing order based upon the policy of the GGT. Third, the judges in higher levels of the colonial court were accustomed to the previous practice of cooperation with the executive branch or basically had a progovernment attitude. Because the government had authority to decide the promotion of judges, those judges who had been promoted to the higher level of court were usually more "obedient" to the executive authority.

It is not clear how many colonial judges would have acted the same as the judges in the district court in the *Taiwan Parliament* case. Because the tenure of judges in Taiwan was weaker than in Japan, a colonial judge took more risk in disregarding the "instruction" of the government. Considering his promotion, a judge perhaps was not willing to irritate his administrative superiors, including the governor-general. Especially when the defendant at the trial was Taiwanese, a Japanese judge who believed in his "racial supremacy" perhaps did not think it worth sacrificing his own interests. Therefore this question and the initial question, to what extent the colonial judiciary was actually independent, have no precise answer. But we must recognize that there were respected Japanese judges who insisted on independent adjudication in Taiwan, as illustrated by the district court's decision in the *Taiwan Parliament* case.

In contrast, even after the 1919 reform the executive authority in the colony often interfered with the procuracy. Since the task of thought control after the late 1920s was undertaken by colonial procurators, the GGT of course wanted to direct the procuracy to do this job in such a way as to advance the interests of colonial rule.[52] As the GGT archives show, in the early 1940s, the prosecution of certain kinds of political criminals had to be approved by the governor-general.[53] During the late period of World War II, some procurators distorted law under the pressure of militarists.[54] The professional integrity of colonial procurators, however, usually made them insist on the principle that no punishments would be meted out except where expressly provided for by law. In the *Taiwan Parliament* case, the procurators did not prosecute the defendants for the offense of insurrection due to their anti-GGT attitudes in general, but for the offense of breaching the prohibition order under the Public Order Police Law to punish their specific behaviors. Moreover, in 1943 a chief procurator objected to the plan of interning about two thousand Taiwanese nationalists and leading figures who would possibly collaborate with a U.S. landing force in the future because he considered such an internment unsupportable by any law.[55]

In conclusion, the independence of the colonial judiciary was not fully guaranteed by legal institutions.[56] However, Japanese judicial officials influenced to a certain extent by the concept of independent adjudication and professional integrity in the homeland brought a Western independent judiciary to Taiwan after the 1919 judicial reform.

JUDICIAL FACILITIES

Number of Courts

The Western-style judicial system depended on the accessibility of its courts and the professionalism of the personnel operating those courts. Moreover, without a sufficient number of modern courts, it would be difficult to implement Westernized law in a society unfamiliar with Western law.

Both the establishment of courts and the employment of legal professionals require money. In colonial Taiwan, the GGT had power to arrange judicial expenditures. Therefore the numbers of courts and personnel were naturally influenced by the colonial government.

During Japanese rule, the number of district courts and their branches in Taiwan basically reflected the development of towns and cities on the island (table 3.2). In 1920, three municipalities (an administrative unit) were established by the colonial government in Taipei, Taichung, and Tainan, the three largest cities on Taiwan before 1920. Correspondingly, three district courts were set up in these three cities situated respectively in the north, middle, and south of the island; meanwhile, three branches of district courts were erected in three other large towns. In 1930, after a decade, the government changed the system to consist of seven municipalities. In 1933, three district courts and four branches were established in six of these seven municipalities. Later, two branches were enlarged to become district courts. In 1945, the last year of Japanese rule, there were eleven municipalities, evenly distributed over the inhabited areas of Taiwan. Five of them (Taipei, Hsin-chu, Taichung, Tainan, Kaohsiung) had a district court; three of them (I-lan, Hua-lien, Chia-i) had branches of district courts. In addition, the Court of Appeal or later the Higher Court was in Taipei, the capital of Taiwan.[57] The establishment by the Japanese of Western-style courts or their branches throughout the island contributed to the development of the modern legal system in Taiwan.

In addition, the Japanese were never stingy in constructing majestic buildings for the GGT Court. Like the imposing Government-General Building, the court building symbolized the permanent authority of the colonial ruler.[58] The GGT invested much money in constructing European-style court buildings to give prestige to the judiciary. For instance, in 1930, 30 percent of the entire expenditure for courts was used to build the GGT Higher Court and the Taihoku District Court.[59] As a result, not only was the continental

TABLE 3.2 Number of Courts in Taiwan, 1897–1943

Year	Higher Court	Court of Appeal	District Court	Branch, District Court	Detached office, District Court
1897	1	1	8	NA	NA
1898	NA	1	3	5	NA
1904	NA	1	2	4	NA
1905	NA	1	2	4	21
1909	NA	1	3	1	24
1912	NA	1	3	1	27
1915	NA	1	3	1	28
1919	1	NA	3	3	27
1921	1	NA	3	3	29
1922	1	NA	3	3	30
1925	1	NA	3	3	31
1927	1	NA	3	3	32
1929	1	NA	3	3	33
1933	1	NA	3	4	35
1936	1	NA	3	5	37
1938	1	NA	4	4	38
1940	1	NA	5	3	38
1942	1	NA	5	3	39
1943	1	NA	5	3	39

SOURCE: *TWTT*, p. 392.
NOTE: Except for 1897 and 1943, this table selects only the years in which the number of courts differs from that of the preceding year.

European court system transplanted by way of legal change, but European court buildings were also erected on the island.

Number of Personnel

In the first two decades of colonial rule the colonial government was reluctant to employ sufficient legal professionals, partly because of the expense; however, from 1919 on the situation gradually improved (table 3.3). The 1898 judicial reform removed about half of all judges and procurators in the colonial court. After the anti-Japanese "bandits" were almost annihilated in 1902, the number of judges and procurators was greatly cut in 1904.[60] As a conse-

TABLE 3.3 Judicial Personnel in Taiwan, 1897–1943

Year	Judges	Procurators	Clerks	Interpreters	Lawyers
1897	55	19	NA	NA	NA
1898	24	10	NA	NA	NA
1899	28	14	91	35	NA
1900	31	13	99	40	NA
1901	32	13	103	41	55
1902	29	13	100	39	NA
1903	30	13	95	33	NA
1904	23	9, 3*	93	28	NA
1905	24	9, 3*	133	32	NA
1906	24	9, 3*	139	28	NA
1907	24	9, 3*	140	31	NA
1908	26	9, 3*	139	27	NA
1909	24	10, 2*	130	27	NA
1910	24	10, 1*	137	27	NA
1911	24	10, 1*	133	26	NA
1912	26	10	134	28	NA
1913	26	10	129	28	NA
1914	27	10	130	28	NA
1915	27	9	129	28	NA
1916	26	11	116	28	NA
1917	26	11	129	28	NA
1918	28	14	144	32	NA
1919	36	15	149	35	NA
1920	37	18	144	35	NA
1921	36	15	146	35	59
1922	38	17	162	35	67

quence, some clerks and police officers who had no professional training were assigned to be agents of procurators in the district courts between 1904 and 1911.[61] Not until the 1919 judicial reform did the number of judges and procurators increase. As a result of the creation of two divisions in the district courts, the number in 1927 rose again. From then to the end of colonial rule, the number of judges and procurators in Taiwan grew steadily.

Judging from the figures of population per judge, the Japanese did not

TABLE 3.3 *(continued)*

Year	Judges	Procurators	Clerks	Interpreters	Lawyers
1923	38	15	166	35	77
1924	37	15	159	33	83
1925	39	16	159	33	93
1926	39	16	163	33	115
1927	48	23	172	40	137
1928	48	26	175	40	NA
1929	48	26	178	40	NA
1930	53	26	184	45	NA
1931	53	26	184	45	158
1932	54	27	183	47	169
1933	56	27	189	47	172
1934	56	29	193	51	177
1935	60	30	201	54	152
1936	60	30	201	54	133
1937	60	30	201	54	127
1938	63	31	212	56	126
1939	63	33	212	56	118
1940	68	34	219	60	122
1941	68	34	214	60	NA
1942	66	33	206	56	NA
1943	66	33	206	56	NA

SOURCES: TWKS, 1: 6 (1901), app.; 1: 10 (1901), p. 88. NTTN, 1917, p. 731; 1927, p. 659; TWTT, p. 392; Hōmukyoku (GGT), *Taiwan shihō ichiran,* pp. 26–27.

NOTES: The figures followed by * indicate the number of clerks or police officers assigned to be agents of procurators in the district courts. The number of lawyers in 1901 is the number of members in the Taiwan Kanshū Kenkyūkai, which did not necessarily include all lawyers in Taiwan at that time.

invest enough money in the judiciary of Taiwan. On average a hundred thousand people in colonial Taiwan were assigned one judge, whereas on average fifty thousand people in metropolitan Japan were assigned one judge (table 3.4). Obviously, Japan paid less attention to Taiwan's judicial system than to its own. But Japan's judicial investment in colonial Taiwan was much better than that in colonial Korea. The population per judge in Korea initially was lower than that in Taiwan but became higher.

TABLE 3.4 Population per Judge
in Japan, Taiwan, and Korea, 1910–40

Year	Japan	Taiwan	Korea
1910	43,719	137,479	51,688
1920	49,164	101,563	88,565
1930	51,139	88,284	103,608
1940	46,334	89,375	98,942

SOURCES: Japan: Hattori, "The Legal Profession in Japan," p. 150, table 2. Taiwan: tables I.1 and 3.3 herein. Korea: Kim Tetsu, *Kankoku no jinkō to keizai*, p. 13; NTTN, 1917, p. 691; 1927, p. 659; 1931, p. 402; Kim Kyu-sung, *Nihon no shokuminchi hōsei no kenkyū*, p. 99, table 3.

LEGAL PROFESSION

Sufficient judicial facilities are not the only necessity in a legal system. Well-trained legal professionals are also essential. In fact, the professional abilities and ethical standards of the legal profession (judges, procurators, and lawyers) determines the quality of justice, which directly influences the interests of the people.

Composition of the Legal Profession in Taiwan

Legal Education. Unlike its actions at home during the Meiji legal reform, Japan did not endeavor to train legal professionals for the Westernization of law in Taiwan. When Japan acquired Taiwan and then enforced several Japanese Westernized laws on the island at the end of the nineteenth century, there was no Taiwanese legal profession versed in Western law because the former regime on Taiwan, the Chinese empire, had never considered adopting Western law. Similarly, Western medicine did not exist on Taiwan. The Japanese strove to train Taiwanese Western-style doctors in Western medical knowledge, for a native medical profession was necessary to improve the sanitary conditions on the island so that Japanese officials and immigrants could live there safely. In contrast, Japan did not want to train a Taiwanese legal profession because it would not be necessary for colonial rule. After thirty years of Westernization of law, Japan already had a large number of legal professionals trained in Western law. Additionally, law, unlike medicine, involved the authority of the Japanese ruler and thus had to be administered by the emperor's own loyal subjects, not Taiwanese.

No law prohibited Taiwanese from studying modern law on or away from the island, but only a few Taiwanese had the opportunity to do so during the first two decades of Japanese rule. Because the colonial education system in Taiwan discriminated against native students, some younger Taiwanese who came from or were sponsored by wealthy families went to Japan for advanced education.[62] In the 1920s about one-fifth of the Taiwanese students in Japan were enrolled in law departments at Japanese universities. During the 1933–37 period the average number of those students studying law increased to two hundred.[63] It was also reported that the total number of Taiwanese students in Japan increased continuously between 1937 and 1942.[64] Within the territory of Taiwan, the Taihoku Imperial University was established in Taipei in 1928, but the majority of students in this university were Japanese.[65] However, the students in the department of political science of the university could study law.[66] A Taiwanese student in this department, Feng Cheng-shu, later became a judge in the colonial court.[67] Despite a few examples of Taiwanese legal professionals during the Japanese rule, pervasive discrimination throughout the colonial education system for the most part kept Taiwanese from becoming legal professionals during this period.

The Japanese colonialists believed that the increasing number of Taiwanese educated in Japanese law would have a negative effect on Japan's government in Taiwan. Scholars in prewar Japanese academic circles often tended to interpret the law in a progovernment fashion so that the government could effectively govern its people.[68] Most Taiwanese did not realize that the colonial government deprived them of many legal rights enjoyed by the Japanese because they did not know Japanese law; once some Taiwanese became familiar with Japanese law, however, they struggled for their rights by law, as illustrated by the *Taiwan Parliament* case of 1923. Meanwhile, many Taiwanese students in Japan studied law so that they could pass the Japanese official examination to become a bureaucrat.[69] Furthermore, many Taiwanese studied in the legal departments of Japanese private universities, which traditionally emphasized civil rights.[70] The colonial authorities naturally considered that Japanese legal education would merely encourage unrest and even rebellion rather than create a group of friendly progovernment jurists.[71]

Japan took the same attitude toward legal education in colonial Korea. Before the annexation in 1910, Korea had somewhat Westernized its own law under Japanese pressure. In 1895, Japanese-trained Korean legal professionals graduated from law schools for the first time in Korea.[72] As subjects of an "independent state," Koreans still had opportunities to be trained and recruited to the court under the Japanese protectorate.[73] In 1909 Korean judges and procurators existed at all levels of the courts in Korea, although the heads and a majority of judges and procurators were Japanese; meanwhile, there were forty-one Korean lawyers compared to twenty-nine Japanese lawyers in the peninsula.[74] Since there had been a law school before the annexation, the Japanese imperial university in Seoul also instituted a department of law to induce Koreans to study law in the colony rather than in metropolitan Japan or Western countries.[75] In 1930 a few Koreans graduated from this law school. But through years of educational discrimination, the number of Koreans increased slowly and decreased slightly as a percentage of all law-school graduates.[76] Obviously, the Japanese colonialists also discouraged Koreans from studying law.

Appointment of Judicial Officials. Passing the Japanese examination for the legal profession was a prerequisite for appointment as a judicial official, but this examination was not the main obstacle for a Taiwanese to be a judicial official under Japanese rule. No legal provision prevented a Taiwanese from taking the national examination for the legal profession.[77] A few Taiwanese law students did pass the judicial section of the Japanese senior examination for public officials (hereafter, "the judicial examination") and thus were qualified to be probationary legal officials or lawyers.[78] From 1923 (the year that the judicial examination began) to 1930, twenty-six Taiwanese law students successfully passed the judicial examination.[79] Taiwanese law students in Japan steadily increased after 1930. But the pass rate of the judicial examination dropped after the mid-1930s.[80] Without statistics, we have no way to know exactly how many Taiwanese passed the judicial examination from 1931 to 1945.

Nevertheless, relatively fewer Taiwanese who were qualified candidates were appointed to be judges or procurators by the Japanese government. In prewar Japan, an average of about a hundred out of three hundred successful candidates for the judicial examination were appointed as probationary legal officials and then became judges or procurators.[81] But this ratio did not hold for Taiwanese candidates. By 1945 only seven or eight Taiwanese had been judges in the district courts in Taiwan, and one Taiwanese had been a probationary legal official in the GGT court (table 3.5). Not until 1931, thirty-six years after the start of Japanese rule, was a Taiwanese appointed as a judge in one of Taiwan's courts. Except for those who shifted to the GGT Court later, before 1945, there were only nine Taiwanese judges in Japan and one Taiwanese judge in Korea. The rest of the Taiwanese who passed the judicial examination became lawyers, whose social status generally was lower than that of judges and procurators in prewar Japan, unless they also passed the administrative section of the senior examination for public officials and took a post in the government. Although only nineteen Taiwanese served as judges (in Taiwan,

Japan, and Korea) during the Japanese period, there were also forty-six Taiwanese lawyers practicing in Taiwan, most of whom had also passed the judicial examination.[82] In addition, other successful judicial examination candidates became administrative officials (if they passed the examination for administrative officials as well; at least five candidates are in this category), practiced law in Japan (at least one), or were appointed to be judicial officials in Japanese-controlled parts of China (at least three). Therefore, we can assume that about seventy-four Taiwanese law students passed the judicial examination. In other words, fewer than a third of the successful judicial examination candidates became Japanese judicial officials, a lower ratio than that for Japanese.

This difference is eventually attributable to discrimination in colonial rule. In metropolitan Japan, the minister of justice, who had power to appoint judges and procurators, always preferred candidates who graduated from imperial universities; private university students who passed the judicial examination often entered private practice.[83] Because of the inequity in colonial education, most Taiwanese students in Japan could not qualify for imperial universities but had to attend private universities.[84] The majority of Taiwanese law students also studied in private universities, especially Meiji University. The few Taiwanese who studied law at imperial universities had better opportunities to be appointed judges in Japan. The majority of Taiwanese judges who served in metropolitan Japan graduated from the most respected university, Imperial Tōkyō University (see table 3.5).[85] In colonial Taiwan, the governor-general of Taiwan, who had power to appoint colonial judicial officials, seemed to think that it was not necessary to recruit Taiwanese judges. In fact, high-ranking official positions in Taiwan were monopolized by the Japanese, and a Taiwanese official was always discriminated against in promotion.[86] Such unfair treatment undoubtedly discouraged Taiwanese law students from searching for jobs in the colonial court. Although the GGT in approximately 1940 began allowing Taiwanese who passed the judicial examination to become judges in Taiwan after training for a year and a half on the Japanese mainland, this measure not surprisingly was not very attractive to them.[87]

It should be noted that the governor-general of Taiwan never appointed a Taiwanese as a procurator in Taiwan. Japanese judges and procurators passed the same examination and received the same training. However, a Taiwanese who was qualified could only be a judge if he served in Taiwan. A few Taiwanese were procurators in the pro-Japanese government on China, but no one in Taiwan.[88] The Japanese colonizers never trusted the colonized in the colony. A colonial procurator had to work closely with the police to fulfill

TABLE 3.5 Taiwanese Judges before 1945

Name	Law school	Service in Japan	Service in Taiwan	Supplement
Huang Yen-sheng	Kyōto	Judge, 1929	Judge, 1931	lawyer later
Huang Yen-wo	Tōhoku	Judge, NA	Judge, 1932	District Court, Tainan; Higher Court?
Tu Shin-ch'un	Kyōto	Judge, 1930	Judge, 1932	Died
Jao Wei-yüeh	Kyōto	Judge, NA	Judge, 1932	District Court, Taichung
Ch'en Ming-ch'ing	NA	NA	Judge, NA	District Court, Hsin-chu
Feng Cheng-shu	Taihoku	no	Judge, NA	District Court, Kaohsiung
Hung Shou-nan	Kyōto	Judge, NA	Judge, 1944	District Court, Tainan
Wang Yu-lin	NA	NA	Probationary legal official	ROC procurator
Liu Tseng-ch'üan	NA	procurator?	Judge?	ROC judge in District Court, Taipei
Lü A-yung	Tōkyō	Judge, 1929	no	
Ch'en Mao-yüan	Tōkyō	Judge, 1929	no	
Wu Wen-cheng	Chūō	Judge, 1930	no	private university
Ts'ai Po-fen	Tōkyō	Judge, NA	no	lawyer later
Chang Yu-chung	Tōkyō	Judge, 1942	no	ROC procurator
Ts'ai Chang-lin	Tōkyō	Judge, NA	no	
Hung Sun-hsin	Tōkyō	Judge, NA	no	
Lin T'ing-sheng	NA	Judge, NA	no	
Ch'en Ch'ing-hua	NA	Judge, NA	no	
Yang Hsing-tang	NA	NA	no	Judge in Korea

SOURCES: See Wu Wen-hsing, pp. 113, 115, 190–94; Chang Tzu-hui, pp. 121, 139, 162, 165; Taiwan Sōtokufu, *Taiwan Sōtokufu oyobi shozoku kansho shokuinroku*, 1944, pp. 54–55, 57; Ssu-fa-yüan (ROC), *Ssu-fa-yüan shih-shih chi-yao*, p. 113; Chang Yu-chung, *Gaichijin*, pp. 62, 215–16; Chang Yu-chung, letter to author; telephone interview with Judge Hung Shou-nan (1990).

NOTE: ? indicates conflicting statements in different sources.

his task of maintaining public order. Since a procurator had extensive power to direct the police, he was in practice like a high-ranking police officer. Just as no Taiwanese were promoted to be high-ranking police officers, Taiwanese were not allowed to be procurators.[89] This is perhaps especially true because the procurator was charged with the duty of "thought control."[90] In the eyes of the Japanese authorities, this job could not be undertaken by Taiwanese, whose loyalty to Japan remained uncertain.[91] A similar situation also prevailed in colonial Korea. Although Japan continued to employ Korean procurators to superficially honor its promise in the annexation treaty of 1910, the total number of procurators who were Korean in 1945 was nearly the same as that in 1909. On the other hand, the total number of procurators who were Japanese in 1945 was double that in 1909.[92]

Most judges and all procurators in the GGT Court were thus Japanese (mainlanders). Based on a *Who's Who* of Taiwan published in 1943, most judges in Taiwan served as judges in Japan before coming to Taiwan.[93] Perhaps the higher payment, more by about half of their original salary, and other bonuses were incentives for their service in Taiwan, where their tenure was less protected by law. Other colonial judges practiced law in Japan before coming to Taiwan. Many such lawyers came to Taiwan because they had a better opportunity gaining the prestigious position of a judge in the colony than on the Japanese mainland.[94] On the other hand, most procurators in Taiwan had previously been procurators in Japan.[95] A few Japanese practicing lawyers became procurators in Taiwan. In addition, several colonial judges later became colonial procurators.[96]

Private Practice. In the early period of Japanese rule, all lawyers in Taiwan of course were Japanese.[97] In 1914, it was still true that all of the members of the Taihoku Bar Association were Japanese.[98] Generally speaking, the Japanese lawyers in Taiwan consisted of two main groups: those who originally practiced in Japan[99] and retired Japanese judges or procurators of the GGT Court.[100]

The number of Taiwanese lawyers grew rapidly after the 1920s. A large number of Taiwanese law students aspired to become practicing lawyers in Taiwan. Not only did most Taiwanese law students graduating from private universities intend to become practicing lawyers, but many graduating from imperial universities also selected private practice. Relatively speaking, a practicing lawyer did not need to depend on the Japanese colonial government and therefore could avoid the discrimination within the bureaucracy. Additionally, sharing the same mother tongue with most inhabitants, Taiwanese lawyers could compete with the dominant Japanese professionals. In 1921 the first Taiwanese lawyer began practicing in Taipei. In 1931, ten years later, 20 of the total 156 lawyers practicing in Taiwan were Taiwanese. By 1935, the number of Taiwanese lawyers had increased to 32. Although the number of Japanese lawyers in 1935 also increased to 145, some Japanese lawyers felt that their law practices were threatened by Taiwanese lawyers.[101] In 1945, the last year of Japanese rule, there were 46 Taiwanese lawyers and only 63 Japanese lawyers practicing law in Taiwan.[102]

The total number of lawyers, either Japanese or Taiwanese, rose rapidly from 1921 to the mid-1930s, reaching its peak (177 lawyers) in 1934 (see table 3.3). Compared to 59 lawyers in 1921, the number nearly doubled by 1926 and tripled by 1934. But in metropolitan Japan, for reasons that are not at all clear, nearly a third of all Japanese practicing lawyers withdrew from their bar association during the 1934–38 period.[103] The number of Japanese lawyers in Taiwan also decreased at the same time. The total number of lawyers therefore began to drop after 1935 and finally dwindled to only 109 lawyers in 1945.

Professional Abilities and Virtue

Fact-Finding and the Application of Taiwanese Customs. In Taiwan, Japanese legal professionals had to face unfamiliar languages in the fact-finding process of lawsuits, one of the special problems in colonial justice. Western colonialists basically thought that native judges were more competent to carry out fact-finding in native lawsuits than European judges, who were not familiar with the indigenous languages and customs.[104] Partly because the Japanese shared the same scripts with the Taiwanese and also studied classical Chinese, they seemed not to seriously consider language an obstacle in fact-finding.

However, the Japanese never overcame the language problem in fact-finding for lawsuits. As in other administrative affairs, the oral interrogation for fact finding in a trial depended on court interpreters.[105] Unfortunately, the reliability of those interpreters was doubtful.[106] Moreover, in the early period of Japanese rule few Japanese knew Taiwanese dialects, and Japanese judges therefore had to first speak to a Japanese interpreter who translated what the judge said into Mandarin Chinese. A Taiwanese interpreter further translated from Mandarin Chinese into Taiwanese dialects, as he did in the Ch'ing period.[107] The system of two interpreters most certainly added obstacles to the process of fact finding. It was reported in 1912 that the native language was directly translated into Japanese, and Japanese judicial officials were encouraged to learn native languages.[108] In any event, the number of interpreters in the GGT court increased gradually after 1919 (see table 3.3). Unlike Japanese policemen in Taiwan, Japanese judges and procurators were not required to learn native languages. With the exception of those judges and procurators who had stayed in Taiwan for a long time and were willing to learn the languages of the colonized, very few actually understood Taiwanese languages. In contrast, quite a few Taiwanese, especially those who lived in cities and towns, gradually learned to speak Japanese. After the policy of assimilation was emphasized in the colony in the 1920s, more Taiwanese began to learn to speak Japanese.[109] Japanese-speaking Taiwanese made up only 8.5 percent of the total Taiwanese population in 1930. Indeed, the GGT recognized in 1935 that there was difficulty in communication between Japanese judicial officials and the Taiwanese population.[110] Not until the policy of Japanization was adopted in the mid-1930s did the Japanese-speaking population greatly increase.[111] In 1943, by which time Japan had governed the island for nearly half a century, 62 percent of the Taiwanese were able to comprehend the Japanese language.[112]

It should not be overlooked, however, that the Japanese colonial authorities took special measures to help the Japanese legal profession to understand Taiwanese customs, seeing this as an important tool for exercising judicial functions. Knowing the customs in a society is frequently an important avenue for fact finding in a lawsuit because certain actions often have specific social meanings based on custom. Furthermore, Taiwanese customary law was applied to civil cases involving only Taiwanese (and Chinese) and Japanese civil cases involving the property rights in land before 1923, as well as civil cases involving Taiwanese family and succession after 1923. Initially what was considered social custom or the customary law in a certain lawsuit was simply determined from the documents collected and the testimony of the Taiwanese witnesses involved; consequently, the legal relations determined by Taiwanese customs were uncertain and unpredictable.[113] In 1901, a special governmental institution, Rinji Taiwan kyūkan chōsakai (Commission for the Investigation of Old Laws and Customs in Formosa), was organized to investigate Taiwanese customs so that Japanese judicial officials could refer to its reports when applying Taiwanese customs.[114] Meanwhile, Japanese judicial officials also organized the Association for the Study of Taiwanese Customs, publishing a monthly journal (*Taiwan kanshū kiji*; TWKS) after 1901. Following the method used by the Ch'ing magistrates, who were also unfamiliar with native customs, Japanese judges and procurators summoned local gentry, strongmen, or merchants and questioned them concerning their customs in every respect.[115]

In the process of applying Taiwanese customs, the Japanese authorities "created" Taiwanese customary law as interpreted by them using their Western concepts of law. It is difficult, sometimes impossible, to use the conceptions and terminology of one legal system to completely interpret the contents of another legal system. However, just as Western colonialists did in their colonies, Japanese officials (especially judges) employed their "own" legal terminology, a terminology recently borrowed from the continental European legal system, which was largely derived from ancient Roman law, to interpret Taiwanese customs under Chinese legal traditions.[116] With their experience of investigating Japanese customs in the Meiji legal reforms and thirty years of learning Western jurisprudence, the Japanese transformed old Taiwanese customs into customary law through the use of systematic European conceptions and terminology. Western colonialists in fact revised substantively the native customs in the name of interpreting or codifying them.[117] Similarly, some old Taiwanese civil customs were inevitably altered in the process of Westernization (see chapter 5). Nevertheless, this process of Taiwanese customary law remains a significant achievement in the legal development of Taiwan.

Honesty of Judicial Officials. The greatest difference in character between Japanese judicial officials and Ch'ing magistrates was their degree of honesty.[118] In the 1920s, many Taiwanese antigovernment political associations frequently criticized the judiciary in Taiwan, but they never doubted the honesty of the Japanese judges and procurators. In the novels written by Taiwanese during Japanese rule, Japanese policemen were sometimes portrayed accepting bribes, but judges and procurators were almost entirely free from such a negative image.[119] In fact, the honesty of judges and procurators was never regarded as an issue in the Japanese period; only one procurator was ever found guilty of accepting bribes, and no judges ever were.[120]

Both their high status and their high pay helped to maintain the honesty of colonial judges and procurators. According to the official table of organization of the GGT, the chief justice and chief procurator in the Higher Court had the same status as the chief of civil administration, the head of the executive department under the governor-general. The judge and procurator in the Re-appeal Division of the Higher Court or the chief justice and chief procurator in the District Court were equal to the head of a bureau in the GGT or a governor of a *shū* (prefecture) in the local government. Other judges or procurators were equal to counselors (*sanjikan*) in the bureaus of the GGT or governors of *chō* (smaller prefectures) in the local government.[121] With high rank came high pay, and they enjoyed high social status. In contrast, the magistrate was the lowest position in the Chinese imperial bureaucratic system. The official salaries of Ch'ing magistrates were kept so low that they could neither support their families and private legal staff nor make "presents" to their superiors. It was only natural that they accepted bribes from litigants.[122]

Impartiality of Decisions. Honesty is a minimum standard for judges; they must also be impartial in making their decisions. A judge indeed does the job that only God could do well. Although not present when an incident occurred, a judge must still decide whether the accused did commit an offense or the plaintiff does have the right of claim. Furthermore, lawsuits always involve conflicting interests relating to at least two parties. They often involve third parties, whole groups of people, or even the state. A judge has to decide which interest more deserves to be protected, usually at the cost of others. Often there is no absolute, concrete criterion to appraise those conflicting values. In this section, I look at the extent to which the environment allowed colonial judges to pursue impartiality.

In criminal cases, it was sometimes not easy for a colonial judge to pursue impartiality. Linguistic obstacles often influenced his ability to uncover the truth. Most important, because criminal cases involve public order, the executive authority typically pays special attention to them. A colonial judge needed moral courage to reject possible administrative interference.[123]

In contrast, colonial judges had a better opportunity to decide civil and commercial cases with impartiality, though their weakness in fact finding impeded them here as well. Further, the extent to which a Japanese judge could and would correctly interpret Taiwanese customs was most certainly limited. Political interference from the executive authorities, however, was probably rare in civil and commercial cases. Meanwhile, since the parties to civil disputes were usually of the same race, racial discrimination could largely be avoided in civil suits.[124]

Service of Lawyers. In the beginning, the role of lawyers in Western-style trial proceedings seemed strange to the Taiwanese who were used to the inquisitorial proceedings of Ch'ing China.[125] In addition, Japanese advocates in the early days of Japanese rule were not necessarily professionally trained.[126] Not until 1901 did the same qualifications that applied to lawyers in Japan become requisite for lawyers in Taiwan, with the exception those who were already practicing as advocates in Taiwan.[127] However, the problem for Japanese lawyers in Taiwan was more language than legal knowledge. Even in 1935 Japanese lawyers still could not easily communicate with their Taiwanese clients and therefore sometimes needed a third party to interpret.[128] In the late period of Japanese rule, the increasing number of Taiwanese lawyers to some degree improved this situation.

During the Japanese period, Japanese lawyers were not concentrated in the capital but evenly distributed to cities and towns throughout the island where there were district courts or their branches.[129] It was therefore convenient for people to hire a lawyer.[130]

As mentioned above, before 1921 there were no Taiwanese lawyers in Taiwan. Nevertheless, the nationality of lawyers (Japanese) seemed not to discourage Taiwanese from employing them. Many Taiwanese litigants retained Japanese lawyers to represent them in trials. In 1910, for example, of all civil trials in the district courts in which Taiwanese plaintiffs won (and most defendants therein were also Taiwanese), 552 cases were conducted by litigants themselves, but there were 440 cases in which either the plaintiff, the defendant, or both were represented by lawyers.[131] In 1920, some 1,220 cases were conducted by litigants themselves, and 399 cases were dealt with by lawyers.[132] Furthermore, most of the increased number of lawyers in Taiwan during the period from the 1920s to the mid-1930s were Japanese.[133] If all Taiwanese had refused to retain a lawyer to represent them in court merely because a lawyer was Japanese, an increasing number of Japanese would not have entered into private practice in Taiwan.

We can observe how large a population a lawyer, Japanese or Taiwanese, could serve in Taiwan. During the period of Japanese rule the population per lawyer in colonial Taiwan was about four times more than that in metropolitan Japan but considerably less than that in colonial Korea (table 3.6). A Taiwanese had far less chance to consult with a lawyer than a Japanese but more chance than a Korean.

Although the Western-style lawyer had become an esteemed professional in Taiwanese society by 1945, in prewar Japan, prejudice against lawyers still persisted both in the general public and among government officials.[134] It has also been pointed out that the Korean bar was apt to be regarded with suspicion by most Koreans because of the bar's close cooperation with the Japanese colonial administration.[135] But there were some differences between colonial Taiwan and these two countries. Lawyers in Taiwan, whether Taiwanese or Japanese, in practice did not receive due respect from the colonial authorities.[136] However, the Taiwanese people were willing to hire lawyers, even though most of them were Japanese. For the Taiwanese who tended to be anti-Japanese (antigovernment), there were plenty of Taiwanese lawyers who participated in the political movement against the oppression of the colonial government, and a few Japanese lawyers were also eager to defend the Taiwanese dissidents who were engaged in the civil rights movement, the farmer movement, or the labor movement.[137] In 1935 the Taiwan Bar Association strongly urged the GGT to protect human rights; and the majority of those active lawyers were Japanese.[138] As a consequence, the lawyer, like the medical doctor, was generally regarded as an esteemed professional by the Taiwanese under Japanese rule,[139] though the judge was also, perhaps more, respected by Taiwanese society.

TABLE 3.6 Population per Lawyer
in Japan, Taiwan, and Korea, 1921–40

Year	Japan	Taiwan	Korea
1921	15,916	65,018	85,975
1925	10,432	44,596	61,539
1931	9,603	30,405	NA
1935	9,705	34,971	56,276
1940	13,386	49,915	66,975

SOURCES: Hattori, "The Legal Profession in Japan," p. 150, table 2; Kim Tetsu, *Kanoko no jinkō to keizai*, p. 13; *NTTN*, 1927, p. 659; 1928, pp. 19, 392; 1932, p. 402; 1939, pp. 6–7; tables 1.1 and 3.3 herein.

NOTE: Because the numbers of lawyers in Taiwan in 1920 and 1930 are not available, 1921 and 1931 are used here.

ACCESS TO COURT

When the provisions in the Westernized positive law were implemented in real disputes decided by modern courts, not only the parties involved but also the friends and neighbors of those involved came into contact with the new legal norms. But modern courts, with sufficient facilities and good legal professionals, cannot automatically perform their task. People must bring cases to court. Accordingly, if people distrust the court, or are denied access to the court, the function of modern courts will be weakened.

Several institutional obstacles prevented people in colonial Taiwan from going to court. In the early period of Japanese rule, Japanese colonial officials rejected about one-fourth of all lawsuits that were brought by Taiwanese to resolve old disputes that had arisen during the Ch'ing period. They later declared that the Taiwanese were neither accustomed to nor willing to seek access modern courts, so that a mediation system had to be restored to meet their needs.[140] Similarly, to "prevent the arrested suspects from suffering the pain of long-distance escort," the heads of local governments, actually police officers, were empowered to make summary judgments imposing criminal sanctions on people.[141] Because the civil disputes settled by this mediation system could not be filed again in courts and few, if any, of the criminal summary judgments were reviewed by the court, these two administrative measures infringed the right to a fair trial. In the next part, I will survey to what extent these measures substituted for court trials so that modern courts in Taiwan had fewer opportunities to bring Westernized law to Taiwanese society.

Civil Litigation vs. Administrative Mediation

Administrative Mediation. Japan's administrative mediation system in Taiwan was a special colonial institution; it did not exist in metropolitan Japan. After the 1904 Civil Disputes Mediation Law was promulgated, the local administrative officials in Taiwan were gradually empowered to mediate civil disputes of the people, and a similar law was enacted by the Korean colonial government in 1910.[142] In metropolitan Japan, even during the wartime period, civil mediation was carried out by judges in courts rather than by administrative officials of local governments.[143]

Based on, but differing in some ways from, its counterpart in imperial China, civil mediation was used by the Japanese state authority to intervene in civil disputes.[144] According to the Civil Disputes Mediation Law in Taiwan, any civil disputes involving status law or property law, irrespective of their monetary value, could be submitted for mediation by a division of mediation in the local government to which the other party to the dispute belonged, with the payment of certain fees. This unlimited scope of matters that could be mediated was greater than that in Korea.[145] A local official in Taiwan could therefore play the role of mediator to settle any possible civil disputes. If a compromise was reached, the entire process of mediation and settlement had to be recorded in an official document by which the parties might apply for compulsory execution and the parties involved thereafter were prohibited from litigating the dispute further.[146] This administrative mediation should be distinguished from the ordinary mediation engaged in by the head of the *hokō* or the policemen in wards. The latter in essence remained an unofficial dispute resolution, although police authority was sometimes involved.[147]

Although the judgments of administrative officials frequently had the same effect as court judgments, administrative mediation differed from the decisions of courts in the following respects. First, administrative mediation was an action of the executive authority rather than the judicial authority.[148] Because the summons to appear in the mediation process was an administrative order and anyone who disobeyed might be punished with detention or be fined by the government, the party summoned in a filed mediation case had little freedom to refuse to participate in the mediation.[149] Second, a judge in court had to find facts and apply the positive law to make decisions, but an official mediator merely persuaded the parties involved to settle their disputes on the basis of "affection and reason."[150] The mediator, however, who was a general administrative official without professional training, frequently coerced the parties to accede to his official authority and "agree" with his decision of the disputes.[151] It is no wonder the majority of mediation cases reached a compromise, while some were withdrawn by parties; only a few were not settled.[152] As a consequence, an administrative mediator actually exercised the power of adjudication over civil disputes without the application of positive civil law.

In any event, administrative mediation was prevalent in Taiwan. In the early period of Japanese rule, the Taiwanese were not familiar with Western-style civil procedure in the court, and therefore tended to employ this mediation system, which was more similar to their old institutions. Later, they had the additional motivation that the expense required for an administrative mediation was much lower than that for filing a suit in the court. The application fee for a suit in the court generally was triple that for an administrative mediation, and there was no appeal and no lawyer in the mediation process.[153]

Formal Dispute Resolution. Like any society in any period, Taiwanese society under Japanese rule maintained some machinery for informal dispute resolution, including negotiation by the parties themselves or mediation involving an accepted third party. But when those methods did not work, people naturally appealed to the official authorities. At this time the Taiwanese people had two choices: to apply for the administrative mediation system mentioned above or to employ various processes in the modern court in accordance with Western-style civil procedure law. In the first half of Japanese rule, the former was more prevalent; but in the last half of Japanese rule, the latter became dominant.

From table 3.7, we can see the interrelationship between the numbers of civil lawsuits and mediation cases. Some civil disputes were first submitted to the compromise procedure after they entered the court system. If compromise failed, the trial commenced upon the request of the parties concerned.[154] Because of the number of suits in which the parties reached a compromise during this procedure was very small, it is omitted here.[155] In contrast, a large number of civil suits involved the "hortatory" proceeding, another special institution in the Japanese Code of Civil Procedure, and therefore should be mentioned here (see (A) of table 3.7). Under Japanese civil procedure law, when the claim of the obligee was one for the payment or delivery of a fixed amount of money or other substitutes or negotiable securities, an application might be made to the court requesting that an order for payment be issued in accordance with the hortatory proceeding rather than the ordinary proceeding. But if, after the order was issued, the obligor made a legal motion objecting to it, the order for payment would become ineffective, and a litigation was deemed to have been brought.[156] In about one-third of the hortatory suits the obligor objected to the claim, and therefore the matter was tried as an ordinary civil case (see (B) of table 3.7). The hortatory suits

TABLE 3.7 Numbers of Various Formal Civil Dispute Resolutions in Taiwan, 1897–1942

Year	Hortatory suits (A)	Objected hortatory suits (B)	Civil trials, court of first instance (C)	Civil lawsuits in court (D)	Administrative mediation cases (E)
1897	NA	NA	2,270	NA	1,451
1898	NA	NA	2,108 (81)	NA	NA
1899	1,490	660	3,068	3,898	4,214
1900	1,371	476	1,417 (52)	2,312	2,808
1901	1,746	696	1,456	2,506	2,056
1902	2,090	660	1,452	2,872	1,858
1903	2,164	821	1,845	3,170	2,375
1904	2,176	952	1,788	3,012	2,525
1905	1,752	816	2,094 (71)	3,030	3,204
1906	1,842	873	3,257	4,226	4,744
1907	2,539	1,122	3,406	4,823	4,785
1908	2,811	1,208	3,356	4,959	4,623
1909	3,073	1,402	3,782	5,453	5,104
1910	3,523	1,445	4,046 (132)	7,124	7,396
1911	3,387	1,282	4,036	6,141	10,139
1912	3,524	1,379	4,694	6,839	11,896
1913	5,093	1,803	5,693	8,983	11,959
1914	7,107	2,908	6,865	11,064	11,221
1915	7,204	3,079	6,330 (181)	10,115	10,113
1916	6,934	2,682	6,330	10,582	9,515
1917	5,546	2,121	6,136	9,561	9,012
1918	4,956	1,746	6,109	9,319	8,533
1919	5,061	1,491	6,831	10,401	7,700
1920	7,122	1,349	7,090 (206)	12,863	6,814
1921	13,901	4,271	10,028	19,658	9,153
1922	14,629	5,520	10,722	19,831	11,140

that were objected to are considered civil trials in the courts of first instance (see (C) of table 3.7). The gross number of civil lawsuits in the court, which were resolved by either hortatory proceeding or ordinary proceeding, therefore, can be calculated from the formula (A) + (C) − (B) (see (D) of table 3.7). During the period 1899–1914, the number of administrative mediation cases was ordinarily greater than all civil suits in the courts ((E) > (D) in table 3.7). But during the period 1915–19, there were for the first time slightly more of the latter than the former ((D) > (E) in table 3.7). The gap gradually enlarged during the period 1920–29. Then, after 1930, the number of hortatory suits

TABLE 3.7 (continued)

Year	Hortatory suits (A)	Objected hortatory suits (B)	Civil trials, court of first instance (C)		Civil lawsuits in court (D)	Administrative mediation cases (E)
1923	9,242	3,470	8,875		14,647	11,718
1924	8,548	3,045	8,527		14,030	13,274
1925	7,325	2,814	8,108	(195)	12,619	9,295
1926	6,617	2,361	7,801		12,057	10,877
1927	7,687	2,714	8,295		13,268	12,880
1928	7,522	2,774	8,522		13,270	10,043
1929	8,870	2,966	8,623		14,527	10,356
1930	13,004	4,543	9,475	(202)	17,936	11,500
1931	17,529	6,436	12,032		23,125	13,474
1932	17,072	6,506	11,839		22,405	12,803
1933	14,349	5,942	11,258		19,665	11,202
1934	12,351	4,498	9,659		17,512	10,923
1935	9,898	3,656	9,150	(171)	15,392	9,711
1936	10,522	3,565	9,471		16,428	9,077
1937	10,268	3,391	9,489		16,366	7,802
1938	10,341	3,372	9,217		16,186	8,145
1939	9,507	3,833	8,452		14,126	7,090
1940	8,054	2,455	7,834	(129)	13,433	6,252
1941	8,125	2,277	6,668		12,516	6,277
1942	7,639	2,054	6,027		11,612	6,304

SOURCES: Dispute-resolution machinery: TWTT, pp. 396–97, 399. Population in Taiwan: Table I.1 herein and NTTN, 1921, p. 21; 1928, p. 19; 1939, p. 7; Barclay, *Colonial Development and Population in Taiwan*, p. 13. The population of 1898 did not include the Japanese residing in Taiwan, but very few Japanese civilians lived in Taiwan at that time.

NOTE: Figures in parentheses indicate the number of new filings for civil trials in the courts of first instance per 100,000 people.

in the court was greater than the number of administrative mediation cases for each year ((A) > (E) in table 3.7). Furthermore, after 1936 the number of disputes dealt with as ordinary civil trials was also greater than the number of administrative mediation cases, except in 1942 ((C) > (E) in table 3.7). In brief, the Taiwanese initially preferred to employ administrative mediation over court litigation. But after the 1920s, people apparently became accustomed to using modern Western-style courts to resolve their civil disputes, and the number of cases litigated in court increased until they eventually surpassed the cases decided by the administrative mediation procedure.

The importance of administrative mediation in colonial Taiwan therefore must not be exaggerated. A commentator has argued that during most of the colonial period the number of administrative mediations was greater than the number of suits brought before the courts, but he excluded the hortatory suits from the "suits brought before the courts" in his calculations.[157] The hortatory proceeding, however, was a special procedure for civil litigation under Japanese law. In this procedure, unlike the in-court compromise procedure or administrative mediation, the judge made a decision in accordance with positive law. In fact, the hortatory proceeding was not a type of traditional dispute resolution, but was rather modern, Western-style legal procedure. Therefore, those involved in civil disputes who resorted to this proceeding certainly hoped to be dealt with by the modern courts with Western-style procedure.

The attitudes of the Taiwanese toward litigation and administrative mediation were a significant factor influencing the reception of Western law in Taiwan. During the early period of Japanese rule, because Japan's modern civil and commercial codes were seldom if at all applied to Taiwanese civil lawsuits, the main difference between civil suits in the court and mediation cases in the local government was that in the court proceedings a Taiwanese was exposed to Western-style civil procedural law. After 1923 the colonial court began to apply most of Japan's Western-style civil and commercial codes to lawsuits involving Taiwanese parties. In contrast, the official mediator without legal training did not begin to apply those Western-style codes. By 1923, however, the Taiwanese had already reduced reliance on administrative mediation so that its effect upon the reception of Western law was no longer a significant factor.

Reasons for Increasing Litigation. During the beginning of Japanese rule, the Taiwanese did not frequently bring suit in the courts, though the Japanese colonialists often accused the Taiwanese of being overly litigious. In Japan, the number of civil cases tried in the courts of first instance was 230 per 100,000 people in 1898.[158] In Taiwan, this number was 81 per 100,000 people for the same year (see table 3.7). Because civil disputes that occurred during the Ch'ing period were not adjudicated after October 1, 1899, a great number of Taiwanese brought their suits before the deadline, causing a sudden rise and then a drop in the number of suits filed in 1899 and 1900.[159] Then, judging from the number of civil cases tried in the courts of first instance per 100,000 people, the civil suits filed in Taiwan gradually increased. The average number of suits brought during the period from the 1920s to the mid-1930s is about triple the average number of suits brought during the early 1897–1905 period, but it is still smaller than the corresponding number in Japan.[160] With the arrival of the war, the number of civil suits brought after the mid-1930s gradually decreased but remained higher than the number of suits brought during the early period of Japanese rule.

Although judicial reform after 1919 contributed to the increase in civil suits from the 1920s to the mid-1930s, it was not the decisive factor. The GGT added two district court branches in 1919 and one more in 1933. In addition, eight judges were added in 1919 and nine more in 1927 (see tables 3.2 and 3.3). But during the period from 1919 to 1932, there were no district courts or branches thereof in one of the five *shū* or any of the three *chō* of Taiwan. Therefore, in these areas, the people had to resort to administrative mediation when they used official machinery to resolve disputes.[161] More important, the number of judges was not increased to meet the increase in civil cases. The heavier caseloads per judge resulted in trial delay. In 1920, 33 percent of all civil cases were tried within one month; in 1930 only 11 percent of all civil cases were tried within one month. In 1920, 27 percent of all civil cases were tried within two months; in 1930, only 18 percent were tried within two months. In 1920, 16 percent of all civil cases took three to six months; in 1930, 27 percent took three to six months. In 1920, 9 percent of all civil cases took six to twelve months; in 1930, 14 percent took six to twelve months.[162] Such trial delay was certainly not good for litigants.[163]

The urbanization of Taiwan after the 1920s contributed to some extent to the increase in litigation. In the traditional agrarian society of Taiwan, the necessity of mutual assistance for economic survival and even personal safety forced people to tolerate the conduct of other people who belonged to the same family, clan, or village. Official lawsuits were regarded as outside interference, and internal affairs were often decided by the heads of the family, clan, or village. Where the disputes involved economic interests, however, the ability of such leaders to influence the involved parties was not as strong. Where a dispute involved outsiders, the families, clans, or villages of the parties involved typically did not exert pressure on the parties to avoid litigation.[164] Starting in the 1920s, Taiwan began urbanization under Japanese rule. As stated before, seven municipalities were formed in 1930, and nine in 1933. The majority of city inhabitants were Taiwanese, who shifted to nonagricultural jobs and settled in a single family unit.[165] They were relatively willing to resort to official authority for settling their disputes because the informal machinery for dispute resolution lost its social foundation in the cities. The establishment of district courts and their branches in those municipalities also encouraged them to use courts rather than the administrative mediation system. However, only 10 percent of all Taiwanese lived in the municipalities in 1920, and only 14.7 percent lived in the municipalities in 1940.[166] The progress of urbanization in colonial Taiwan was too slow to result in a great increase in litigation during the period from the 1920s to the mid-1930s.

The modern Japanese education system in Taiwan to a certain extent inspired Taiwanese to receive Western-style law and courts. However, its influence on the great increase of litigation during the 1920s and the mid-1930s is limited. Unlike traditional institutions of learning, which taught only Confucianism, Japanese modern education included some recently imported Western ideas. Although in the early period of Japanese rule colonial education largely emphasized the Japanese language and modern practical knowledge, it did help Taiwanese to have access to the Japanese courts and come in contact with some modern media, like newspapers and radio, which occasionally reported the decisions of the courts and therefore had an effect on the standards being applied in popular settlement of similar disputes.[167] However, the content of the official program of education in practice suppressed the development of Western legal ideas. A Taiwanese was always required to act like an obedient, hard-working Japanese subject, but he was not taught much about the privileges or opportunities that a Japanese might be tempted to claim.[168] To struggle for individual interests through litigation was of course not encouraged by the schools. Moreover, Japanese primary education was extensively promoted on the island only after the 1920s.[169] This educational reform therefore did not influence the Taiwanese litigants in the 1920s and early 1930s.

It is worth noting that the average Taiwanese were relatively richer during the period from the 1920s to mid-1930s than they were during other periods of Japanese rule. Money was undoubtedly needed to file a case in courts. During the colonial period, the average real wage earned by male Taiwanese rose sharply in the 1920s. Wages continued to increase in the first half of the 1930s, but fell in the second half of the 1930s. Meanwhile, the per capita consumption of food, cotton cloth, paper, and so on increased rapidly in colonial Taiwan until the late 1930s.[170] A wealthy man influenced by Confucianist antilitigation ideas, however, was probably not willing to use the courts to settle disputes. In addition, on a cost-benefit basis, litigation was not necessarily more desirable than other methods for resolving disputes. Hence, the improvement in the economic ability of the average Taiwanese did not directly result in an increase in lawsuits in courts.

Examination of Taiwanese plaintiffs' rate of success in civil trials (in which the defendants were mostly Taiwanese as well) filed during the 1920s and mid-1930s reveals an interesting fact: an increase in this rate is always met by a corresponding increase in the number of civil suits during the same period. During the 1910–20 period, 32 percent of Taiwanese plaintiffs were completely

TABLE 3.8 Results of Civil Trials in the Court of First Instance
Where the Plaintiff Was Taiwanese, 1910–42 (percentage)

Year	Complete success	Partial success	Complete failure
1910	31.5	9.4	20.6
1912	30.5	7.2	17.9
1914	33.7	7.5	13.4
1916	33.8	6.3	11.8
1918	30.0	7.8	15.0
1920	31.0	5.3	14.9
1922	36.2	6.4	12.4
1924	37.8	6.5	14.7
1926	33.8	5.8	15.6
1928	34.7	5.1	12.9
1930	38.5	6.1	12.3
1932	43.3	2.7	8.9
1934	43.2	3.7	10.9
1936	38.8	4.1	10.4
1938	40.7	3.8	10.0
1940	37.7	4.0	9.0
1942	40.2	2.0	9.7

SOURCE: TWTT, pp. 408–9.
NOTE: Other results for suits (e.g., withdrawal of the suit) are not included here.

successful in their civil suits; only 16 percent of plaintiffs were completely unsuccessful in their suits (table 3.8). During the period from 1920 to 1934, a plaintiff's rate of success in a civil trial rose considerably. In the early 1930s, when suits drastically increased, the rate of complete success in a civil trial rose to about 43 percent, and the rate of complete failure fell to about 10 percent. Furthermore, the period during which the highest number of suits was filed coincides with the period during which plaintiffs met with the highest rate of success. After 1935, the rate of success did not vary considerably but the amount of litigation gradually decreased. The inconvenience arising out of the war may explain the decrease in litigation in the late Japanese period; administrative mediation cases also decreased considerably at the same time (see table 3.7). But why is there such relation between Taiwanese plaintiffs' rate of success and the quantity of litigation during the peaceful period?

In the early period of Japanese rule, Taiwanese customs were applied in civil cases involving Taiwanese parties, but Taiwanese plaintiffs often lost their suits. This result perhaps caused Japanese judges to concur with the myth that the Taiwanese had a habit of "abusing litigation," as the Ch'ing officials declared.[171] In fact, Taiwanese plaintiffs were not necessarily to blame for their failure in civil trials. Only the old customs that were recognized by the Japanese authorities became Taiwanese customary law, which was applied in Taiwanese civil suits. Taiwanese plaintiffs therefore had to adapt themselves to the Japanese version of the customary law, though in name they were Taiwanese customs. Moreover, the Western-style proceeding in the court was entirely strange to the Taiwanese litigants. Needless to say, the obstacles in language deepened the problems arising from facing an alien legal system.

The situation changed after the early 1920s. After 1923, Japanese Western-style civil substantive and procedural codes were applied to Taiwanese cases. Since the substantive law applied by the courts was not indigenous law but foreign law, one might expect that it would be more likely for a Taiwanese plaintiff who knew only customary legal rules to file a civil suit but lose it because the court applied the new law. In fact, the Taiwanese plaintiffs' rate of success in civil suits actually increased during this period. From their observations of daily life in Taiwan, more Taiwanese gradually enhanced their knowledge of Western civil law and civil procedure. Taiwanese thus had more opportunity to successfully use modern law and courts for the settlement of disputes after a quarter century of Japanese rule.

That there were more hortatory cases but fewer administrative mediation cases can illustrate this development. Administrative mediation was relatively close to the traditional dispute resolution method of the Taiwanese. In the early period of Japanese rule it was frequently employed to settle civil disputes involving less than 500 yen.[172] The hortatory procedure was designed for the efficient resolution of such monetary disputes. The Taiwanese initially were not familiar with this new Western-style procedure. However, by the 1920s the number of hortatory cases was almost equal to the number of administrative mediation cases. By the 1930s the number of hortatory cases exceeded the number of administrative mediation cases (see table 3.7). The increase in the number of hortatory cases illustrates that the Taiwanese learned to use the more efficient modern court procedures, including lawyers, to replace traditional-style mediation.

The more Taiwanese who successfully employed the court to protect their interests, the more Taiwanese brought suits to the modern courts. A person who observes that in many instances other people have, without much difficulty, acquired benefits by filing proceedings in court will also be willing to resort to the courts when he or she is involved in a dispute. In the period from the 1920s to mid-1930s, 40 percent of the Taiwanese who filed court proceedings were completely successful in their suits. Only 12 percent of those who filed court proceedings met with complete failure during such period. Two-thirds of those who filed hortatory proceedings gained an order for payment with compulsory execution. It was only natural that the Taiwanese would turn to the courts to settle disputes.

In conclusion, under the new environment brought about by governmental judicial reforms, urbanization, colonial modern education, and economic development, the Taiwanese slowly but gradually learned to use the Western-style legal system to settle disputes. This increased familiarity with the new system was reflected in their improved rate of success in civil trials. Such a newly acquired ability encouraged more people to go to court, resulting in the great increase of civil suits during the period of the 1920s and mid-1930s. When the war began, however, many Taiwanese who were capable of using modern law and the courts were forced to employ other informal means of dispute resolution instead of official lawsuits or administrative mediation.

Criminal Trial vs. Police Summary Judgment

Police Summary Judgment. Under the summary judgment system, the local administrative authority in colonial Taiwan, as in colonial Korea, had jurisdiction to try misdemeanors.[173] Early in 1896, the GGT transplanted the Japanese system of summary judgment for police offenses to Taiwan, providing that the offenses for which the statutory punishments were detention and/or a police fine might be decided summarily by police superintendents or police inspectors. The 1904 Summary Judgment Law provided that two other types of offenses could be decided by summary judgment, namely, (1) offenses of gambling (punishable with penal servitude of not more than three months and/or a fine of not more than 100 yen or a police fine) and offenses of assault (violent conduct) (punishable with detention and/or a police fine), and (2) violations of administrative regulations punishable with penal servitude of not more than three months or detention and/or a fine of not more than 100 yen or a police fine. Those offenses were, according to the statute, to be decided by "the summary judgment officer," which in name was the head of local government but in practice was the police superintendent or inspector, as before. The Summary Judgment Law allowed the executive authority in the colony to summarily decide not only police offenses but also certain misdemeanors that would have been decided by judges in metropolitan Japan.[174]

Two channels existed under the law by which cases decided by the administrative (police) authorities under the summary judgment procedure could be submitted to the courts for review. First, if a case involved an offense that could not be decided by the summary judgment procedure or was inappropriate for this method, it was to be shifted to the procuracy.[175] In addition, after a case was decided by the summary judgment procedure, people convicted might apply for trial by court within the statutory period set out in the judgment.[176] However, according to the figures for May–December 1904, of the 28,770 cases decided by summary judgment during that period, only 39 cases were submitted to the procuracy. In only 12 cases of conviction was there a request for trial by a court; in most cases there was a final summary judgment by the police officer.[177] This situation appears to have been common throughout the period of Japanese rule. In later years, once a case was received by the summary judgment officer, the result was always a guilty judgment.[178] Very few summary judgments later saw application for trial by court.[179]

The GGT Court, however, was not a rubber stamp for the police officer's summary judgment. From 1904 to 1934, among those convicted under summary judgment proceedings who applied for trial by court, 588 people (38.4 percent) received the same punishments; 118 (7.7 percent) were given heavier punishments; 581 (37.9 percent) were given lighter punishments; and 244 (15.9 percent) were acquitted.[180]

Courts and Police Summary Judgment. To what extent were criminal cases decided by police officers rather than by judicial officials (judges and procurators)? In table 3.9 I compare the criminal cases handled by the procuracy under the Western-style law of criminal procedure and the cases decided by police officers under the summary judgment procedure. The cases handled by the procuracy are divided into four categories: (1) those investigated and then prosecuted, (2) those investigated but not prosecuted, (3) those prosecuted and tried by preliminary examination, and (4) those prosecuted and tried by the summary procedure or the ordinary procedure in the courts of first instance. These cases were all dealt with by procurators only or by both judges and procurators, and thus belong to the category of criminal cases disposed of by the modern court system.

The police summary judgment system was prevalent in colonial Taiwan. To reduce the number of criminal cases prosecuted in the courts following an increase from 1900 to 1903, the GGT brought the Summary Judgment Law into effect on May 1, 1904. Their goal was achieved (see table 3.9). The number of criminal cases prosecuted in the court during the 1905–15 period was not considerably higher than the number in the early 1900s. From the mid-1910s to the 1920s, judicial officials dealt with criminal cases more frequently than before. However, those criminal cases prosecuted in the court still made up only one-fourth of all criminal cases in colonial Taiwan. In the early 1930s, administrative summary judgment cases played a dominant role in colonial criminal justice. After the mid-1930s, the ratio of criminal cases prosecuted in the courts to the police summary judgment cases was nearly the same as the ratio in 1905 (see the ratio of (A) to (B) in Table 3.9). For every criminal case disposed of by procurators or judges, six criminal cases were decided by police officers outside the court.

The Japanese authorities' arguments in support of the police summary judgment system were not persuasive. In 1904, the official reasons for enactment of the Summary Judgment Law were the shortage of courts and poor communication on the island as well as the people's ignorance concerning the separation of the judiciary from the executive branch.[181] Even supposing that those reasons were true in the first decade of this century, they could not justify the increasing number of summary judgment cases from the late 1920s to the 1930s unless the Japanese authorities denied the improvement of the judicial facilities, communications, and education on the island during the intervening three decades.

Many Japanese colonialists argued that it was proper for police officers who were familiar with local affairs to decide criminal cases under the summary judgment system because few of them were retried by courts, and when they were, the judges seldom gave judgments more favorable to the accused than the original judgment.[182] However, few applications for trial by court also meant that this remedial provision was in fact ineffective and thus reveals the unassailable fact that the police virtually had the power to make final decisions upon some misdemeanors without judicial review. As stated above, more than 50 percent of those convicted under the summary judgment system received lighter punishments or acquittal from the court and only 10 percent received a heavier punishment. However, the police in practice usually prevented the accused from applying for trial by court within the statutory period. An application for trial by court might be regarded as a challenge against police authority and thus could provoke the revenge of policemen, who controlled every aspect of daily life. To avoid such problems, many of those accused preferred to give up the potential advantage of being tried by a court. In fact, the real purpose of the GGT for continuing to employ this summary judgment system was to reinforce the authority of policemen who, in the eyes of the Taiwanese, represented the Japanese colonial government.[183]

As a result of police summary judgment, Taiwanese had fewer opportu-

TABLE 3.9 Criminal Cases Disposed of by Court
or Summary Judgment Office in Taiwan, 1897–1942

Year	Cases of the procuracy in courts of first instance (A)	Police summary judgment cases (B)	Applications for trial by court (C)
1897	3,246	NA	NA
1898	4,258 (164)	NA	NA
1899	5,645	NA	NA
1900	7,600	NA	NA
1901	8,979	NA	NA
1902	9,199	NA	NA
1903	9,861	NA	NA
1904	6,220	28,008	46
1905	5,892 (189)	37,965 (1,217), 1:6.4*	41
1906	6,236	39,095	51
1907	7,751	47,944	30
1908	7,162	43,940	26
1909	7,820	41,977	21
1910	8,333 (253)	40,146 (1,217), 1:4.8*	99
1911	9,723	39,807	23
1912	10,018	40,885	15
1913	10,774	42,985	47
1914	10,832	39,562	31
1915	10,737 (309)	36,177 (1,040), 1:3.4*	33
1916	12,231	42,064	49
1917	13,789	43,039	58
1918	15,340	45,569	43
1919	15,339	50,366	35
1920	14,347 (383)	37,500 (1,000), 1:2.6*	18
1921	17,214	50,436	20
1922	17,917	56,383	49

nities for access to modern courts with Western-style criminal procedure. But the Taiwanese under Japanese rule still appeared in courts more for criminal matters than for civil matters (see tables 3.7 and 3.9). Therefore, going to court frequently implied being punished. The court remained an unwelcome place for the general public.

TABLE 3.9 (continued)

Year	Cases of the procuracy in courts of first instance (A)	Police summary judgment cases (B)	Applications for trial by court (C)
1923	19,535	61,058	31
1924	19,402	68,737	53
1925	21,616 (521)	72,044 (1,736), 1:3.3*	34
1926	24,581	88,969	39
1927	24,681	91,870	51
1928	26,389	103,632	89
1929	27,517	131,738	79
1930	27,197 (581)	129,103 (2,759), 1:4.7*	54
1931	26,137	143,179	77
1932	26,332	159,456	56
1933	26,670	161,754	48
1934	26,152	181,702	49
1935	27,340 (514)	172,712 (3,246), 1:6.3*	16
1936	31,344	214,203	19
1937	27,985	196,432	10
1938	24,206	171,434	6
1939	24,665 (418)	165,584 (2,807),1:6.7*	NA
1940	30,030 (500)	NA	NA
1941	39,817	NA	NA
1942	33,896	NA	NA

SOURCES: The numbers in (A) are from *TWTT*, p. 436. The numbers in (B) and (C) are from *KSEK*, pp. 353–55. Population in Taiwan: Table I.1 herein; *NTTN*, 1921, p. 21; 1928, p. 19; 1939, p.7, and Barclay, *Colonial Development and Population in Taiwan*, p. 13. The population of 1898 did not include the Japanese in Taiwan, but very few Japanese civilians lived in Taiwan at the time. Additionally, the population of 1939 is from Kondō Ken'ichi, ed., *Taiheiyō senka no Chōsen oyobi Taiwan*, p.3.

NOTES: Figures in parentheses indicate the number of cases per 100,000 people. The ratio followed by * indicates (A):(B).

SUMMARY

The Japanese established the first modern Western court system in Taiwan in 1896. After the 1898 judicial reform the GGT instituted a special colonial judicial system independent of the courts in metropolitan Japan, with two levels of courts to handle the first instance and appeal of lawsuits. After the 1919 judicial reform Taiwan's court system was actually similar to Japan's, with four levels of courts to handle the first instance, appeal, and re-appeal. However, Taiwan's court system remained independent of the Japanese mainland court system.

The Japanese gradually brought a Western-style independent judiciary to Taiwan. Before the 1919 reforms the independent judiciary had little opportunity to develop in colonial Taiwan. Even after the 1919 reforms, judges in colonial Taiwan, unlike judges in metropolitan Japan, did not have sufficient security of tenure. However, as a result of their legal training in Japan, colonial judges struggled to maintain independent adjudication in Taiwan.

The Japanese established Western-style courts in most large cities on Taiwan. However, Japan's judicial investment in colonial Taiwan was worse than that in metropolitan Japan. Because of various forms of discrimination in colonial rule, very few of the judges in Taiwan and none of the procurators in Taiwan were Taiwanese, although many Taiwanese legal professionals entered private practice beginning in the 1920s. Because most judicial officials were Japanese, language problems plagued colonial justice in Taiwan. Japanese jurists successfully interpreted Taiwanese customs, however, and merged them into Japan's European-style legal system. Furthermore, the honesty of Japanese judges and procurators was above reproach, although their impartiality was not without doubt. In addition, lawyers became esteemed professionals in Taiwan under Japanese rule.

Taiwan's courts therefore were capable of performing their task in bringing Western-style positive law into Taiwanese society, but two special colonial institutions, namely, administrative mediation and the police summary judgment, largely obstructed the function of the courts. However, the Taiwanese gradually learned how to use the modern court system to resolve their civil disputes and thereby lessened the negative effects resulting from the administrative mediation system. On the other hand, under the suppression of colonial police authorities, the Taiwanese were seriously deprived of many opportunities to make use of the Western-style criminal procedure in the modern courts throughout Japanese rule.

4 / Criminal Justice and Changing Society

The main concern in this chapter is the effect of Western-style criminal justice upon Taiwanese society under Japanese rule. Under Chinese legal traditions, in addition to the state, some social organizations such as the family, clan, and village to a certain degree possessed the authority to impose punishments on their members.[1] These "private punishments" were in practice prevalent in Ch'ing Taiwan.[2] To maintain its governance and social order, however, a modern state monopolizes the authority to punish its citizens. Since the early Meiji era, Japan strove to forbid private punishments so that the unifying authority of the state could be established.[3] How did Japan establish the authority of the state over Taiwanese society, which was hostile to alien Japanese rule and had experienced unrest for a long time before Japan's arrival? To what extent did the Westernized and colonized criminal law enforced by the Japanese state authority influence Taiwanese society? Through the fifty years of Japanese rule, did the Taiwanese change their perceptions about criminal justice? This chapter attempts to answer these questions.

GOVERNING ORDER AND POLITICAL CRIMES

Military Suppression (1895–1902)

Military Conquest. The political chaos at the beginning of Japanese rule derived mainly from the weak imperial control upon Taiwan in late Ch'ing. After the Treaty of Shimonoseki, which ceded Taiwan to Japan, was ratified by the two nations on May 8, 1895, Taiwan legally belonged to Japan. However, the central Ch'ing government had only weak control upon this frontier island. Without the authorization of the Ch'ing government, local Ch'ing officials in Taiwan and some high-level Taiwan gentry established the Republic of Formosa on May 23, 1895.[4] In addition, local strongmen in Taiwan organized the Righteous Army to protect their land. Fearing that Japan might blame it for breaching its obligation under the treaty, the Ch'ing government told Japan that "since Taiwan's people have declared independence, the Ch'ing government has lost its original jurisdiction over the people; therefore, the Ch'ing government can merely ritually transfer Taiwan to Japan to perform its obligation to the treaty."[5] The two empires completed all documents concerning the transfer of sovereignty over Taiwan on a ship near the port of Keelung on June 2, 1895.[6] But Japan knew that military conquest would be necessary to govern the island and thus had already sent a Japanese army to land on Taiwan. Fighting broke out between the Japanese army and the army of the newly established republic (the former Ch'ing army), accompanied by the Taiwanese Righteous Army.

From the Japanese perspective, the army of the republic was merely soldiers of the defeated Ch'ing, but the members of the Taiwanese Righteous Army were "rebellious subjects." The Japanese authorities on Taiwan declared that those Ch'ing soldiers who were ordered to fight by treasonous Ch'ing officers would be sent back to China if they surrendered to Japan. In contrast, the Japanese called the Taiwanese Righteous Army "bandits" and declared that any armed resistance by them was to be severely punished pursuant to the Disposition for Taiwanese Military Criminals.[7]

Under the Japanese military administration, Taiwanese resisters were killed in battle rather than tried in court. From the Japanese landing on Taiwan in May 29, 1895, to the collapse of the republic in late October of 1895, about ten thousand members of the former Ch'ing army and Taiwan Righteous Army were killed in battle.[8] Continuing the work of the Righteous Army, Taiwanese anti-Japanese guerrillas persisted in fighting with the Japanese army after the former Ch'ing army left Taiwan in late 1895. By law, those Taiwanese resisters should have been tried by the military tribunal or the bureau of civil affairs.[9] However, few resisters were tried by any tribunal.[10] From the actual establishment of the military tribunal in late November of 1895 to the end of the military administration on March 31, 1896, only 41 of 345 criminal cases in the tribunal involved the offenses of resistance against the government.[11] Most armed resisters were killed by the Japanese army in the name of "urgent disposition."[12]

Taiwanese Armed Resistance from Late 1895 to 1902. The resistance of the Taiwanese was to a large extent aroused by the misrule of the Japanese authorities in the early days of colonial rule. Several leaders of anti-Japanese guerrilla groups initially did not object to the presence of the Japanese, and some even assisted them at first; but they soon turned against the Japanese after suffering unjust treatment under them.[13] The Japanese army slaughtered many people and recklessly burned houses and thus provoked many Taiwanese into participating in anti-Japanese guerrilla groups.[14] Such a tragedy resulted at least in part from the difference between the languages and customs of the Taiwanese people and their new rulers. Moreover, the belief by the Japanese in the supremacy of the Japanese master race certainly led to the abuse of power by the Japanese.[15]

Owing their origins to a tradition of antigovernment sentiment and activities in Ch'ing Taiwan, Taiwanese dissidents with abundant experience in fighting naturally selected force to challenge Japanese authority. Although called "bandits" by the government, the goal of most armed resisters was in fact political, that is, to oust the Japanese invaders.[16] Since the majority of leaders among the armed resistance were local strongmen who had frequently been the leaders of popular uprisings during the Ch'ing period, it is not surprising that they employed force to express their dissatisfaction with the new government.[17] However, some anti-Japanese guerrillas who started out as "Chinese Robin Hoods" in Ch'ing Taiwan gradually lost their original political goal and threatened the general public, demanding money after their supplies became scarce.[18]

The political ideas of those Taiwanese resisters had their origins in traditional China, with its feudal relations. In the negotiation for their submission, influential anti-Japanese leaders frequently demanded partial autonomous authority, including judicial powers over their followers.[19] They were unfamiliar with any machinery for protecting the people of a modern state. Because of their distrust of the Japanese, they hoped to erect a small "kingdom" within the larger Japanese kingdom, as they had done under the Ch'ing administration.[20] Japan, however, was not interested in such prospects and instead threatened the Taiwanese dissidents with military annihilation.

Suppression by Force. Before the Kodama administration era, the task of suppressing bandits (including political "bandits" and real bandits) was undertaken mainly by the army. Although the military administration had officially ended, the Japanese army continued to suppress the Taiwanese guerrillas. In June 1896, the army vengefully burned 4,295 houses and brutally massacred countless Taiwanese inhabitants in Yun-lin, an act that was criticized by the British press. The GGT Temporary Court system was subsequently established in Taiwan to deal with "offenses relating to politics." This kind of court could be organized in any place whenever necessary, regardless of ordinary jurisdictions.[21] The Taiwanese resisters were not severely punished by the Temporary Court from mid-1896 to 1897; statutory punishments for offenses against the internal security of the state were not severe;[22] in addition, the Takano court had sympathy for the accused Taiwanese.[23] Of 421 cases tried before the Temporary Court in 1896, some 349 cases were not prosecuted; in 44 cases there were acquittals; only 2 defendants were given the death penalty (table 4.1). Such high rates of nonprosecution and not-guilty decisions were largely attributed to reckless investigation by the police and gendarmerie.[24]

TABLE 4.1 Disposition of Accused Bandits
in the Temporary Court in Taiwan, 1896–1915

Year, place	The Procuracy			The Trial		
	Suspect	Not prosecuted	Administrative disposition	Defendants	Death penalty	Not guilty
1896, Chang-hua	421* 100%	349* 82.9%	NA	58 100%	2 3.4%	44 75.9%
1898, Tou-liu, Chia-i, A-kung-tien	148 100%	93 62.8%	NA	51 100%	35 68.6%	7 13.7%
1907, Pei-p'u	NA	3	97	9 100%	9 100%	0
1912, Lin-i-p'u	NA	NA	NA	13 100%	8 61.5%	1 7.7%
1913, Miao-li	NA	578	4	339 100%	20 5.9%	34 10.0%
1915, Tainan	1,950 100%	303 15.5%	217 11.1%	1,430 100%	866 60.6%	86 6.0%

SOURCE: Yamabe Kentarō, ed., *Gendai shi shiryō: Taiwan*, pp. 19–20, 26, 29, 47, 77.

NOTE: * : number of cases rather than number of suspects arrested

Meanwhile, the ordinary courts—in which there were three instances for a lawsuit (first trial, appeal, re-appeal)—retained jurisdiction over the bandit cases.[25] In 1897, district courts imposed death sentences on 54 of 526 suspected bandits (table 4.2). However, not all suspected bandits were brought to the Temporary Court or ordinary courts at that time. Between mid-1896 and early 1898, the Japanese army, gendarmerie, and police continuously suppressed the Taiwanese armed resistance throughout the island. A large number of suspected bandits were either killed in combat or summarily executed upon arrest in the name of "urgent disposition."[26]

After early 1898, the Kodama administration began relying more heavily on judicial sanctions as an instrument to exterminate the Taiwanese armed resistance. Instead of the army and gendarmerie, the police became the main suppressing force after 1898.[27] The police successfully employed the *hokō* system to separate the general public from the anti-Japanese guerrillas and further demanded that the militia of *hokō* participate in the official quelling

CRIMINAL JUSTICE

TABLE 4.2 Disposition of Accused Bandits
in the District Courts in Taiwan, 1895–1906

Year	No. of defendants	Death penalty	Penal servitude for life	Not guilty
1895	89	35	3	31
(%)	100.0	39.3	3.4	34.8
1896	298	71	29	63
(%)	100.0	23.8	9.7	21.1
1897	526	54	99	42
(%)	100.0	10.3	18.8	8.0
1898	935	247	162	79
(%)	100.0	26.4	17.3	8.4
1899	1,436	863	142	128
(%)	100.0	60.0	9.9	8.9
1900	1,336	582	259	151
(%)	100.0	43.6	19.4	11.3
1901	1,325	910	87	92
(%)	100.0	68.7	6.6	6.9
1902	686	510	38	63
(%)	100.0	74.3	5.5	9.2
1903	133	82	13	11
(%)	100.0	61.7	9.8	8.3
1904	25	13	1	6
(%)	100.0	52.0	4.0	24.0
1905	17	6	1	9
(%)	100.0	35.3	5.9	52.9
1906	6	0	1	3
(%)	100.0	0	16.7	50.0

SOURCE: Yamabe Kentarō, ed., *Gendai shi shiryō: Taiwan*, pp. 21–23.
NOTE: Other results for suits (e.g., penal servitude) are not included here.

actions.[28] Meanwhile, the Bandit Punishment Law was enacted to punish various resistance activities with death, a punishment far more severe than the punishments for offenses of insurrection under the Japanese Criminal Code; the law was even applied retroactively to those acts that occurred before it was promulgated.[29] As a result, the use of the death penalty against those accused of violating the Bandit Punishment Law rose suddenly in 1899 and reached almost 75 percent in 1902 (see table 4.2). Moreover, the GGT instructed the quelling force to shift the suspected bandits to three Temporary Courts to avoid mass carnage in 1898. Nevertheless, the Japanese forces continued to summarily execute innumerable suspects.[30]

Based on the Kodama administration's carrot and stick policy, the GGT promised to pardon armed resisters in return for their submission. According to an internal regulation, the head of local government was empowered to decide whether or not to pardon the "bandits" who had been prosecuted or tried without the presence of defense.[31] Because this measure was criticized for infringing the constitutional power of the emperor to grant pardons, the colonial government argued that the pardon was the result of applying article 6 of the Bandit Punishment Law, which provided that the punishment might be reduced or remitted if the offender surrendered himself (legal term *jishu*) before the official.[32] However, the GGT in fact disregarded the specific legal meaning of *jishu*.

The GGT Court explicitly held that the fact of submission to the government was irrelevant to the question of whether or not an offender had in fact surrendered himself under law, thus constituting *jishu*. In 1901 the district court in a certain bandit case remitted the punishments of the defendant on the ground that when he submitted to local government, he had also voluntarily submitted himself for trial for his offense as a bandit. The procurator appealed. The Court of Appeal considered that administrative permission for submission and *jishu* in law were two different things; the offenses of the defendant in that case had been discovered by the police before his submission and thus did not meet the legal requirement of *jishu*.[33] Later the Court of Appeal concluded clearly, "Those defendants who submitted to local government and stated their offenses as bandits who had already been discovered by the police could not enjoy the favor of *jishu* according to article 6 of the Bandit Punishment Law"[34] (emphasis added). Certainly the punishments of some "bandits" submitting to the government were remitted by the court because the circumstances met the requirement of *jishu*.[35] But how did the colonial government plan to fulfill its promise of pardon for those accused bandits who had been prosecuted or even tried, when their offenses obviously had already been discovered by the procurator or judge? One possibility is that after the submission was approved by the government, those "bandits" were not reported to the procuracy or the court.

The GGT, in certain cases, also promised not to arrest or try political "bandits" according to the ordinary procedure for criminal cases if the "bandits" submitted themselves to the Japanese authorities. This promise recognized factually the extraterritoriality of those "bandits." But the colonial government still agreed to it because "once they surrendered to the government, those promises automatically became empty; it was not necessary to care for the wording of the conditions."[36]

The law as distorted by Kodama in fact was a "poisonous carrot." From the submission of bandits, the GGT acquired a complete list of Taiwanese dissidents and then prepared to kill them at the proper time. In late 1901 the Japanese authorities decided to dispose of all the Taiwanese dissidents, irrespective of their submission. In May 1902, the GGT intentionally irritated the Taiwanese guerrillas who had submitted to the government in "repentance" ceremonies held at six places and then killed all of them, about 275 people, on the pretense that they had resisted in the ceremonies.[37] In mid-1902, the Japanese quelling force opened cannon fire upon a former leader of the guerrillas, even though he did not want to resist the Japanese authority any further.

Thus, under the so-called civilian administration the majority of Taiwanese bandits were killed without trial. According to the information gathered by Gotō Shimpei, who was charged with the job of ending Taiwanese resistance, 11,950 bandits were killed between 1898 and 1902. Among them, 5,673 (47.5 percent) were killed after being arrested; 3,279 (27.4 percent) were killed by the quelling force; only 2,999 (25.1 percent) were sentenced to death[38]—that is, only one-fourth of the bandits killed were punished through the legal process.

Moreover, the courts under the Kodama administration were more harsh than the previous Takano court. Although the GGT conducted numerous large-scale military actions against bandits from 1898 to 1902, the Temporary Court was instituted only in 1898 at three places. Most bandit cases were tried by the ordinary courts (see tables 4.1 and 4.2). If a Taiwanese resister who was arrested between the years of 1899 and 1902 was lucky enough not to be summarily executed, he still faced more than a 60 percent chance of being sentenced to death. Although the rate of not-guilty sentences for bandit cases was about 9 percent in the 1899–1902 period, this rate was not high at all considering the reckless investigation of the police.

The costs of establishing modern state authority in Taiwanese society were extremely high. It is estimated that during the 1895–1902 period, 32,000 Taiwanese, more than 1 percent of all the population, were killed by the new Japanese authorities,[39] and one of twenty-five young Taiwanese men died resisting Japan.⁴⁰ Additionally, 2,459 Japanese, including innocent dependents of officials and civilians, were killed by Taiwanese guerrillas between 1897 and 1902.⁴¹

Judicial Sanction of Armed Resisters (1907–16)

The Nature of Taiwanese Resisters. Despite the military suppression in mid-1902, several anti-Japanese armed uprisings occurred during the period between 1907 and 1916. Generally speaking, organized Taiwanese forces had been severely diminished by the end of 1902; as a result, the number of bandit cases in the court gradually began decreasing in 1903. In 1906, for the first time, no Taiwanese were accused of bandit and thus sentenced to death (see table 4.2).⁴² These facts notwithstanding, in 1907 an anti-Japanese armed uprising broke out in Pei-p'u. At the same time, a number of similar uprisings were planned or conducted, such as the Lin-i-p'u Incident in 1912, the T'u-k'u Incident in 1912, the Miao-li Incident in 1913, the Liu-chia Incident in 1914, and the Hsi-lai-an Incident in 1915–16.⁴³

Most of the anti-Japanese armed resisters were not so much modern nationalists as traditional resisters. Like the popular uprisings in Ch'ing Taiwan, these incidents were largely caused by the government's oppression of the Taiwanese, experienced by the Taiwanese daily. For example, the Lin-i-p'u Incident resulted from the government's depriving a community of a bamboo grove on which the lives of the inhabitants depended heavily.⁴⁴ The Taiwanese armed resisters used the hostility of the Taiwanese people toward the Japanese to mobilize the Taiwanese against the Japanese government. Most anti-Japanese leaders were motivated by traditional political ideas of "changing dynasties." Many leaders declared themselves to be the emperor of Taiwan. The overthrow of the Manchu government in China in 1912 inspired some Taiwanese to try to overthrow the Japanese government and establish a Han Chinese kingdom on Taiwan. For example, Yu Ch'ing-fang, the leader of the Hsi-lai-an Incident, announced the establishment of a "great-Ming merciful kingdom" (*Ta-ming tz'u-pei kuo; ming* implied the Ming dynasty, representing a kingdom of Han Chinese) on the island. Except for Lo Fu-hsing, the anti-Japanese leaders during this period were far from modern nationalists.⁴⁵ The Japanese authorities on Taiwan also commented that those incidents were merely instances of individual, irritated political resistance rather than the result of a modern colonial independence movement.⁴⁶

Judicial Sanctions. The Temporary Court harshly punished the Taiwanese resisters. Those involved in the incidents of T'u-k'u and Liu-chia, and some of those involved in the Hsi-lai-an Incident, were tried by the ordinary courts, and some of those defendants brought their cases to the court of appeal.⁴⁷

But the majority of cases in those incidents were tried by the brutal Temporary Court (see table 4.1). In Pei-p'u, all defendants were put to death; in Tainan (the Hsi-lai-an Incident), 866 defendants were sentenced to death. No appeal was allowed.

Judicial sanctions were not the only means used to suppress anti-Japanese resisters. In 1915, the Japanese authorities massacred the entire population (5,000–6,000 people) of a village in southern Taiwan. They coaxed the villagers who had fled into the mountains to return to the village by declaring the "bandits" pardoned. Upon their return, all the villagers were shot down by machine-gun fire and then thrown into a trench they had previously been ordered to dig. Such a horrible slaughter indeed terrified every Taiwanese, as the authorities expected.[48] Additionally, in 1916, the GGT failed to fulfill its promise to pardon those Taiwanese suspected of banditry in the Hsi-lai-an Incident on the ground that "the state law must not be distorted."[49] In fact, this so-called law was merely an instrument of control used by the Japanese empire and was often distorted to serve the objectives of oppression.

Numerous innocent Taiwanese suffered tremendous persecution and even death. Most anti-Japanese incidents during this period were discovered by the police and its auxiliary machinery, the *hokō*.[50] The police were quick to regard any slightly suspicious people as "bandits." Therefore, a large number of people arrested as "bandits" in the Miao-li and Liu-chia incidents were not prosecuted or, if they were, were later acquitted (see table 4.1). In another incident in 1922, in which all suspects were forced to confess under police torture, the procurator released them because of insufficient evidence. This incident also illustrated that the colonial police were accustomed to employing violent and illegal means to secure confessions from suspected bandits.[51]

Suppression of the Modern Political Movement (1914–37)

Nonviolent Political Movement. After two decades of Japanese rule, Taiwanese society began to employ nonviolent measures to resist oppression from the state authority. From the time of Dutch rule, armed resistance (popular uprisings) had been the only way for the Taiwanese to express their dissatisfaction with the government. This tradition continued into the early period of Japanese rule. In the face of a suppressive modern-style government, however, Taiwanese armed resistance was useless and resulted in the loss of many lives. Under such circumstances, the Taiwanese had to search for another way to resist Japanese oppression. Therefore, in 1914 several members of the Taiwanese elite vigorously supported the Assimilation Society, led by a leader in the Japanese liberty and civil rights movement of 1880, Itagaki Taisuke. In the name of assimilation, Taiwanese wanted to struggle for their rights against colonial discrimination.[52] For the first time, Taiwanese found that they could object to state authority through nonviolent, lawful means rather than armed revolution.

From 1921 to 1937, Taiwanese dissidents actively organized various modern social and political associations to object to the colonial administration.[53] In the 1920s, the new generation of Taiwanese, who had received Western-style education, organized the Taiwan Cultural Association to spread modern ideas that threatened the arbitrary methods of the GGT. They advocated a Taiwan parliament and brought about the *Taiwan Parliament* case in 1923. When the GGT began to arrest the Taiwanese dissidents participating in the petition drive, many Taiwanese feared a repeat of the Hsi-lai-an Incident eight years previously.[54] But the public trials—in which political arguments were allowed and relatively minor punishments for defendants were meted out— told the Taiwanese people that the arbitrary methods of the GGT had become part of the past. As a result of this change, Taiwanese began to engage in a modern political opposition movement.[55] Thereafter, Taiwanese farmer movements led by the Farmer Association and labor movements led by various labor associations became widespread. In 1927, the first Taiwanese political party, the Taiwan Popular Party, was legally organized on the island. In the next year, the Taiwanese Communist Party was secretly formed in Shanghai. After 1931, when other relatively radical political associations were banned, the League for the Attainment of Local Autonomy composed of Taiwanese dissidents nevertheless existed lawfully until the Sino-Japanese War broke out in 1937.

Most Taiwanese modern political movements between 1914 and 1937 protested the GGT's policies from within the legal establishment. With the overthrow of Japanese imperial rule in Taiwan as their goal, Taiwanese Communists did not care whether the means were legal.[56] One Taiwanese secret association prepared an armed uprising but was uncovered in 1934.[57] Armed resistance, however, was the exception rather than the norm in the 1920s and mid-1930s. From the establishment of the Assimilation Society in 1914 to the dissolution of the League for the Attainment of Local Autonomy in 1937, most Taiwanese modern political movements shared two common goals: the attainment of freedom and rights for Taiwanese society and for individual Taiwanese. The first cause was manifest in terms of nationalism, the autonomy of colonial Taiwan, and the petition for a Taiwan parliament. The second goal was manifest in terms of assimilation, the extension of the Japanese mainland (metropolitan Japan), and the petition for local autonomy.[58] Those political movements did not deny the Japanese state's fundamental authority over Taiwanese society.

Suppression by Law. Like the authoritarian government in Japan, the colonial government in Taiwan employed various laws to repress political movements. Because the Taiwanese had already moved away from traditional armed resistance, the Bandit Punishment Law had not been applied since the Hsi-lai-an Incident in 1915–16.[59] Instead, many Japanese oppressive laws were employed to deal with the Taiwanese new-style resistance movements emerging in the 1920s.

Many of these laws were specially designed to punish political criminals. For example, the Public Order Police Law, applied to Taiwan in 1923, was used to prevent antigovernment or anti-Japanese lectures and to dissolve the assemblies held by dissidents' associations such as the Taiwan Cultural Association, the Popular Party, the Farmer Association, and some labor unions. Under this law, the League for the Creation of a Taiwan Parliament was quashed in Taiwan in 1923, and the Popular Party was forced to dissolve in 1931.[60] Another such law, the Peace Preservation Law, which was applied to Taiwan in 1925, was used to punish Taiwanese Communists and anarchists in the late 1920s and early 1930s.[61] The Violence Punishment Law, applied to Taiwan in 1926, was used to suppress mass movements led by the Cultural Association, the Farmer Association, the League of Labor and other political associations.[62] The Press Law was used to control antigovernment publications and to punish some members of the Farmer Association in 1929.[63] The crime of disrespectful actions against the imperial family in the Criminal Code was also used to to punish some Taiwanese dissidents after the late 1920s.[64]

In addition, certain Criminal Code provisions such as the provisions prohibiting disturbance of the peace, assault and battery, and interference with public functions were also used to punish Taiwanese dissidents. Some special laws, like the Executive Enforcement Law, the Taiwan Forest Regulation, and the Taiwan Police Offense Law, were used to punish Taiwanese dissidents as well.[65] For instance, a Taiwanese who presented antigovernment (anti-Japanese) ideas was sometimes not convicted for serious political crimes but rather was punished by the police in accordance with the Taiwan Police Offense Law.[66]

It is clear that the Japanese authorities did not always depend on those special laws concerned with mass movements or thought control to deal with Taiwanese dissidents. For example, only one-fourth of all members of the Taiwanese farmer movement accused of committing crimes between 1927 and 1929 were punished under the laws specially designed for political criminals (see table 4.3). Nevertheless, the very existence of those laws has led some to overestimate their actual role in the administration of justice.

TABLE 4.3 Crimes of Which Members of the Taiwanese
Farmer Movement Were Accused, 1927–29

Offenses	Number of accused	Percentage
Laws for political criminals		
Disrespectful actions	3	0.2
Peace Preservation Law	7	0.5
Public Order Police Law	59	4.4
Violence Punishment Law	175	13.0
Press Law	87	6.5
Subtotal	331	24.7
Laws for general public		
Disturbing the peace and interference with public functions	188	14.0
Bodily harm	75	5.6
Assault and threat	19	1.4
Theft, misappropriation fraud, and intimidation	163	12.2
Destruction and obstruction of business	174	13.0
Forest Regulation	130	9.7
Various police regulations	189	14.1
Other	71	5.3
Subtotal	1,009	75.3
Total	1,340	100.0

SOURCE: Yamabe Kentarō ed., *Gendai shi shiryō: Taiwan*, pp. 443–44.

As in metropolitan Japan, the notorious "special high police" and "thought procurators" undertook the task of repressing political dissidents in colonial Taiwan. Acquiring their legitimacy from the 1925 Peace Preservation Law, the special high police (commonly called *tokkō*) were assigned to police departments throughout the prewar Japanese empire, including Taiwan.[67] Similarly, certain procurators, called thought procurators, were charged with prosecuting criminals with "dangerous thought" in Taiwan, as in Japan and Korea.[68]

Punishment of Taiwanese dissidents from the 1920s to the mid-1930s was far less cruel than during the early period of Japanese rule. As table 4.3 shows, less than 1 percent of the members of farmer movements were accused of committing disrespectful actions against the imperial family or violating the Peace Preservation Law, for which the penalties were severe.[69] Taiwanese dissidents were more frequently punished under the Violence Punishment Law and the Public Order Police Law, for which the penalties were less severe.[70] In practice, criminals were not ordinarily sentenced to the highest statutory punishments. For instance, the severest punishment for the members of the League for the Creation of a Taiwan Parliament was a sentence to four months of imprisonment (without mandatory labor) in accordance with the Public Order Police Law.

The most severe Peace Preservation Law was applied less frequently in Taiwan than in Japan or Korea. In metropolitan Japan, the Peace Preservation Law was employed extensively to suppress Communists, anarchists, extreme rightists, scholars, students, intellectuals, and members of various religions. The number of suspects arrested under the law reached a peak of 14,622 in 1933, and the total number of suspects between 1928 and 1941 was 65,921.[71] In Japanese colonies, the conflict between master race and ruled race became the main contradiction in society, and the political criminals dealt with under the Peace Preservation Law were largely anti-Japanese elements. Because the Taiwanese anti-Japanese movement primarily changed to a lawful political movement in the 1920s and mid-1930s, the Peace Preservation Law had less relevance in Taiwan. In the Taiwan Communist Incident of 1931, fewer than a hundred suspects were arrested under the Peace Preservation Law, and between 1931 and 1940 the total number of suspects arrested in cases involving the Peace Preservation Law was 856, far fewer than the number of suspects arrested in metropolitan Japan.[72] In contrast, with their strong anti-Japanese passion, the Koreans were more frequently accused of offenses against the Peace Preservation Law than the Taiwanese (18,600 Korean suspects were arrested under the law between 1928 and 1935).[73]

The government's primary aim in applying the Peace Preservation Law was to reform thought criminals rather than to harshly punish them. In cases involving the Peace Preservation Law in Taiwan, prosecution was suspended against 418 (48.8 percent) of the total 856 suspects; there was no prosecution because of insufficient evidence or other reasons in 203 cases (23.7 percent); and criminal proceedings were terminated for other reasons (e.g., that the accused had died) in 22 (2.6 percent). Only 235 (27.5 percent) suspects arrested under the law were prosecuted; 213 (24.9 percent) were found guilty. However, no one was acquitted after prosecution.[74] That only about a quarter of the suspects arrested were actually prosecuted largely reflects the official emphasis on the conversions (*tenkō*) of "dangerous thought."[75] Since prosecution was almost equivalent to a guilty sentence, those principally involved in the application of the Peace Preservation Law were the special high police and thought procurators.[76]

For Taiwanese dissidents, the real threat from Japanese suppression was the likelihood of brutal torture by the police. In metropolitan Japan and colonial Korea, suspects arrested for political crimes frequently suffered from illegal torture, and some even died in police custody.[77] The same situation occurred in colonial Taiwan, especially in those cases brought under the Peace Preservation Law.[78]

Wartime Political Crimes (1937–45)

Taiwanese Nonresistance. Anti-Japanese movements nearly disappeared in Taiwan during the wartime period. After ten years of democratic experience, most Taiwanese dissidents were used to nonviolent forms of political expression. However, during the war, it was not possible to continue such political expressions.[79] On the other hand, after being stably governed by Japan for more than thirty years, the Taiwanese had in fact lost their ability to resist the government by force as they had done in the Ch'ing period or the early era of Japanese rule.[80] After years of Japanese rule, the Taiwanese had largely succumbed to the strict control of Japan's state authority. Only a few Taiwanese left for China to continue their anti-Japanese activities.

Unlike the situation in Japan or Korea, the level of antigovernment activities in Taiwan was not so high that the Japanese authorities had to resort to new repressive measures. For example, the Japanese authorities in Taiwan did not employ two important "thought control" measures employed in Japan and Korea, namely, (1) the 1936 Law for Protection and Observation of Thought Criminals, which was enacted for the supervision of those people whose prosecution or execution under the Peace Preservation Law was suspended, and (2) the system of preventive detention for those who could not be reformed under the 1941 revised Peace Preservation Law.[81] These two measures were not enforced in Taiwan probably because the number of Taiwanese violators of the Peace Preservation Law was quite low compared to the number in Japan and Korea. In addition, the original *hokō* system and vagrant discipline system in Taiwan, which did not exist in Japan and Korea, to a certain extent performed the same function of supervising or detaining prospective political criminals.

In fact, "thought control" was still prevalent in Taiwan throughout the wartime period. For instance, any Taiwanese who traveled to China and then returned to Taiwan during this period was always put under close supervision by the special high police.[82]

Oppressor's Suspicion. Despite the passive acceptance of the state authority by the Taiwanese, a large number of Taiwanese were falsely accused of political crimes by overly zealous police authorities. According to official records, a considerable number of Taiwanese dissidents engaged in resistance against Japanese authorities. In fact, most of them were framed by the police, who might appear not to be doing their job if they did not arrest any Taiwanese dissidents. Actually, many suspects were not sentenced to death but were tortured to death when they were required to "confess."[83] The procuracy often suspected that the cases of political crimes were manufactured by the police and thus declined to prosecute many of them.[84] Still, since evidence was often well manufactured by the police, many innocent Taiwanese were found guilty under the Peace Preservation Law and sentenced to penal servitude for life in accordance with the Peace Preservation Law.[85] Such severe punishments never occurred in the 1920s and mid-1930s.[86]

SOCIAL ORDER AND ORDINARY CRIMES

Crime Control Structure

Completion of the Structure (1903–9). Before the anti-Japanese guerrillas were annihilated in 1902, the GGT paid little attention to nonpolitical crimes. At the beginning of Japanese rule, the government brought few criminal cases to courts because it was unwilling to devote administrative resources to the prosecution of relatively minor nonpolitical crimes.[87] In 1895, the GGT gave clear instructions that opium smoking and ordinary gambling, although illegal, need not be prosecuted, and the punishment for other crimes depended on "actual necessity."[88] From 1898 to 1902, with the increase of areas actually controlled by the GGT, more nonpolitical crimes were brought to the Japanese courts than before (see table 3.9). After the "bandits" were virtually annihilated in mid-1902, the suppression of nonpolitical crimes became a priority of the colonial administration.

The GGT took preventive measures to cope with vagrants—supposedly to stop the proliferation of crime, actually to maintain the settled political order. Vagrants, after all, were prospective members of anti-Japanese "bandit" groups.[89] In 1903, without any basis in law, the GGT warned all suspected vagrants that they had to have the guarantee of local chiefs that they would abide by the law and find a job soon. The government would arranged employment for anyone who remained unemployed. In the same year, more than forty so-called vagrants were sent to T'ai-tung, a frontier of the island, for compulsory labor.[90] Using the excuse that Western powers also had compulsory labor systems in colonies, the GGT enacted the Taiwan Vagrant Discipline Regulation of 1906 by which vagrants would be warned to have fixed residences or jobs and, failing that, would be sent to work in a specific place.[91] The vagrant camp (*shūyōjo*) in T'ai-tung was established in 1908. This camp was no different from a prison (*keimuyo*).[92] The decision to send a person to the vagrant camp was in practice a serious sanction, depriving of freedom a person who had not committed a crime. It was made by the police in the name of the chief of the local government, with the approval of the governor-general.[93] No judicial means existed to appeal this decision.

To reduce the number of convicts in prison, the GGT in 1904 restored traditional flogging and emphasized the imposition of fines (as opposed to imprisonment). The Japanese colonialists argued that there were many advantages of flogging over short-term imprisonment from the perspective of those who were sentenced to the punishment. (However, they never explained why, if flogging was so good, it was not extended to Japanese residing in colonial Taiwan and was abolished in metropolitan Japan after the Meiji reform). Flogging was actually revived because it ordinarily took not more than four days to carry out and therefore could clear out the prisons. Similarly, the Japanese began relying more heavily on monetary sanctions to save money being spent on prisons. Reluctant to express their real motivation, the GGT again argued that monetary punishment was more suitable for the Taiwanese, who were concerned only with money and frequently preferred to be imprisoned because of their low living standard.[94]

According to the Fine and Flogging Law, when the sentence of a Taiwanese was (1) penal servitude of not more than three months, (2) a fine of not more than 100 yen (and if the convicted had no domicile in the island or no assets), or (3) detention or a police fine, his sentence could be changed to flogging. When a Taiwanese was convicted and sentenced to three months or less, his sentence could be changed to a fine.[95] If a Taiwanese was sentenced to a fine of not more than 100 yen or a police fine but he or she did not pay the entire amount, this sentence might also be executed by flogging to compensate for the unsatisfied part of the fine.[96] The formula for substitution was "one day = one yen = one stroke."[97]

As we have seen, to further reduce the caseload in the criminal court and reinforce the Fine and Flogging Law, the GGT in 1904 strengthened the police summary judgment system. Here it should be further pointed out that the scope of the police summary judgment as enlarged in 1904 corresponded to the statutory scheme of substituting fines and flogging. Offenses subject to the police summary judgment system were (1) those offenses punishable by "detention and/or a police fine"; (2) gambling offenses that carried a sentence of "penal servitude of not more than three months and/or a fine of not more than 100 yen or a police fine" as well as the offense of assault (violent conduct, article 208 of the Japanese Criminal Code of 1907), which carried a sen-

TABLE 4.4 Crime Control Structure in Taiwan under Japanese Rule, 1909–45

	Investigated by	Tried by	Executed by

Court system	→ procurator	→ judge
		⎡ **penal code**
		⎣ **offenses**
		⎣ special law
		   violations
		   opium
		   taxation
		   political
		   crimes etc.
			→ procurator,
			in the prison

police (hokō)			

Police summary judgment system	→ **summary judgment officer (police)**	→ the same
		⎡ penal code
		⎣ offenses
		   gambling
		   assault
		⎣ **special law**
		   violations
		   police offenses
		   opium etc.
			→ the same
			in the police
			station, or
			procurator, in
			the prison

Vagrant discipline system	↳ head of local government (police)	→ the same, approval by governor-general	→ the vagrant camp

NOTE: Boldface means that this item occurred more frequently than other items in the same category.

tence of "detention and/or a police fine"[98]; and (3) violations of administrative regulations with sentences of "penal servitude of not more than three months or detention and/or a fine of not more than 100 yen or a police fine." Accordingly, summary judgment officers could inflict a number of punishments, including flogging and fines. They could execute the sentences they imposed—flogging, fines, and sometimes penal servitude—within the police station, although offenders sentenced to penal servitude were often sent to prison.[99] A complete crime-control structure was thus set up by the Japanese colonialists in Taiwan between 1903 and 1909 (table 4.4).

TABLE 4.5 Offenses Punished by the Courts of First Instance in Taiwan, 1910–43 (percentage)

	Penal code offenses				Special law violations		Total
Year	Subtotal	Gambling	Bodily injury	Theft and robbery	Subtotal	Economic regulations	Total cases
1910	92.3	6.4	13.9	41.6	7.7	NA	100.0
1915	89.6	2.8	13.3	42.6	10.4	NA	100.0
1920	82.4	7.6	13.7	33.5	17.6	NA	100.0
1925	82.7	7.4	11.9	34.2	17.3	NA	100.0
1930	82.9	4.5	16.1	36.2	17.1	NA	100.0
1935	80.5	6.2	9.6	37.5	19.5	NA	100.0
1940	89.0	3.5	5.4	50.8	11.0	4.3	100.0
1943	77.7	4.1	3.3	51.2	22.3	11.2	100.0

SOURCE: *TWTT*, pp. 447–51, table 165.
NOTE: This table lists only certain offenses in Japanese criminal law. However, the entire number of penal code offenses or special law violations is presented under "subtotal." The percentage is calculated from the number of cases involving a particular offense and the total number of all criminal cases in the courts.

In this structure, investigation was initiated by the police, who penetrated the daily lives of the people, frequently with the assistance of the heads of the *hokō*.[100] Those suspected of crimes then were handled by either the procurator in the court system or the summary judgment officer in the police system. The majority of them in fact were shifted to the latter (see table 3.9).

The court system mainly disposed of penal code offenses. As table 4.5 shows, most cases in the district courts consisted of penal code offenses, such as homicide, bodily harm, theft, fraud, rape, and the like. Some cases involving special law violations were also disposed of by the court. Those special laws included the Taiwan Opium Law, taxation law, wartime economic regulations, the laws for political criminals, and so on. If the punishments involved were minor, however the cases could be decided by police summary judgment.

Because only those penal code offenses of gambling and assault that were not subject to severe punishments were under the jurisdiction of the summary judgment office, most cases decided by the police summary judgment system involved special law violations, especially police offenses.[101] Meanwhile, only a few criminal cases in the summary judgment system were dealt with by the court system (see chapter 3).

The third approach used to control crimes was an administrative disposition imposed under the vagrant discipline system. An unemployed Taiwanese who was regarded by the police as having criminal tendencies would typically be sent to the vagrant camp for a year or sometimes two or three years.[102] The Japanese authorities argued that this system was instituted to accustom vagrants to work.[103] Inasmuch as treatment in the vagrant camp was almost the same as that in prison, being sent to the camp was actually equivalent to being sent to prison. The duration of incarceration in the vagrant camp as decided by the police was in fact longer than the terms of imprisonment of most real criminals convicted by the court.[104]

Continuity of the Structure. In the 1920s, a relatively democratic period in the Japanese rule, some measures in this crime control structure that constituted serious violations of human rights were criticized. Therefore, in 1921 the first civilian governor-general of Taiwan abolished the flogging system, hoping to convince the Taiwanese that the Japanese colonial authorities were in fact benevolent leaders. Still, the vagrant discipline system was neither abolished nor improved. In fact, this system was abused to cope with Taiwanese dissidents.[105] The vagrant discipline system became a tool for political oppression rather than a means for preventing crimes. Nine vagrants were sent to the camp in 1928, 91 in 1929, 47 in 1930, and 16 in 1931. Such abrupt fluctuations were apparently a result of the rising and falling predominance of the Taiwanese democratic movement between 1929 and 1931.[106]

In the first half of the 1930s some Japanese criminal laws were enforced in Taiwan under the assimilation policy, such as the 1930 Japanese Law for Prevention and Disposition of Banditry and the 1933 Japanese Criminal Indemnity Law. However, the special crime control structure in colonial Taiwan was kept intact.

During the wartime period, this crime control structure was used to punish violations of economic and military regulations. After the Sino-Japanese War broke out in 1937, although Taiwan was sometimes bombed, especially during the late period of the Pacific War, martial law was not enforced on the island. The judicial and police organs, not the military agency, continued to perform their functions in suppressing crime. In addition, the court system played an important role in punishing the violations of many wartime economic regulations (for example, the National Mobilization Law of 1938) and military regulations (for example, the National Defense Security Law of 1941) because the punishments for those offenses were severe and thus the offenses came under the jurisdiction of the courts (see table 4.5).[107]

Crime in Taiwanese Society

The Late Ch'ing Period. The Tanshui-Hsinchu Archives (Tan-hsin tang-an), a collection of documents of two local Ch'ing governments in northern Taiwan during the late Ch'ing period, provide a useful source for understanding crime in late Ch'ing Taiwan. According to the classification of Tai Yen-hui, a Taiwanese legal historian, there are 365 "criminal cases" in the archives. The most common property offense is theft (39 cases), the next, robbery (30 cases). Among offenses against freedom and the person, injury by beating appears most frequently (17 cases). Among offenses against morals, gambling is the most prevalent offense (13 cases). In addition, nearly half the cases involving offenses against public order are banditry (9 cases).[108]

However, the number of criminal cases in the archives does not accurately reflect the number of such offenses in Taiwanese society at that time. In Ch'ing Taiwan only "serious" crimes—that is, those related to the interests of the government—were tried by magistrates; cases involving "petty" crimes—which must have greatly exceeded the number of cases filed in the office—were ordinarily settled by general members of the community.[109]

Crime in late Ch'ing Taiwan corresponded with the turbulent social order prevalent at the time. The "banditry" in the above classification usually refers to offenses of bandit gangs. The prevalence of these kinds of cases reflects their serious threat to the public order of late Ch'ing Taiwan. Meanwhile, the high rate of robbery illustrates that bandits were very active at that time. Additionally, while according to the official criminal cases theft was the largest of all categories, the actual number was probably still greater because some cases of theft were regarded as petty theft and thus not filed. Similarly, the actual number of cases involving injury by beating must have been higher than the official number because communal strife and beating were prevalent in Ch'ing Taiwan. Finally, gambling was certainly a petty crime in the eyes of Ch'ing magistrates, but it was a popular activity in Ch'ing Taiwan. Therefore, gambling most certainly occurred far more frequently than indicated by the official records.[110]

The Japanese Period. Under Japanese colonial law, serious crimes were disposed of by the court, but petty crimes were dealt with by the summary judgment office (the police). As stated above, the GGT court in principle decided only the more serious penal code offenses and the violations of special law that earned heavier punishments. All other offenses were decided by the summary judgment office. The offenses of gambling and assault (not involving bodily injury), although they were penal code offenses and were the most frequent crimes in Taiwan, were relatively minor crimes, so most of them were decided by the police summary judgment.[111] Violations of the Taiwan Opium Law, another legacy of Ch'ing Taiwan, were also numerous. Most of these violations were also decided by the police summary judgment.[112] In addition, numerous police offenses, the main target of the police summary judgment system, were minor crimes. Thus, during Japanese rule, unlike the Ch'ing period, the state, through the court and the police summary judgment system,[113] monopolized criminal punishment.

The Japanese administration to a large extent managed to suppress serious offenses against public order originating in Ch'ing Taiwan. By the extremely harsh Bandit Punishment Law, the GGT eradicated not only the armed Taiwanese dissidents but also genuine bandits.[114] After 1916 the Bandit Punishment Law was never applied, and the number of cases involving robbery was also very small.[115] Resolution of communal strife, a special style of private justice in Ch'ing Taiwan, was still heard of in the early Japanese period; however, it disappeared later because the state strictly controlled public order and prohibited private force.[116] At a high cost in human rights, the GGT also lessened the seriousness of the Taiwanese vagrant problem, a main source of social disorder in Ch'ing Taiwan. Consequently, in the 1930s only a few Taiwanese were sent to the vagrant camp, and during the late wartime period almost no Taiwanese were imprisoned in the vagrant camp.[117] Although the lack of people in the vagrant camp did not mean that there were no vagrants any more, the number of them certainly diminished during the Japanese period.[118]

On the other hand, under Japanese rule relatively minor crimes in Taiwan did not decrease. Theft, a basic property offense, resulted from the hard living conditions of the general public.[119] Therefore, when the economic situation improved in the 1920s, the cases of theft declined relatively; but the numbers rose again as a result of the hardship in the late Japanese period (see table 4.5). Meanwhile, bodily injury did not decline until the early 1930s (see table 4.5).[120] The tradition of fighting remained prevalent in the immigrant society, although it declined somewhat in the late period of Japanese rule. Gambling, the most common crime, did not decline in the Japanese period.[121] The Japanese also did not make great efforts to diminish the prevalence of opium smoking, and violations of the opium law still occurred frequently except during the late wartime period.[122] In addition, violators of colonial administrative regulations were frequently punished by criminal sanctions, thereby becoming criminals, even though their punishments were relatively light.

In fact, during the entire Japanese period, the number of Taiwanese convicted by courts and summary judgment offices ("criminals") increased (table

TABLE 4.6 Average Number of Convicted Criminals in Taiwan, 1905–42 (per 10,000 people)

Year	Taiwanese	Japanese	Chinese	Average
1905	31.9	112.7	356.3	NA
1906	37.7	96.6	355.7	NA
1907	49.1	109.3	318.5	NA
1908	43.5	91.7	272.3	NA
1909	41.0	100.9	314.2	43.9
1910	46.5	79.8	356.8	48.8
1911	53.0	77.1	325.0	55.1
1912	NA	NA	NA	NA
1913	61.9	82.7	362.7	64.4
1914	59.7	83.2	285.5	62.0
1915	54.9	72.6	486.7	57.9
1916	58.5	78.1	571.9	62.0
1917	63.1	78.4	563.7	66.4
1918	62.7	78.5	640.2	66.8
1919	68.7	87.8	466.2	72.1
1920	59.8	84.5	433.6	63.4
1921	67.7	89.3	609.9	72.8
1922	73.4	83.8	618.7	78.1
1923	78.9	70.5	585.9	82.5
1924	84.1	76.9	627.7	88.1
1925	93.9	70.7	591.7	96.8

4.6). According to official statistics on crime in colonial Taiwan, during the 1905–10 period there were 41.6 criminals per 10,000 Taiwanese, but 98.5 criminals per 10,000 Japanese residing in colonial Taiwan. In the 1920s, however, the number of Taiwanese criminals rose rapidly; in contrast, as of 1923, the percentage of criminals in the Japanese population dropped to a level lower than the equivalent figure for Taiwanese. During the 1925–29 period, the peak crime period during Japanese rule, there were 95.4 criminals per 10,000 Taiwanese. A possible reason for this phenomenon is that during the 1920s the Japanese authorities relaxed their control over the Taiwanese. In contrast, during the same period the number of resident Japanese criminals decreased. After 1930, the number of Taiwanese criminals was stable but was more than that in the early Japanese period. From 1930 to 1942, there were 77.9 criminals per 10,000 Taiwanese. Additionally, the percentage of criminals among Chinese (nationals of the Ch'ing Empire or the ROC) residing in Taiwan, most

TABLE 4.6 *(continued)*

Year	Taiwanese	Japanese	Chinese	Average
1926	102.4	76.0	599.1	105.4
1927	106.7	65.4	555.4	108.7
1928	85.7	33.8	448.2	86.6
1929	88.5	42.0	468.5	89.8
1930	76.1	38.1	339.9	76.9
1931	76.9	38.5	424.2	78.3
1932	82.4	36.2	419.3	83.0
1933	82.7	33.8	385.7	82.8
1934	77.4	33.2	365.4	77.9
1935	79.3	35.6	331.1	79.6
1936	85.1	34.9	379.5	85.7
1937	76.9	28.0	443.6	77.4
1938	78.8	27.8	376.0	78.3
1939	78.5	26.1	357.8	77.7
1940	62.7	17.9	385.9	62.6
1941	82.9	26.2	462.7	82.5
1942	72.6	15.9	404.3	71.8

SOURCE: Taiwan Sōtokufu, *Taiwan Sōtokufu hanzai tōkei,* 1909–42.
NOTE: The figures given did not include those people who were convicted of police offenses or sentenced to detention of not more than ten days or given a police fine of not more than two yen. In the original statistics, "Chinese" were called "foreigners."

of whom were laborers away from home, was severalfold higher than other groups in Taiwan. But the largest number of criminals were still the Taiwanese (see tables 4.6 and I.1).

THE ROLE OF WESTERN-STYLE CRIMINAL LAW

Promulgation of Crime and Punishment

Under imperial Chinese law, magistrates were required to cite the legal provisions they were applying. This requirement was enacted to ensure that magistrates would observe the law promulgated by the emperor under a strictly disciplined bureaucracy.[123] Chinese magistrates could convict a person by analogy (that is, according to a legal provision that was provided for punishing different, though similar, criminal conduct) only if approved by the emperor who had power to punish his subjects without any legal basis. In contrast, in the modern Western world, the principle that no punishment is to be meted out except when an express provision of the law allows for it has been established to protect individuals against the state. With a sinicized legal tradition itself, Japan had only recently learned this Western-oriented criminal principle during the early era of Meiji reform.

This principle, at least in form, was gradually enforced by Japanese rulers and thus became known by the Taiwanese. In the early Japanese period, the principle that no one was punished for an act that was not a crime when he did it was disregarded. The best illustration is article 7 of the Bandit Punishment Law, which allowed newly enacted harsher punishments to be imposed on offenses that occurred before the law was promulgated.[124] Following the establishment of a stable governing order in the colony, this fundamental ex post facto principle of modern Western criminal law was followed in form. With its broad legislative power, the GGT enacted a great number of criminal laws to regulate the people's life so that various crimes could be "defined and made clear" in advance. As Lai Ho, an anti-Japanese Taiwanese writer, described the situation in the 1920s, "all times a man is being observed by the eyes of the law all around."[125] To ensure that any possible situation would be covered by legal proscriptions, the colonial authorities employed vague phrasing in defining criminal conduct, such as "there exist sufficient facts to indicate the interference with public order or disturbance against morals and customs."[126] On the other hand, Lai also noted that if restricted to the extent that law provided, local officers could not punish at all the people challenging their authority.[127] Therefore, although the basic spirit of this principle, that is, protection for the people, was not completely carried out by the law that Japanese rulers made, the Taiwanese did understand that where there was no law, there could be no punishment.

Due Process

Under modern Western law, due process is deemed necessary as a guarantee that the judge will decide cases as correctly as possible. Therefore, a person should not be punished by the state without due process. The people are entitled to object to the state authority's summons, arrest, detention, and decision if it violates statutory procedure. In contrast, imperial Chinese law considered that a capable magistrate could find the truth based on his social experience and skills (for example, eavesdropping, terrifying suspects by a ghost); the statutory criminal process was thus not viewed as a vehicle for securing individual justice.[128] Although in imperial China a detailed set of rules existed to guide magistrates in adjudicating criminal cases, these legal guidelines for procedure encompassed little of what modern Western law considers fundamental procedural "due process." Furthermore, the accused did not normally know of these procedural guidelines and had no rights to demand magistrates to abide by them.[129]

Generally speaking, Western-style criminal procedure was followed in Taiwan from the end of the nineteenth century.[130] In one case, the court explicitly pointed out that a military court was different from the ordinary courts and the former had no jurisdiction over the crimes of civilians after the termination of military administration on March 31, 1896.[131] This decision expressed a fundamental idea in modern Western criminal process: that civilians should not be tried by military courts. Thus, with the exception of police summary judgment cases, all crimes should be decided by a court in accordance with statutory procedure.[132]

To protect individuals from unforeseen punishments imposed by the state, modern Western law forbids the court from trying the accused on any charge he or she was not accused of in the complaint. The GGT Court also held that the scope of trial might not exceed the offenses being charged and the facts alleged.[133] However, it was also decided that the defendant might be convicted according to an article in the statute that was different from the one applied by the procurator.[134] Further, if several offenses constituted "an offense in law," the court could try all offenses including the parts not being prosecuted. For instance, if the defendant consecutively stole trees in areas A, B, and C, although the act in area A was not prosecuted, the court still could decide that he committed the offense of consecutive theft in areas A, B, and C.[135] From the perspective of human rights protection (Western legal theory), the scope of matters the court could consider under such interpretations was too broad.

To avoid prejudice against a person suspected of committing a crime, Western criminal procedure provides that the prosecutor be different from the adjudicator. In Taiwan the separation of procurators and judges in criminal proceedings was carried out by Japan from late 1895.[136] In practice, there did exist a few cases in which people prosecuted by the procurators were acquitted by the judges. But Taiwan's criminal procedural law explicitly granted colonial procurators and the police broad powers to summon, interrogate, search, arrest, or detain persons not in flagrante delicto, powers that in metropolitan Japan belonged only to the preliminary judge, who held a preliminary examination of serious or complicated cases referred to him by the procurator.[137] The GGT Higher Court further held in 1924 that when exercising those mandatory powers of the preliminary judge, the procurator or judicial police officer might decide at his own discretion whether or not the concrete facts met the legal requirements, namely, (1) that a suspect had no fixed domicile or residence, that there were sufficient facts to indicate that suspects might destroy or forge evidence, or that a suspect had absconded or there were facts sufficient to believe that he might abscond; and (2) that the situation constituted an emergency and therefore had to be disposed of.[138] In addition, before 1919 the opinion of the procurator was important in the judge's decision on whether the high amount of deposit for appeal could be waived, so that the procurator in practice deeply influenced whether or not an appeal was made by an accused.[139] State authority, then, was extensive, the rights of the accused, marginal, in practice.

In any event, the most serious threat to Western-style criminal justice in colonial Taiwan was police use of illegal means of investigation.[140] In law, the police had the duty of investigating crimes. During investigations, the police officer had almost the same powers to restrict personal freedom as the procurator had.[141] Unfortunately, policemen frequently abused their broad powers. Early in 1897, Chief Justice Takano had pointed out that the Japanese police publicly arrested and tortured Taiwanese at their will.[142] Some policemen and police spies (*mittei*) even extorted money from people by threatening to charge them with crimes.[143] In 1900, however, the Court of Appeal still considered that confessions and interrogatory records acquired by illegal means would not necessarily be rejected by the judge; based on his own discretion, the judge could take them as proof of guilt.[144] The result is that, as a Taiwanese lawyer pointed out in 1921, the police always employed illegal violence when interrogating suspects.[145] In 1925, under the pressure of Taiwanese political movements, a Japanese patrolman who tortured a Taiwanese suspect to death was sentenced to four years of penal servitude.[146] In 1935, the police arbitrarily detained many innocent tenant farmers and thus caused the Taiwan Bar Association to publicly advocate that the police be forbidden to exercise their compulsory powers in the investigation.[147] But the situation got worse during the wartime period; the police seemed to arrest or detain people without any regard for statutory procedures.[148]

Meanwhile, Taiwanese intellectuals became familiar with Western ideas of due process. The political platform of the Taiwanese opposition party between 1927 and 1931 called for many institutions from the Western criminal justice system, including the jury system and a criminal indemnity system. The platform also objected to extension of the duration of preliminary examination; to punishment, arrest, or detention without trial; and to police entrance into private homes without a warrant.[149] Many Taiwanese knew that the police ought to follow statutory procedures, but they did not dare to resist illegal arrest and detention. Lai Ho, for example, fully understood that the police needed a warrant of arrest to apprehend him. But during the wartime period, when he received an extralegal "notice" from the police, he went voluntarily to the police station, where he was detained, and did not challenge the legality of the proceedings.[150] When the war ended and Japan lost its authority over the island in 1945, Taiwanese intellectuals naturally considered that the wrongdoing of the Japanese authorities, including violations of due process, ought not to happen again. Two years after the end of Japanese rule, the Taiwanese people clearly demanded that no agents of the Chinese Nationalist government except the police be allowed to arrest people. They also demanded that the military police be empowered to arrest only those actively serving in the military.[151] The above facts illustrate that during the Japanese period, the Taiwanese people, at least intellectuals, certainly learned Western concepts of due process, although such ideas were not respected by the Japanese authorities.

EQUALITY OF PUNISHMENT

In contrast to the differentiation by social status in imperial Chinese criminal law, equality is emphasized in modern Western criminal justice.[152] Some colonial statutes in Taiwan also created inequality between resident Japanese and Taiwanese. For instance, like Manchus, the mainland Chinese, and Mongol bannermen in Ch'ing Taiwan, resident Japanese were excluded from collective responsibility under the *hokō* system.[153] In addition, after 1908 the sentence of a convicted Taiwanese could not be suspended unless the procurator suggested such a suspension to the judge.[154] Consequently, the sentences of only four Taiwanese were suspended from 1908 to 1915, compared to sixty-two Japanese.[155] Not until 1920 was the policy of discrimination against Taiwanese in the suspension of sentence abandoned.[156]

The Japanese authorities gradually began to enforce the criminal law without differentiation by race. In the 1910s one of the reasons for fighting between Japanese and Taiwanese was that low-ranking Japanese officials often favored resident Japanese in their disputes with Taiwanese.[157] But judging from the number of Japanese criminals, if a resident Japanese committed crimes, he could not escape punishment. Meanwhile, there were many cases involving malfeasance in office by Japanese in the court every year. In the majority of these cases, the patrolmen and assistant patrolmen who received bribes were punished.[158] The court seemed not to favor Japanese officials as much as one would expect. In fact, this practice was beneficial to colonial governance. A Taiwanese who lived during the late period of Japanese rule said, "I was very impressed. It was not just the Taiwanese who had to pay when

TABLE 4.7 Kinds of Punishments against Defendants in the Court of the First Instance in Taiwan, 1912–40

Year	Death penalty	Penal servitude for life	Penal servitude	Fine	Police fine	Flogging
1912	6	9	2,157	1,133	306	2,440
1915	879	6	2,437	1,064	360	2,101
1920	4	2	2,131	10,720	7,417	2,994
1925	5	2	3,925	14,572	20,780	0
1930	0	2	3,182	14,242	17,827	0
1935	1	2	3,156	17,770	20,637	0
1940	1*	7*	3,271*	NA	NA	0

SOURCES: Number of defendants: NTTN, 1921, p. 660; 1928, pp. 313, 315; 1933, pp. 324, 327; 1937, pp. 334, 337; 1939, pp. 317, 319. Number of new convicts in the prison: TWTT, pp. 500–501.
NOTES: The numbers of defendants sentenced to imprisonment and detention were insignificant and are not included in this table. The defendants in the court of first instance include both penal code offenders and special law violators. Defendants in the administrative summary judgment system are not included herein. * : number of new convicts in the prison, which was not the same, but close, to the number of the defendants convicted by the court of first instance.

they broke the law; Japanese law-breakers had to pay fines too."[159] The equality of punishment made Taiwanese more accepting of the numerous laws and regulations that controlled daily life.

Assurance of Punishment

The stable public order in Taiwan under Japanese rule was not entirely attributable to the severity of criminal punishments. When discussing criminal justice under Japanese colonial rule, many authors have emphasized the extremely harsh criminal sanctions that were imposed.[160] That is true for Japanese disposition of Taiwanese political criminals during the first two decades of Japanese rule. But from the 1920s to the mid-1930s, most Taiwanese political criminals were not severely punished. In connection with the ordinary crimes of the general public, the principle of severe punishment can to a certain degree describe the Japanese practice before 1920.[161] After 1920 the fine and the police fine were to a large extent used to punish criminals by the courts whose punishments were supposed to be more severe than those of the summary judgment office;[162] meanwhile, the number of defendants sentenced to death and penal servitude for life was very low (table 4.7). Furthermore, as early as 1910, more than half of all sentences to penal servitude were terms

TABLE 4.8 Terms of Penal Servitude of the Newly Convicted in the Prisons in Taiwan, 1910–42

Year	More than 10 years	37 months– 10 years	13–36 months	7–12 months	6 months or less	Total
1910	21	139	399	453	1,800	2,812
(%)	0.7	5.0	14.2	16.1	64.0	100.0
1915	87	509	367	522	1,701	3,186
(%)	2.7	16.0	11.5	16.4	53.4	100.0
1920	13	148	530	599	819	2,109
(%)	0.6	7.0	25.2	28.4	38.8	100.0
1925	12	116	352	626	2,292	3,398
(%)	0.3	3.4	10.4	18.4	67.5	100.0
1930	18	143	445	801	1,465	2,872
(%)	0.6	5.0	15.5	27.9	51.0	100.0
1935	20	207	646	1,080	980	2,933
(%)	0.7	7.1	22.0	36.8	33.4	100.0
1940	28	199	1,185	1,395	464	3,271
(%)	0.9	6.1	36.2	42.6	14.2	100.0
1942	8	248	1,139	1,390	490	3,275
(%)	0.2	7.6	34.8	42.4	15.0	100.0

SOURCE: *TWTT*, pp. 500–501.

of not more than six months (table 4.8). In the 1920s the punishment of flogging was abandoned and in practice replaced by fines and police fines; meanwhile, the majority of terms of penal servitude remained short. After the mid-1930s, the terms of penal servitude generally became longer, but the punishments of death and penal servitude for life did not increase significantly (see tables 4.7 and 4.8).

Public order in Taiwan under Japanese rule was maintained by the assurance of, not the severity of, criminal punishments. Accordingly, the colonial government emphasized the certainty of punishment, even at the risk of false accusation for minor crimes. The certainty of punishment is very important in stopping recidivism and deterring other people from committing the same crimes. In addition to their severe treatment of serious crimes, the Japanese

TABLE 4.9 Rates of Nonprosecution, Dismissal of Prosecution, and Acquittals in the Taiwan Court, 1897–1942 (percentage.)

Year	Nonprosecution	Dismissal of prosecution	Acquittal
1897	13.4	20.6	5.3
1900	28.2	26.5	5.7
1905	42.4	48.4	5.2
1910	50.0	53.1	3.6
1915	55.8	44.1	2.8
1920	66.1	19.2	1.7
1925	69.4	15.0	1.6
1930	79.1	7.5	2.2
1935	70.3	0.0	3.7
1940	59.2	6.3	1.0
1942	50.0	2.7	1.9

SOURCE: *TWTT*, pp. 436–37, 440–43.

NOTE: The rate of nonprosecution is calculated from the number of cases that resulted in nonprosecution and the total number of cases disposed of by procurators. The rate of dismissal of prosecution is calculated from the number of cases that resulted in dismissal of prosecution and the total number of cases decided by the preliminary judges. The rate of acquittals is calculated from the number of cases that resulted in acquittals and the total number of cases decided by judges in criminal trials.

authorities in Taiwan never loosened their punishment of minor crimes except during the initial period of Japanese rule. Almost all of those tried under the police summary judgment procedure for minor crimes were found guilty.

In the Western-style court system of Taiwan, however, the assurance of punishment did not mean that everyone being processed by the criminal procedure had to be put in jail. The rate of nonprosecution of the GGT procuracy was consistently over 50 percent after 1910, and was nearly 80 percent in 1930 (table 4.9). Although officials most often decided not to prosecute because there was insufficient evidence, sometimes they simply decided that punishments were not necessary.[163] Additionally, in some cases charges were dismissed after the preliminary examination.[164] After the rate of nonprosecution rose during the 1910–35 period, the rate of acquittals in criminal trials dropped to about 2.5 percent. However, during the wartime period, human rights seemed to be of less concern, and thus the rate of nonprosecution and the rate of acquittals both dropped (table 4.9).

Prison and Rehabilitation

There were no Western-style prisons in Chinese legal tradition. None of the "five punishments" of imperial Chinese law consisted of a stay in prison. Jails were merely designed to imprison those who were not convicted or who were awaiting transfer to the place of execution of their sentences.[165] In the first year of Japanese rule, Japan introduced into Taiwan certain Western forms of criminal punishments, including penal servitude to be served in a prison, but the Western-style prison did not in fact exist in Taiwan yet.[166] From 1899 to 1903, the GGT invested a large amount of money in constructing huge, well-designed modern prisons.[167] Because modern prisons were expensive, the GGT restored the traditional punishment of flogging. The abolition of flogging in 1921 thus promoted prison construction.[168] At the end of Japanese rule, there were eight prisons in Taiwan, corresponding to the eight district courts and their branches.[169] Even if a Taiwanese was never put into prison, he was impressed by the lofty prison building and felt the State authority that it represented.

Similarly, imperial Chinese law provided no rehabilitation fitting the outcast for a better future role in society.[170] Learning from the West, Japan paid attention to rehabilitation of convicts who were sentenced to prison. The GGT thus sent juvenile criminals to a special juvenile reformatory in Hsin-chu. Additionally, quasi-official associations for judicial protection (shihō hogo) were instituted extensively in towns throughout the island so that an ex-convict who had served his sentence could find a job or assistance and would not commit crimes again.[171] Taiwanese people therefore gradually came to understand the idea of rehabilitation of criminals, and some of the Taiwanese were sponsors of the associations for judicial protection.[172]

Non-Western Criminal Measures

In establishing their system of criminal justice on Taiwan, however, Japanese colonialists preserved some traditional measures of imperial Chinese law and excluded the related criminal principles of modern Western law. First was the physical punishment of imperial Chinese law, namely flogging, as discussed before. The Japanese made only a "humanitarian" reform with respect to this punishment. The GGT had a doctor examine the convict in advance to make sure that he could tolerate the flogging and provided that the flogging could not exceed twenty five strokes per day.[173]

The second was collective responsibility for others' offenses. As under the traditional Chinese *pao-chia* system, a Taiwanese would be punished because of his neighbor's commission of a crime. That is far different from the spirit of modern Western law, in which everyone is basically responsible for only his own behavior. According to the statistics of the GGT, under the *hokō* system there were 18 cases in 1919 involving collective criminal responsibility, by which members of a *hokō* were fined for not reporting the crime of one of the members. Although the GGT had no statistics about the number of this type of case before 1919, it is reasonable to presume that the number was not low since imperial Chinese law was still emphasized and society was not entirely stable during the first half of Japanese rule. According to the GGT, such cases did not occur any more after 1925. In any event, in the 1920s another kind of collective responsibility for other members' breaching the *hokō* regulations was still prevalent. In 1920 there were 246 cases involving this kind of collective responsibility. After 1936, this kind of case in fact did not occur.[174] Not until 1945, when the GGT formed other institutions to substitute for it, was the *hokō* system abolished.[175]

The third and most important area where Chinese-style principles were retained was the combination of executive and judicial power in the administrative summary judgment system. This system greatly modified Western due process. In a Western-style criminal law system, the criminal suit should be tried by a judge who is neutral to the two parties involved, that is, the suspect and the state. But the GGT had the state become both referee and a player in the police summary judgment cases, in which the police not only undertook the task of prosecution but also were in charge of adjudication. This traditional system was maintained and further strengthened in the late Japanese period.

THE LAW-ABIDING TAIWANESE AND THE RECEPTION OF LAW

Few appraisals were so generally accepted by commentators of various backgrounds as the remark that the Taiwanese under Japanese rule were a law-abiding and obedient people. In addition to Western and native scholars, the prime minister of the Chinese Nationalist government, who was typically unwilling to make any positive comment concerning the Japanese administration on Taiwan, also stated in 1947 that the Taiwanese under Japanese rule respected law and order.[176] Such an impression of the general public was reasonable. Compared to Korea or Japan, Taiwanese political criminals were few in number. Compared to the Ch'ing period, Taiwanese under Japanese rule were certainly law-abiding. Although there were more Taiwanese criminals in the last half of Japanese rule than in the first half (see table 4.6), people did not think the social order was threatened by crime, probably because serious crimes were greatly reduced; many of those convicted had violated some administrative regulation, an action not considered a crime by the general population in Taiwan. What could make a turbulent society filled with disrespect for law only fifty years earlier transform so rapidly?

Taiwanese obedience originated in eventual submission to this alien ruler. Under Japanese rule, the Taiwanese, regarded by the Japanese as Chinese, by the Chinese as Japanese, were "orphans in Asia." The outside world seemed not to care about this isolated island. When the Taiwanese resisted the Japanese invaders, no one came to their aid.[177] Facing useless sacrifice of life, the pragmatic Taiwanese chose to be obedient subjects. They were indifferent to politics but engaged in their livelihoods out of concern for their own lives and the lives of their families.[178] For the sake of their own safety they had to observe whatever law the Japanese authorities promulgated. In addition, the political and judicial system was not fully effective during the Ch'ing period, in part because of the Ch'ing's lack of commitment to Taiwan. Therefore, when problems arose that could not be resolved through local Taiwanese customary means, there was no effective judicial system to satisfactorily settle matters. The Japanese colonialists, however, brought a systematic, effective political and judicial mechanism to Taiwan in the form of a Westernized government. Thus, Taiwanese obedience was perhaps practicality as the Taiwanese accepted what was a largely accessible and reliable system.

This law-abiding spirit led the Taiwanese to accept the Japanese-imposed Western-style criminal justice system. The Taiwanese did not at first understand the basis of Western-style criminal law. But, out of practical concern, they had to obey the state laws. Through effective enforcement over a long time, those Western-style criminal laws gradually were taken for granted by the general public. Some legal concepts derived from Western culture therefore were unconsciously received by the Taiwanese people. In sum, the Japanese "created" a Taiwanese version of submission to authority (at high costs to the Taiwanese), by which Japan implemented Westernized criminal law in Taiwan, as the Meiji reform did in Japan.

Taiwanese reception of Western criminal law was thus restricted to the progovernment character of the legal reform in the colony. The protection of human rights in the Western criminal process was often overlooked in reality by the colonial authorities. The illegal massacre of "bandits," arbitrary disposition of so-called vagrants, prevalent police torture, and so on illustrate this point. Therefore, what Taiwanese people learned about from experience with the colonial legal reform was not individual-rights-oriented Western criminal justice.

On the other hand, it is also true that some democratic ideas in Western criminal justice that are not to be found in the colonial legal reform were also received by some Taiwanese intellectuals. Objecting to Japan's colonial positive law, many antigovernment Taiwanese intellectuals viewed "law" in a different way. They advocated what the law should be by modern Western legal standards, emphasizing the interests of the people. Based on their normative ideas of what "the law should be," they publicly demanded the colonial government to improve criminal justice on Taiwan. Those Taiwanese intellectuals proposed far more legal and criminal justice reforms than their ruler was prepared to give them.

SUMMARY

At the beginning, the greatest threat to Japan's establishment of governing order in the colony was the Taiwanese armed resistance, influenced by Taiwan's tradition of antigovernment action by force. In 1895–1902, Japan resorted primarily to military force to terminate this armed resistance. Later, in 1907–16, the Temporary Court became the main forum for the trial of Taiwanese armed resisters. Not until the 1920s, when the Taiwanese employed modern political movements to resist Japanese oppression within the fundamental legal framework of the state, did the ordinary court finally have exclusive authority to try political crimes. In the 1920s and mid-1930s, the punishments for political dissidents sentenced by the court were not as harsh as before; but the brutal police never loosened their tight control upon Taiwanese dissidents. During the wartime period, severe punishments were imposed on Taiwanese political criminals, although the Taiwanese on the island for the most part had given up resistance against Japan.

To use state authority to suppress ordinary crimes, Japan shaped a crime control structure between 1903 and 1909 that continued until the end of Japanese rule in 1945. Under this structure, the court system prudently disposed of the minority of serious criminal cases; the police summary judgment system on the other hand hastily decided the majority of minor criminal cases. In addition, under the vagrant discipline system, the police could arbitrarily send so-called vagrants to labor camps. Because of the state's involvement in imposing punishments for crimes, the nature and incidence of crimes changed. Generally speaking, serious crimes threatening the public order were reduced, but relatively minor crimes still occurred frequently, so that the number of Taiwanese criminals did not drop under Japanese rule.

Many Western-style criminal institutions played a significant role in the transformation of Taiwanese criminal justice. The principles of requiring the promulgation of a law before a penalty could be imposed as well as due process were observed in form by the Japanese authorities, and thus by 1945 the Taiwanese people had already been exposed to the basic concepts of those principles. In the last half of Japanese rule, Japan also followed the principle of the equality of punishment regardless of race, social status, and so on. Meanwhile, although after the 1920s the Japanese in practice did not emphasize the severity of punishments on Taiwan, throughout their rule they insisted on the assurance of punishments. Additionally, the Western-style prisons and policies of rehabilitation were introduced to the island. These efforts notwithstanding, Japan still employed some elements of the Chinese legal tradition so that the use of Western-style criminal justice on Taiwan was not complete.

That the Taiwanese abode by the law because they found it useless to resist meant that in time the Taiwanese accepted as normal the Western-style criminal law to the extent that it had been adopted in the colonial legal reform.

5 / Westernization of Civil Justice

This chapter investigates whether Japan also employed state authority in the form of positive law to directly and immediately transform the civil customs of the Taiwanese, as the Japanese government did in colonial criminal law, and also assesses the reaction of the Taiwanese toward Japan's Westernized civil law, which had relatively few connections with the political oppression of the new rulers. These two topics influence the extent to which the Taiwanese received Western civil law under Japanese rule.

APPROACH FOR WESTERNIZATION

Taiwanese Customary Law

Application of Old Customs. After the annexation of Taiwan to Japan, old Taiwanese customs were considered the law in Taiwanese civil matters. Early in 1895, the Japanese military administration stipulated that Taiwanese civil lawsuits were to be adjudicated in accordance with local custom and legal theory.[1] In 1898, such a measure was adopted by a *ritsurei* of the GGT (having the same effectiveness as Japan's statute), providing that Taiwanese customs be applied to these civil matters involving only Taiwanese (and Chinese).[2] Although after 1899 Japanese civil procedural law was enforced in Taiwanese lawsuits, for the most part the content of Japanese civil substantive law was not extended to regulate Taiwanese civil matters until 1923.[3] During the period of "*ritsurei* civil law" (1898–1922), meaning that the positive civil law was constituted by *ritsurei* rather than by Japan's statutes, Taiwanese civil matters were legally bound by their own "old customs," as during the Ch'ing period.[4]

Under *ritsurei* civil law, the Taiwanese in principle could not help but be governed by the old customs in civil matters. Before 1923, only those Taiwanese civil matters that involved a Japanese and did not involve property rights in land were governed by Japanese law rather than Taiwanese customs. In theory, a change in ethnic status meant that the governing law for civil matters would change as well. But only those people who were registered according to Japan's Household Registration Law in metropolitan Japan were "Japanese mainlanders" (*naichijin*) in colonial Taiwan.[5] This Japanese law was never applied to Taiwan and thus there was no legal device to allow a Taiwanese to become a Japanese mainlander in colonial Taiwan.[6] Furthermore, under *ritsurei* civil law, a Taiwanese was not allowed to voluntarily select Japanese civil law to be the governing law for his or her own civil matters.[7]

Recognition of Customary Law. The term "old customs" in *ritsurei* civil law referred to the legal rules effective in Ch'ing Taiwan. Two elements of law in Ch'ing Taiwan were the written law (the Ch'ing Code) and local customs. The Ch'ing Code contained some rules, though relatively few in number that would now be categorized as civil matters: rules on family relations, marriage, transactions in land and other objects, and loans. Those rules were expressed as proscriptions or commands and punished as crimes. Moreover, because the Ch'ing Code was, in form, a directive from the emperor to magistrates, those rules were not direct statements about the relations of individual citizens with each other, as the term "civil" law would imply under Western law.[8] For example, a statute in the Ch'ing Code provided that any debtor who failed to pay a valid debt when due should be punished with beating. Although in this statute the magistrate was also commanded by the emperor to demand payment of debt and then return it to the creditor, the statute did not provide any measures that the creditor, a citizen, could take to directly force the debtor, another citizen, to repay a debt.[9] On the other hand, local customs in Ch'ing Taiwan often dealt with sophisticated legal relationships between parties, including various obligations, as they would be called now, of parties and remedies for their breach.[10] However, those rules in local customs were ordinarily carried out by parties' voluntary compliance or by unofficial dispute resolution machinery such as community or kin mediation. Only in a small number of "civil" cases were local customary rules enforced by the magistrate (governmental agency). Moreover, customary rules were sometimes set aside for the sake of harmony among community or kin.[11] For instance, even though a creditor lent a certain sum of money to a debtor and the debtor did not repay it, the dispute resolution tribunal might require that the creditor settle for less than the full sum because the debtor was too poor to pay it all.[12]

The enforcement of obligations under Taiwan's old customs was therefore different from enforcement under Western-style civil law. Neither the "civil" rules in the Ch'ing code nor local customs included the concept of legal rights as developed in Western law, by which citizen claimants can activate and control the process for enforcing substantive legal rules.[13] When an obligation is not performed, the obligee under Western law is granted a legal right to decide whether or not to demand that the obliger perform such obligation (or, when its performance is impossible, demand indemnity). If, after the demand, the obliger fails to perform, the obligee can require the court to force the obliger to perform the obligation, rather than merely impose a criminal penalty. If the obligation involved is considered to exist, the court is bound to do as the obligee requests unless otherwise provided in law. Under Western-style civil law, a citizen, as a bearer of rights, therefore plays an active role in the enforcement of obligations. Under traditional Chinese law, which had no concept of rights, the enforcement of obligations always depended on the voluntary performance of the obliger and the discretion of the arbitrator (such as a magistrate or a community or kin leader).

As Taiwanese old customs were incorporated into colonial law, they needed to be accommodated to Japan's Western-style legal system. By 1895, Japan had already received modern European law, which was a system of rights defined by specific procedures and remedies as the claims of individuals.[14] Taiwanese customs, originally composed of the Ch'ing Code and local customs, therefore had to be interpreted through Western concepts of legal rights so that they could function in the whole legal system of Japan. The colonial authorities soon established an institute to take on this task. Led by Okamatsu Santarō, a Japanese legal scholar, the Commission for the Investigation of Old Laws and Customs in Taiwan (hereafter the Survey Commission) was organised.[15] The Survey Commission first confirmed which usages in Taiwan were recognized as "law," which everyone ought to obey. Those rules in the Ch'ing Code that were not observed in Taiwan were to be excluded from customary rules; in contrast, those Taiwanese customs that were in conflict with the Ch'ing Code but were generally followed were now to be considered as customary rules.[16] The accepted customary rules were then interpreted through the concepts of legal rights derived from Western Roman law.[17] In the commentaries on Taiwanese customs written by the Survey Commission, the rights under specific legal relations were listed, and their acquisition, transfer, and loss were explained in detail.[18]

Only those customary rules recognized by courts and other competent authorities constituted the customary law. What the Survey Commission hoped to "discover" was merely the customary rules, the existence of which depended on habit and community consensus. In a modern state the customary rules have to be recognized through a specific institutional process and then become law, which acquires its legitimacy from political authority. Under *ritsurei* civil law in Taiwan, this institutional process was undertaken by courts and, in certain circumstances, by executive authorities of the GGT that were to apply old customs to the cases they handled. The GGT court and other competent authorities interpreted the legal relations in old customs, granting rights and imposing obligations to the parties concerned. Old customs were thus redefined as institutionalized legal rules, called the customary law.[19] Through such lawmaking and law enforcing, Taiwan's old customs evolved into customary law under the Western-style legal system.

In connection with the same civil matters, the old customs explained by the Survey Commission were sometimes different from the customary law judged by the court. The reports of the Survey Commission aimed at discovering the old customs. In practice, however, those reports were used by the GGT Court for reference only. As a Japanese judge in the colony said, a judge should not merely discover local customs but also take into account "improvement" when he applied Taiwanese customs to make decisions.[20] In law, the applied customs might not be contrary to public order or good morals. It was argued that because of Taiwan's status as a special legal zone within the Japanese empire, the standard of "public order or good morals" ought to be based on Taiwan, not Japan.[21] But Japanese judges were inevitably influenced by Japan's Westernized law in deciding whether or not a Taiwanese custom should be recognized by the court, an institution representing state law. As a result, customary law in Japan's Taiwan was different from customary rules in Ch'ing Taiwan.[22]

Customary law in Japan's Taiwan more closely resembled Western civil law. The colonial officials, unlike the investigating scholars, preferred to employ Japanese legal terms rather than indigenous terms, and therefore frequently interpreted Taiwanese customs by similar legal relations in Japan's civil law. Through the process of interpretation, some substantive contents of old Taiwanese customs were changed by Japanese civil law. Moreover, by the term "legal theory," certain provisions in Japanese modern civil law were also incorporated into Taiwanese customary law. In fact, the Japanese authorities consciously or unconsciously unified the customary law in Taiwan and the positive law in metropolitan Japan.[23] Since Japan's modern civil law was virtually received from Continental Europe, this attitude consequently made a contribution to the Westernization of Taiwanese customary law.

Statutory Regulation. Furthermore, some statutes promulgated by the colonial government directly changed old Taiwanese customs. It was because of a general delegation of authority by *ritsurei* that Taiwanese customs were to be applied by the courts. Therefore, when a *ritsurei* specially regulated a certain civil matter, this *ritsurei* would supersede the customary law recognized by the courts. For instance, under Taiwanese customary law, the transfer of certain rights concerning land without any official registration was considered valid by the courts, but after a *ritsurei* specially regulating land registration in Taiwan was put into force in 1905, such a transfer became invalid unless it was registered in the office.[24] In sum, even though Taiwanese customary rules were recognized as customary laws by the colonial officials, the rules were often invalidated by later statutes.

Common Law System for Civil Matters. Under Japanese rule, a common law system for Taiwanese civil matters was thus established. Before the Japanese Civil Code became applicable to Taiwanese in 1923, there was no written code in Taiwan to govern civil matters involving only Taiwanese. A colonial judge had to apply customs or legal theory to decide Taiwanese lawsuits.[25] The Court of Appeal or the Re-appeal Division of the Higher Court after 1919 was in charge of unifying different legal interpretations between courts in Taiwan.[26] The lower courts in Taiwan had to follow the preexisting legal interpretation in the decisions of Taiwan's supreme court in applying customs to decide Taiwanese civil matters. The supreme court in Taiwan in practice followed its own decisions but also was expected to respond to the changing situation in Taiwanese society.[27] Such practice is similar to the doctrine of *stare decisis* (let the decision stand), the essence of the common law system developed in England and transferred to most of the English-speaking world. That doctrine states that courts should adhere to the law as set forth in previous cases decided by the highest court of a given jurisdiction as long as the principle derived from those cases is logically essential to their decision, is reasonable, and is appropriate to contemporary circumstances.[28] It should be noted, however, that in Taiwan's courts the reasoning of judgments applying customary law did not necessarily have to cite related precedents, especially when the content of customary law was not in dispute.[29]

In addition to recognizing customary rules, colonial judges were involved in lawmaking. For instance, the 1907 Japanese Criminal Code provided that the legal definition of "relatives" was contained in the Civil Code; however, because the Civil Code was not applied to Taiwanese, there was no statute in Taiwan to stipulate the legal definition of relatives. The Council of Judges, composed of all judges in the Court of Appeal and all heads of district courts, thus made a legal "interpretation" to provide such a definition, based on neither old Taiwanese customs nor Japanese civil code.[30]

Codification of Taiwanese Customary Law

The Japanese government did not wish to maintain this common law system and intended to enforce written civil codes in Taiwan. Probably because the Japanese legal system itself had already adopted the approach of codification, it was taken for granted that a civil code would be used in the colony. The question left was what kind of civil code should be used in Taiwan, a civil code specially enacted for Taiwan or Japan's preexisting civil code. In 1908, Okamatsu strongly supported the former model and further asserted that a special code for Taiwan should contain Taiwanese customs as well as Japanese Western-style law.[31] In the same year, the GGT started to codify Taiwanese customary law.[32]

The GGT spent five years completing the drafts of Taiwan civil codes. A committee led by Okamatsu drafted several civil codes for Taiwan between 1909 and 1914. The draft Taiwan codes basically codified Taiwanese customary law, with some modification, using the organization of the Japanese civil and commercial codes.[33] In discussions carried on during the preparation of drafts, scholars on the drafting committee ordinarily supported Taiwanese customary law, as Okamatsu said in 1908: "It is improper to break the customs of three million Taiwanese for the sake of a minority number of (Japanese) mainlanders."[34] Some judicial officials in the committee, on the other hand, frequently advocated incorporating Japanese civil law into the drafts.[35] These proposals were the first modern civil codes to be drafted on the basis of the conditions of Taiwan society itself (or on the basis of the Japanese understanding of Taiwanese society).

When the central government decided to adopt the principle of assimilation as colonial policy, the project of codifying Taiwanese customary law and promulgating it as a code was destined to fail. The existence of unique Taiwan civil codes would, to a certain degree, emphasize the special legal status of Taiwan within the Empire of Japan. The GGT, whose members hoped to maintain their extensive powers in an "independent Taiwan," thus sent the draft codes to the central government for approval in 1914. Although the central government never explicitly objected to the drafts, it presumably disagreed with the GGT's scheme; in any event, it did not approve the drafts. Not until 1919, when the existing colonial policy was seriously criticized in Japan, did the central government decide to implement the policy of assimilation in the colonies. Since the special status of Taiwan was weakened by this policy, there was little hope that a special law like a Taiwan civil code would be promulgated.

Japanese Civil Code except Status Law

Instead of enacting a Taiwan civil code, the decision was made to have the Japanese Civil Code applied to Taiwan. In 1922, an ordinance declared that Japanese civil law would be applied to the Taiwanese, beginning January 1, 1923.[36] However, Taiwanese customary law would still apply to family and succession matters involving only Taiwanese under a common law system.[37]

The rights under Taiwanese customary law were therefore transformed into the rights under Japan's Westernized civil law insofar as Taiwanese civil matters were governed by Japanese law. The Taiwanese thus had to adapt themselves to a modern civil code that originally had been enacted for another society.

With the ultimate goal of assimilating the Taiwanese and extinguishing Taiwanese ideas of self-determination, the colonial government next tried to apply the books of Family and Succession in the Japanese Civil Code to the Taiwanese. When the books of General Provisions, Rights over Things, and Obligations in the Civil Code as well as the Commercial Code were applied to Taiwanese, a few special civil provisions in Taiwan were promulgated to supersede the related provisions in the two codes.[38] In 1929–30, the GGT wanted to follow the same approach and suggested that the books of Family and Succession in the Japanese Civil Code apply to Taiwanese, with some special provisions. However, the Ministry of Colonial Affairs (Takumushō) did not adopt such a proposal. The GGT discussed similar proposals again in the late 1930s, to promote the Japanization movement, but to no effect.[39] In March of 1945, the GGT declared in the Imperial Diet that Japanese family and succession law would apply to Taiwanese, with some exceptions, to "improve the treatment of the Taiwanese." But Japan surrendered in August, and the plan was never realized.[40]

WESTERNIZATION OF LAW RELATING TO REAL ESTATE

During the Japanese period, the main occupation of Taiwanese was agriculture,[41] and the legal rules regarding real estate (especially fields) therefore deeply influenced the livelihood of the people. In fact, the old customs concerning real estate were the first subject that the Survey Commission investigated.[42] Here, I will discuss how the law relating to real estate developed from old customs to Japanese Westernized civil law.[43] Through this discussion, the Westernization of Taiwanese civil law, discussed generally above, will be illustrated more concretely.

Old Customs and Various Rights in Customary Law

Yeh-chu and Its Rights. According to Taiwanese custom, a private subject could not acquire full ownership of land in the sense understood in modern Western law, but only the legal status of *yeh-chu* (proprietor, landlord). Influenced by the Chinese concept that "all land under heaven belongs to the sovereign," Taiwanese, especially the better educated, thought the land was the king's. The maximum power in regard to land that could be enjoyed by a private subject were those of a *yeh-chu*. To ask who was the *yeh-chu* of a certain piece of land was the same as to ask to whom the land belonged. Nevertheless, the *yeh-chu* as "owner" was subjected to certain restraints, not only in theory but also in fact.[44]

The existence of certain substantial restraints upon the *yeh-chu* can be illustrated by the relationship between the *ta-tsu-hu* (large-lease holder) and the *hsiao-tsu-hu* (small-lease holder). As stated in chapter 1, in late Ch'ing Taiwan *ta-tsu* holders, who were originally *yeh-chu*, lost their actual power over land. *Hsiao-tsu* holders in contrast were regarded as *yeh-chu* by Taiwanese society at that time. However, *hsiao-tsu* holders had to pay rent (*tsu*) to *ta-tsu* holders. Accordingly, although *hsiao-tsu* holders were *yeh-chu*, they were subject to what might be called private law obligations toward others in connection with their rights.

Because the rights of the *yeh-chu* were not precisely the same as "ownership" in Japanese modern civil law, the term "*yeh-chu* right" was created in Taiwanese customary law by the colonial authorities. A *yeh-chu* in Taiwan's old customs could possess, use, or dispose freely and independently of his land. After those powers were described within a system of legal rights, he could activate and control the process for enforcing those interests he enjoyed through the court. But because certain obligation that is, to pay rent) to others might be imposed on a *yeh-chu* through a *ta-tsu–hsiao-tsu* relationship, his rights to land could not be classified as "ownership" in Japanese civil law with German root, wherein means the owner has exclusive rights to land in private law. Japanese jurists in Taiwan thus first defined the rights possessed by a *yeh-chu* as "*yeh-chu* rights." Those *hsiao-tsu* holders who had "*hsiao-tsu* rights" were considered to possess the *yeh-chu* rights to land under Taiwanese customary law. On the other hand, those *ta-tsu* holders who had "*ta-tsu* rights," by which they were entitled to collect rent from *hsiao-tsu* holders, did not enjoy *yeh-chu* rights.

Ti-chi and Its Rights. In Taiwanese custom, the *ti-chi* (or *ts'uo-ti*, building lot) relation was entered into when one paid rent on a piece of land and erected a building on it. The builder was the *yeh-chu* of the building, but legal relations between the builder and the *yeh-chu* of the property were not the same in all circumstances. There were three possible relations in the old customs. (1) The original *yeh-chu* of the lot had lost his actual control over the land. The builder had become the *yeh-chu* of the lot, but he had to pay rent to the original *yeh-chu* for the *ti-chi* relation. (2) The original owner of the lot maintained his *yeh-chu* right to land, but the builder had the right to permanently use the lot. (3) By a lease contract, a builder erected a simple house on land in town for nonagricultural purposes, but the lot owner maintained the *yeh-chu* right. Under Taiwanese customary law, the builder in circumstance (1) had *yeh-chu* rights to the lot with the obligation to pay rent, as the *hsiao-tsu* holder did. The legal right of the builder over the building lot was called the *ti-chi* right (or *ts'uo-chu* right) in the relations of (2), and the *po* right (tenant right) over the lot in situation (3).[45]

Tien *Lease and Its Rights.* In Taiwan's old customs the *tien* lease was a tenancy of a farm owned by others. This relation was created by a contract between the *yeh-chu* (for example, *hsiao-tsu* holder) and the tenant (*tien-jen*). The contract was usually called a *po-keng*. The object of the lease was ordinarily cultivated land. A *tien* lease was usually for a fixed term of three to six years. Where the duration of a *tien* lease was not fixed in advance, this relation might be terminated by the *yeh-chu* after a year. The tenant could cultivate the fields freely during the lease term and enjoyed the fruits thereof at the cost of rent paid to the *yeh-chu*. In Taiwanese customary law, the tenant therefore was said to have a *tien* lease right, but he could not dispose of or sublet fields without the consent of the *yeh-chu*. Moreover, the *tien* lease right could not be exercised against a third party, for example, a new owner of leased land.[46]

Yung-tien *and Its Rights.* In Taiwanese customs *yung-tien* meant a long-term (exceeding ten years) or permanent lease relation. The tenant under *yung-tien*, however, could dispose of the leased land without the consent of the *yeh-chu*. His right, called a *yung-tien* right in customary law, was enforceable against a third party. *Yung-tien* relations ordinarily arose in circumstances where the tenant had to invest much labor to cultivate wasteland to make it usable and therefore needed to have the use of it for a long period to profit from it.[47]

Tien *Pledge and Its Rights.* Tien pledge is similar to, but not identical with, the pledge in Japanese civil law (*shichi*). Under the *tien* pledge in Taiwanese customary law, the possession of certain immovable objects (for example, farms, hill lots, and building lots) or immovable rights (for example, the right to receive rent for a building lot) was transferred to the *tien* pledge buyer, who then became the holder of a *tien* pledge (*tien-chu*) and could use and collect the fruits of the property. The *tien* pledge seller received a sum of money from the *tien* pledge buyer and had no obligation to pay interest on the loan. Sometimes the wording *chi-keng* (literally, "establish cultivation") was added to make it clear that *tien* pledge holders were allowed to use and take fruits therefrom. But the ownership of the transferred objects or rights remained in the hands of the *tien* pledge seller. If the *tien* pledge seller failed to pay back the money at the stipulated time, *tien* pledge holders could not obtain payment of their claims by selling or disposing the transferred objects or rights but could continue to use and take fruits until the debts were paid. In fact, the duration specified in *tien* pledge agreements was simply the time for the *tien* pledge seller to redeem the transferred objects or rights. From this aspect, *tien* pledge may perhaps be regarded as a sale, subject to the conditions of repurchase. Accordingly, the *tien* pledge right under Taiwanese customary law in fact was not equal to the right of pledge in Japanese civil law. Japan's pledge of immovable objects resembled *tien* pledge insofar as it also allowed the creditor to use and take the fruits of the object pledged; however, according to the pledge in Japanese law, the creditor was entitled to dispose of the object pledged when the debtor failed to perform, whereas the creditor with a *tien* pledge right could not do so.[48]

T'ai and Its Rights. In Taiwanese custom, *t'ai* usually referred to the deposit of a title deed in an immovable object or immovable rights, which traditionally served as the evidence of a proprietary right, as security for a loan. The holder of *t'ai*, however, neither possessed the immovable objects or immovable rights nor could he use and take the fruits therefrom, although he could receive interest from the debtor. He had no way to obtain payment by selling the debtor's immovable objects or immovable rights. The *t'ai* right under Taiwanese customary law therefore only made the payment secure indirectly. Accordingly, many *t'ai* contracts in Taiwan in practice changed this general rule by adding a special agreement in which the creditor was entitled to get possession, use, and take the fruits from the immovables or immovable rights if the debtor failed to perform his obligation or to do so for the purpose of receiving interest for the loan within the duration of the *t'ai* agreement.[49]

Ekiken of Land. In the early period of Japanese rule, some customary relations relating to using others' land for certain purposes of one's own land were legally defined as *ekiken* (in Japanese, literally, "service right") of land. In Ch'ing Taiwan people sometimes entered into contracts to use the land belonging to others for such purposes as irrigating their own fields, securing a passage way thereto, or preventing the view of their ancestors' tombs from being impaired by buildings on others' land. The Japanese used a similar legal term in their own law, *chiekiken* (servitude, easement), to collectively refer to those Taiwanese customary land relations. But the so-called *ekiken* of land in Taiwanese customary law, unlike the easement in Japanese civil law, was not necessarily effective against a third party, for example, a new landowner or holder of a *tien* pledge.[50]

Land Survey and Yeh-chu Rights. Based on its land survey on Taiwan and in the light of its experiences in the Meiji reform, the Japanese government confirmed who had *yeh-chu* rights and clarified the ownership of land in colonial Taiwan. Such clarification made taxation more efficient and safeguarded the legality of transactions involving land. Under the 1898 Land Survey Regulation,[51] Taiwanese landlords (or *tien* pledge holders) were required to report their land to the colonial government. After looking at the documents submitted, the government confirmed who had *yeh-chu* right and whether there were legal restrictions such as *ta-tsu* or *tien* pledges on the land, then registered these facts.

Some Taiwanese landlords were unfortunately sacrificed during this process. Article 7 of the Land Survey Regulation provided that the *yeh-chu* right of land not reported was transferred to the state. The decision of the land survey agency could not be challenged; those owners who did not report their rights to the survey agency were unprotected in private law. The GGT Higher Court held in 1921 that the Land Survey Commission's decision (registration) on who was a landlord was absolutely final; nothing that had occurred before the registration under the land survey could affect the validity of this registration.[52] It is true that in another case in 1932 the GGT Higher Court decided that a person who had not reported his ownership so that his land was not registered under the land survey did not lose his ownership (namely, *yeh-chu* right in the early days of Japanese rule) in private law,[53] but in that case the unreported land was not registered as belonging to someone else.[54] As a 1924 decision shows, in the event that this unreported land was already registered as another's land, the original real owner would unfortunately lose his ownership.[55] And it was easy for a Taiwanese landlord to neglect to report his land rights to the new Japanese government. At the time the land survey was conducted (between 1898 and 1904), under the Taiwanese customary law recognized by the courts, the acquisition, transfer, and loss of the rights relating to real estate took place regardless of any official registration.[56] Some Taiwanese landlords thus paid little attention to the requirement to report land rights for official registration. They were also undoubtedly influenced by the practice of avoiding taxation in Ch'ing Taiwan by not reporting their fields to the government. As a consequence, their land was often "lawfully" appropriated by others, including the state. Thus the land survey, while codifying land rights, deprived some Taiwanese landlords of their rights.

Modification by Western Civil Law

Duration of Rights. In 1900, the GGT began to regulate the duration of certain land rights in Taiwanese customary law. Customarily, there were no limits on the duration of these rights. Probably because there were statutory limitations on the duration of the rights of emphyteusis and lease in Japan's civil law,[57] the GGT enacted a *ritsurei* to restrict the duration for the lending and borrowing of land in Taiwan. The original unlimited duration of *ti-chi* rights, *po-keng* rights, *yung-tien* rights, or *ekiken* of land were thereafter restricted to one hundred years; and the duration of *tien* lease rights could not exceed twenty years.[58]

Abolition of Ta-tsu Rights. In 1903, the GGT enacted a *ritsurei* to clarify the *ta-tsu* right, which was still a burden in private law for the *hsiao-tsu* holder, who now had the *yeh-tsu* right. This regulation clearly provided that the *ta-tsu* right was thereafter not allowed to be established, and the amount of rent of *ta-tsu* was not permitted to increase.[59] The Japanese authorities wanted to freeze the relationship of *ta-tsu* rights so that these rights could be further disposed of by the government.

The *ta-tsu* right was abolished in 1904, and therefore the substance of the *yeh-tsu* right under Taiwanese customary law was similar to that of ownership under Japanese Western-style civil law. After the clarification of *ta-tsu* rights, the GGT provided that all these rights were to be terminated by June 1, 1904, with compensation from the government.[60] Those who possessed *yeh-chu* rights under the relationship of *ta-tsu* and *hsiao-tsu* were thus freed from their burdens in private law that originated from *ta-chu* rights. Like the owner under European law, the person with *yeh-chu* right had exclusive rights to land in private law. This development also corresponded to the principle of "one land, one owner" in European civil law.

Changes by the Land Registration Regulation. In 1905, a registration system for certain civil law rights in land (not including buildings) was established in Taiwan.[61] Under the 1905 Land Registration Regulation, all *yeh-chu* rights, *tien* pledge rights, *t'ai* rights, and *po-keng* rights (that is, *yung-tien* rights and *tien* lease rights) in the land that had already been registered under the land survey were to be registered in the land register (*tochi tōkibo*). Other kinds of civil law rights in land (for example, *ti-chi* right, *ekiken* of land) as well as the civil law rights in the land that had not been registered under the land survey did not have to be registered therein. More important, rights could not be acquired, transferred, or lost if they were required to be registered in this regulation unless their registration was completed, with the exception of a transfer based on the death of the rights holder or in accordance with his will. In connection with those rights occurring before the effective date of this regulation (July, 1, 1905), the *yeh-chu* right was allowed not to be registered, but the other three kinds of rights in land were to be registered within one year after the effective date; otherwise, they could not be asserted against a third party.[62] However, under Taiwanese customary law, as interpreted by the colonial court, these four kinds of rights could be lawfully acquired, transferred, or lost if the parties concerned each agreed.[63] The 1905 Land Registration Regulation had obviously changed the substance of Taiwanese customary law.

Japan emphasized the requirement of registration in colonial Taiwan more than in metropolitan Japan. Under Japanese civil law, the rights over things concerning real estate were to be registered in the office for public information, and those rights could be asserted against a third party. However, even without registration, the transactions remained valid between the parties. Under the *ritsurei* civil law in Taiwan, the *tien* lease right, one of the *po-keng* rights in land, though not a right over things, was still required to be registered in the office.[64] Without the registration, any transfer of the four kinds of rights in land mentioned above became absolutely invalid. The colonial government ignored whether or not the Taiwanese could adapt to the requirement of registration; it was concerned only with expressing land relations in the register so that transactions in land could be conducted smoothly.

At the same time, the substantive contents of rights in Taiwanese customary law were changed by the 1905 regulation, although the terms for rights were left intact. The Land Registration Regulation granted the person having a *tien* pledge right or *t'ai* right a priority in receiving performance of an obligation from the sale of the land that given as security for the obligation. The provisions in Japan's Auction Law relating to pledge were applied, with modifications, to the enforcement of a *tien* pledge right, and those relating to mortgage were applied, with modifications, to *t'ai* rights.[65] As mentioned before, the holder of the *tien* pledge or *t'ai* right in original Taiwanese customary law usually had no power to sell or dispose of the objects of their rights to obtain payment of their claims. But the 1905 regulation gave them such a power. In addition, the *yeh-chu* right was to be subject to the provisions in Japanese civil law relating to modern ownership with necessary modifications.[66] Evidently, Japan was employing "old bottles" (*tien* pledge, *t'ai*, and *yeh-chu*) to accommodate "new wine" (similar rights in Japan's civil law).

Transformation into Western Civil Law Rights

By directly applying Japanese civil law to the Taiwanese, Japan comprehensively transformed all kinds of rights relating to real estate in Taiwanese customary law into Western civil law rights. On January 1, 1923, the Westernized Japanese Civil Code (excluding the books on Family and Succession) became applicable to the Taiwanese. Meanwhile, under the 1922 Exceptions of Applied

Statutes, preexisting Taiwanese customary civil law rights were to be treated as if they were comparable rights in the Japanese Civil Code after January 1, 1923, as follows: (1) the *yeh-chu* right was to be regarded as ownership (*shoyūken*); (2) the *ti-chi* right and the *po-keng* right, and *yung-tien* rights to buildings, bamboo, and trees with a duration of not less than twenty years were to be treated as superficies (*chijōken*); (3) the *po-keng* right and *yung-tien* rights to cultivate fields or to rear horses and cattle on others' land with a duration of not less than twenty years were to be treated as emphyteusis (*eikosakuken*); (4) the *tien* pledge right and *ch'i-keng-t'ai* right (which was actually one of the *tien* pledge rights because of the creditor's possession of the real estate) were to be treated as pledges (*shichiken*); (5) the *t'ai* right (except the *ch'i-kenq-t'ai* right) was to be treated as a mortgage (*teitōken*); (6) the *po-keng* right and *yung-tien* rights that did not meet the requirements in (2) and (3) above as well as the *tien* lease right were to be treated as leases (*chin-shakuken*).[67] Additionally, the requirement of official registration in Taiwan now had the same effect in private law as it did in Japan: it did not influence the relations between the parties, but it did affect the relations with third parties. Rights that had not been registered under the 1905 regulation, now had to be registered within one year from January 1, 1923; otherwise, they would not become rights over things and could not be asserted against a third party.[68]

Thus from the early era of Japanese rule, the substantive contents of rights relating to land under Taiwanese customary law were gradually altered by the Japanese authorities: (1) The *yeh-chu* right was almost transformed to modern ownership in 1905. (2) The *ti-chi* right was transformed into the superficies in 1923, but its unlimited duration had been reduced to one hundred years under the 1900 regulation.[69] (3) The *tien* lease right and the *yung-tien* right (the *po-keng* right) were divided into either a right over things or an obligation right (*saiken*) according to whether or not the duration of the right was "not less than twenty years." The rights over things were further divided into either superficies or emphyteusis according to the purposes of their creation. The duration of those rights that became superficies was limited to one hundred years in 1900, as stated above. The duration of those rights that became emphyteusis was also restricted to one hundred years under the 1900 regulation and then fifty years under the Japanese Civil Code.[70] (4) The *tien* pledge right was virtually transformed to the pledge in Japanese law in 1905. But after direct application of the Civil Code in 1923, the *tien* pledge right and *ch'i-keng t'ai* right in original Taiwanese customary law were limited in duration to not more than ten years.[71] (5) The *t'ai* right was virtually transformed into the mortgage in Japanese law in 1905 as well. (6) The legal relations that were

TABLE 5.1 Transformation of Land Rights in Taiwan, 1895–1945

Rights in Taiwanese customary law	Changes in 1900	Changes in 1905	Changes in 1923
ta-tsu right		abolished in 1904	
hsiao-tsu right		yeh-chu right ≒ ownership, R.	ownership, R.
ti-chi right	≤ 100 years		superficies, R.
tien lease right	≤ 20 years	po-keng right, R.	lease (≤ 20 yrs)
yung-tien right	≤ 100 years	po-keng right, R.	superficies, R., emphyteusis (≤ 50 yrs), R., or lease (≤ 20 years)
tien pledge right		tien pledge right ≒ pledge, R.	pledge (≤ 10 years), R.
t'ai right		t'ai right ≒ mortgage, R.	mortgage, R.
Ekiken of land	≤ 100 years		servitude, R.

NOTE: Those *tien* lease rights and *yung-tien* rights that were not regarded as *po-keng* rights under the 1905 Land Registration Regulation are omitted in this table. R. means that rights in land were to be registered so that transactions of rights became valid (1905–22) or could be asserted against third parties (1923–45). ≒ : similarity.

called *ekiken* of land under Taiwanese customary law by the Japanese became easements under the Japanese Civil Code after January 1, 1923, and thus were effective against third parties, as they had not been before (see table 5.1). In conclusion, under the policy of extension of Japanese law in the early 1920s, Japan was employing "new bottles" (the terminology of Japanese law, not Taiwanese customary law) to accommodate "new wine" (rights in Japanese law).

Effect on Taiwanese Society

The Japanese authorities spent a quarter century (1898–1922) gradually transforming the nature of the legal interests in land in Taiwan from those that had existed in traditional Chinese law to those recognized in a Western civil code. Furthermore, for another quarter of a century (1923–45), Japan effectively enforced this modern legal code. Inasmuch as the majority of Taiwanese were farmer-tenants and landlords, those changes in real estate law undoubtedly influenced most Taiwanese during this period. Today,

Taiwanese sometimes still use the terms from their old customs, but with the meanings given to them by the Japanese, which come from Japanese Western-style real property law. Two examples below illustrate such a development.

A hundred years ago, *kuo-hu* (literally, "changing of the holder") in Taiwanese custom meant transferring the interest of a *yeh-hu* (landholder, the same meaning as *yeh-chu*) or *hsiao-chu-hu*.[72] Presently, the Taiwanese who lived under Japanese rule, as well as their offspring, continue to use this term, but now they mean any transfer of the ownership of real estate or other property. No one is reminded of the *yeh-hu* or *hsiao-chu-hu* when he or she utters this word. The process whereby the *hsiao-chu-hu* was recognized as the *yeh-chu*, and the *yeh-chu* right then was transformed into the modern Japanese right of ownership has been completely forgotten.

When reading the advertisement column relating to loans in any newspapers in modern-day Taiwan, one often finds terms like *i-t'ai*, *erh-t'ai*, or *san-t'ai* (literally, the "first," "second," or "third" *t'ai*). *I-t'ai* refers to a mortgage with first priority in obtaining payment of the claim by the sale of the mortgaged immovable objects; *erh-tai* refers to a mortgage having second priority; *san-t'ai* refers to a mortgage having third priority. Accordingly, people use *t'ai* as a synonym for "mortgage" in modern Western civil law (which was created in 1905). They have no idea about the original *t'ai* relations, under which a creditor could not sell the immovable object for performance of his claim, and practically never inquire about who had the first, second, or third priority in obtaining payment under such a situation. In other words, the change of *t'ai* relations into the mortgage in the Japanese Western-style civil code in 1905, which had already been received by the Taiwanese under the Japanese rule, continues to prevail in postwar Taiwan.

WESTERNIZATION OF BUSINESS LAW

Law for Ordinary Commercial Transactions

Because Ch'ing Taiwan had a commoditized economy, a highly developed commercial contract law did exist at the time of the Japanese arrival. However, as Brockman has pointed out, because there was no effective means for formal legal enforcement, a sophisticated system for ordinary commercial transactions in Taiwan was developed to incorporate a mechanism of self-enforcement and self-execution directly into the contracts themselves, a mechanism that never worked perfectly.[73] Under Japanese rule, those traditional commercial contract rules were preserved, and two important elements were added to strengthen their enforcement: the Western concept of legal rights and the modern court. Thus, under Japanese rule a Taiwanese creditor could activate and control the process for performance of his claims under the old customs or, as a last resort, take the matter to the modern courts.

As they did with the old customs relating to real estate, Japanese judges always interpreted old Taiwanese commercial customs with the concepts in Japan's Westernized civil law. The commercial customs used by Taiwanese litigants may have differed from the Taiwanese customary law applied by colonial courts. However, for the sake of effective enforcement of their claims, Taiwanese litigants were willing to accept the court's "customary" law. Furthermore, because the Japanese dominated Taiwan's economy, Taiwanese businessmen were inevitably influenced by modern Japanese business law. In 1922, when preparations were being made to apply the Japanese Civil Code to the Taiwanese, the GGT reported to the Japanese central government that in Taiwan the legal obligations that arose in ordinary commercial transactions, such as sales, gifts, loans, and so on, were largely the same under Taiwanese customary law as under the Japanese Civil Code.[74]

Thus, partly because the Taiwanese themselves already had a developed contract law, modern civil law relating to ordinary commercial transactions was received rapidly and smoothly under Japanese rule.

Modern Capitalistic Commercial Law

The key question in Westernization of business law in an East Asian society with a Chinese legal tradition is how to adopt the commercial laws that were developed in modern Western capitalistic economies. In Japan's reception of modern European law, when the enforcement of European-style civil and commercial codes was suspended in the early 1890s, the provisions concerning companies, bills, and bankruptcy were nevertheless allowed to take effect because they were urgently needed.[75] This example fully illustrates the importance of these laws in a modern society with a capitalistic economy.

Modern Company Law. The traditional institution that was most similar to a modern company was the *ho-ku* (literally, "combined shares"). Under Taiwanese customary law, *ho-ku* was a contract whereby several people agreed to pool contributions for managing an enterprise. As a rule, a *ho-ku* contract included a statement of the purposes of the enterprise, the name of firm, the names of contributors (*ku-tung*), their individual contributions, and so on, and was signed by the contributors. Then, using the assets of the *ho-ku,* managers did business in a fixed office using the firm name.[76] After the annexation of Taiwan to Japan, some Taiwanese *ho-ku*, especially those running industries, were influenced by certain characteristics of Japan's modern companies. For instance, some of them practically named their firms "companies" (*kaisha*) and organized "shareholders' meetings." Such *ho-ku* can be called "new-style *ho-ku*."⁷⁷

Whereas a company (*kaisha*) was legally considered to be a juristic person, under Taiwanese customary law conceptually a *ho-ku* did not have the same status. The *ho-ku* assets therefore belonged to all contributors, and managers of firms worked on behalf of all the contributors rather than on behalf of the *ho-ku*. Thus, in litigation relating to the enterprise, all contributors were parties.⁷⁸ In fact, individual contributors had close ties with their *ho-ku*. The share of a contributor might not be transferred to others without approval of all contributors.⁷⁹ The GGT court also held in the 1910s that every contributor to a *ho-ku* was liable for the obligations of the *ho-ku* jointly and severally.⁸⁰

When Japanese civil and commercial laws were not applied to the Taiwanese, the GGT court ordinarily employed the legal theory of partnership (*kumiai*) in Japanese civil law to interpret *ho-ku* relations. However, some precedents concerning *ho-ku* were not decided according to the provisions of Japanese partnership law. For example, a partner in Japanese civil law was not liable for the obligations of the partnership jointly and severally unless the obligations had arisen from commercial acts (transactions) under Japanese commercial law.⁸¹ Therefore, the *ho-ku* in this period of Japanese rule was a unique institution governed by Taiwanese customary law.⁸²

If one of the shareholders of a *ho-ku* was Japanese, the *ho-ku* could legally incorporate as a modern company under Japanese commercial law because civil and commercial matters involving any Japanese were to conform to Japanese civil and commercial law rather than Taiwanese customary law. Therefore, Taiwanese investors sometimes invited a Japanese to join their enterprise so that they could legally incorporate a Western-style company. In light of such a situation, the colonial court decided that such a Taiwanese company would lose its status as a juristic person if the Japanese shareholder left the company.⁸³ In addition, any *ho-ku* (including the new-style *ho-ku* mentioned above) organized under Taiwanese customary law was legally prohibited from using the name "company."⁸⁴

After 1923, the enterprises organized by Taiwanese only were legally allowed to select either the modern company or the *ho-ku* as the legal form for their business enterprises. After Japanese civil and commercial law was applied to the Taiwanese, a Taiwanese had in law the same right to incorporate a company as a resident Japanese had had for two decades.⁸⁵ However, after 1923, a *ho-ku* was directly governed by the provisions of partnership in Japanese civil and commercial law.

Taiwanese had already incorporated modern companies to do business during the Japanese period. Because a modern company is legally a juristic person, the manager can conveniently represent his company in commercial transactions. Additionally, a shareholder of a joint-stock company (*kabushiki kaisha*) is not liable for any of the company's obligations. Because of these advantages, many Taiwanese of course wanted to incorporate a modern company. Discrimination discouraged some Taiwanese from doing so. After the new law became effective in 1923, the situation was much improved. Still, in 1926, the GGT exercised its powers to hinder a large joint-stock company in the trust industry, incorporated by Taiwanese dissidents, from doing business.[86] Nevertheless, exactly because the GGT in law could not forbid the incorporation of a Taiwanese company, it had to harass this company and prevent its activity indirectly. Moreover, in colonial Taiwan, although the Japanese dominated large enterprises, the Taiwanese dominated medium and small enterprises.[87] There is no example to show that that GGT also interfered with the incorporation of medium or small companies whose shareholders were all Taiwanese. In fact, when Japan's Limited Company Law,[88] which was designed for the medium or small enterprise, was applied to Taiwan in 1940, a regulation was at the same time promulgated to allow the number of Taiwanese shareholders in a limited company to exceed the fifty-person limit in the law, if this situation resulted from the Taiwanese succession system under which all sons had the right to inherit the deceased shareholder's property.[89] The GGT obviously acknowledged that Taiwanese might incorporate their medium or small enterprises as modern limited companies.

Japanese modern company law had a considerable effect on Taiwanese society, although that effect should not be exaggerated. There are no figures to show how many modern companies there were whose shareholders were all, or mostly, Taiwanese during the Japanese period. Of the entire capital investment in modern companies, the Japanese investment was more than the Taiwanese.[90] But there were not necessarily fewer Taiwanese shareholders; possibly there were even more. In fact, the majority of Japanese holdings were controlled by a very few large Japanese shareholders, and the total population of Japanese in colonial Taiwan was very small (6 percent at most). When the number of modern companies rapidly increased in Taiwan in the 1930s and early 1940s,[91] the majority of shareholders in those new companies were possibly Taiwanese, who now were entitled to incorporate modern companies. In any event, the GGT did not want Taiwanese modern companies to be so prosperous that Japanese economic interests in the colony were threatened. The continuity of *ho-ku* and new-style *ho-ku* also slowed down the development of Taiwanese modern companies. Even today, a few Taiwanese businessmen still consider that their "companies," which are incorporated under the modern company law, are partnerships, like the new-style *ho-ku* during the Japanese period, in which the entity of *ho-ku* (company) was not independent of the contributors (shareholders).[92]

Modern Law of Bills of Exchange. Taiwan old customs allowed for some kinds of bills of exchange, but they seldom could be transferred merely by endorsement or delivery. In Ch'ing Taiwan, the *hui-p'iao* (literally, "bill for remittance") was frequently used in the trade between Taiwan and the Chinese mainland. To receive a sum of money from a debtor who lived in a distance place, a drawer of a *hui-p'iao* ordinarily issued a bill to a drawee, requesting that the debtor (the payor in the bill) pay a certain sum of money on a future date to the payee, who was nominated by the drawee and lived in the same place as the debtor. On issuing this bill, the drawer received this sum of money from the drawee; the drawee then obtained reimbursement because the payee he nominated would receive the same sum of money from the payor in the bill. A sum of money was thus remitted to a distant place. In addition, for local business or ordinary transactions between two people, Ch'ing Taiwan had *p'ing-tan* (literally, "paper for evidence") or *chien-tan* (literally, "paper for presentation"). The drawer of *p'ing-tan* himself promised to pay a certain sum in money or deliver a certain quantity of other things to the specified (sometimes, not specified) payee upon presentation of the paper. In contrast, the drawer of the *chien-tan* ordered a third party to pay a certain sum in money or deliver a certain quantity of other things to the specified payee. These three kinds of bills are similar in form to bills of exchange (*kawase-tegata*), promissory notes (*yakusoku-tegata*), and checks (*kogitte*), respectively, in Japan's Westernized commercial law. With the exception of the *p'ing-tan* that did not specify the payee, they lacked an important characteristic of Japanese modern negotiable instruments (*tegata*)—the negotiability of bills, through which a bill can legally be transferred by endorsement or delivery. Under the Japanese negotiable instrument law, a holder (or endorsee) of a bill could prove his rights by continuity of endorsements, exercise his rights according to the meaning of the words in the bill, and make claim against endorsers, the issuer, and other parties liable under the bill when the bill was not paid on the due date. In contrast, Taiwanese traditional bills were ordinarily only evidences of obligations between specified parties.[93]

As with incorporation, not until 1923 could the Taiwanese in law extensively employ modern negotiable instruments.[94] Before 1923, Taiwanese could only make use of Japanese modern negotiable instruments when one of parties was Japanese. Those Taiwanese who had business relations with the Japanese residing in Taiwan or out of the island thus became aware of these Western-style negotiable instruments. Finally, after 1923, the Taiwanese were legally allowed to use Japanese modern negotiable instruments. Inasmuch as the term *tegata* appeared in a novel written by a Taiwanese under Japanese rule,[95] it would seem that in the 1920s, common people in Taiwan already used Japanese *tegata* as an instrument of payment. Today, the names of these old bills are not used in Taiwan except for *hui-p'iao*, which means either an evidence of remitting a certain sum in money or a bill of exchange. In addition, some Taiwanese with Japanese experience continue to use the Japanese term *tegata*, pronounced in their own Chinese dialect (Southern Fukienese), to refer to negotiable instruments. It is safe to say that most Taiwanese learned the concepts of modern negotiable instruments from Japanese Western-style commercial law.

Modern Bankruptcy Law. According to Taiwanese custom, when a businessman's assets were insufficient to pay his debts, either the debtor himself or creditors would assemble a creditors' meeting, at which the debtor had to explain his assets and liabilities and the causes of insolvency and ask the creditors to prolong the time of performance or remove some parts of his obligations. If the creditors disapproved of this proposal or the debtor could not perform the approved proposals later, the process of *tao-hao* (literally, "fallen shop") started. All properties belonging to the debtor declared *tao-hao* went into a special estate managed and sold by the creditors to evenly pay off the debts. After the *tao-hao* estate was distributed to all the creditors, the claims for unpaid portions were deemed extinguished.[96]

Japan's Western-style bankruptcy law has also applied to the Taiwanese since January 1, 1923.[97] In contrast to the traditional *tao-hao*, bankruptcy proceedings in modern Western law are controlled by the court. But the involvement of the court makes the proceedings more expensive so that the creditors receive less money. Furthermore, the waiving of unpaid debts, a great advantage to debtors under Western-style bankruptcy law, was also available under *tao-hao*. Not surprisingly, it seems that few Taiwanese resorted to modern bankruptcy proceedings during the Japanese period.[98] Even today, Taiwanese businessmen usually apply traditional concepts of *tao-hao* to deal with insolvency.[99]

LIMITED WESTERNIZATION OF FAMILY AND SUCCESSION LAW

Probably because family relations and succession were governed by Taiwanese customs during the entire period of Japanese rule, it is usually thought that Taiwanese family and succession law was never modernized by Japan.[100] One commentator even argued that, influenced by the feudal nature of Japan's status law, the indigenous Taiwanese status law was unfortunately led backward by Japan.¹⁰¹ However customary law for Taiwanese family and succession matters, being free from the restrictions of a written civil code, could be changed by court precedents. Therefore the decisions of the colonial courts have to be carefully reviewed before any comments on Taiwanese family and succession matters under Japanese rule can be made. It is possibly true that Japan's status law maintained certain feudal ideas and thus influenced colonial courts' decisions, which were made by Japanese judges; however, the Japanese family and succession law was also influenced by Western law, and Taiwanese status law was possibly affected in the same way.

Family System

Japanese-style Head of House. Under old Taiwanese customs, the leadership of a family included the family head (*chia-chang*) and elders (*tsun-chang*). The powers of the head of the family and the powers of elders were conceptually different. Because of the needs in actual common life, the family head managed family affairs, especially the family estate, and represented the family in dealing with the government and nonfamily members. In practice, the position of family head was usually, but not always, undertaken by the eldest male in a family.¹⁰² The elders supervised and protected the bodies and properties of the younger people in the family; these duties were derived from ethical principles. During the early period of Japanese rule, both of these positions were recognized by the GGT court.¹⁰³

The 1906 Taiwan Household Regulation for the first time brought Japan's unique concept of head of house (*koshu*) to Taiwan.¹⁰⁴ It should be noted that the regulation was merely administrative law and therefore did not regulate family relations and succession in private law. According to Taiwan's civil law, Taiwanese family and succession matters were to conform to Taiwanese customs. As a result, in the law concerning household registration the head of house actually meant the head of house under the Japanese Civil Code, who had power to approve the entry or exit to or from the household, order house members to leave, approve the marriage and adoption of house members, allow members to create a new house, and so on.¹⁰⁵ But in civil law, those provisions relating to the Japanese head of house were not applicable to the Taiwanese, since they were not Taiwanese customs.

Japanese colonial courts, however, gradually made Taiwanese customary status law adopt the concept of the Japanese head of house, which was used in Taiwan's household registration law.¹⁰⁶ In 1911 the colonial court employed the concept of head of house in a Taiwanese lawsuit relating to family matters. Under old Taiwanese customs, parents could exile their son from the family according to "the powers of elders," although such a practice was not provided in the Ch'ing Code.[107] The colonial court thus considered that according to "the powers of head of house," the head of the house might decide to exile any house members who did not obey his instructions.[108] Then, in a decision in 1920, the GGT court held that only the eldest in the family could qualify as family head under Taiwanese customary law. The court also decided that the Japanese-style head of house was the same as the family head in Taiwan, who was the leader in a family.[109] Accordingly, both the powers of the family head and the powers of elders were granted to the same person, who was also called "head of house."[110] The same year, the court further held that the concept of the head of house introduced by the 1906 regulation was new in Taiwan and therefore was not governed by old customs; the rights and obligations of the head of house should be decided by legal theory insofar as they were not contrary to Taiwanese customary law.[111] "Legal theory" meant the provisions relating to head of house in Japanese civil law.

After 1923, although the GGT did not extend Japanese family law to directly enforce the Japanese household system in Taiwan, the colonial courts considered that the idea of head of house had become a part of "Taiwanese customs" because of the implementation of the household regulation for nearly two decades. They further tried to employ as much Japanese family law as possible to regulate a Taiwanese head of house. An influential Japanese judge specializing in Taiwanese family and succession law expressed his view in 1938 that, with very few exceptions, the customary law concerning Taiwanese the family system could be generally decided by the principles in the book of Family in the Japanese Civil Code as well as the spirit of the Japanese Household Registration Law. Therefore, under the Taiwanese customary law as interpreted by the Japanese authorities, when the original head of house died, the eldest son would become the head of house, by which he had power to govern and represent the house.[112]

In any event, the powers of a Taiwanese head of house under the Taiwanese customary law was not exactly the same as those of a Japanese head of house under Japanese civil law. For example, unlike his Japanese counterpart, the eldest son, who alone could become head of house, could not exclusively inherit all family properties.[113] In addition, some rights of the head of house explicitly provided in Japanese civil law were not yet clearly granted to the Taiwanese head of house.[114] Because of the differences between a Taiwanese head of house under customary law and a Japanese head of house, the GGT considered it necessary to circumvent customary law and directly apply the books of Family and Succession in the Japanese Civil Code to Taiwan. In fact, the powers of the Taiwanese head of house basically derived from original positions of family head and elders under old Taiwanese customs which were deeply influenced by the Chinese legal tradition. The Japanese authorities merely combined these two kinds of powers into the hands of one person, as usually happened in Ch'ing Taiwan.

Division of Family. Under Taiwanese customs, a family was a body whose members shared a life in common. As a unit of production and consumption, the family was established and maintained on the basis of the family estate. In the joint family, comprising parents, their unmarried children, and their married sons (more than one) and sons' wives and children, the family estate was jointly owned by the prospective new families led by the sons (*fang*); these would usually become independent family units after the eldest male in the original family died. The division of the original (joint) family depended on the partition of the family estate as well as the separation of domicile (customarily called the division of stove) of original family members. However, in Ch'ing Taiwan the partition of the family estate and separation of domicile were in principle not permitted when parents were alive unless the parents consented. It is also to be noted that such joint families were factually a minority in Taiwanese society.[115]

During the early period of Japanese rule, the colonial court generally followed this Taiwanese custom in dealing with the division of Taiwanese families. First, the colonial court maintained the principle that when parents, especially the father, were alive, the family estate could not be partitioned.[116] The family division was closely connected with the partition of the family estate. The GGT court in a 1909 decision held that as a consequence of the partition of the family estate, the family had of course been divided.[117] Moreover, the family division that derived from the partition of the family estate and separation of domicile was effective, even if it had not yet been recorded in the household registry.[118] A decision in 1924 also insisted that when the joint family was divided, a new family took away its share in the original family estate, and thus the head of this new family lost the rights of inheritance from his parents staying in the original family.[119]

During the late period of Japanese rule, family division in civil law was determined by the consent of the head of house, similar to the consent of parents in Ch'ing days. In fact, during the early period in some civil lawsuits the colonial courts had ruled that the head of the house had to consent before anyone could leave a household to establish a new one,[120] and that even though the family estate was already partitioned, the head of the original house did not have to allow the establishment of a new house.[121] In 1930, the GGT Higher Court for the first time abandoned the required connection between family division and the partition of the family estate, holding that if a new family was capable of independently making money for their own livelihood and if the parents approved, the new family could be divided from the original joint family in spite of the fact that the family estate was not yet partitioned.¹²² A decision in 1936 confirmed the rule that according to the customary law the division of a family should be initiated by family members and consented to by the head of (the original) house.¹²³ Another decision in the same year further pointed out that the division of a family, even without registration in the household registry, became effective when the head of (the original) house consented to it.¹²⁴ Hence, the key requirement for family division became the consent of the head of house. The facts of the partition of the family estate and separation of domicile (including the separation of the two households in household registers) were merely used to give rise to a presumption of such consent.¹²⁵ Consequently, under Japanese rule a Taiwanese family, whose customary function and identity were fundamentally economic, became in civil law a group of people controlled by the head of the house.¹²⁶

These changes in the Japanese-style head of house and family division added few, if any, new feudal-style elements to Taiwanese status law, although modern democratic status law was certainly excluded from the Taiwanese family system under Japanese rule. The superiority of the elder and the male to the younger and the female was prevalent in Taiwan's old customs concerning the family system. That was substantively similar to the Japanese household system. What the colonial court did was to maintain the Taiwanese conservative family system in the terms of Japan's family law (for example, Japanese head of house). Modern Western family law, which emphasizes equality among all members in a family, was therefore not introduced to Taiwan, as it was to prewar Japan.

Marriage and Adoption

With regard to Taiwanese marriage and adoption, Japanese judges on the one hand continued to support Taiwanese conservative customs but on the other hand sometimes modified old customs through the concepts of freedom and equality in modern law.

Requirements for Marriage. According to old Taiwanese custom, parents decided marriage contracts. The GGT Court therefore held in 1908 that a contract of marriage could not be made merely based on the agreement of the parties concerned (the bride and groom), but should be under the direction of the parents of the parties.¹²⁷ However, in 1919 the court ruled that a marriage decided on by parents was invalid because the bride and groom did not agree.[128] This idea that the prospective bride and groom were the main parties in a marriage contract, was seldom recognized in old Taiwanese custom.

Money was an important concern under Taiwanese custom. When a man wanted to get married to a woman he had to give her parents a sum of money as bridewealth (*p'in-chin*). A marriage was thus sometimes like a sale.[129] The GGT court continued to recognize bridewealth as a customary ritual requirement in a marriage,[130] although the claim to recover bridewealth in the case of divorce was not permitted as discussed below. On the other hand, the court considered the exchange of money under marriage contracts invalid on the grounds that it contradicted "public order and good morals."[131] Based on the same reason, the custom of selling, giving, pledging (*tien* pledge), or mortgaging (*t'ai*) one's wife was held to be invalid.[132] A covenant in which the bridewealth was paid only in part, and if the rest was not paid, the marriage ended, was also held invalid.[133]

Kinds of Marriage. Taiwanese customs allowed for some exceptional marriages in addition to ordinary marriage. A family that wanted to maintain a livelihood, secure sons to inherit a family name, or keep a daughter at home (women normally became members of the husband's family when they married), sometimes invited a man to enter into their family. A man invited to marry a daughter who stayed in her own family was called an "invited son-in-law" (*chao-hsü*); if the bride was a widow who stayed in the family of her former husband after the marriage, the new husband was an "invited husband" (*chao-fu*). Such "invited" men did not change their original surnames to the wife's surname and had no right to inherit the estate of the wife's family.[134] Accordingly, they were equivalent neither to the Japanese adoption of a son-in-law (*mukoyōshi*), in which the husband was also an adopted son and therefore had the right to inherit the estate of the wife's family, nor to Japanese uxorilocal marriage (*nyūfu*), in which the husband became the head of house of the wife's family and enjoyed comprehensive powers as such.[135] Inasmuch as the husbands in these two Japanese marriages, like the Taiwanese invited son-in-law and invited husband, had to enter the wife's family, however, it is not surprising that Japanese judges recognized the validity of Taiwanese invited sons-in-law and invited husbands.[136]

According to old customs, a Taiwanese, to save a large sum of bridewealth, often adopted a young girl who was expected to become the wife of his specified or nonspecified son in the future. This relationship of adopted daughter-in-law (*t'ung-yang-hsi*) was recognized by the GGT court. Even when the prospective husband died, an adopted daughter-in-law could not leave the adopting family; she could, however, be "transferred" to another family.[137] In 1931 the court held that the specified prospective husband could marry another girl; under this circumstance the relationship of adopted daughter-in-law should be ended because it had lost its original purpose.[138] There was never a decision holding that an adopted daughter-in-law could reject marriage to her prospective husband.

Another controversial form of exceptional marriage in Taiwan under Japanese rule was marriage to a concubine. In traditional Taiwan, a married man sometimes married someone in addition to his original wife, either to secure sons or to satisfy his desire for more than one wife. The subsequent wife (or wives) was a concubine. Early in 1906, the GGT court decided that marriage to a concubine was not contrary to public order and good morals in Taiwan and hence was valid.[139] In 1922 the court changed the old customs by holding that, according to "legal theory," since the husband could terminate the relationship without any restraints, the concubine should have the same right to release herself from the relationship. Therefore, without any causes for divorce, a concubine was entitled to end the concubine relationship.[140]

Divorce. In Ch'ing Taiwan, an agreement to divorce was allowed, but it was to be approved by the parents of the husband and wife. When divorce occurred all or part of the original bridewealth was usually recovered by the groom's family. Moreover, in old Taiwanese customs, a wife could not actively demand divorce.[141]

In 1908, the colonial court held that an agreement to divorce had to be approved by the parents of the divorcing partners as well as by the husband and wife themselves.[142] In 1912, the court further supported the old custom that when the husband died, the wife could not leave the husband's family unless the husband's parents agreed.[143] In addition, the GGT court originally allowed the bridewealth to be recovered when divorce occurred unless a special covenant in the marriage contract provided otherwise.[144] A decision in 1917, however, denied the right to recover bridewealth on the ground that a husband who in practice negotiated how much bridewealth could be recovered and then decided whether or not to consent to divorce actually looked upon marriage as a sale and bridewealth as the price.[145] In fact, in 1916, the court had already considered any agreement to allow divorce on the condition of paying a certain amount of money to be void.[146]

More important, under Japanese rule, a wife might apply to the court for a divorce. Although a wife was not granted a divorce merely because her husband was married to concubines, she was granted a decision for divorce, for example, when her husband committed a "dishonest crime," refused to reside with her, or married another woman as wife (not as concubine) and lived with this woman.[147] Generally speaking, the reasons for filing a suit for divorce under the Taiwanese customary law were almost the same as those under the Japanese Civil Code.[148] During the Japanese period suits for divorce in courts were ordinarily brought by the wife[149] because she, as the weaker partner in the marriage, could not gain a divorce agreement from her husband but had to search for help from the state authority.

Adoption. Adoption was prevalent in the immigrant society of Taiwan, and people adopted not only boys with the same surname but also boys with different surnames. The reasons for an adoption included continuation of the memorial service of the *fang* or increasing the number of descendants. Most adoption in Taiwan was conducted by transferring a sum of money to the adopted child's original parents. This practice extended to the adoption of girls.[150]

The GGT court in a 1908 decision still recognized an adoption contract in which an adopted son was "bought outright."[151] In 1920, however, the court expressly decided that the practice of buying other people's children was contrary to public order and good morals and thus became invalid.[152] Another innovative decision in 1929 held that an adoption should be agreed to by the adopting parents and the adopted child, who was presented by his original parents, rather than the adopting father and original father as in the old custom.[153]

Succession System. The fundamental principles for property succession in old Taiwanese customs were maintained by the Japanese authorities. In Taiwan, unlike Japan, all sons were entitled to inherit family properties under the customary law. The GGT never tried to change this rule, even when it attempted to apply Japanese family law to the Taiwanese in the late period of Japanese rule.[154] Although a daughter had no right to inherit the family properties of her deceased parents under Taiwanese customary law, she to a certain degree received her share in the original family estate when she got married.[155] In this respect, the Taiwanese customary succession system is closer to modern Western law than the prewar Japanese succession system, in which only the eldest son was entitled to inherit the family properties.

However, the Taiwanese customary succession law was not completely free from the effect of Western law. Because the Japanese Civil Code relating to succession was not applied to the Taiwanese, many Continental European succession rules included in the code were not directly applied in Taiwan. But the colonial court sometimes applied those Western succession rules in the Japanese Civil Code to Taiwanese lawsuits in the name of "legal theory." For instance, Japanese civil law provided the system of limited inheritance, by which an heir might limit the payment of the deceased's debts to the extent of the property acquired by the inheritance, and the right to waive an inheritance. These two provisions, adopted from Continental European law, did not exist in old Taiwanese customs, under which a son was responsible for all the debts of his deceased father. However, in 1936 the General Meeting of Judges in the GGT Higher Court considered that the provisions in the Japanese Civil Code relating to the system of limited inheritance and the right to waive an inheritance might be regarded as "legal theory" and hence were applied to the Taiwanese.[156]

Social Effects of Family and Succession Law

It was not an easy task for the state authorities to immediately change the customs on family and succession. Early in 1917, the contract for female indentured servants was held invalid.[157] But an official report in 1931 stated that people frequently used the term "adopted daughter" to hire female indentured servants.[158]

In fact, the effect of the court's decisions on the Westernization of family and succession matters was relatively restricted. If parties did not bring their family disputes to courts, the courts could not easily change the behavior of the people. Litigation for divorce was recognized by law, but most divorce was effected by agreement rather than judicial decisions.[159] Furthermore, inasmuch as the degree of Westernization of the Taiwanese customary law relating to family and succession matters was not high, we can only presume that the actual societal Westernization was lower. For example, the existence of concubines reflects the superiority of males in society. The colonial court did not wield state authority to invalidate this relationship, but in 1922 granted a concubine the right to leave her husband at will. But the effects of this innovation were in practice very limited. The number of concubines in Taiwan during the 1930s actually increased rather than diminished.[160]

SUMMARY

Western civil law gradually entered Taiwanese society under Japanese rule. The old Taiwanese customs under Chinese legal traditions at first were analyzed and expressed in terms of the Western concepts of legal rights and interpreted by Westernized courts within the framework of Western law. The substantive contents of the Taiwanese customary law recognized by the Japanese authorities were therefore to a certain extent different from Taiwanese customs in the Ch'ing period. Some colonial statutes further pushed Taiwanese civil law to be more Western-oriented. Although a modern civil code specially designed for Taiwan was not enacted, after 1923 another Western-style civil code originally enacted for Japan was put into effect in Taiwan, except for its family and succession law.

The development of the law relating to real estate in Taiwan is an important and illustrative example of Westernization of Taiwanese civil law. At first old Taiwanese customs concerning real estate were incorporated into a legal system based on legal rights. Then certain kinds of civil rights in land under Taiwanese customary law were modified to be similar to the rights recognized in Japan's Westernized civil law. After the Japanese Civil Code was applied to Taiwan in 1923, all the Taiwanese customary rules relating to real estate were replaced by relevant modern rights in the Japanese Civil Code. By the end of Japanese rule, Taiwanese society had largely received Western-style law relating to real estate.

Because the law for ordinary commercial transactions was already well developed in the Ch'ing period, traditional Taiwanese commercial contract law was merged smoothly into a modern civil law system. On the other hand, the Taiwanese were originally less familiar with some modern capitalistic commercial laws, such as the laws relating to companies, bills of exchange, and bankruptcy. The general population, however, gradually became acquainted with much of the law of negotiable instruments and got some ideas of company law, but few of them knew about Western-style bankruptcy law.

Compared to other civil matters, the Taiwanese law regarding family relations and succession was influenced by Western law under Japanese rule only to a limited extent. It is not fair to say that Japan never imposed Western legal concepts upon Taiwanese family law. Based on "public order and good morals," the colonial court invalidated some traditional customs in the Taiwanese family system. In the name of "legal theory," some Western family and succession laws that had been adopted by the Japanese Civil Code were applied to the Taiwanese. However, Japan's status law generally had the same conservative nature as old Taiwanese customs. Not surprisingly, then, unlike the laws relating to real estate, Japan did not endeavor to effect much change in old Taiwanese customs on family relations and succession. But it should be taken into account that family and succession law was not particularly amenable to alteration by the state.

6 / Appraisal and Legacy

To appraise the results of Japan's colonial rule on Taiwan is in itself a controversial move. As Mark R. Peattie has told us, in connection with the colonial economy, some scholars concentrate on Japanese economic activities in the empire that collectively merit the term "exploitation," whereas others emphasize the creation of modern economic infrastructures in the colonies; a conclusion on which most might agree is that there was a mixed pattern of development and exploitation.[1] The situation is similar when assessing Japan's colonial law. This law is sometimes described as brutally suppressive, sometimes praised for establishing a modern legal order. Scholars tend to find what they want to find. Acknowledging that the results of colonial rule are mixed, we would do better to observe both the good and the ill effects of Japan's legal reform on Taiwan. An understanding of both the positive and negative aspects of this Japan-led legal reform on Taiwan can help a legal historian explore where Taiwan's law came from, where it is today, and where it should be going.

APPRAISAL OF THE JAPAN-LED LEGAL REFORM

Irrespective of its motives, Japan indeed conducted legal reform in Taiwan during its fifty-year rule. The core of this reform was Westernization of law, a process many non-Western countries went through at that time. The process and results of Japan's modernization of Taiwan's law, especially civil and criminal law, have been discussed in detail. In this part, I appraise Japan's legal reform in Taiwan from two directions: (1) What merits or flaws can be found in Japan's role as reformer of Taiwanese law, and would other regimes have done better? (2) What advantageous or disadvantageous conditions for Westernization of law already existed in colonial Taiwan?

Japan as a Reformer

Merits. Affinities of culture between Japan and Taiwan gave this non-Western colonialist power many advantages in understanding Taiwanese customs and then transforming them into Western-style legal rules. In the early period of French rule in Cochinchina, the French encountered great difficulty in translating the Vietnamese legal code and establishing a legal system for the native people to fill the vacuum left by Vietnamese mandarins.[2] Compared to that case, we can understand how much more easily the Japanese, who shared traditional Chinese culture with the Taiwanese, could grasp the meanings of Taiwanese customs and rapidly establish their own courts to deal with Taiwanese lawsuits so quickly after arriving on the island. Furthermore, with more than twenty years of experience in learning Western law before taking possession of Taiwan, Japan had its own legal experts versed in Western law who nevertheless were also imbued with Chinese traditions. As we see in colonial civil law, those Japanese legal experts skillfully Westernized many of Taiwan's old customs and finally transformed them into Westernized forms.

The Japanese also had a unique asset that other powers did not have, that is, their Meiji reform experiences. The Meiji reform was in essence a process by which Western law was imposed on an East Asian society influenced by Chinese traditions. By the time Japan defeated Ch'ing China, acquired Taiwan, and thereby demonstrated its acquisition of Western military technique, the Japanese had also successfully copied Western institutions to establish a modern state that nevertheless retained many traditional elements. Japan applied this model to modernize another traditional East Asian society in Taiwan.

In establishing their colonial legal system, the Japanese at first largely followed the methods they had used in the early Meiji era. Although after 1898 many Western colonial laws and Chinese traditional laws were adopted in Taiwan's colonial legislation, Meiji experiences still deeply influenced Japanese legal reforms on Taiwan (as, for example, in the clarification of ownership of land). More important, as a result of the Meiji reform Japan had a large number of legal professionals, including a body of judges with the idea of independent adjudication, who were able to implement Westernized positive law in Taiwan. The serious deficiency of legal professionals in the early Meiji era was thus avoided in Taiwan's legal reform. In addition, the Meiji reform established a strong modern government in Japan, and a similar efficient centralized government was duplicated on the island of Taiwan. Generally speaking, after 1902 public order in Taiwan became stable under the control of the Japanese colonial government. There were thus about forty tranquil years to allow some Western law to penetrate Taiwanese society. In contrast, contemporary China also tried to receive Western law, but there was no powerful centralized administration in that vast territory during either the late Ch'ing period or the Republican era. With incessant wars, China in practice was not able to establish a governmental system including courts that could effectively administer the entire country; as a result, China's Western-style codes existed on paper but functioned only in parts of the country.

Flaws. On the other hand, the Japanese regime was not really qualified to administer Western law. Prewar Japan itself carried out merely the formalistic rule-by-law, a commitment to administration under law but with a complete lack of legal limitations on law-making power and formalistic limits on administrative power, rather than Western rule-of-law, whereby both official discretion and policy formulation are limited by law in favor of fundamental human rights and the electoral process.[3] Japan was of course unable to give Taiwan any more than it itself had, but some Westernized institutions such as universal suffrage and the administrative court system, which existed in metropolitan Japan, were not introduced into colonial Taiwan. The question is, if the reformer had been a Western power that respected the rule of law in its own country, would it have implemented this principle in Taiwan? The answer unfortunately tends to be no; history has shown that what a Western power had at home it did not necessarily give to its colonial peoples. France, which declared its ambition to spread civilization to its colonies, did not want to further politically modernize its colonies in African when African intellectuals demanded that it do so.[4] The United States, which was originally a British colony and finally became an independent state, in 1916 promised colonized Filipinos their own independent state but in 1921 retreated from this promise and maintained a colonial system.[5]

So the Japanese should not be blamed merely because of their failure to enforce modern Western law. Like most Western powers in their colonies, Japan did not entirely implement its Westernized codes in Taiwan, especially in the first half of Japanese rule. But it was not practical or reasonable to demand that Japanese rulers immediately enforce all of their Westernized codes in Taiwan when they had just arrived on the island in 1895. Japan had prepared to enforce Western law for at least twenty years, and it was doubtful that before this Taiwanese society had favorable conditions allowing for the immediate application of Japan's modern codes. If those codes had been applied in Taiwan, they probably would have become either empty words or sources of the people's hatred. Factually, there is no absolute answer to such questions as whether a certain Western law is "better" and therefore should be enforced to replace old Taiwanese customs. If the old ought to be replaced, should a statute be enacted or should the new law be introduced through common law? When should the new law begin to be enforced—immediately or after a transitional period? It is to be noted that contemporary Taiwanese jurists themselves have different opinions about those questions (see chapter 2).

The real flaw of Japanese implementation of Western law was that the policy decision about whether Western law was to be enforced in Taiwan was made by the Japanese rulers on the basis of their colonial interests. The Taiwanese had no power to select their own methods, so that their interests were subordinated to the interests of the rulers. Such a procolonialist attitude resulted in differences in the implementation of Western law in Taiwan and Japan. This attitude—that the interests of the rulers were the most important consideration in policy decisions—was always adopted by colonialist or monarchical regimes. From the standpoint of Taiwan's history, the Japanese government was probably not any worse than other regimes. A colonialist government like the Dutch and Spanish (1624–62), an independent Han Chinese government like the Cheng regime (1662–83), and a local government of Chinese empire like the Ch'ing regime on Taiwan (1683–1895) all pursued the rulers' interests in enacting law for Taiwan. Had the 1895 Republic of Formosa composed of former Ch'ing officers succeeded in establishing a government on Taiwan, the leaders of the Republic, who were accustomed to monarchical governance, might not have had the will or ability to modernize the legal system for the Taiwanese people. Nevertheless, Japan cannot escape the label "oppressor" just because others might have been as bad or worse.

Original Conditions of Taiwan

Taiwan actually showed great potential for receiving legal reform in the nineteenth century. Basically, Taiwanese society was composed of Han Chinese immigrants who had been settled on the island for only one or two hundred years and thus, unlike the inhabitants in the Chinese mainland or Korea, they were less bound by long-standing political and social traditions.[6] Meanwhile, Taiwan, unlike Korea and the inland areas of China but like Japan, did develop extensive commercialization of agriculture and prosperous international trade with the West in the late nineteenth century.[7]

At that time the real obstacle for Taiwanese modernization of law was the lack of a centralized authority capable of implementing legal reform over the entire island. In Ch'ing Taiwan there was no political authority that could effectively push legal reform. Disrespect for the law and disturbances of public order were commonplace on the island. In addition, Taiwan's inhabitants were divided into four ethnic groups that distrusted one another, and there was no common Taiwanese identity to inspire them to improve the law of Taiwan as a whole.

Japan, with its successful reform experience, met this defect of the

Taiwanese in 1895. This newly emerged Asian power arbitrarily but effectively modernized Taiwan's legal system. Having little choice, the Taiwanese people obeyed Japan's leadership. After not too long, the pragmatic Taiwanese learned of the advantages in those modern institutions and shared in them.

Korea's case is a good contrast to Taiwan's. The most significant difference between Korea and Taiwan was that when the Japanese conquerors came, the Koreans already had their own government, working to receive modern law, but the Taiwanese did not. Before the annexation of Korea by Japan in 1910, the Korean people had been unified in an independent nation with a highly developed culture, which they felt to be superior to that of Japan. The Koreans wanted to engage in legal reform and receive some Western law, but Japan violently occupied the country and took over the government.[8] Consequently, all of Japan's legal reforms were met with hostility by the Koreans.

The Taiwanese, however, have no need to thank the Japanese. The Taiwanese paid tremendous costs for the advantages of Japan's legal reform. As second-class citizens, Taiwanese had to tolerate Japanese discrimination in political rights, the appointment of officials, education opportunities, and so on.[9] In the 1920s, when new-generation Taiwanese wanted to take back the leadership over legal reform to develop their own type of society, Japan rejected their requests without hesitation—primarily because Japan enjoyed a majority of the gains from Taiwan's legal reform. Like a man who cannot help but buy certain products under duress, the Taiwanese were coerced to "buy" Japan-made legal reform. They gained some benefits from this Japanese "product" but had to pay a high price for it. Should a coerced man be thankful for such a deal?

LEGACY TO POSTWAR LEGAL DEVELOPMENT

Unlike the transfer of political authority, a society's legal system cannot be changed in a moment. Just as the Japanese regime had to face the legacy left by the Ch'ing administration, the regime that succeeded Japan after its withdrawal from Taiwan in 1945 had to face the legacy resulting from the fifty years of effective Japanese rule.

In 1945, Taiwan, a colony of the defeated Japanese, was to be returned to the hands of the Chinese regime in accord with the 1943 Cairo Declaration. Irrespective of the issue of Taiwan's status in international law,[10] Taiwan was in fact governed by the Nationalist government (Nanking government, or Kuomintang government) of the Republic of China (hereafter called the "ROC regime") after 1945. In 1949, because the forces of the ROC regime were defeated in China by the Chinese Communist Party (which became the ruler of China and established the People's Republic of China [PRC]), the central government of the ROC regime retreated to its only safe haven, the newly acquired area of Taiwan (two very small islands off the coast of Fukien are omitted here). The PRC did not go on to occupy Taiwan. Thus, since 1949 the ROC regime has been the de facto supreme authority over the island. When the ROC regime arrived on Taiwan in 1945, it was, from the perspective of the Taiwanese originally governed by Japan, actually an alien, Han Chinese regime (like the Cheng regime on Taiwan). Unlike Japanese colonialists, the ROC regime had no "homeland" from which to continue its alien governance after 1949. Today, a half century after the ROC's arrival on Taiwan, the ROC regime, unlike the Cheng regime, has become a nonalien government composed of Taiwanese people, including aborigines, original Taiwanese ("the Taiwanese" in this book), and new immigrants, who were also called Chinese-mainlanders.

Continuity of Legal Institution

Similar Modern Codes. The example of the Meiji legal reform influenced not only the Taiwanese in the colony but also the people of China. Japan's success in ending extraterritoriality through Westernization of law attracted the attention of Ch'ing China, which also suffered the same problem. During the late Ch'ing period, numerous Chinese students were sent to Japan to learn the Western law, which had been trimmed by the Japanese, and many Japanese scholars taught law in China. It is therefore not surprising that Chinese codification of modern law in the late Ch'ing period was deeply influenced by Japanese legal experts and sources. Three Japanese jurists, Okada Asatarō, Matsuoka Yoshimasa, and Shida Kōtarō, were very active in drafting the Chinese criminal code, civil code, and commercial code, respectively.[11] Those draft codes were thus largely modeled on related Japanese codes with some modifications to accommodate Chinese traditions or new legal theories; unfortunately, Ch'ing was overthrown in 1912, before the codes were adopted.[12] Except for the criminal code, the new Republic of China under the Peking government (1912–28) did not put them into force. Japanese influences continued to dominate Republican legislation. Many Japanese special criminal statutes in the Meiji era have their counterparts in the Chinese law under the Peking government. For instance, the Japanese Public Order Police Law (Chian keisatsu hō), repeatedly mentioned in this volume, was promulgated in 1900 and later extended to Taiwan in 1923. In 1914, the Chinese Peking government used the same Chinese script as the title of a law (Chin-an ching-cha fa) to promulgate similar provisions to restrict political organization and assembly.[13]

Not until 1928, when the Nationalist government (the ROC regime) replaced the Peking government, did most draft codes take effect one by one.[14] The Nationalist government made some revisions to the original draft codes, especially with reference to the newly enacted German codes. However, a large number of legal terms and concepts in the German-rooted Japanese codes that had already been adopted in the original draft codes were maintained in the Nationalist ROC codes. These modern ROC codes thus still preserved strong Japanese influences.[15] Furthermore, Nationalist law continued to be modeled on Japanese law. For wartime economic regulation, the Japanese National General Mobilization Law (Kokka sōdōin hō) was enacted in 1938 and applied in Taiwan during the same year. In 1942, the Chinese Nationalist government in Chungking enacted a statute with the same title (Kuo-chia tsung-tung-yüan fa), providing the same legislative purposes, the same "materials for general mobilization," and similar "businesses for general mobilization," and imposing similar restrictions. It is safe to say that the Nationalist ROC code is to a large extent similar to the prewar Japanese code.

The prewar Japanese codes were mostly extended to Taiwan after 1923 and had been effectively implemented there for two decades by the time the Nationalists arrived in 1945; therefore, the similar modern code of the ROC regime was not strange to the Taiwanese. The ROC law became effective in Taiwan on October 25, 1945. In November of 1945, the ROC's local government on Taiwan declared that Japanese colonial law remained temporarily effective except those laws enacted to oppress the people or those contrary to ROC law.[16] After October 25, 1946, most Japanese laws were rescinded, and all public or private matters were decided by ROC law, with the exception that the matters not being provided for in ROC law might be decided according to the customs that were effective under Japanese colonial law.[17] After 1949, the ROC central government applied only its own law in Taiwan. But the old Japanese code was substantively preserved in Taiwan—not because the new ruler intentionally maintained them, as in the Korean case[18]—but because most of the new ROC codes were initially modeled on the old Japanese codes. The result is that the Taiwanese governed by Japan could continue to receive Western law through the Japanese-oriented ROC codes without interruption despite the change of regimes, although neither the Japanese codes nor the ROC codes were originally enacted for Taiwan's society.

Taiwanese Lack of Lawmaking Power. The new ROC regime, on the other hand, intentionally maintained the political structure left by Japanese colonialists. When the ROC regime prepared to take possession of Taiwan, it encountered a basic question that Japan had met fifty years before: whether to treat Taiwan within an entire national system, as a special district, or as an ordinary administrative area (see chapter 2).[19] The ROC regime finally adopted the former method, as Japan had in 1896. Under this, the central government delegated extensive powers to the resident government on Taiwan.[20] The political system thus reverted almost completely to the one that had existed fifty years before. As under Japanese rule, Taiwan was regarded as a special zone within the country, and a new governor-general of the Taiwan Provincial Administration was appointed. Based on the same reasoning as Japan's enactment of the 1896 Title 63, the ROC regime announced that a special zone was merely a transitional measure.[21] The issue of application of constitutional law to Taiwan followed. The ROC regime declared that the newly enacted ROC Constitution would not be immediately applied in Taiwan.[22]

The Taiwan administration of the ROC regime was virtually equivalent to the GGT. In fact, the 1945 Organic Regulations of Taiwan Provincial Administrative Executive Office was largely the same as the Japanese Organic Regulations of the Government-General of Taiwan.[23] Like the governor-general of the GGT, the governor-general of the Taiwan Provincial Administration managed all administrative affairs in Taiwan under the supervision of the cabinet of the central government; he also headed the Garrison Command.[24] The ROC's governor-general likewise directed and supervised all officials in Taiwan, including judicial officials.[25] The administrative structures of these two governments were alike.[26] The ROC regime established an Administrative Council (*cheng-wu hui-i*) similar to the GGT Consultative Council, but adopted the 1896 version of the GGT Consultative Council, which was composed of high-ranking officers and presided over by the governor-general, rather than the 1919 version, to which several resident Taiwanese were appointed as members.[27] In addition to issuing executive ordinances of the resident government on Taiwan, the ROC's governor-general himself could also draft proposed statutes for the special needs of Taiwan and then send the draft to the central government for promulgation.[28] That was not different from the practice followed by the Japanese colonial government after Title 3 took effect in 1922, under which the GGT drafted the contents of the ordinance for exception by itself and then sent it to the central government for promulgation. Therefore, although the ROC's governor-general had no power to issue an ordinance like the GGT's *ritsurei* (which was further restricted under Title 3), he actually still possessed extensive legislative power for Taiwan. Moreover, in practice the high-ranking officials of the Taiwan administration of the ROC regime were always people who came from the Chinese mainland, few of whom were original Taiwanese.[29]

Both in law and in practice, most original Taiwanese did not have any opportunities to participate in the process of legislating law for Taiwan. The bitterest fruit in Japan-led legal reform for the Taiwanese appeared again at the hands of their "beloved brethren." From the perspective of original Taiwanese, the only difference after 1945 was that Japanese mainlanders were replaced by Chinese mainlanders.[30] Like their forerunners in the 1920s and early 1930s, original Taiwanese again pursued autonomous legal reform. Taiwanese intellectuals who had suffered Japanese discrimination were deeply dissatisfied that a Chinese regime under a republic treated them the same as a Japanese imperial regime did. Since the new regime recognized the uniqueness of Taiwan, as the Japanese in theory had, they naturally wanted to have power to enact their own law to address this uniqueness, which had been suppressed for a long time by the Japanese colonialists. After the February 28 Incident, angry original Taiwanese demanded that Taiwan be made a self-governing autonomous unit under the jurisdiction of the ROC.[31] This request was virtually the same as that contained in the petition for establishing a Taiwan parliament under the jurisdiction of the Empire of Japan; that movement had ended only thirteen years earlier, in 1934, under pressure from Japanese militarists.

The response of the new ROC regime was a ruthless military massacre in 1947 and later terrifying suppression. Similar terrorism had been employed by the Japanese colonialists on Taiwan, especially during the early period of Japanese rule. The terrible experiences of the Japanese period naturally emerged again in the minds of the original Taiwanese, telling them that when "cold winter" came, reform by peaceful measures was impossible, but bleeding was also in vain; therefore, the best way to ensure one's safety was to make money and not pay any attention to politics.[32]

Thus, the nightmare in people's memories deriving from Japanese colonial rule deeply discouraged most original Taiwanese from pursuing legal reforms. The ROC law was in form enacted by the Legislative Yuan, composed of members elected by the people. After 1949, the areas that the ROC regime could control were almost limited to Taiwan, but it declared that it had authority over the entirety of mainland China, including Outer Mongolia. Its "people" temporarily could not exercise their suffrage; therefore, the reelection of the members of the Legislative Yuan was suspended. As a result, the original Taiwanese could have only a few representatives in the Yuan, as they were the people of only one of China's thirty-five provinces. Inasmuch as the ROC law took effect only on Taiwan, however, the vast majority of people actually affected by the ROC law were the original Taiwanese—who could not decide the contents of their law under the interpretation of the ROC regime.[33]

This was the same result that had obtained under the Japanese interpretation of "complete" application of Japan's constitution to Taiwan. Nevertheless, the memory of their previous Japanese colonial experiences evoked by the February 28 Incident forced most original Taiwanese not to challenge this injustice, which resulted from the ROC's myth of its sovereignty. Only as the ROC regime needed more original Taiwanese supporters and time lowered the number of those nonreelected members through retirement or death did reelection become possible.[34] In 1992, the Legislative Yuan was finally no longer "occupied" by those nonreelected members but composed of representatives elected by the Taiwanese people. It took nearly fifty years (1945–92) for the original Taiwanese to get out of the political frame left by the Japanese. Taiwan's new legislature is actually a "Taiwan parliament," an aim that was pursued by the majority of Taiwanese intellectuals under Japanese rule seventy years ago.[35]

Because Japan did not introduce the Western concept of rule of law in the reforms it imposed on Taiwan, many Taiwanese educated under Japanese rule still consider law as merely an instrument of the ruler, as imperial Chinese law had taught them. Further legal reform had to wait for new-generation Taiwanese people to take on this issue through their own legislature. A new Westernization of law oriented to the interests of the people and based on the conditions of Taiwan is expected.[36]

Disconnection of Judiciary

Judicial Facilities. The Japanese left sufficient buildings for Taiwan's judiciary in 1945. In 1947 the ROC regime on China said that the most important task in Chinese judicial reform was to establish district courts, independent from administrative authorities, in the country.[37] In Taiwan, the ROC regime needed only to change the names of preexisting district courts and their branches, jails, and so on, and with a few adjustments make them correspond to the ROC system.[38] Today, the Judicial Yuan, the highest authority in the ROC judicial system, sits in the building of the former GGT Higher Court, which was also the highest authority in Japan's Taiwan. In addition, the ROC's Taiwan High Court uses the same office of the former GGT Taihoku (Taipei) District Court. The physical facilities left by Japan have of course contributed to the enforcement of modern ROC codes in postwar Taiwan.

Judicial Personnel. Japan did not, however, leave sufficient Taiwanese personnel to continue the operation of the courts. And the new rulers were not prepared to let original Taiwanese manage Taiwan's courts. The ROC regime planned to assign judicial officials from the Chinese mainland to fill the positions in Taiwan's courts; all heads of courts had already been appointed before the ROC regime came to take over Taiwan's courts. But by late 1945 only a few mainland officials had arrived on the island.³⁹ So the ROC regime sent Taiwanese judges who had originally served in the colonial courts as temporary agents of the heads of district courts and appointed a few Taiwanese lawyers to be judges to operate the courts that had been taken over.⁴⁰ Unfortunately, because of Japanese discrimination, few Taiwanese law graduates became judicial officials in Taiwan or Japan, even though there were significant numbers of Taiwanese lawyers. Most Taiwanese legal experts who had been educated under Japanese rule could not grasp this opportunity to be judicial officials of the new regime. In addition, many Taiwanese who had been judges or lawyers during the Japanese period suffered arrest or death in the ROC regime's suppression of the February 28 Incident.⁴¹ Furthermore, because more judicial officials came from the Chinese mainland in 1949, and the ROC regime tended to distrust original Taiwanese, especially after the 1947 incident, the Taiwanese jurists educated under Japanese rule were mostly excluded from high positions in postwar Taiwan courts. According to a report made in 1965, twenty years after the ROC regime came to Taiwan, there were sixteen people in the highest class (*chien-jen*) in the court hierarchy, but none were original Taiwanese.⁴² Consequently, although many colonial laws were not substantively changed in postwar Taiwan, few of the people enforcing those laws had been influenced by Japanese rule on Taiwan.

With different enforcing officials, similar codes resulted in different effects. As an original Taiwanese who was a judge in prewar Japan and then became an ROC procurator in 1945 said in his memoir, he had no difficulty in understanding the ROC code because of its similarity to Japan's, but he felt uncomfortable writing judgments in Chinese.⁴³ What really shocked him was the practical operation of this basically similar code. Being a procurator, he disposed of many criminal cases by nonprosecution when he considered the evidence insufficient to prove the suspect's guilt or when the offenses were minor. However, the chief procurator from the Chinese mainland told him that too many nonprosecutions would induce others to suspect him of receiving bribes or being lobbied. In another case, he refused to issue a warrant of arrest because there was no evidence against the accused, but the chief procurator issued the warrant himself because the mayor (who was from the same county as the chief procurator) required him to do so.⁴⁴ Having been a judge in Japan, this Taiwanese jurist was unable to tolerate a practice in which application of the law depended on these sorts of elements outside the law, but he could do nothing to change matters since the head of the court came from a society in which this practice was commonplace.⁴⁵

Chinese judicial traditions thus dominated postwar Taiwan's judiciary. Judicial independence, the honesty of judicial officials, and other aspects of the judicial system in Taiwan during the Japanese period (see chapter 3), were almost irrelevant to postwar Taiwan. In this respect, the Japanese legacy on Taiwan was nearly nonexistent.

But the present Taiwan judiciary is not free from Japanese influence. In 1947 an American jurist, Roscoe Pound, who was adviser to the Ministry of Justice of the ROC, pointed out that most Chinese judges were influenced by Japan, indirectly by Germany.[46] Presently, the style of writing judgments of ROC courts still follows that of the Japanese courts.[47] Nevertheless, it must be realized that like the modern code in today's Taiwan, those Japanese influences in present Taiwan come not from the legacy of Japanese rule on Taiwan but are derived from the fact that the original ROC court system was based on that of Japan.

Legacy in Criminal Justice

Political Crimes. The Japanese treatment of political crimes during the latter period did not carry over into the ROC period. Generally speaking, when the alien Japanese regime had just come to Taiwan, it did not dispose of Taiwanese dissidents entirely by law; anyone who threatened the safety of the regime was seriously punished, even though the person had not violated a law. After the 1920s, however, the Japanese authorities employed law to sanction the behavior of Taiwanese dissidents, and the punishments against them were not so harsh as those in the early days. When new alien rulers came, a similar cycle began. In the 1947 incident, the ROC regime killed or arrested Taiwanese without legal process, and some of them were sentenced to death only to set an example for the people.[48] For original Taiwanese dissidents, the principle of rule by law disappeared again. Another cycle in the treatment of political crimes began.

Ordinary Crimes. Some Japanese-style crime-control institutions were left in Taiwan. The summary judgments made by police, an important measure in the colonial crime-control structure, though restricted to the police offenses, were maintained by the ROC regime, which in fact had imitated this system directly from Japan before coming to Taiwan.[49] In 1980 the use of police punishment power to punish police offenses was declared unconstitutional by the ROC's Council of Grand Justices.[50] However, the ROC government continued to implement this system, and the people continued to obey it, in large part because the original Taiwanese have been accustomed to such a system since Japanese rule. Similarly, the vagrant discipline system, another special measure for crime control created by the Japanese regime on Taiwan, has continued to be used by the ROC regime. Such an institution never existed in China under the ROC.

On the other hand, some other aspects of the administration of criminal justice during the Japanese period do not influence present Taiwan. For instance, the assurance of punishment no longer exists, but punishments are quite severe. The high rate of nonprosecution of colonial procurators has ceased. Once the crime rate rose, an increasing number of the convicted were sentenced to death.[51]

Obedience to Law. The most valuable asset that Japan left to the new regime is the Taiwanese characteristic of being law-abiding. During the fifty-year Japanese rule, "rebellious Taiwanese" became obedient subjects who followed the law (will) of the ruler. By means of this legacy, the ROC regime easily "imposed itself over a society in which it had no power base."[52] But after half a century of the ROC regime's implementation of law, the Taiwanese people might have lost their law-abiding nature.

Legacy in Civil Law

Property Law. Westernization of the real property law and business law under Japanese rule certainly helped in the application of the ROC Civil Code in Taiwan. Modern Continental European civil law relating to real estate and business transactions and enterprises had been extensively used in Taiwan, especially since the Japanese Civil Code became effective for Taiwanese in 1923 (see chapter 5). The provisions in the ROC Civil Code relating to the civil matters mentioned above are close to those in the Japanese Civil Code. In this respect, we can say that most of the provisions concerning property law in the ROC Civil Code had been effectively applied in Taiwan for more than two decades at least before the ROC regime came to the island, even earlier than the year of promulgation of the ROC Civil Code, 1929.

In particular the complete registration of real estate on Taiwan left by the Japanese has greatly contributed to the enforcement of the book of Rights over Things in the ROC Civil Code. Under the ROC Civil Code, official registration was required for the transactions of the right over things relating to real estate. Anyone can trust the information on the official register to give accurate information on the ownership of interests in a particular piece of land or building. Without the official registration of real estate, this law could not be implemented. Moreover, incomplete official registration surely results in numerous civil disputes. When the ROC regime came to Taiwan, it did not need to worry about such problems because the Japanese had done well.

APPRAISAL AND LEGACY

Status Law. As David C. Buxbaum has pointed out, the ROC status law was more Westernized than prewar Japanese status law, but it was little enforced in China.⁵³ Japanese colonial authorities had, however, already applied some Western concepts to change old Taiwanese customs concerning the family and succession system. The numerous court buildings left by the Japanese, which made using the court system convenient, also contributed to the enforcement of the more-progressive provisions in the ROC Civil Code.

SUMMARY

The Japanese regime was competent, at least not worse than other regimes, in carrying out legal reform of Taiwanese law because Japan shared a similar cultural background with the Taiwanese and had already successfully established an efficient modern government in the Meiji reform. The real flaw in this Japan-made legal reform is that Japan pursued its own interests in the reform. But because Taiwanese society itself tended to accept the new reforms, legal modernization was more smoothly implemented in Taiwan than in other colonies.

Japanese colonialists on Taiwan left many legacies to postwar Taiwan's legal development. Because the codes of the ROC regime were to a large extent modeled on the modern Japanese codes, Japan's fifty-year imposition of modern Japanese law on Taiwan laid a firm foundation for later implementation of the ROC codes. In addition, because the Japanese regime had thoroughly suppressed Taiwanese political participation in the colony, the new ROC regime could easily replace the Japanese as rulers and effectively prevent the Taiwanese people from pursuing any legal reform for themselves for a long time. Unfortunately, the Japanese regime left only a few Taiwanese judicial officials to operate the courts in Taiwan, whose physical facilities had been established by the Japanese. Therefore, some merits of the colonial judiciary—for example, the honesty of judicial officials—did not influence postwar Taiwan. In addition, a relatively tolerant treatment for political criminals in the latter period of Japanese rule, earned at the cost of numerous lives of Taiwanese in the early Japanese period, also disappeared with the arrival of another alien regime. The new ROC regime did preserve some Japanese crime-control institutions but implemented them differently. In any event, the best legacy of Japanese rule for the Taiwanese people was Japan's Westernization of Taiwanese civil law, especially property law.

Conclusion

This book, from the perspective of emerging Taiwan studies, raises and answers the question To what extent did the Taiwanese under Japanese rule receive Western legal concepts, replacing traditional Chinese concepts?

Before discussing this question, we first have to observe Taiwanese society in the late nineteenth century, upon which modern Western law was imposed, and also examine the Westernization of Japanese law in the period of the Meiji reform, which of course influenced the legal reforms Japan imposed in Taiwan. Generally speaking, Taiwanese society at that time was a frontier society composed of Han Chinese settlers. Transplanting several customs from their native regions in the Chinese mainland, these settlers formed their new society on the island, where although the control of political authority was weak and social disorder was serious, commercial activities prospered. During this time Japan, under the pressure of Western powers, had gradually adopted Western law. When Japan occupied Taiwan in 1895, it had nearly completed its Western-style codes. These Westernized codes had been instituted to suit the needs of the government, not the people; but most Japanese people, imbued with traditional feudal obedience, still passively accepted the new laws.

The threshold question concerning Taiwanese reception of Western law is How many Western-style laws were adopted in colonial legislation? As a rule, legislation was a primary method of introducing Western law to East Asian societies such as Taiwan. Because most of the Japanese laws had been modeled on Western law, the number of Western laws in Taiwan was virtually identical to the number of Japanese laws that were enforced in colonial Taiwan. Between 1895 and 1922, only a limited number of Japanese laws went into effect in Taiwan; instead, colonial special laws prevailed; after 1923, most of the Japanese Westernized laws were finally applied in Taiwan. In fact, unlike the situation in Japan during the Meiji reform, since there was no Western pressure, the colonial administration did not intend to adopt Western law to apply in the colony from the beginning. In the early period of Japanese rule, colonial legislation was largely influenced by imperial Chinese law, old Taiwanese customs, and Western colonial institutions rather than modern Western law. Not until the late period was most Japanese law extended to Taiwan, and then it was intended to rapidly assimilate the Taiwanese people into Japanese society. As in the period of the Meiji reform, Western-style law was still an instrument for the rulers in colonial Taiwan. Many modern Taiwanese intellectuals wanted to play a significant role in the process of the modernization of the legal system of Taiwan, but they failed.

Westernized positive law in the colony then was implemented by Western-style courts. In Taiwan, a Continental European court system had been established in 1896; after the 1919 reform, Taiwan's court system was virtually the same as Japan's court system. Similarly, after 1919, an independent judiciary was to a large extent in existence in Taiwan. The colonial court basically possessed sufficient facilities and competent legal professionals to use Western-style positive law. But the administrative civil mediation system and police summary judgment for criminal cases to some degree blocked the courts from carrying out their function of allowing Western law to penetrate Taiwanese society. From the 1920s on, however, the Taiwanese people preferred to use Western-style courts rather than administrative mediation when they resorted to official dispute-resolution.

In criminal law, the Japanese government initially dealt with Taiwanese political criminals primarily by military suppression instead of by the use of criminal sanctions in a criminal law system. But after 1902, serious suppression by the army was replaced by the use of criminal sanctions to punish Taiwanese resistors. Then, after the 1920s, because most Taiwanese dissidents carried on their opposition by means of a modern political movement against Japanese rule within the legal framework, the colonial government generally depended on various Western-style criminal laws to dispose of them. Interestingly, in the 1930s there were fewer political criminals in Taiwan than in Japan or Korea. To maintain social order, the Japanese established a crime-control structure in Taiwan composed of the court system, the summary-judgment system, and the vagrant-discipline system. At the cost of human rights, the Japanese successfully suppressed the serious offenses against public order originating in Ch'ing Taiwan, although minor crimes in Taiwan did not decrease. In the process of this transformation of the criminal justice system, the Taiwanese people were exposed to the basic concepts of Western criminal law as applied by the colonial authorities. Those colonial criminal institutions that paid little attention to human rights were accepted by the people because they represented state authority, not because they were presumed to be just.

In civil law, the colonial government did not immediately impose Western-style law but applied the old customs, which were deeply influenced by the Chinese legal tradition, to Taiwanese civil matters. However, the contents of old customs were in fact changed through the process of their recognition by the colonial courts. In 1923, Japanese Westernized civil and commercial codes became applicable to the Taiwanese, and therefore Taiwanese customary civil law was completely transformed to Western-style civil law, except for family and succession law. This process can be illustrated by the development of the law relating to real estate. At first, the various relations that existed in connection with land under old customs were interpreted by the Japanese authorities within the framework of the Western legal concept of "rights." Then, some customary rights in land were modified to be similar to the rights described in the Japanese Westernized civil code. Finally, after 1923 all of the customary rights relating to real estate were transformed into corresponding rights in the Japanese Civil Code. Because the Taiwanese had already had a sophisticated contract law for ordinary commercial transactions in the Ch'ing period, they easily received Western-style commercial law. Meanwhile, modern company law and the law for negotiable instruments were widely accepted in Taiwanese society (to the extent they were used). In contrast, Taiwanese family relations and succession were less influenced by Western law under Japanese rule, but they were to a certain extent modified by Western ideas through courts' decisions.

Finally, it should be admitted that the Japanese regime indeed was a competent agent for the reform and Westernization of law in Taiwan's unique context. However, it also should not be forgotten that the ultimate goal of this legal reform was to advance Japanese imperial interests. The Taiwanese surely gained some benefits from the reform, but they paid tremendous costs for such indirect benefits and therefore need never thank the Japanese. Furthermore, the Japanese practice whereby the original Taiwanese people were excluded from deciding the contents of legal reform was unfortunately maintained by the new ROC regime for nearly half a century after the Japanese left Taiwan in 1945. Because the ROC codes were originally modeled on Japanese codes, Taiwanese reception of Western law was not significantly interrupted by the change of political authority.

In sum, because they needed to assimilate the colonized people, Japanese imperialists—who in fact still preserved some Chinese legal ideas—finally extended most of their Western-style laws to Taiwan. Because of effective Japanese enforcement of colonial Westernized positive law, the Taiwanese became familiar with modern Western criminal law and, more important, modern Western civil law. However, the general public was merely exposed, through this Japan-led legal reform, to the Western law that was selected by the colonial government. Thus the fundamental spirit of modern Western law—that the primary function of law is to protect people from an arbitrary government and to realize justice—was not yet generally known.

APPENDIX A

Development of Taiwanese Law

Based on the discussion in the texts, this section briefly explains the effects of Chinese law and Japanese law on Taiwan from the perspective of the reception of Western law (table A.1). In the latter half of the nineteenth century, imperial Chinese law was applied to Taiwan, a part of Ch'ing China. For several years after the Meiji Restoration of 1868, Japan to a large extent retained imperial Chinese law; from 1872 on, however, the Japanese government began to adopt modern Western law. After the annexation of Taiwan in 1895, Japanese Westernized law was brought to Taiwan starting from the next year (although the Japanese administration in Taiwan still employed some parts of imperial Chinese law). Not until 1906, a decade after Taiwan had come into contact with Western law through Japanese rule, did Ch'ing China promulgate its first Westernized law for its judicial system, which was deeply influenced by Japanese law.[1] From 1912 on, the legislation of the new Republic of China was continuously influenced by Japanese law; however, the Chinese government was unable to enact Western-style codes, in part because China was governed by several warlords who fought each other; thus only a few Chinese courts applied some Western legal concepts in the name of "legal theory." In contrast, Japan was able to apply Japanese Western-style laws in Taiwan, and did so almost fully after 1923. Not until the Chinese Nationalist government nominally unified China in 1928 were ROC Westernized codes (which were still influenced by Japanese law) gradually enacted. Soon, because of the 1937 Sino-Japanese War not only China but also Japan and Taiwan were led to wartime legal institutions.[2] During this period, as before, Japanese wartime laws applied to Taiwan and even influenced Chinese law. With the end of World War II in 1945, China took over Taiwan and then applied the ROC Westernized codes (and accompanying wartime special statutes) to Taiwan.[3] At that time, prewar Japanese law was further reformed toward Western law (American law), but postwar Japanese law could not apply to Taiwan any more. After the establishment of the People's Republic of China in 1949, Westernization of law in China was stopped; socialist law replaced Western-style law. Taiwan was still governed by the ROC code under martial law, which was similar to prewar Japanese Westernized law during the wartime period, until martial law was lifted in 1987. Such wartime institutions existed in Taiwan for about fifty years (1938–87). However, after having come into contact with Western law for a century (1896–present), the Taiwanese people have gradually, although not completely yet, received modern Western law.

TABLE A.1 Relationships among Taiwanese Law, Chinese Law, and Japanese Law, 1868–present

Event	China	Taiwan	Japan
1868: Meiji Restoration	Imperial Chinese law	⇒ Imperial Chinese law	≫ Native Japanese law and Imperial Chinese law
			†1872
1895: China cedes Taiwan to Japan	†1906	†1896	
1912: ROC established	Chinese Westernized law in courts	Imperial Chinese Law and prewar Japan Westernized Law	prewar Japan Westernized Law
		†1923	
1928: Kuomintang unifies China	†1928 ROC Westernized codes (≅ prewar Japan Westernized codes)	≪ prewar Japan Westernized Law	⇐
1937: Sino-Japanese War	†1937 (wartime law)	≪ †1938 (wartime law)	†1938 (wartime law)
1945: ROC takes over Taiwan	†1949	⇒ †1945	⇐ †1945
1949: PRC established	Socialist Chinese law	▶◀ ROC Westernized law (≅ prewar Japanese Westernized law) (wartime law)	▶◀ Postwar Japanese Westernized law
*1987 Taiwan lifts martial law		†1987	

NOTES: ⇒ ⇐: direct application; ≫ ≪: indirect influence; †: watershed; ≅: similarity; ▶◀: independent.

APPENDIX B

The Law Relating to Laws and Ordinances to Be Enforced in Taiwan

I. TITLE 63, 1896

Article 1
The Governor-General of Taiwan may issue ordinances that have the same effect as the (Japanese) statute within his governing jurisdiction.
Article 2
Ordinances mentioned in the preceding article shall be determined first by the GGT Consultative Council and then receive imperial approval through the Minister of Colonization.
The Organization of the GGT Consultative Council shall be provided by ordinance.
Article 3
In the situation of extraordinary emergency the Governor-General of Taiwan may immediately issue ordinances mentioned in article 1 without the procedure provided in the first paragraph of the preceding article.
Article 4
After the promulgation of ordinances mentioned in the preceding article, imperial approval shall be immediately obtained and the GGT Consultative Council shall be informed.
Where imperial approval is not obtained, the Governor-General of Taiwan shall immediately promulgate that the ordinances be invalid from this point on.
Article 5
Those portions of statutes in the present day or in the future that are to be applied to Taiwan shall be provided by ordinance.

Article 6

This Law shall become invalid after a three-year duration beginning from the effective day.

II. TITLE 31, 1906

Article 1

In Taiwan the Governor-General of Taiwan may issue ordinances that have the same effect as the statute to regulate those matters that shall be provided by the statute.

Article 2

Ordinances mentioned in the preceding article shall receive imperial approval through the responsible minister.

Article 3

In the situation of extraordinary emergency the Governor-General of Taiwan may immediately issue ordinances mentioned in article 1.

After the promulgation of ordinances mentioned in the preceding paragraph, imperial approval shall be immediately obtained; where imperial approval is not obtained, the Governor-General of Taiwan shall immediately promulgate that the ordinances be invalid from this point on.

Article 4

Those portions of statutes that are to be applied to Taiwan shall be provided by ordinance.

Article 5

Ordinances issued mentioned in article 1 shall not be in conflict with those statutes that have been applied to Taiwan or those statutes or ordinances that are specially enacted for Taiwan.

Article 6

Those *ritsurei* that have been issued by the Governor-General of Taiwan are still effective.

Appendix

This Law shall be effective from January 1, 1907, to December 31, 1911.

III. TITLE 3, 1921

Article 1

Those portions of statutes that are to be applied to Taiwan shall be provided by ordinance.

In the case of the preceding paragraph, when it is necessary to make an exception for Taiwan's unique situation, special provisions may be promulgated by ordinance to regulate the matters concerning the duties of an office or an agency, legal durations, and others.

Article 2

In Taiwan the Governor-General of Taiwan may issue ordinances that have the same effect as the statute to regulate those matters that shall be provided by statute only if no (Japanese) statutes are available, or available statutes are hard to be applied to Taiwan in accordance with the preceding article, and at the same time it is necessary to respond the unique situation of Taiwan.

Article 3

Ordinances mentioned in the preceding article shall receive imperial approval through the responsible minister.

Article 4

In the situation of extraordinary emergency, the Governor-General of Taiwan may immediately issue ordinances mentioned in article 2.

After the promulgation of ordinances according to the preceding paragraph, imperial approval shall be immediately obtained; where imperial approval is not obtained, the Governor-General of Taiwan shall immediately promulgate that the ordinances be invalid from this point on.

Article 5

Ordinances issued according to this law shall not be conflict with those statutes and ordinances that have been enforced in Taiwan.

Appendix

This Law becomes effective on January 1, 1922.

Those ordinances that were issued by the Governor-General of Taiwan according to Title 63, 1896, and Title 31, 1906, and are still in force at the time this law takes effect shall temporarily remain effective as before.

APPENDIX C

The Civil, Commercial, and Criminal Law
(Ritsurei No. 8, 1898)

Article 1
Civil, commercial, and criminal matters shall conform to the (Japanese) Civil Code, Commercial Code, Criminal Code, Code of Civil Procedure, Code of Criminal Procedure, and statutes attached to those codes, but matters mentioned below shall specially conform to present practice:
  i. Civil and commercial matters involving only Taiwanese or Chinese.
  ii. Criminal matters relating to Taiwanese or Chinese.

Article 2
Those statutes mentioned in article 1 shall not affect the validity of the provisions specially enacted for Taiwan.

Article 3
Attached statutes (mentioned in article 1) shall be designated by executive ordinance (*furei*) of the GGT.

Article 4
Ritsurei No. 4 of 1896 is rescinded.

APPENDIX D

The Bandit Punishment Law
(Emergency Ritsurei No. 24, 1898)

Article 1

Regardless of their aim, those who band themselves in groups and resort to violence or threat of violence to achieve their aim shall be considered as bandits and be dealt with according to the following classifications:
   i. The leader and instigators shall be punished with death.
   ii. Those who participate in plotting or directing the activities of bandits shall be punished with death.
   iii. Those who blindly follow or serve odd jobs shall be punished with penal servitude.

Article 2

Anyone who is tried under the third item of the preceding article and is found guilty of any one of the following acts shall be punished with death:
   i. resisting Japanese officials or army;
   ii. destroying by fire or other means buildings, trains, ships, or bridges;
   iii. setting fire to forests, fields, bamboo forests, or harvested grains;
   iv. destroying railways and their signs, lighthouses and their accessories or causing danger to transportation;
   v. destroying telegraph and telephone facilities or obstructing postal communications;
   vi. murdering or raping;
   vii. kidnaping or plundering.

Article 3

Once attempted, the crimes listed in the preceding article shall be considered accomplished.

Article 4
   Anyone who aids bandits by means of sponsoring firearms, ships, money, rice, or other objects, or supplying a place to assemble, or other acts shall be punished with death or penal servitude for life.

Article 5
   Anyone who harbors or conceals bandits or intends to free bandits convicted of banditry shall be punished with penal servitude.

Article 6
   The punishment of anyone who committed the offenses punishable in this law who surrenders himself before the official (*jishu*) shall be reduced or remitted depending on the individual situation; anyone whose punishment has been remitted shall be kept under surveillance for not more than five years.

Article 7
   This Law shall apply to any punishable acts, even though the acts occurred before this Law comes into force.

Appendix
   This Law takes effect as of the day it is promulgated.

Glossary

(C): Mandarin Chinese; (J): Japanese

A-kung-tien (C) 阿公店
Amoy (C) 廈門

Bakkin oyobi chikei shobun rei (J) 罰金及笞刑處分例
banchi (J) 蕃地
banjin (J) 蕃人
Bōryoku kōi to shōbatsu ni kansuru hōritsu (J) 暴力行為等処罰ニ関スル法律

Chang-chou (C) 漳州
Chang-hua (C) 彰化
Chang Yu-chung (C) 張有忠
chao-fu (C) 招夫
chao-hsü (C) 招婿
Ch'en Ch'ing-hua (C) 陳慶華
Ch'en Mao-yüan (C) 陳茂源
Ch'en Ming-ch'ing (C) 陳明清
Cheng Ch'eng-kung (C) 鄭成功
Cheng Chih-lung (C) 鄭芝龍
Cheng Ching (C) 鄭經
cheng-wu hui-i (C) 政務會議
Cheng Sung-yü (C) 鄭松筠
chi-keng (C) 起耕

chi-keng-t'ai (C) 起耕胎
chia-chang (C) 家長
Chia-i (C) 嘉義
Chian iji hō (J) 治安維持法
Chian keisatsu hō (J) 治安警察法
Chiang Pao-ch'eng (C) 江保成
Chiekiken (J) 地役権
chien-jen (C) 簡任
chien-tan (C) 見單
Chihō hōin (J) 地方法院
Chihō saibansho (J) 地方裁判所
chijōken (J) 地上権
Chin-an ching-cha fa (C) 治安警察法
Chinshakuken (J) 賃借権
Chizaihō (J) 治罪法
chō (J) 庁
Chōchō o shite minji sōshō chōtei tō o toriatsukawashimuru ken (J) 庁長ヲシテ民事争訟調停等ヲ取扱ハシムル件
Ch'üan-chou (C) 泉州
chūkaminkokujin (J) 中華民國人

199

GLOSSARY

Chung-yu-hui (C) 眾友會
Chungking (C) 重慶

Dai Nappon teikoku kempō (J)
　大日本帝国憲法
Daishin'in (J) 大審院
Dai-so-ken seiri ni kansuru ken (J)
　大租権整理ニ関スル件
Den Kenjirō (C) 田健治郎

eikosakuken (J) 永小作権
ekiken (J) 役権
erh-t'ai (C) 二胎
Etō Shimpei (J) 江藤　新平

fang (C) 房
Fen-lei-hsieh-tou (C) 分類械鬥
Feng Cheng-shu (C) 馮正樞
Fukien (C) 福建
fukoku-kyohei (J) 富国強兵
Fukushin-bu (J) 覆審部
Fukushin hōin (J) 覆審法院
fuon-bunsho (J) 不穩文書
furei (J) 府令

gaichi (J) 外地
goningumi (J) 五人組
Gotō Shimpei (J) 後藤　新平

Hai-lan (C) 海南
haihan chiken (J) 廃藩置県
han-jen (C) 漢人
hanseki hōkan (J) 版籍奉還
Hanzai sokketsu rei (J) 犯罪即
　決例
Hara Kei (Takashi) (J) 原　敬

Hishō jiken tetsuzu hō (J) 非訟事
　件手続法
Hito keibatsu rei (J) 匪徒刑
　罰令
hō no sesshu (J) 法の摂取
Hoan jōrei (J) 保安条例
hokō (J) 保甲
Hōko jorei (J) 保甲条例
ho-ku (C) 合股
Hōmubu (J) 法務部
hontōjin (J) 本島人
hōritsu (J) 法律
hsiao-tsu (C) 小租
hsiao-tsu-hu (C) 小租戶
Hsi-lai-an (C) 西來庵
Hsin-chu (C) 新竹
Hsu Tsung-kan (C) 徐宗幹
Hua-lien (C) 花蓮
Huang Yen-sheng (C) 黃炎生
Huang Yen-wo (C) 黃演渥
Hung Shou-nan (C) 洪壽南
Hung Sun-hsin (C) 洪遜欣
Hyōgikai (J) 評議会

I-lan (C) 宜蘭
i-t'ai (C) 一胎
ie (J) 家
Inoue Kaoru (J) 井上　馨
isshi dōjin (J) 一視同仁
Itagaki Taisuke (J) 板垣　退助
Itō Hirobumi (J) 伊藤　博文

Jao Wei-yüeh (C) 饒維岳
Jinji soshō tetsuzu hō (J) 人事訴
　訟手続法
jishu (J) 自首

200

GLOSSARY

Jiyū minken undō (J) 自由民権運動
jōkoku (J) 上告
Jōkoku-bu (J) 上告部
Jun-yō (J) 準用
junsa (J) 巡査
junsaho (J) 巡査補

kabushiki kaisha (J) 株式会社
kaisha (J) 会社
Kaitei ritsu-rei (J) 改定事例
kakyō (J) 華僑
Kantōshu (J) 関東州
Kaohsiung (C) 高雄
kawase-tegata (J) 為替手形
k'e-chia-jen (C) 客家人
Keelung (C) 基隆
keibu (J) 警部
keibuho (J) 警部補
Keihō (J) 刑法
Keiji soshō tokubetsu tetsuzu (J) 刑事訴訟特別手続
keimuyo (J) 刑務所
keishi (J) 警視
Kodama Gentarō (J) 児玉源太郎
kogitte (J) 小切手
Kokka sōdōin hō (J) 国家総動員法
kōminka (J) 皇民化
koshu (J) 戸主
kōso (J) 控訴
Kōsoin (J) 控訴院
Kōtō hōin (J) 高等法院
Ku saibansho (J) 区裁判所
Ku-tung (C) 股東

kumiai (J) 組合
kuo-hu (C) 過戶
Kuo Huai-i (C) 郭懷一
Kuomintang (C) 國民黨
Kwangtung (C) 廣東
Kwantung (C) 關東

Lai Ho (C) 賴和
Lin Ch'eng-lu (C) 林呈祿
Lin-i-p'u (C) 林圯埔
Lin Ting-sheng (C) 林挺生
Liu-chia (C) 六甲
Liu Ming-ch'uan (C) 劉銘傳
Liu-pu ch'u-fen tse-li (C) 六部處分則例
Liu Tseng-ch'üan (C) 劉增銓
Lo Fu-hsing (C) 羅福星
lo-han-chiao (C) 羅漢腳
Lü A-yung (C) 呂阿墉

Matsuoka Yoshimasa (J) 松岡義正
Meiji (J) 明治
Miao-li (C) 苗栗
Mimpō (J) 民法
Minji ni kansuru hōritsu o Taiwan ni shikō suru no ken (J) 民事ニ関スル法律ヲ台湾ニ施行スルノ件
Minji shōji oyobi keiji ni kansuru ritsurei (J) 民事商事及刑事ニ関スル律令
Minji soshō tokubetsu tetsuzu (J) 民事訴訟特別手続
min-nan-jen (C) 閩南人
mittei (J) 密偵

mukoyōshi (J) 婿養子

naichi (J) 内地
naichihō (J) 内地法
naichijin (J) 内地人
Nan'yōchō (J) 南洋庁
Nichirei (J) 日令
nyūfu (J) 入夫

Okada Asatarō (J) 岡田 朝太郎
Okamatsu Santarō (J) 岡松 参太郎
Okinawa (J) 沖縄
ōsei fukko (J) 王政復古
Otsu (J) 大津

pao-chia (C) 保甲
P'eng-hu (C) 澎湖
Pei-p'u (C) 北埔
p'in-chin (C) 聘金
p'in-tan (C) 憑單
P'in-tung (C) 屏東
po (C) 贌
po-keng (C) 贌耕

Rinji Taiwan Kyūkan Chōsakai (J) 臨時台湾旧慣調査会
ritsurei (J) 律令
Ritsuryō (J) 律令

Saibansho kōsei hō (J) 裁判所構成法
Saibansho kōsei hō senji tokurei (J) 裁判所構成法戦時特例
saiken (J) 債権
sakoku (J) 鎖国
Sakuma (J) 佐久間

samurai (J) 侍
sanjikan (J) 参事官
san-t'ai (C) 三胎
seirei (J) 制令
Senji keiji tokubetsu hō (J) 戦時刑事特別法
Senji minji tokubetsu hō (J) 戦時民事特別法
shichi (J) 質
shichiken (J) 質権
Shida Kōtarō (J) 志田 鉀太郎
shihō hogo (J) 司法保護
Shihō shokumu teisei (J) 司法職務定制
shikō chokurei (J) 施行勅令
Shin ritsu kōryō (J) 新律綱領
shinkokujin (J) 清国人
shokusan kōgyō (J) 殖産興業
shoyūken (J) 所有権
shū (J) 州
Shu-lin (C) 署令
shūyōjo (J) 収容所
soshō dainin (J) 訴訟代人

Ta-ming tz'u-pei kuo (C) 大明慈悲國
ta-tsu (C) 大租
ta-tsu-hu (C) 大租戸
t'ai (C) 胎
T'ai-tung (C) 台東
T'ai-wan pien-ch'a liu-yü (C) 台灣編查流寓
T'ai-wan-sheng tan-hsing kuei-chang (C) 台灣省單行規章
Tai Yen-hui (C) 戴炎輝
Taichung (C) 台中
Taihoku (J) 台北

Tainan (C) 台南
Taishō (J) 大正
Taiwan ahen rei (J) 台湾阿片令
Taiwan furōsha torishimari kisoku (J) 台湾浮浪者取締規制
Taiwan hoan kisoku (J) 台湾保安規則
Taiwan jimmin gunjihan shobun rei (J) 台湾人民軍事犯処分令
Taiwan jūmin chizai rei (J) 台湾住民治罪令
Taiwan jūmin keibatsu rei (J) 台湾住民刑罰令
Taiwan jūmin minji rei (J) 台湾住民民事令
Taiwan keiji rei (J) 台湾刑事令
Taiwan minji rei (J) 台湾民事令
Taiwan ni shikō subeki hōrei ni kansuru hōritsu (J) 台湾ニ施行スヘキ法令ニ関スル件
Taiwan ni shikō suru hōritsu no tokurei ni kansuru ken (J) 台湾ニ施行スル法律ノ特例ニ関スル件
Taiwan rin-ya chōsa kisoku (J) 台湾林野調査規則
Taiwan saihyō (J) 台湾彩票
Taiwan shimbunshi jōrei (J) 台湾新聞紙条例
Taiwan Sōtokufu hōin jōrei (J) 台湾総督府法院条例
Taiwan Sōtokufu hōin shokusei (J) 台湾総督府法院職制
Taiwan Sōtokufu kōbun ruisan (J) 台湾総督府公文類纂
Taiwan Sōtokufu rinji hōin jōrei (J) 台湾総督府臨時法院条例

Taiwan tochi chōsa kisoku (J) 台湾土地調査規則
Taiwan tochi tōki kisoku (J) 台湾土地登記規則
Takano Takenori (J) 高野　孟矩
takasagozoku (J) 高砂族
Takumushō (J) 拓務省
Tan-hsin tang-an (C) 淡新檔案
Tanshui (C) 淡水
tao-hao (C) 倒號
tegata (J) 手形
teitōken (J) 抵当権
tenkō (J) 転向
tennō (J) 天皇
tennō-taiken (J) 天皇大権
ti-chi (C) 地基
tien-chu (C) 典主
tien (lease) (C) 佃
tien (pledge) (C) 典
tien-jen (C) 佃人
tochi tōkibo (J) 土地登記簿
Toguchi kisoku (J) 戸口規則
tokkō (J) 特高
Tokugawa (J) 徳川
tokurei chokurei (J) 特例勅令
tonarigumi (J) 隣組
Tou-liu (C) 斗六
Toyotomi Hideyoshi (J) 豊臣秀吉
Ts'ai Chang-lin (C) 蔡章麟
Ts'ai Po-fen (C) 蔡伯汾
ts'uo-chu (C) 厝主
ts'uo-ti (C) 厝地
T'u-k'u (C) 土庫
Tu Shin-ch'un (C) 杜新春
t'ung-yang-hsi (C) 童養媳

Wang Yu-lin (C) 王育霖
wu-hsing (C) 五刑
Wu Wen-cheng (C) 吳文中

yakusoku-tegata (J) 約束手形
Yang Hsing-tang (C) 楊杏鏜
yeh-chu (C) 業主

yeh-hu (C) 業戶
Yokai rei (J) 予戒令
yoru (J) 依る
Yu Ch'ing-fang (C) 余清芳
yüan-chu-min (C) 原住民
Yūgengaisha hō (J) 有限会社法
yung-tien (C) 永佃

Abbreviations

Fukuinshū	*Fukushin hōin hanrei zenshū* [Collection of the precedents of the Court of Appeal]
GGT	Taiwan Sōtokufu [The Government-General of Taiwan]
GGT Ac.	Taiwan Sōtokufu kōbun ruisan [Archives of the GGT]
Hōinroku	*Taiwan Sōtokufu hōin hanketsuroku* [Collection of the decisions of the GGT Court]
J. Ac.	Jih-chü ch'u-ch'i ssu-fa chih-to tang-an [Archives for the judicial system in the early period of Japanese occupation]
Kōinshū	*Kōtō hōin hanrei zenshū* [Collection of the precedents of the Higher Court]
KSEK	*Taiwan Sōtokufu keisatsu enkaku shi, dai-ni-hen: Ryō-Tai igo no chian jōkyō, (gekan)* [A history of the GGT's police, part 2: The circumstance of public peace after the possession of Taiwan, the last volume]
NTTN	*Nihon-teikoku tōkei nenkan* [Statistics of the Empire of Japan]
ROC	The Republic of China
THGP	*Taihō geppō* [Monthly report of Taiwan's law]

ABBREVIATIONS

TTK   *T'ai-wan-sheng t'ung-chi kao, chuan san, cheng-shih chih, ssu-fa p'ien* [Draft gazetteer of Taiwan Province, political affairs, division of judiciary]

TWKS   *Taiwan kanshū kiji* [Records of Taiwanese customs]

TWSH   *Taiwan shihō* [Taiwanese private law]

TWSN   *Taiwan seinen* [Taiwanese youth]

TWTT   *T'ai-wan-sheng wu-shi-i-nien-lai t'ung-chi t'i-yao* [Statistical summary of Taiwan Province for the past fifty-one years]

Notes

INTRODUCTION

1. Fix, "Mei-kuo hsüeh-sui-chieh te T'ai-wan shih yen-chiu," pp. 57–58.
2. See, e.g., Gordon, ed., *Taiwan*. An English writer even excluded all Japanese from his list of "the makers of Taiwan" (Goddard, *The Makers of Taiwan*, p. 3).
3. Fix, pp. 56–57.
4. See Gallin, *Hsin Hsing, Taiwan*, p. 1; Freedman, ed., *Family and Kinship in Chinese Society*, pp. vi–vii; Buxbaum, "Some Aspects of Substantive Family Law and Society Change in Rural China (1896–1967)," pp. ix–xiii.
5. See Gallin, pp. 1–2, 16–18; Freedman, ed., p. vii; Wolf, *Women and the Family in Rural Taiwan*, pp. 5–6; M. Cohen, *House United, House Divided*, p. 3. At least one researcher, however, considered that the Japanization in Taiwan since the late 1930s had somewhat converted traditional Chinese customs to Japanese ways. Pasternak, *Kinship and Community in Two Chinese Villages*, pp. 134–36.
6. See, e.g., Moser, *Law and Social Change in a Chinese Community*, pp. 24–33. Cf. Buxbaum, pp. 183–86, 193–96, 200–3, 210–14.
7. See also Ch'en K'ung-li, "Ch'ing-tai T'ai-wan she-hui fa-chan te mo-shih wen-t'i," pp. 70–75.
8. The Tan-Hsin archives collection of documents of local Ch'ing governments in North Taiwan has been used to study traditional Chinese law. See, e.g., Chang Bin Liu, "Chinese Commercial Law in the Late Ch'ing (1842–1911)"; Allee, *Law and Local Society in Late Imperial China*.
9. See, e.g., Gallin, ; Wolf, ; M. Cohen,; Ahern, *The Cult of the Dead in a Chinese Village*.
10. See, e.g., Barclay, *Colonial Development and Population in Taiwan*, p. 52; Gallin, p. 2; Wolf, p. 5.
11. See, e.g., Buxbaum, pp. 184–85.
12. Ch'en Shao-hsiang, *T'ai-wan te jen-k'ou pien-ch'ien*, pp. 171–72. For instance, Taiwanese in the urban areas were more likely to have had contact with Japanese colonial education. Tsurumi, *Japanese Colonial Education in Taiwan 1895–1945*, p. 156.

13. Fix, pp. 58–59.

14. Gates, "Introduction," in *The Anthropology of Taiwanese Society*, ed. Ahern and Gates, p. 8. See, e.g., Gold, *State and Society in the Taiwan Miracle*, p. 16.

15. Gates, p. 9. Douglas Fix has strongly argued that if the history of the Japanese period is not well studied, the development of Taiwan in the twentieth century cannot be understood; and if the intention and process involved in this unique development of Taiwan are not kept in mind, it is impossible to analyze socioeconomic changes in postwar Taiwan. Fix, p. 58.

16. See, e.g., Barclay; E. Chen, "Japanese Colonialism in Korea and Formosa"; C. Chen, "Japanese Socio-political Control in Taiwan"; Ho, "Economic Development of Colonial Taiwan," pp. 417–39; Tsurumi.

17. One of the important incentives of Japan and China for importing Western law was to end the extraterritorial rights of the Western powers. See Matsui Yoshirō, "Jōyaku kaisei," pp. 241–52, 259; Rice, "Notes on International Law," p. 891; Chan Heng-chü, *Chung-kuo chin-tai fa-chih shih*, p. 100.

18. In discussions about the influence of modern European laws (e.g., French, German, or Swiss law), three groups of countries are ordinarily listed: (1) other European countries with a Christian civilization, (2) former colonies ruled by European powers, and (3) independent countries with non-Western civilization. Mizuta Yohio, "Gaikokuhō no eikyō to wa nani ka," p. 25. The Taiwan case does not belong to any of these groups.

19. See Chang Lung-chih, *Tsu-ch'ün kuan-hsi*, pp. 5–11.

20. Early in 1946, one year after Japan's defeat, the Chinese Nationalist government presented such an official comment upon the fifty years of Japanese rule on Taiwan. T'ai-wan-sheng hsing-cheng chang-kuan kung-shu Min-cheng ch'u (ROC), *T'ai-wan min-cheng*, pp. 6, 465.

21. See, e.g., Lin Mei-jung, *Jen-lei-hsüeh yü T'ai-wan*, pp. 7–9; Chang Yen-hsien, "Tui T'ai-wan shih yen-chiu te ch'i-tai," pp. 4–5.

22. See, e.g., Wu Wen-hsing, "Jih-chü shih-ch'i T'ai-wan te fang-tsu tuan-fa yün-tung," p. 69; Ts'ai Shu-lin, "She-hui ti-wei ch'ü-te," pp. 2–3; Chou Wan-yao, *Jih-chü shih-tai te T'ai-wan i-hui*, p. 8.

23. See, e.g., Tai Yen-hui, "Wu-shih nien lai chih T'ai-wan fa-chih," *T'ai-wan wen-hua*, 5: 1 (1948), modified and reprinted in "Jih-pen t'ung-chih shih-ch'i te T'ai-wan fa-chih," pp. 79–86; *TTK*, vol. 1, pp. 141–318, vol. 2, pp. 1–367; Huang Ching-chia, *Jih-chü shih-ch'i chih T'ai-wan chih-min-ti fa-chih*.

24. See Ts'ai Tun-ming, "Opening Remarks," pp.3–5; Wang Tse-chien, "Min-fa wu-shih nien," p. 8. These two scholars currently teach criminal law and civil law respectively at National Taiwan University.

25. As noted in *TTK*, Taiwan was ceded to Japan more than two decades before China began to adopt Western law; Japan had Westernized its legal system thirty years

before China and generally extended its Westernized law to colonial Taiwan. *TTK*, vol. 1, p. 6.

26. In 1989, some 17,331,254 people in Taiwan (86.2 percent of the population) or their ancestors had experienced the Westernization of law in Taiwan under Japanese rule; in contrast, 2,776,186 (13.8 percent) people in Taiwan or their ancestors had experienced the Westernization of law in China before 1945. See Hsing-cheng-yüan Chu-chi-ch'u (ROC), *Chung-hua min-kuo t'ung-chi nien-chien*, pp. 68–69.

27. For instance, one Japanese scholar has argued that because Japanese modernization took into consideration the national characteristics of the colonized, the Taiwanese had been somewhat assimilated. Mukōyama Hiroo, "Nihon tōchi ka ni okeru Taiwan no hō to seiji," pp. 61–106.

28. Most Japanese scholars who study China have regarded Taiwan as a part of China (the People's Republic of China) and further consider that independent study of Taiwan would imply "two Chinas" or "one China, one Taiwan," positions that irritate the People's Republic. But one Japanese professor has pointed out that the image of Taiwan held by those scholars reflects their ignorance of the situation of Taiwanese society; and even supposing that Taiwan were a part of China, it is useful to make an academic comparison between the development of Taiwan after 1949, the year that the PRC was established, and that of mainland China. Ishida Hiroshi, "Taiwan-kenkyū to Chūkoku-kenkyū," p. 5.

29. Myers, "Post–World War II Japanese Historiography of Japan's Formal Colonial Empire," in *The Japanese Colonial Empire, 1895–1945*, ed. Myers and Peattie, pp. 455–77.

30. See, e.g., Kō Se-kai, *Nihon tōchika no Taiwan*; To Shōgen, *Nihon teikokushugika no Taiwan*; Mukōyama Hiroo, *Nihon tōchika ni okeru Taiwan minzoku undō shi*. See also Taiwan Kingendaishi Kenkyūkai, comp., "Sengo Nihon ni okeru Taiwan kingaidaishi kenkyū bunken mokuroku," pp. 152–204.

31. See, e.g., Nakamura Akira, "Shokuminchi hō," pp. 175–206. The author was a legal professor at Imperial Taihoku (Taipei) University in colonial Taiwan. Ibid., p. 302.

32. This institute is the Taiwan-shiryō Kenkyūkai [The Society for the Study of Taiwan's Historical Material] in Chūkyō Daigaku Shagai-kagaku Kenkyūjo [Social Science Institute, Chūkyō University]. See Sung Chin-hsiu, "Jih-pen chung-ching ta-hsüeh she-hui k'o-hsüeh yen-chiu-so, T'ai-wan shih-liao yen-chiu-hui," pp. 30–31.

33. See Sawaki Takao, "Hō no keiju," pp. 124–42, 152–58.

34. Such research will probably contribute to a general theory of the reception of modern Western law in East Asia. This reception is frequently called "modernization" or "Westernization."

35. On the lack of modern nationalism, see also Wolf, p. 5.

36. See Wang Shih-ch'ing, "Chieh-shao jih-chü shih-ch'i T'ai-wan tsung-tu-fu tang-an," p. 157. In the past, the archives kept by the Government of Taiwan Province

(in Nan-t'ou) were accessible only to those who had been approved by the authorities. Therefore, these archives, although they had been known for a long time, were seldom used for the study of Japanese colonial rule in Taiwan. The author was fortunately permitted to read the entire archives in the summer of 1992. Recently, the archives have become open to the public and thus have been often used by researchers.

37. See T'ai-wan-sheng wen-hsien wei-yüan-hui (ROC), trans. and ed., *Jih-chü ch'u-ch'i ssu-fa chih-to tang-an*.

38. See Hsü Hsüeh-chi et al., comps., *Hsien tsang T'ai-wan tsung-tu-fu tang-an tsung mu-lu*. Some of these catalogs have already been revised and published by Japanese Chūkyō University. See also note 32.

39. The decisions of the GGT courts were also occasionally used to research colonial law. Buxbaum cited a few decisions in his dissertation but did not mention the publications reporting those decisions. See Buxbaum, pp. 184–85, 220–21. Ts'ai Chang-lin listed a number of case citations but did not discuss the content of them. See *TTK*, vol. 1, pp. 263–91.

40. *Taiwan shihō* was published by Rinji Taiwan Kyūkan Chōsakai, a special agency instituted by the Japanese government. *Taiwan kanshū kiji* was published by Taiwan Kanshū Kenkyūkai, organized largely by Japanese judicial officials in Taiwan. *Taihō geppō* was published by Taihō Geppō Hakkōsho managed by the department of judicial affairs in the GGT. After *TWKS* stopped publishing in 1907, the papers concerning Taiwanese customs were published by *THGP*.

41. The GGT published annual reports of *Taiwan Sōtokufu tōkeisho* [Statistical yearbooks of GGT, 1897–1942] and *Taiwan Sōtokufu hanzai tōkei* [Criminal statistics of GGT, 1909–1942]. In addition, *Nihon-teikoku tōkei nenkan* [Statistics of the Empire of Japan], published by the Japanese central government, included some statistics concerning colonial Taiwan. In 1946, the Chinese Nationalist government on Taiwan (T'ai-wan-sheng hsing-cheng chang-kuan kung-shu) also compiled the statistics made by the former Japanese government and then published *T' ai-wan-shenq wu-shih-i-nien-lai t' ung-chi t' i-yao* [A statistical summary of Taiwan Province for the past fifty-one years].

42. This magazine was published by Taiwanese engaged in a modern political movement against the GGT in the 1920s. Those Taiwanese intellectuals also published *Taiwan minppō* (1923–1930) and *Taiwan shin minppō* (1930–1941). These two publications paid more attention to reporting news and had few academic articles concerning criminal and civil laws.

43. In civil and criminal law, the definition of *hontōjin* did not include mountain aborigines, although the Taiwan Household Regulation incorporated mountain aborigines into its definition of *hontōjin* for the specific purpose of the regulation. In addition, beginning in 1933, those people who were not *hontōjin* were allowed to enter

the *hontōjin*'s household through marriage or adoption. Those people who entered the household of *hontōjin* became *hontōjin*, but they lost this status if they later left the *hontōjin*'s household. Aneha Shōhei, *Hontōjin nomi ni kansuru shinzokuhō*, pp. 10–12.

44. According to the 1895 treaty ceding Taiwan to Japan, Japan allowed Taiwan's inhabitants to decide their nationality before May 8, 1897. In practice, those inhabitants who did not want to be Japanese subjects had to report their selecting Ch'ing nationality to the colonial authorities within these two years. The rest of Taiwan's inhabitants became Japanese subjects, namely, Taiwanese in this book. The number of Taiwan's inhabitants who selected Ch'ing nationality was about 4,500 (0.16 percent of the population). See Huang Chao-t'ang, *T'ai-wan tsung-tu-fu*, pp. 65–67. On the nationals of Ch'ing or ROC in Taiwan during the Japanese period, see Sanka Shiho, "Taiwan kakyō, ni," pp. 56–59, 69–71.

45. For description of the four different groups of people in Taiwan under Japanese rule, see Aneha, pp. 6–12. From the standpoint of Taiwan's history, the term "mainland" may mean either mainland China or mainland Japan.

46. Today, in my opinion, the term "Taiwanese" includes all people who live on the island of Taiwan now, including (1) "aborigines," i.e., the aborigines who inhabited the island before Han Chinese arrived and who maintain their indigenous culture, as well as their descendants; (2) "original Taiwanese," i.e., the Southern Fukienese and Hakka who migrated to Taiwan before 1895 and the plains aborigines, and their descendants; and (3) "Chinese-mainlanders," i.e., the "Chinese" as defined in this book and the people immigrating from the Chinese mainland after 1945 and their descendants. See also Wang, "Chapter 4: Taiwan," pp. 125–27. I use "original" to name the second category because they were called Taiwanese in the Japanese period. Because "mainlanders" in Taiwan's history may mean either Japanese mainlanders (*naichijin*) or Chinese mainlanders, I use "Chinese-mainlanders" to refer to the people in the third category.

47. As an exception, the names of old Taiwanese civil customs that were applied by Japanese colonial courts are still romanized from Mandarin Chinese rather than the official language, Japanese, because they originated from customs in the Ch'ing period and were not found in Japan's law.

48. Gold, p. 11.

49. See, e.g., Stead, ed., *Japan by the Japanese*, pp. 581, 586.

1 / BACKGROUND OF LEGAL REFORM

1. See Hsieh, "The Physical Setting of Taiwan," p. 1; U.S. Department of the Navy, *Civil Affairs Handbook: Taiwan (Formosa)* OPNAV 50E-12, p. 1. Since 1949,

Kinmen Island and Matsu Island, very small islands off the coast of China (PRC), may be regarded as "politically subordinate islands" of Taiwan. These islands, however, were not a part of Taiwan under Japanese rule.

2. Hsieh, p. 2.

3. U.S. Department of the Navy, *Civil Affairs Handbook: Taiwan (Formosa)*, pp. 1, 4.

4. See Mukōyama Hiroo, *Nihon tōchika ni okeru Taiwan minzoku undō shi*, p. 3; Kondō Ken'ichi, ed., *Taiheiyō senka no Chōsen oyobi Taiwan*, p. 1.

5. Ts'ao Yung-he, "Ming-Cheng shih-ch'i i-ch'ien chih T'ai-wan," p. 40.

6. See Shih Ming, *T'ai-wan-jen ssu-pai-nien shih*, pp. 14–16.

7. See Campbell, ed., *Formosa under the Dutch*, pp. 9–13.

8. See Shih, pp. 20–28. Cf. Ts'ao, pp. 41–44; Kuo, "Early Stages of the Sinicization of Taiwan, 230–1683," pp. 21–22.

9. See Ts'ao, pp. 44–47; Kuo, pp. 22–24; Hung, "Taiwan under the Cheng Family 1662–1683," pp. 25–34.

10. In 1620 a band of Chinese pirate-traders from southern Fukien immigrated to the southern coast of Taiwan Island. Most of them later returned to the Fukien coast, where they formed the Cheng band led by Cheng Chih-lung and then his son, Cheng Ch'eng-kung (Koxinga). See Lien Heng, *T'ai-wan t'ung-shih*, pp. 697–701.

11. See Mukōyama, p. 6; Takekoshi, *Japanese Rule in Formosa*, pp. 49–53; Hung, pp. 34–35, 60.

12. Ts'ao, p. 51; Shih, p. 52.

13. See Ts'ao, p. 52; Shih, pp. 54–55; Hung, pp. 49–50.

14. See Beckmann, "Brief Episodes—Dutch and Spanish Rule," pp. 34–36; Ts'ao, pp. 56–57; Shih, pp. 56–58.

15. According to modern international law, as derived from Western Europe, Dutch sovereignty over the island was recognized by international society on the grounds that no other states, including Ming China and Tokugawa Japan, protested against the exercise of Dutch authority in these areas. See P'eng Ming-min and Huang Chao-t'ang, *Taiwan no hōteki chi-i*, p. 6. The Dutch occupied only the southern plain of Taiwan Island in 1624 but extended their reach to the northern part of the island in 1642.

16. Hsu, "Chinese Colonization of Taiwan," p. 54.

17. See Angelino, *Colonial Policy*, vol. 2, pp. 2–3; see also Yanaihara Tadao, *Shokumin*, p. 316.

18. P'eng and Huang, p. 7.

19. Angelino, p. 3.

20. See Hsu, p. 61; *TTK*, vol. 1, pp. 2–5.

21. This may explain why the company in Batavia did not show much concern over the loss of Formosa. See Angelino, p. 5. In 1663, to seek revenge, the Dutch helped

NOTES

the Manchu government defeat the Cheng force, landing a force of two hundred men at Keelung. But because of the lack of trade, they finally departed again in 1668. See Beckmann, p. 56.

22. The Dutch did not welcome Han Chinese after a Han Chinese uprising against the Dutch occurred in 1652; furthermore, the Manchu maritime prohibition of 1656 obstructed travel to Taiwan.

23. See Hsu, pp. 62–63, 71.

24. Shih, p. 96.

25. See ibid., pp. 67, 81–82. Cf. Beckmann, p. 47.

26. See Shih, pp. 94, 110, 190–91; Hung, p. 192; Hsu, p. 79. The "crown fields" owned by the Dutch East India Company were nominally changed into "government fields" owned by the Cheng family and officials.

27. See Hsu, pp. 54–59, 77–78; Hung, pp. 50–56.

28. See Hung, p. 125; P'eng and Huang, pp. 9–10, 23.

29. Cf. Hung, p. 123.

30. Koxinga's son, Cheng Ching, also retreated to Taiwan after the Chengs were defeated by the Ch'ing forces in China. Fearing the inhospitability of Taiwan, many high-ranking officers of the Cheng government refused to leave for Taiwan and even defected to the Ch'ing. See Hung, pp. 89, 130–31, 166–68, 175, 279; Hsu, p. 84.

31. See Hung, p. 238; Hsu, p. 89.

32. In the peace talks of 1662, Cheng Ching demanded that Taiwan be treated in accordance with the precedent of Korea. Thus, for example, Taiwan's people were not required to adopt the Manchu queue. Hung, pp. 146–47.

33. See Wang Yu-te, *T'ai-wan*, pp. 62–64; Hung, p. 266.

34. See Hung, pp. 123–27, 177–79; 229–38; Hsu, p. 80.

35. The Dutch influences on Taiwan were not completely erased by the Cheng regime. Some measures being advantageous to the ruler, like crown fields, were maintained by the Cheng regime. Cf. Hung, p. 137.

36. Cf. Hung, p. 267.

37. The traditional Chinese regarded Westerners as "barbarians" and considered international trade to be subsumed under the tributary system. Hung, pp. 208, 210, n. 127. After Ch'ing China conquered Taiwan in 1683, Taiwan's prosperous international trade ended. Hsu, p. 102.

38. Hsu, p. 92.

39. For instance, Japan became Taiwan's largest trading partner during this period. Hung, p. 208.

40. Most of the Han Chinese settlers hated the Dutch after the 1652 Kuo Huai-i Incident, and they remained dialectically and culturally Southern Fukienese, the same as Koxinga. Besides, in the view of the settlers, a Han Chinese ruler presumably could help them acquire land from the aborigines.

41. See Hsu, p. 97. The exact number of the increase is not known. According to another source, the estimated number of Han Chinese during this time is 150,000 to 200,000. See Shih, p. 113. This increase was mainly attributed to the migration of Cheng's soldiers and some Fukien residents who refused to be relocated by the coastal removal policy. They became new settlers of Taiwan society during the Cheng period. Hsu, pp. 92, 97.

42. See Hsu, pp. 89–90; Hung, pp. 192–95.

43. See Hsu, pp. 247–50. An emperor of Ch'ing initially said that "Taiwan is only a tiny island. We add nothing if we obtain it; we lose nothing if we do not obtain it."

44. Hai-nan is another large island neighboring mainland China. But Hai-nan is much closer to mainland China than is Taiwan and thus was controlled by the regime on the Chinese mainland from a much earlier time. In fact, early in 111 B.C., Hai-nan Island was governed by the Han dynasty. In contrast, not until 1662 did a Han Chinese regime (the Cheng) govern Taiwan Island, but the Cheng regime virtually did not govern mainland China. See Chang Shih-hsien, "Ch'ing-tai chih-T'ai Cheng-ts'e te hua-chan," pp. 221–22.

45. See ibid., pp. 223, 227.

46. *T'ai-wan pien-ch'a liu-yü*, in the *Liu-pu ch'u-fen tse-li* (Punishment Regulations of the Six Boards). Liu, "Chinese Commercial Law in the Late Ch'ing (1842–1911)," p. 93.

47. Tai Yen-hui, *Ch'ing-tai T'ai-wan chih hsiang-chih*, pp. 274–76.

48. For the legal provisions, see ibid., p. 276; Liu, p. 95.

49. See Shih, pp. 141–42.

50. See Tai, pp. 276–80.

51. Liu, p. 98.

52. Shih, p. 122; Chang Shih-hsien, pp. 226–27.

53. Ting Yüeh-chien, ed., *Chih-T'ai pi-kao lu*, pp. 150, 159. All writings collected in this book were written by high-ranking officials of the Ch'ing government on Taiwan. See also Tai, pp. 280–81.

54. Ting, p. 160. During Lin Shuang-wen's revolt and Ts'ao Ch'ien's disturbances, a small number of Taiwan people were recruited to the Ch'ing army. Hsu, p. 582.

55. See Liu, p. 99.

56. See Chang Shih-hsien, pp. 227–29, 233–35.

57. See Hsu, pp. 108–32, 148, table 8.

58. Huang Fu-san, "Ch'ing-tai T'ai-wan Han-jen chih keng-ti ch'ü-te wen-ti," pp. 198–201.

59. Hsu, p. 316; Chang Sheng-yen, *T'ai-wan shih yen-chiu*, pp. 64–65.

60. See Hsu, pp. 312–14, 479–80.

61. Ch'en Ch'iu-k'un, "T'ai-wan t'u-ti te k'ai-hua (1700–1756)," p. 168.

62. The collection of taxes has been a problem throughout Chinese imperial history. For a general overview of how it has affected various dynastic regimes, see Fairbank, Reischauer, and Craig, *East Asia*, pp. 100–2, 118–22, 127–29.

63. See Ch'en Ch'iu-k'un, pp. 164–65, 167.

64. See Ting, p. 349; Tai, p. 283; Hsu, p. 265.

65. On the introduction of the magistrate, clerks, and runners in imperial China, see Ch'ü, *Local Government in China under the Ch'ing*, chaps. 2, 3, 4. On the situation in Taiwan, see Tai, pp. 281–87.

66. See Hsu, p. 267; Tai, pp. 301–2.

67. Two rival ethnic, professional, or otherwise related groups fought each other. For example, within a certain area, all of the Southern Fukienese settlers fought with all of the Hakka settlers.

68. Tai, pp. 323–24.

69. Hsu, pp. 464, 472–78; Tai, pp. 323–26.

70. HSu, pp. 478–82.

71. Tai, pp. 305–6, 310, 331.

72. Hsu, pp. 493–94; Tai, pp. 301–2.

73. Harrell, "From Xiedou to Yijun," pp. 111–14.

74. Tai, pp. 298–99, 302–3.

75. But communal strife between different surnames, among people with identical surnames, and among groups with the same occupation still prevailed. See Hsu, p. 502. The transformation of settler society after the 1860s turned the focus of internal conflict away from ethnic conflict. On the one hand, trade with the West after the 1860s brought some economic profit to Taiwan, which relaxed the economic tension between the three groups and encouraged them to cooperate. On the other hand, some local strongmen became agents of the state and discouraged the occurrence of communal strife. See Harrell, pp. 107, 117–19; Lin Man-hung, "Mao-i yü Ch'ing-mo T'ai-wan te ching-chi she-hui pien-ch'ien (1960–1895)," pp. 257–58.

76. See Harrell, p. 122; Weng Chia-yin, *T'ai-wan Han-jen wu-chuang k'ang-jih*, pp. 42–43. Cf. Hsu, p. 523.

77. The Hakka were the least likely to revolt because they were a minority group and generally sided with the government. Among various social strata, the landlords who could mobilize their tenant peasants revolted against the government most frequently. See Hsu, pp. 555, 557–58, 569, 574.

78. See Hsu, p. 526; Weng, p. 43.

79. Hsu, pp. 563–64.

80. Ibid., pp. 572–73. See also Tai, pp. 291–93.

81. See Hsu, pp. 535, 564–72; Weng, p. 22. Cf. Shih, p. 200.

82. That various clan and worship organizations were instituted in Taiwan actu-

ally meant that settlers wanted to live and die on the island, not return to the Chinese mainland. See Ch'en Ch'i-nan, "T'ai-wan pen-t'u i-shih te hsing-ch'eng chi ch'i han-i," pp. 94–95.

83. For the origin of this system, see TWSH, vol. 1, pt. 1, pp. 268–74.

84. See Tai, pp. 320–22; Wichberg, "Continuities in Land Tenure, 1990–1940," pp. 212–17.

85. See TTK, vol. 1, pp. 94–95; Allee, *Law and Local Society in Late Imperial China*, pp. 53–54; P. Huang, "Codified Law and Magisterial Adjudication in the Qing," pp. 142–43 The question of whether the magistrates decided those civil suits in accordance with the Chi'ng Code is still controversial.

86. See Liu, p. 99.

87. Ch'en Ch'iu-k'un, pp. 166–67; Shih, pp. 161–64.

88. Harrell, pp. 112–14.

89. See also Ch'en K'ung-li, "Ch'ing-tai T'ai-wan she-hui fa-chan te mo-shih wen-t'i," p. 71.

90. Harrell, pp. 116–19.

91. See also Ch'en K'ung-li, p. 71. A similar process of economic development might have occurred in some parts of mainland China, but the number of such areas is relatively small in comparison to the entire Chinese mainland.

92. See Higashi Yoshio, *Taiwan kenzaishi kenkyū*, pp. 318–69.

93. See Lin, pp. 240–42, 260–61; Weng, pp. 23–24.

94. Myers, "Taiwan under Ch'ing Imperial Rule, 1684–1895," p. 408.

95. Chu, "Liu Ming-ch'uan and the Modernization of Taiwan," p. 52.

96. These Asian societies included independent countries like Japan and other Western colonies in Asia. Then, in the early twentieth century, Siam and China also tried to Westernize their laws under Western pressure.

97. Ishii, ed., *Japanese Legislation in the Meiji Era*, pp. 15–16.

98. As a matter of law, a centralized government was established through the measures of "return of the people and land to the emperor" (*hanseki hōkan*) and "abolition of fiefs and establishment of prefectures" (*haihan chiken*). See Fairbank, Reischauer, and Craig, pp. 502–3, 505–6.

99. Fukushima Masao, "Hō no keiju to shakai=keizai no kindaika (I)," pp. 11–12.

100. Shin ritsu kōryō (Dec. 20, 1870); Kaitei ritsurei (Declaration No. 206, 1873). See also Ishii, p. 17.

101. Mukai and Toshitani, "The Progress and Problems of Compiling the Civil Code in the Early Meiji Era," pp. 34–35; Noda, *Introduction to Japanese Law*, p. 8.

102. See Mukai and Toshitani, pp. 32–33.

103. D. Henderson, "Law and Political Modernization in Japan," pp. 432–33.

104. See Matsui Yoshiro, "Jōyaku kaisei," pp. 232, 241–45.

105. Mukai and Toshitani, pp. 37–39; Noda, pp. 43–47.

106. Japan already had a tradition of courtlike bodies, but no modern courts were established until the 1870s. See Henderson, pp. 407–8.

107. See Mukai and Toshitani, p. 40.

108. Shihō shokumu teisei, 1872.

109. Saibansho kōsei hō (Law No. 6, 1890).

110. See Yokoyama Kōichirō, "Keibatsu chian kikō no seibi," pp. 309–11, 347–48; Ishii, pp. 275–95, 479–89.

111. Chizaihō (Declaration No. 37, 1880).

112. See Yokoyama, pp. 309–11, 315–16, 332–36, 345–46; Ishii, pp. 320–35, 512–24.

113. Minji soshō hō (Law No. 29, 1890).

114. Jinji soshō tetsuzu hō (Law No. 13, 1898); Hishō jiken tetsuzu hō (Law No. 14, 1898). See Ishii, pp. 295–320, 490–511; Henderson, pp. 409–10.

115. Keihō (Declaration No. 36, 1880).

116. See Yokoyama, pp. 314–17, 329–32, 335, 343; Takayanagi, "A Century of Innovation," pp. 15–17. On special criminal statutes, see note 129 and accompanying text.

117. See Mukai and Toshitani, pp. 41–44.

118. Mimpō (Law No. 89, 1896; Law No. 9, 1898).

119. See Mukai and Toshitani, pp. 49–58; Ishii, p. 591.

120. To balance the demands of traditionalists and radical innovators, the Meiji government preserved some old practices in the new Westernized system. See Epp, "Threat to Tradition," pp. 211–16.

121. Noda, p. 49. The essence of the Meiji Restoration is the establishment of an antipopular authoritarian rule. Igeda, Yamanaka, and Ishikawa, *Nihon kindaihō shi*, p. 7.

122. Mukai and Toshitani, pp. 36–37.

123. See Noda, p. 50; Igada, Yamanaka, and Ishikawa, pp. 122–24.

124. Fukushima Masao, "Hō no keiju to shakai=keizai no kindaika (III)," p. 26.

125. Noda, p. 50.

126. See Mukai Ken, "Mimpō-ten no hensan," pp. 387–93. But it should be noted that German scholarship was very useful for Japanese analysis and exegesis of their new codes. Henderson, p. 437.

127. *Dai Nippon teikoku kempō* (Feb. 11, 1889), arts. 60, 61. See Henderson, pp. 426–28.

128. See Yokoyama, pp. 331–32; Ishii, pp. 536–37.

129. Henderson, p. 419. See also Yokoyama, pp. 343–49.

130. See Mukai and Toshitani, pp. 51, 56–58.

131. Kuroki, "Modernization on the Law," p. 4.

132. See Noda Yoshiyuki et al., "Nihon in okeru gaikokuhō no sesshu," pp. 166–67; Mizuta Yohio, "Gaikokuhō no eikyō to wa nani ka," pp. 34–35, n. 14; Masaji Chiba, *Legal Pluralism*, pp. 154–56.

133. See Ishii, p. 23; Fukushima, "Hō no keiju to shakai=keizai no kindaika (I)," p. 21.

134. Noda, pp. 42, 62.

135. Ibid., pp. 13, 15; Ishii, p. 23.

136. See Nakamura Hideo, "Shihō seido to Nihon no kindaika," pp. 9, 16–17; Henderson, pp. 455–56.

137. Haley, *Authority without Power*, p. 19.

138. Aoyagi Tsunatarō, *Sōtoku seiji shi ron*, p. 198.

139. See Bodde and Morris, *Law in Imperial China*, pp. 23–25.

140. See Kerr, *Formosa, Licensed Revolution, and the Home Rule Movement, 1895–1945*, pp. 18–19; Takekoshi, "Japan's Colonial Policy," p. 96.

141. Jansen, "Japanese Imperialism," p. 64.

2 / RECEPTION OF WESTERN LAW IN COLONIAL LEGISLATION

1. See Wu Mi-ch'a, *T'ai-wan chin-tai shih yen-chiu*, pp. 270–72; Mukōyama Hiroo, *Nihon tōchika ni okeru Taiwan minzoku undō shi*, pp. 15–18.

2. See E. Chen, "Japan's Decision to Annex Taiwan," pp. 61–72.

3. Peattie, "Japanese Attitudes toward Colonialism, 1895–1945," p. 80 (hereafter cited as "Japanese Colonialism").

4. Itō Hirobumi, ed., *Taiwan shiryō*, pp. 143–46, 407–8.

5. See Betts, *Assimilation and Association in French Colonial Theory, 1890–1914*, pp. 10–32, 50.

6. This instruction expressed in the last paragraph that the governor-general should first govern the island in accordance with listed items and then produce detailed reports; according to them, the central government would decide on appropriate permanent institutions. Itō, pp. 434–39.

7. E. Chen, "The Attempt to Integrate the Empire," pp. 250–51; Itō, pp. 32–34.

8. Grajdanzev, "Formosa (Taiwan) under Japanese Rule," p. 311.

9. See Mukōyama, pp. 59–119.

10. See Gaimushō Jōyakukyoku Hōkika (Japan), *Nihon tōchika gojunen no Taiwan*, pp. 141–47 (hereafter cited as *Gojunen no Taiwan*).

11. Itō, p. 33.

12. E. Chen, "Attempt to Integrate," p. 247. Although Taiwan was thus regarded as a colony, the Japanese central government was unwilling to call Taiwan a "colony" but used the term "new territory" or later "outer area" (*gaichi*). See Nakamura Akira, *Shokuminchi tōchihō no konpon mondai*, pp. 105–9.

13. Taiwan ni shikō subeki hōrei ni kansuru hōritsu (Title 63, 1896).

14. Ibid., arts. 1, 5. See Gaimushō Jōyakukyoku Hōkika (Japan), *Taiwan no inin rippō seido*, pp. 7–8 (hereafter cited as *Inin rippō*).

15. Taiwan Sōtokufu kansei (Ordinance No. 88, 1896), arts. 3, 5, 8. See *Gojunen no Taiwan*, p. 148; E. Chen, "Japanese Colonialism in Korea and Formosa. A Comparison of the Systems of Political Control," pp. 132–40 (hereafter cited as "Political Control").

16. In the draft of the central government, a special colonial law should be enacted by a "legislative council" that was recommended by the two foreign advisers. But such provision was deleted because it was considered improper to have native members join this council under the circumstances of prevalent anti-Japanese activities in Taiwan. See *Inin rippō*, p. 32.

17. Nakamura Akira, "Shokuminchi hō," p. 177; Haruyama Meitetsu, "Kindai Nihon no shokuminchi tōchi to Hara Kei," 1895–1934 p. 12.

18. See Naikaku Kirokuka (Japan), comp., *Taiwan ni shikō suru hōrei ni kansuru hōritsu so no enkaku oyobi genkō ritsurei*, pp. 3–291.

19. See Shimizu Chō, *Chikujō teikoku kempō kōgi*, pp. 62–64; Sasaki Sōichi, *Nihon kempō yōron*, pp. 156–57; Uesugi Shinkichi, *Teikoku kempō jutsugi*, pp. 404–6; Hozumi Yatsuka, *Kempō teiyō, jōkan*, pp. 328–29. The principal arguments they put forward were as follows. (1) The acquisition of new territory was foreseen and the provisions concerning the territory of the empire as well as the jurisdiction of the Constitution were intentionally omitted. This meant that Japanese territory included not only the original territory but also any territory acquired after the time of the Constitution's enactment, and that any territory of the empire of course was under the jurisdiction of the Constitution. (2) If the application of the Constitution depended on the social conditions of the new territory, the ambiguity of degree of social conditions would make the application of the Constitution unclear; if the question whether or not the Constitution was applied could not be determined by review to the Constitution itself, the Constitution would lose its nature as supreme law. (3) Any special laws, if necessary, could still be enacted for the new territory under the jurisdiction of the Constitution.

20. See Ichimura Mitsue, *Teikoku kempō ron*, pp. 235–43. The early opinion of Minobe Tatsukichi also supported this argument. See Haruyama, p. 15. He argued that the territory of the empire was not coincident with the jurisdiction of law that included the Constitution and that the Constitution, like other Japanese law, was enacted for Japanese society, not other societies with different cultures and customs, as expressed in the Preamble to the Constitution. In connection with the fact that Title 63 was enacted by the Diet, these influential legal scholars argued that since Taiwan should be governed by the powers of the emperor (*tennō-taiken*; that is, the powers of the executive and military organs) beyond the Constitution, the legislative process was only one of the several means that the emperor might select to exercise his power.

21. See *Gojunen no Taiwan*, pp. 37–39. In contrast, because Kwantung Leased Territory (Kantōshū) and Micronesia (Nan'yōchō) were considered to be beyond the jurisdiction of the Constitution, the legislation of the two territories did not need to be regulated by Diet-enacted law but merely by imperial ordinance. Yamazaki Tanshō, *Gaichi tōchi kikō no kenkyū*, p. 5.

22. Stead, ed., *Japan by the Japanese*, p. 599.

23. Nakano, *The Ordinance Power of the Japanese Emperor*, pp. 135–36.

24. See *Gojunen no Taiwan*, pp. 34, 40–41; Nagao Keitoku and Ōda Shūkichi, *Taiwan gyōseihō taii*, pp. 3–5; Tanino Tadasu, *Taiwan shin minjihō*, pp. 46–47. Tanino was head of the colonial supreme court in 1923 (Tanino, *Taiwan*, p. 9). Nagao was head of the Department of Legal Affairs of the GGT from 1918 to 1923, and the first edition of his book cited above was published in 1923 (Kōnan Shimbunsha, ed., *Taiwan jinshi kan*, p. 303).

25. J. Ac., p. 983.

26. See Nakamura, *Konpon mondai*, pp. 98–100; *Gojunen no Taiwan*, p. 43.

27. See Sasaki Chūzō and Tagahashi Buichirō, *Taiwan gyōseihō ron*, p. 8. See also Nakamura, *Konpon mondai*, p. 102, n. 7.

28. *Gojunen no Taiwan*, pp. 44–45.

29. See, e.g., Minobe Tatsukichi, *Chikujō kempō seigi*, pp. 35–41; Nakamura, *Konpon mondai*, p. 13. See also Haruyama, pp 15–16.

30. Most Western colonialist powers legally excluded the colony from the jurisdiction of the constitution of the mother country. Nakamura, *Konpon mondai*, pp. 7–21.

31. See Lin Ch'eng-lu, "Liu-san wen-ti chih yün-ming," pp. 23–25.

32. See Haruyama, pp. 29–30, 49; Nakamura, *Konpon mondai*, pp. 75–80.

33. Wu Mi-ch'a, p. 144. This political party supported the extension of the effective duration of Title 63, and in return the government agreed to prepare a budget for establishing this university in the constituency of many members of the party. Since Taiwan was not the constituency of any members of political parties, they of course did not need to argue the issue of Title 63 for the people in Taiwan.

34. See Ichimura, pp. 240–41. See also Nakamura, "Shokuminchi hō," p. 178; Tai Yen-hui, "Jih-pen t'ung-chih shih-ch'i te T'ai-wan fa-chih," p. 79; Huang Ching-chia, *Jih-chü shih-ch'i chih T'ai-wan chih-min-ti fa-chih*, p. 60.

35. See Nakamura, "Shokuminchi hō," pp. 192–93.

36. See *Inin rippō*, pp. 58–64.

37. Japan proper was called "mainland" (*naichi*) in contrast to the colonies, ordinarily called "outer areas." See, e.g., Stead, p. 582. Those Japanese who lived in the colonies were called "mainlanders" (*naichijin*) by themselves and the colonized people.

38. See Nakamura, *Konpon mondai*, p. 137; Yamazaki, pp. 310–13.

39. See *Inin rippō*, app., pp. 27–61.

40. E. Chen "Political Control," p. 138. Such difficulty in extending Japanese statutes to Korea was actually the result of the greater degree of legislative power of the governor-general of Korea, who, unlike his counterpart in Taiwan, was always a man of top prominence in Japanese politics and thus considered to have power to decide the colonial law without interference from the central government. See ibid., pp. 131, 156–57.

41. Title 3, art. 2. See also Nagao and Ōda, pp. 34–35.

42. *Gojunen no Taiwan*, p. 68.

43. Title 63, art. 2.

44. See *Inin rippō*, pp. 10–11.

45. In viewing the GGT's judicial archives, I found very few cases in the initial period of Japanese rule in which the council disapproved a bill drafted by legal bureaucrats of the GGT. See J. Ac., p. 128. After the Kodama administration (1898–1906), no such cases could be found. In fact, the chief administrator of the GGT promised the central government to modify the content of *ritsurei* that had already been determined by the council and then convened the council to "determine" this modification. See, e.g., J. Ac., pp. 289–99. Considering the arbitrariness of this process, it is no wonder that the process of the GGT Consultative Council for enacting *ritsurei* was abolished in Title 31 and Title 3. See Title 31, art. 2; Title 3, art. 3.

46. For instance, the GGT drafted a *ritsurei* that would have enacted a civil code for Taiwan in 1914, but it never received the imperial approval from the central government. See GGT Ac., 1914, permanent vol. 36, pt. 6, nos. 2, 3.

47. The term *yoru* was similar to the meaning of *jun-yō*, that is, to be applicable mutatis mutandis. I therefore translate *yoru* as "conform to." See also Nakamura, "Shokuminchi hō, p. 200, n. 3.

48. When the Japanese statute itself was amended later on, the revision did not become a part of *ritsurei* as a matter of course. Accordingly, Ritsurei No. 21 of 1899 had to provide that any later amendment of the Japanese statute named should be a part of the *ritsurei* naming it unless otherwise provided. Similarly, even though the Japanese statute was repealed later, the *ritsurei* having named it was still effective on Taiwan. In practice, such a *ritsurei* was often amended in accordance with the newly enacted Japanese statute. Yamazaki, pp. 252–54.

49. See, e.g., J. Ac., pp. 121–23.

50. *Gojunen no Taiwan*, p. 65.

51. Kambō Shingishitsu (GGT), *Ritsurei seido no enkaku*, pp. 232–33. In the draft for Title 3, the extension of Japanese law was to be decided by the *ritsurei* of the governor-general. Finally Den agreed to change it to be decided by ordinances. Haruyama, p. 68. Such a resolution of the cabinet was probably made in return for Den's agreeing to this change.

52. On the agency in charge of colonial affairs in the Japanese central government, see Kodansha, comp., *Kodansha Encyclopedia of Japan*, vol. 1, p. 336. The Japanese

central government ordinarily issued ordinances as the GGT expected, but in a few cases the central government rejected the GGT's proposals. For example, the GGT suggested in 1929 that the books of Family and Succession in the Japanese Civil Code apply to Taiwanese by ordinance; however, the central government did not adopt such a proposal. See chap. 5.

53. See, e.g., GGT Ac., 1922, permanent vol. 140, pt. 6, nos. 4, 5, 6. The process of the Consultative Council in enacting *ritsurei* was abolished in Title 3. On the change of supervisory agency in the central government, see *Gojunen no Taiwan,* pp. 167, 171.

54. For practical instances, see *Inin rippō,* pp. 72–74. Nakamura named this kind of imperial ordinance "ordinance for enacting *ritsurei.*" Nakamura, *Konpon mondai,* pp. 150–51.

55. See p. 26. Nakamura, *Konpon mondai,* p. 26.

56. See, e.g., TTK, vol. 1, pp. 144–46. On other sources of law, see Chen, "Attempt to Integrate," pp. 254–62.

57. *Gojunen no Taiwan,* pp. 70–72.

58. Many mainland statutes that were applied to Taiwan by ordinances under Title 3 were not effective in Taiwan until January 1, 1923. Thus, the special colonial law was still dominant in 1922. See Ordinance No. 406, 1922; Ordinance No. 521, 1922.

59. Taiwan jimmin gunjihan shobun rei (Admonition, July 6, 1895). The offenses provided in article 1 of this order were (1) resisting the Japanese army, (2) destroying railroads, bridges, firearms, etc., (3) harboring enemies or setting them free, (4) revealing the location and also of the army to enemies, (5) committing fraud in guarding the Japanese army or ships, (6) spreading rumors, making noise, or shouting that interfered with the quiet of the army or ships, (7) poisoning or polluting rivers used by the army, (8) giving opium to Japanese soldiers. Except (8), all the above items probably described various actions of the Taiwanese guerrillas. See Weng Chia-yin, *T'aiwan Han-jen wu-chuang k'ang-jih,* p. 76.

60. Taiwan Sōtokufu hōin shokusei (Nichirei No. 11, Oct. 7, 1895). This tribunal had no jurisdiction over the civil cases involving Japanese. See J. Ac., p. 55.

61. Taiwan jūmin keibatsu rei (Nichirei No. 21-1, Nov. 17, 1895). The Japanese were not subject to this regulation. J. Ac., p. 50.

62. See J. Ac., pp. 48–49. According to article 11 of this law, the punishment for attempting or abetting a crime or being an accessory to a crime could not be reduced. This was harsher than the original Dispositions for Taiwanese Military Criminals.

63. Taiwan jūmin chizai rei (Nichirei No. 21-2, Nov. 17, 1895). See J. Ac., pp. 50–51. The term *chizairei* followed the Army Criminal Instruction rather than the 1890 Code of Criminal Procedure.

64. Taiwan jūmin minji rei (Nichirei No. 21-3 Nov. 17, 1895), art. 2.

65. J. Ac., p. 51.

66. Judgment No. 16 of June 30, 1898, in *Fukuinshū* 124 (Ct. App.).

67. See Peattie, "Introduction," p. 18.
68. See also Barclay, p. 7.
69. Taiwan Sōtokufu hōin jōrei (Ritsurei No. 1, 1896).
70. Emergency Ritsurei No. 4 Aug. 14, 1896. As a matter of law, military orders did not continue after a colony came under civilian administration. See also Washinosu Atsuya, *Taiwan keisatsu shijūnen shiwa*, p. 258.
71. Aneha Shōhei, *Chi-ssu-kung-yeh yü T'ai-wan t'e-shu fa-lü*, p. 131.
72. See D. Henderson, "Law and Political Modernization in Japan," p. 416.
73. Taiwan Sōtokufu rinji hōin jōrei (Ritsurei No. 2, 1896).
74. The 1896 GGT court Organization Law, arts. 4 (2) (4), 7 (2) (5).
75. Ritsurei No. 7, 1896.
76. Furei No. 2, 1898. A *furei* (executive ordinance), also promulgated by the governor-general of Taiwan, did not have the same effect as a Diet-enacted statute. It was often enacted to implement the provisions in *ritsurei*.
77. Someno Yoshinopu, "Shihō seido," pp. 115–17, 127–28; Yokoyama Kōichirō, "Keibatsu chian kikō no seibi," pp. 314, 320, n. 43.
78. Western powers did not demand that Western-style law be enforced in colonial Taiwan. Furthermore, the consular jurisdiction of Western powers in Taiwan was abolished in 1899, the same year as in metropolitan Japan. See Huang Chao-t'ang, *T'ai-wan tsung-tu-fu*, pp. 63–64.
79. See Mukōyama, p. 221.
80. Gotō Shimpei, *Taiwan keiei jō kyūkan seido no chōsa o hitsuyō to suru iken*, pp. 14–18.
81. Ibid., pp. 21, 25–27.
82. See also Chang and Myers, "Japanese Colonial Development Policy in Taiwan, 1895–1906," p. 448.
83. See also Takekoshi, "Japan's Colonial Policy," p. 96; Gann, "Western and Japanese Colonialism," p. 502. Gotō said "Our nation's history as a colonial power commences with the story of our administration in Formosa, and our failure or success there must exercise a marked influence on all our future undertakings." See Takekoshi, *Japanese Rule in Formosa*, p. v.
84. Girault, *Shokumin oyobi shokumin hōsei genron*, p. 521.
85. Minji shōji oyobi keiji ni kansuru ritsurei (Ritsurei No. 8, 1898), art. 1.
86. Taiwan keiji rei (Ritsurei No. 9, 1908), arts. 1, 7. For the reasons for enactment, see GGT Ac., 1908, permanent vol. 16, pt. 6, no. 14.
87. The 1895 Penalty Order for Inhabitants of Taiwan provided that the Japanese Criminal Code was to be applied to offenses on which this order did not expressly impose punishment. However, official statistics on crimes for the period of military administration do not include the number of cases involving offenses punished by the Criminal Code. See J. Ac., pp. 75–77.

88. See Girault, pp. 538–39.

89. Hito keibatsu rei (Emergency Ritsurei No. 24 1898).

90. The main features of this law were (1) almost all offenses were punished by death; (2) without specifying offenses, it provided that any members in a violence-oriented association were guilty of committing bandit offenses; (3) an attempt was punished the same as the consummation of the offense; (4) an act was punished in spite of its not being expressly provided for by the law at the time of its commission. Mukōyama, p. 233.

91. Taiwan ahen rei (Ritsurei No. 2, 1897). This law was applied to resident Japanese as well. See, e.g., Judgment No. 204 of July 15, 1899, in *Fukuinshū* 371 (Ct. App.).

92. Taiwan shimbunshi jōrei (Ritsurei No. 3, 1900). See, e.g., GGT vs. *Hayashi*, in *Hōinroku* 1: 4 (criminal), 74 (Ct. App., March 31, 1903); *Mizuno vs.* GGT, in *Hōinroku* 1: 5 (criminal), 83 (Ct. App., Feb. 26, 1903).

93. Taiwan hoan kisoku (Ritsurei No. 21, 1900).

94. Hoan jōrei (Ordinance No. 67, 1887). See Mukōyama, p. 155; Igeta, Yamanaka, and Ishikawa, *Nihon kindaihō shi,* pp. 123–24.

95. Hokō jōrei (Ritsurei No. 21, 1898). See, e.g., Mukōyama, pp. 233–39.

96. Bakkin oyobi chikei shobun rei (Ritsurei No. 1, 1904).

97. Taiwan furōsha torishimari kisoku (Ritsurei No. 2, 1906).

98. Hozumi Nobushiga, *Goningumi seido ron,* pp. 401, 445.

99. Hosokawa Kameichi, *Nihon kindai hōseishi,* p. 139.

100. Yokai rei (Ordinance No. 11, 1892; repealed in 1914). See Mukōyama, pp. 295–96; Igeda, Yamanaka, and Ishikawa, p. 124.

101. According to article 1 of this law, Taiwanese should be tried according to existing procedure. It was said that in practice before 1899 the colonial courts for convenience followed Japanese criminal procedural law in criminal trials. But there was not a unified procedure in all of the GGT courts. See Washinosu, p. 267.

102. Ritsurei No. 8, 1899. See Hōmubu (GGT), ed., *Taiwan shihō seido enkaku shi,* p. 20.

103. The 1908 Taiwan Criminal Law, art. 1.

104. Itō, p. 147; Girault, p. 545.

105. Ritsurei No. 9, 1899; J. Ac., pp. 327–28.

106. Ritsurei No. 4, 1901; J. Ac. pp. 500–1.

107. Keiji soshō tokubetsu tetsuzu (Ritsurei No. 10, 1905); see J. Ac., pp. 1019–74.

108. Hanzai sokketsu rei (Ritsurei No. 4, 1904); Mukōyama, pp. 136–37.

109. Article 12 of this law.

110. The 1908 Taiwan Criminal Law, art. 7.

111. Itō, pp. 147, 407; Girault, p. 524.

112. Taiwan minji rei (Ritsurei No. 11, 1908).

113. The Taiwanese civil matters could conform to only the Japanese Civil Code relating to lost things, concealed treasure, and deposit. See the 1908 Taiwan Civil Law, art. 3; Huang Ching-chia, pp. 96–97.

114. See Yanaihara Tadao, *Shokumin*, pp. 443–78.

115. Ritsurei No. 9, 1898.

116. Taiwan tochi chōsa kisoku (Ritsurei No. 14, 1898); Dai-so-ken seiri ni kansuru ken (Ritsurei No. 6, 1904). On the Japanese reform on land system in the early Meiji era, see Igeta, Yamanaka, and Ishikawa, pp. 17–22.

117. Taiwan rin-ya chōsa kisoku (Ritsurei No. 7, 1910). See Huang Ching-chia, pp. 209–11.

118. Taiwan tochi tōki kisoku (Ritsurei No. 3, 1905). This will be discussed in detail in chapter 5.

119. Itō, pp. 147, 407.

120. Minji soshō tokubetsu tetsuzu (Ritsurei No. 9, 1905).

121. Article 1 of this law.

122. Chōchō o shite minji sōshō chōtei tō o toriatsuka-washimuru ken (Ritsurei No. 3, 1904; No. 2, 1912).

123. Ritsurei No. 21, 1898; Mukōyama, p. 233. The new rulers frequently provided for collective criminal responsibility, as in the *pao-chia* system, to force newly conquered people to supervise each other. For example, when William I conquered England in the eleventh century, when the Manchu emperor conquered China in the seventeenth century, or when the Tokugawa Shogunate dominated Japan in the seventeenth century, the new conquerers instituted a system of collective criminal responsibility. Based on the same principle, the GGT adopted the traditional *pao-chia* system in Taiwan. See Hozumi Nobushiga, pp. 51, 411–12, 508–9, 543.

124. J. Ac., p. 321; Girault, p. 538.

125. J. Ac., pp. 402–3, 407–8. For Japan's temporary court, see Someno, pp. 116–19.

126. J. Ac., p. 327.

127. Ibid., p. 501.

128. Mukōyama, pp. 327–28. For instance, Mr. A sold his land to Mr. B without registration. According to social concepts, Mr. B of course became the new owner of the land, but by law he did not. Later, anyone who considered Mr. A as owner in accordance with the land registry was legally able to acquire the land ownership from Mr. A, and Mr. B could not claim that he was the real owner of the land. However, Mr. B could claim back the payment from Mr. A.

129. Tōgō Minoru, *Taiwan shokumin hattatsu shi*, p. 79; J. Ac., pp. 769–70.

130. See Yanaihara Tadao, *Jih-pen ti-kuo-chu-i hsia chih T'ai-wan*, pp. 21, 49, n. 9. However, by joining a Japanese shareholder, a Taiwanese enterprise could incorporate a modern company under the Japanese company law. This will be discussed in detail in chapter 5.

131. Gotō, pp. 16–17.

132. In Japan, the West demanded the abolition of these two measures (which were regarded as "uncivilized"). Compared to the interest in the revision of the unequal treaties, these two measures' benefits in reducing judicial expenditure were minor, and therefore the measures were abandoned.

133. Gotō, p. 9, 13–14, 22. Japanese judges had to decide Taiwanese civil suits relating to commercial transactions in accordance with old Taiwanese customs.

134. The GGT allowed the Taiwanese with licenses to continue to smoke the opium, which was sold only by the government. In 1906 the GGT issued the Taiwan lotto (*Taiwan saihyō*) for the Taiwanese and Chinese; they stopped it in 1916. See Mukōyama, pp. 138, 142.

135. See, e.g., Washinosu, p. 194.

136. In 1897, the next year that Japanese civilians were allowed to migrate to Taiwan, there were 128 resident Japanese in prison. See TWTT, p. 490.

137. See Washinosu, pp. 195–200.

138. See, e.g., GGT Ac., 1915, permanent vol. 37, pt. 6, no. 4.

139. Peattie, "Japanese Colonialism," pp. 104–7.

140. See ibid., pp. 114–18; Wakabayashi Masahiro, *Taiwan kōnichi undō shi kenkyū*, pp. 75–102. Yanaihara commented that "compulsory assimilation is an infringement upon the collective personality of a group"; Yanaihara, *Shokumin*, p. 385.

141. Peattie, "Japanese Colonialism," pp. 119–21.

142. See Wakabayashi, pp. 56–59.

143. Kambō Shingishitsu (GGT), pp. 62, 68–69, 74, 130–31.

144. Minji ni kansuru hōritsu o Taiwan ni shikō suru no ken (Ordinance No. 406, Sept. 16, 1922).

145. Taiwan ni shikō suru hōritsu no tokurei ni kansuru ken (Ordinance No. 407, Sept., 16, 1922).

146. See, e.g., GGT Ac., 1923, permanent vol. 124, pt. 6, the second category, no. 1.

147. Ritsurei No. 6, Sept. 18, 1922.

148. See Ordinance No. 521, 1922.

149. In 1919, the GGT enacted *ritsurei* to enable Taiwan's judicial system to become more similar to the Japanese metropolitan system. This will be discussed in more detail in a later chapter.

150. For the periodization of the Japanese wartime legal system, see Watanabe Yōzō, "Nihon fashizumu hō-taisei," pp. 16–17.

151. Mukōyama, pp. 593, 723–24, 1264. In fact, in 1941 original *kō* had been organized as Japanese *tonarigumi* with a different name, a variation of *goningumi*, which was established to mobilize and control the population. Therefore, after the *hokō* system was abolished, its original function of controlling the population was replaced by Taiwan's

tonarigumi, but the collective criminal responsibility was abandoned. See Mukōyama, pp. 1253–54; Kodansha, comp., *Kodansha Encyclopedia of Japan*, vol. 3, p. 45.

152. GGT Ac., 1930, permanent vol. 6, pt. 6, the second category, no. 1.

153. Chian keisatsu hō (Law No. 39, 1900), applied to Taiwan in 1923; Chian iji hō (Law No. 46, 1925), applied to Taiwan in 1925; *Bōryoku kōi tō shōbatsu ni kansuru hōritsu* (Law No. 60, 1926), applied to Taiwan in 1926. See Mukōyama, pp. 604–8.

154. Ritsurei No. 1, 1936. See Mukōyama, p. 1217.

155. See *Inin rippō*, app. pp. 20–22.

156. Kokka sōdōin hō (Law No. 55, 1938). See *Gojunen no Taiwan*, pp. 101–5.

157. The 1922 Code of Criminal Procedure (Law No. 75, 1922), applied to Taiwan by Ordinance No. 526, 1923.

158. Ordinance No. 514, 1923.

159. Senji keiji tokubetsu hō (Law No. 64, 1942), applied to Taiwan by Ordinances No. 177, 1942, and No. 89, 1943.

160. The 1922 Exceptions of Applied Statutes, art. 5. This will be discussed in detail in chapter 5.

161. See *Inin rippō*, app. pp. 20–22; *Gojunen no Taiwan*, pp. 101–5; TTK, vol. 1 pp. 229–60.

162. Senji minji tokubetsu hō (Law No. 63, 1942), applied to Taiwan by Ordinance No. 88, 1943.

163. The Japanese government did not need to adopt Western-style law in Taiwan to revise the unequal treaties. Western-style law was probably necessary to develop Taiwan's capitalism, but since 1898 the Japanese could apply Japan's modern codes to develop Japanese capitalism in Taiwan. It was not important for the Japanese rulers to promote Taiwanese capital.

164. In 1921, the first civilian governor-general told the Diet that the application of Japanese commercial law had no influence on Taiwanese interests but the application of Japanese family and succession law would seriously affect their interests. Kambō Shingishitsu (GGT), pp. 66–67.

165. See Mukōyama, p. 603.

166. See also Izumi Akira, *Shokuminchi tōchi ron*, p. 247.

167. Huang Ching-chia, p. 134.

168. See Tsurumi, *Japanese Colonial Education in Taiwan, 1895–1945*, pp. 177–82.

169. Lin, who had been a clerk in the colonial court, was a graduate of the legal department of Meiji University. As a leading Taiwanese dissident, he provided a theoretical foundation for the movement for creation of a Taiwan parliament based on his knowledge of modern jurisprudence and the theory of colonial governance. See Chou Wan-yao, *Jih-chü shih-tai te T'ai-wan i-hui*, pp. 40, 50.

170. Lin, "Liu-san wen-ti chih yün-ming," pp. 26, 29.

NOTES

171. Chou, pp. 51–56, 144–45, 188–203. In 1927, some Taiwanese intellectuals already advocated the enactment of a Taiwan constitution based on the separation of powers, in which Taiwanese people would have legislative power for colonial affairs. Such demand for complete home rule, however, was not adopted in official petitions. Chou, pp. 126–27.

172. See Lin Ch'eng-lu, "Kai-cheng T'ai-wan t'ung-chih chi-pen-fa yü chih-min-ti t'ung-chih fang-chen," pp. 1, 12. See also Wakabayashi, p. 69; Tsurumi, pp. 183–84.

173. Wakabayashi, p. 45.

174. Cheng Sung-yü, "Chiu min-shang-fa shih-hsing erh yen," pp. 17–21.

175. Lin Ch'eng-lu, "Shih-hsing min-fa shang-fa i chih ch'u-wai-li," pp. 21–26; Lin Ch'eng-lu, "Minpō no shinzoku kitei o Taiwan-jin ni tekiyō suru hōan no gigi," pp. 21–35.

176. For instance, see *TWSN*, 1: 5 (Dec. 1920), Japanese version, pp. 60–64; 2: 1 (Jan. 1921), Chinese version, pp. 34–36; 2: 4 (May 1921), Japanese version, pp. 23–32; 5: 1 (April 1924), Japanese version, pp. 66–68; 5: 2 (May 1924), Japanese version, pp. 59–61.

177. Lin, "Shih-hsing min-fa shang-fa i chih ch'u-wai-li," p. 26; Cheng, p. 20.

178. Lin, "Minpō no shinzoku kitei o Taiwan-jin ni tekiyō suru hōan no gigi," pp. 27–28, 31.

179. Hsiu Hu-sheng, "Taiwan gikai to musan kaikyū kaihō," pp. 43–48.

180. See Wu San-lien et al., *T'ai-wan min-tsu yün-tung shih*, pp. 367–68.

181. See Lu Hsiu-i, *Jih-chü shih-tai T'ai-wan Kung-ch'an-tang*, pp. 61–63.

182. See Robinson, "Nationalism and Human-Rights Thought in Korea under Colonial Rule," pp. 114, 118.

183. Chou, pp. 76, 119, 175–76, 182.

184. Wakabayashi, pp. 151–53.

3 / MODERN JUDICIARY IN THE COLONY

1. See *TTK*, vol. 1, pp. 17, 19–20, 94, 105, 108–9.

2. Hōmubu (GGT), *Taiwan shihō seido enkaku shi*, p. 3 (hereafter cited as *Shihōshi*).

3. Hosokawa Kameichi, *Nihon kindai hōseishi*, pp. 97–101. After 1876, there were four levels in the court hierarchy. The courts below the Great Court of Cassation were the High Court (Kōtō hōin, after 1890 the Appellate Chamber [Kōsoin]), the District Court (Chihō saibansho), and the Ward Court (Ku saibansho).

4. The GGT court Organization Law (Ritsurei No. 1, 1896), art. 2.

5. Ritsurei No. 2, 1896.

6. *Shihōshi*, p. 4.

7. See, e.g., Teshima Heijirō, comp., *Shokumin hōsei chosho mokuji shū*. The author was the head of the Department of Judicial Affairs in the GGT from 1909 to 1914. See *Shihōshi*, pp. 40–41.

NOTES

8. See Izumi Akira, *Shokuminchi tōchi ron*, pp. 230–31; Girault, *Shokumin oyobi shokumin hōsei genron*, pp. 530–36.

9. Ritsurei No. 16, 1898.

10. Ritsurei No. 1, 1899, and Ritsurei No. 25, 1898. The cases involving rights occurring in the Ch'ing period occupied more than one-fourth of all civil lawsuits, and Japanese judges had difficulties in dealing with them. See J. Ac., pp. 291–92. The Japanese deposit for criminal appeals was criticized as seriously hindering appeals. See Someno Yoshinopu, "Shihō seido," p. 124. Surprisingly, the amount of such deposits was higher in Taiwan than in Japan.

11. Izumi, p. 251.

12. See J. Ac. pp. 349–60.

13. After 1899, some members of the Imperial Diet repeatedly proposed unifying the Japanese judicial system in the home land and the colony, but their proposals failed. See *Shihōshi*, app. pp. 1–9.

14. The Higher Court of the Government-General of Korea had jurisdiction over re-appeal cases and could present its own legal interpretation different from the Japanese Supreme Court's. See Chōsen Sōtokufu, *Shisei nijūgonen shi*, p. 41 (hereafter cited as *Nijūgonen shi*); see generally Chōsen Sōtokufu Hōmukyoku, *Kōtō hōin Daishin'in ishushi hanrei yōshi*.

15. The GGT court Organization Law (Ritsurei No. 4, 1919), arts. 2, 3, 4, 8–5, app. para. 1; KSEK, pp. 27–29.

16. The Japanese Court Organization Law (Law No. 6, 1890), art. 50; Ritsurei No. 4, 1919; the 1919 GGT court Organization Law, art. 4.

17. Ritsurei No. 6, 1919.

18. TTK, vol. 2, pp. 14, 46. See Ritsurei No. 9, 1905; the Japanese Court Organization Law, arts. 11, 14, 16, 19, 26, 27.

19. The 1919 GGT court Organization Law, arts. 2, 7; KSEK, pp. 27–28, 31, 33–34, 37, 40–43.

20. KSEK, p. 39. See also the Japanese 1890 Court Organization Law, art. 27.

21. In fact, the Korean court initially adopted four levels and three instances from January 1908 to March 1912. But after April 1912, only three levels were left. See *Nijugonen shi*, pp. 38–41.

22. Saibansho kōseihō senji tokurei (Law No. 62, 1942), art. 5. Applied to Taiwan by Ordinance No. 87, 1943.

23. See GGT Ac., 1943, permanent vol. 6, pt. 7, the first category, no. 26. The GGT objected to the application of Japanese Court Organization Law in Taiwan.

24. Hattori, "The Legal Profession in Japan," p. 111.

25. Nakamura, "Shokuminchi hō," p. 191. On the *Otsu* case, see chap. 1, n. 110, and accompanying text.

26. See Kusunoki Seiichirō, *Meiji rikkensei to shihōkan*, pp. 115–30, 147–52.

27. Walz, "A Constitutional Struggle in Japan," p. 33.
28. The 1896 GGT court Organization Law, art. 4 (3).
29. *KSEK*, p. 14.
30. Kusunoki, p. 144.
31. See *KSEK*, p. 12.
32. Izumi, pp. 228–30.
33. A Japanese colonialist defended the lack of an independent judiciary in Taiwan, arguing that conflict between the executive and the judicial branches would cause Taiwanese to disrespect colonial authorities; therefore an independent judiciary would threaten colonial rule. Similar reasons were applied by a French scholar to argue in support of French judicial institutions in the colony. See Mochiji Rokusaburō, *Taiwan shokumin seisaku*, p. 104; Girault, pp. 540–43.
34. Naikaku Kirokuka (Japan), *Taiwan ni shikō subeki hōrei ni kansuru hōritsu*, p. 134.
35. The Japanese originally seriously criticized the lack of separation between the judiciary and the administrative branch in Korea, but after its annexation of Korea in 1910, Japan did not separate the administrative and judicial powers. See Chōsen Sōtokufu Hōmukyoku Hōmuka, *Chōsen no shihō seido*, pp. 2–3; Baker, "The Role of Legal Reforms in the Japanese Annexation and Rule of Korea, 1905–1919," p. 194.
36. The Japanese Court Organization Law, arts. 57–58, 73–74, 80. See Hattori, pp. 120–21.
37. Hattori, pp. 121–22.
38. The 1898 GGT court Organization Law, arts. 1, 5, 9.
39. The 1898 GGT court Organization Law, arts. 15–17. Kodama said that those provisions referred to the tenure of military judges. See *Shihōshi*, p. 10.
40. Kobayashi Masahito, *Taiwan keiei ron*, pp. 32, 56–57. Cf. *KSEK*, p. 35.
41. Ordinance No. 300, 1899. The 1898 GGT court Organization Law, art. 10. On the number of police officers who undertook the duties of procurators in district courts, see table 3.3.
42. Shirai Masaaki, "Senzen no shihō," p. 34.
43. See, e.g., GGT Ac., 1910, permanent vol. 49, pt. 6, no. 6.
44. Mochiji, pp. 103–4.
45. *Naichi oyobi Taiwan shihō kyōtsū ni kansuru ikensho*, p. 3.
46. J. Ac., pp. 230–31.
47. See GGT Ac., 1915, permanent vol. 37, pt. 6, no. 4.
48. Kambō Shingishitsu (GGT), *Ritsurei seido no enkaku*, pp. 89–91.
49. The 1919 GGT court Organization Law, arts. 15, 16.
50. In Korea, the governor-general's power to suspend judges with lowered salary was rescinded in 1921. See *Nijugonen shi*, p. 343. But a judge in Korea was guaranteed not to be removed from office against his will only if he had not been sentenced to

penal servitude or subjected to disciplinary measures. See Article 26-4 of the Government-General of Korea Court Organization Law (Seirei No. 4, 1911).

51. *Chianq et al. vs.* GGT, in *Kōinshū* 109 (Re-app. Div., Higher Ct., February 20, 1925). See Wu San-lien et al., *T'ai-wan min-tsu yün-tung shih,* pp. 212–76.

52. See, e.g., GGT Ac., 1930, permanent vol. 6, pt. 6, the second category, no. 2.

53. See, e.g., GGT Ac., 1941, permanent vol. 8, pt. 6, no. 13; GGT Ac., 1943, permanent vol. 6, pt. 7, the first category, no. 24.

54. In a 1944 case, the army demanded that a Taiwanese fisher who gave a ride to a U.S. officer inspecting Taiwan's coast be shifted to the jurisdiction of the martial court. The charging procurator finally yielded to this demand. See Mukōyama, pp. 1271–72.

55. See ibid., p. 1267.

56. Further reform for an independent judiciary was still suggested even late in Japanese rule. In 1937 GGT asked all members of local councils to submit reformative proposals for administrative organization. One of the proposals was that the judicial power should be independent from the executive authority. See Haruyama Meitetsu, ed., *Taiwan tōnai jōhō,* pp. 72–73.

57. See Taiwan Sōtokufu, *Taiwan tōchi gaiyō,* p. 10 (hereafter cited as *Tōchi gaiyō*); Barclay, *Colonial Development and Population in Taiwan,* pp. 115–16; Yang P'eng, *T'ai-wan ssu-fa chieh-shou pao-kao shu,* pp. 39–40.

58. See Peattie, "Japanese Attitudes toward Colonialism, 1895–1945," p. 88.

59. In 1930, the ordinary expenditure for courts was 1,222,000 yen; the special expenditure for constructing these two buildings was 531,000 yen. The entire expenditure for court was thus 1,753,000 yen. See NTTN, 1933, pp. 361–63.

60. It is still unknown how the GGT dismissed seven judges within a year (1904) because after the 1898 reform colonial judges were guaranteed not to be removed from office and transferred to other offices against their will.

61. NTTN, 1917, p. 731, table 733.

62. Huang Chao-t'ang, *T'ai-wan Tsung-tu-fu,* pp. 239, 243–46.

63. See Wu Wen-hsing, "Jih-chü shih-ch'i T'ai-wan she-hui ling-tao chieh-ts'eng," pp. 110–13.

64. Mukōyama, pp. 1221–22.

65. Tsurumi, *Japanese Colonial Education in Taiwan, 1895–1945,* p. 124.

66. The curriculum of this department was similar to that of law schools in present-day Taiwan. See U.S. Department of the Navy, *Civil Affairs Handbook: Taiwan (Formosa) Taihoku Province,* p. 118.

67. Chang Tzu-hui, *T'ai-wan shih-jen chih,* p. 121. There were few Taiwanese students in the department of political science.

68. See Igeda, Yamanaka, and Ishikawa, pp. 192–96.

69. Wu Wen-hsing, p. 113.

70. Nakamura Hideo, "Shihō seido to Nihon no kindaika," p. 11.

71. Tsurumi, p. 214.
72. Hahm, "Korea's Initial Encounter with the Western Law," pp. 175–76.
73. *Nijūgonen shi*, pp. 38–39.
74. NTTN, 1911, p. 959.
75. Wu Mi-ch'a, *T'ai-wan chin-tai shih yen-chiu*, p. 174.
76. G. Henderson, "Human Rights in South Korea, 1945–1953," p. 135.
77. A biography of the first Taiwanese law student who passed the Japanese bar examination in 1918 recorded that Taiwanese were originally forbidden to take the examination until this student petitioned the Minister of Justice. See Chuang Yung-ming, "T'ai-wan ti-i-wei fa-hsüeh po-shih: Yeh Ch'ing-yao," p. 64. I suspect that a legal prohibition, if it existed, could not be rescinded so easily, and that in fact there were not any Taiwanese who tried to take the bar examination until this student did. A former Taiwanese judge under Japanese rule also said that no legal provision prevented a Taiwanese from being a Japanese judge. Chang Yu-chung, letter to author, April 5, 1991.
78. In prewar Japan the examination for judges and procurators initially was separate and distinct from the bar examination. In 1923, the two examinations were combined into the judicial section of the senior examination for public officials. Hattori, pp. 127–28.
79. See Wu Wen-hsing, pp. 113, 119, n. 9.
80. Haley, "The Myth of the Reluctant Litigation," p. 385.
81. Hattori, p. 128, n. 63.
82. Yang P'eng, p. 15. On the qualifications of Taiwanese lawyers in 1935, see GGT Ac., 1935, permanent vol. 13, pt. 6, no. 7.
83. Nakamura Hideo, pp. 11–12.
84. It was estimated that during the period of Japanese rule, only one thousand Taiwanese students in Japan studied in imperial universities, twenty thousand in other public or private universities, forty thousand in colleges. Wu Wen-hsing, pp. 114–15.
85. Being a graduate of Imperial Tōkyō University was helpful in obtaining a judicial position. See, e.g., Chang Yu-chung, *Gaichijin*, pp. 26–27.
86. See Wu Wen-hsing, p. 190; Huang Chao-t'ang, pp. 239–43.
87. See, e.g., Chang Yu-chung, *Gaichijin*, p. 26.
88. Three Taiwanese had been procurators in the Amoy District Court of the Republic of China controlled by Japan by 1945. See Kōnan Shimbunsha, *Taiwan jinshi kan*, p. 153; Gaijibu (GGT), *Nan-Shi hōmen shihō jimu shisatsu hōkokusho*, p. 190.
89. On Taiwanese police officers, see Huang Chao-t'ang, p. 242. The ranks of colonial police were (1) police superintendent (*keishi*), (2) police inspector (*keibu*), (3) assistant police inspector (*keibuho*), (4) patrolman (*junsa*), and (5) assistant patrolman (*junsaho*). In 1931, no Taiwanese were police superintendents or inspectors; only

2 of 189 assistant inspectors in plains areas were Taiwanese. See Keimukyoku (GGT), *Taiwan no keisatsu*, pp. 35–36. This situation was largely unchanged in 1938. See Washinosu Atsuya, *Taiwan keisatsu shijūnen shiwa*, pp. 124–25.

90. Chang Yu-chung, *Watashi no aisuru Taiwan*, p. 193. See also Shirai, p. 35.

91. The following stories illustrate that after ruling for nearly half a century, the GGT still distrusted the Taiwanese. On February 18, 1938, the Taihoku airfield was bombed by Chinese planes. All public buildings and strategic crossings in the city were barricaded by sandbags and machine guns directed not at the invading airplanes, but at the Taiwanese population. Not until these barricades were up did the GGT sound the air alarm. See U.S. Department of Navy, *Civil Affairs Handbook: Taiwan (Formosa)* OPNAV 50E-12, pp. 176–77. In 1944, the commander-in-chief of the Taiwan garrison, who later became the last governor-general of Taiwan, said to a group of high-level Japanese residents in Taiwan that he did not have complete confidence in Taiwanese loyalty to Japan. See Huang Chao-t'ang, pp. 191–92.

92. Article 7 of the annexation treaty provided that "the Japanese government... appoint qualified Koreans as imperial officials when circumstances allow." In 1909, 7 of 64 procurators in the Residency-General courts were Korean. In 1945, only 8 of 120 procurators in the colonial courts were Korean. Moreover, Japan decreased the number of Korean judges. In 1909, 87 of 279 judges in the Residency-General courts were Korean. But in 1945, only 46 of 235 judges in the colonial courts were Korean. See *NTTN*, 1911, p. 959; G. Henderson, p. 135.

93. See Kōnan Shimbunsha, pp. 1, 16, 20, 21, 31, 37, 48, 51, 52, 72, 85–86, 92, 123, 133, 172, 180, 220, 227–28, 287, 300, 302, 307, 337–38, 347, 360, 387, 398, 411, 425.

94. See ibid., pp. 10, 56, 103, 121, 166, 235.

95. See ibid., pp. 18, 30, 36, 144, 162, 178–79, 180, 190–91, 238, 288–89, 299, 326, 355, 413.

96. See ibid., pp. 3, 105, 286, 300, 376.

97. See *TWKS*, 1: 6 (June 1901), app.

98. Wu San-lien, p. 30.

99. See Kōnan Shimbunsha, pp. 1, 64, 76, 81, 94, 123, 200, 334, 412.

100. See ibid., pp. 27, 50, 85–86, 92, 133, 185, 235, 238–39, 286, 300, 303, 355.

101. See GGT Ac., 1935, permanent vol. 13, pt. 6, no. 7; GGT Ac., 1936, permanent vol. 9, pt. 2, the second category, no. 2. The number of total lawyers in 1931 herein (156) is different from the number in table 3.3 (158). In the latter archives cited above, some resident Japanese, including lawyers, suggested outlawing Taiwanese lawyers. Such an unreasonable proposal reflected their fear of Taiwanese lawyers.

102. See Yang P'eng, p. 15.

103. Haley, p. 385.

104. Girault, pp. 530–31.

105. Mukōyama, p. 251.

106. See Takekoshi, *Japanese Rule in Formosa*, p. 193. For instance, a Taiwanese interpreter receiving bribes intentionally misinterpreted to mislead Japanese judges.

107. See J. Ac., p. 286. It was said in 1905 that the system of two interpreters was maintained in the Court of Appeal but was not used in the District Court any more. Takekoshi, pp. 189–90.

108. Mochiji, pp. 105–6.

109. Tsurumi, pp. 147–57.

110. GGT Ac., 1935, permanent vol. 13, pt. 6, no. 8.

111. The percentage of Japanese-speaking Taiwanese in the total Taiwanese population was 0.4 in 1905, 1.6 in 1915, 2.9 in 1920, 8.5 in 1930, 37.8 in 1937, and 45.6 in 1939. Kirk, "Social Change in Formosa," p. 21.

112. Kondō Ken'ichi, ed., *Taiheiyō senka no Chōsen oyobi Taiwan*, p. 20. The ratio in Korea was lower than in Taiwan. In 1942, only 20 percent of indigenous population were able to comprehend the Japanese language. Ibid.

113. Gotō Shimpei, *Taiwan keiei jō kyūkan seido no chōsa o hitsuyō to suru iken*, pp. 7–9.

114. Ordinance No. 96, 1901.

115. See, e.g., TWKS, 1: 6 (June 1901), p. 78; 1: 7 (July 1901), p. 81; 1: 12 (Dec. 1901), p. 20. Additionally, a GGT official was sent to the Chinese mainland to investigate Ch'ing administration of law. See TWKS, 2: 3 (March 1902), p. 251.

116. Okamatsu Santarō, "Dai-so-ken no hōritsu jō seishitsu," pp. 5–6.

117. See Girault, pp. 529–30.

118. Some stories show that at the beginning the Taiwanese still tried to bribe judges, as in the past, when they went to the GGT court. See Takekoshi, pp. 192–93.

119. See, e.g., Li Nan-heng, ed., *Jih-chü hsia T'ai-wan hsin-wen-hsüeh, ming chi 2*, pp. 54–57. Wu Cho-liu, a famous Taiwanese author, even wrote favorably about colonial procurators. See, e.g., Wu Cho-liu, *T'ai-wan lien-ch'iao*, pp. 66, 146.

120. According to a telephone interview of Judge Hung Shou-nan in 1990. See also Washinosu, pp. 286–89.

121. See Taiwan Sōtokufu, *Taiwan Sōtokufu oyobi shozoku kansho shokuinroku*, 1942, pp. 93–95.

122. See Chang Wei-jen, *Ch'ing-tai fa-chih yen-chiu*, vol. 1, pp. 371–72.

123. The impartiality of the criminal justice system will be discussed in chapter 4.

124. Most civil lawsuits in Taiwan involved Taiwanese on both sides of the dispute. Civil lawsuits involving Taiwanese and Japanese were relatively rare. For instance, of the civil lawsuits in the district courts in 1910, some 3,307 cases involved Taiwanese on both sides of the dispute; 466 cases involved Japanese on both sides of the dispute; and only 296 cases involved Taiwanese and Japanese. Of the lawsuits in the district courts in 1940, some 5,949 cases involved Taiwanese on both sides of the

dispute; 297 cases involved Japanese on both sides of the dispute; 458 cases involved Taiwanese and Japanese. See Taiwan Sōtokufu, *Taiwan Sōtokufu tōkeisho*, no. 14 (1910), p. 125; no. 44 (1940), p. 154 (hereafter cited as *Tōkeisho*).

125. It was said that in the early period, some Taiwanese imagined that fees paid to an attorney at law were nothing else than bribes for judges. Takekoshi, p. 193.

126. Those who had a license of advocator in Japan before the stricter requirements were imposed were allowed to be advocators in Taiwan. See J. Ac., pp. 241–42.

127. Ritsurei No. 5, 1900; Ritsurei No. 2, 1901.

128. GGT Ac., 1935, permanent vol. 13, pt. 6, no. 8.

129. See *TWKS*, 1: 6 (June 1901), app.; 1: 10 (Oct. 1901), p. 88.

130. For the period from 1931 to 1935, see GGT Ac., 1935, permanent vol. 13, pt. 6, no. 7.

131. Of these 440 cases, there were 204 cases in which only plaintiffs retained lawyers, 49 cases in which only defendants retained lawyers, and 147 cases in which both of them retained lawyers. See *Tōkeisho*, no. 14 (1910), p. 126, table 144.

132. See *Tōkeisho*, no. 24 (1920), pp. 184, 190, tables 203 and 204.

133. In 1921, there were 59 lawyers in Taiwan; only one of them was Taiwanese. In 1931, there were 156 (158?) lawyers in Taiwan; only 20 lawyers were Taiwanese. In 1935, the total number of lawyers in Taiwan reached 177; only 32 lawyers were Taiwanese.

134. Hattori, p. 129.

135. Hahm, *The Korean Political Tradition and Law*, p. 213.

136. See U.S. Department of Navy, *Civil Affairs Handbook: Taiwan (Formosa), Taichu Province*, p. 111.

137. See, e.g., Wu San-lien, pp. 213–14, 221–30, 248–65, 271; Mukōyama, pp. 786, 798, 849.

138. Mukōyama, pp. 1179–80.

139. Ch'en Shao-hsiang, *T'ai-wan te jen-k'ou pien-ch'ien*, pp. 520, 524.

140. See Mochiji, p. 91.

141. Ibid., p. 94.

142. Ritsurei No. 3, 1904; Seirei No. 11, 1910 (in Korea). For the content of this *seirei* (ordinance), see Gaimushō Jōyakukyoku Hōkika (Japan), *Seirei*, p. 235. However, before the 1904 Civil Disputes Mediation Law was enacted, local administrative officials in Taiwan had sometimes mediated civil disputes. See Tōgō, p. 90.

143. Inoue Masahiro, "Taiwan minji chōtei zakkō," p. 2. In metropolitan Japan only labor disputes were mediated by administrative officials because labor law was an administrative law.

144. In Ch'ing Taiwan, during each step of the formal legal process, magistrates urged parties to compromise with each other. In most cases, the parties were ordered to seek mediation through the social group such as the family, lineage, village, or guild.

Occasionally, the magistrate himself acted as mediator. Only in the latter cases was the state authority involved in civil mediation. See Liu, "Chinese Commercial Law in the Late Ch'ing (1842–1911)," pp. 253–54.

145. In Korea only the civil matters that belonged to the jurisdiction of Japanese Ward Courts under the civil procedure law could be dealt with by administrative mediation. Seirei No. 11, 1910 (revised by Seirei No. 10, 1912), art. 1.

146. See *TTK*, vol. 2, pp. 207–10.

147. See, e.g., Buxbaum, "Some Aspects of Substantive Family Law and Society Change in Rural China (1896–1967)," p. 201. See also Judgment No. 212 of Nov. 30, 1918, in *Fukuinshū* 344 (Ct. App.).

148. Nagao Keitoku and Ōda Shūkichi, *Taiwan gyōseihō taii*, p. 309; Tōgō, p. 92.

149. Tanino Tadasu, *Taiwan shin minjihō*, p. 32.

150. Nagao and Ōda, pp. 309–10.

151. *TTK*, vol. 2, p. 211.

152. See *TWTT*, pp. 428–29.

153. See *TTK*, vol. 2, pp. 205–6, 210–11.

154. See *TTK*, vol. 2, p. 47.

155. For the number of compromised cases, see *TWTT*, p. 398. Such cases increased during the wartime period, but the number was still small.

156. The 1890 Code of Civil Procedure, arts. 382, 390; the 1926 Code of Civil Procedure, arts. 430, 442.

157. Moser, *Law and Social Change in a Chinese Community*, pp. 28–29. Additionally, the author did not distinguish administrative mediation from unofficial mediation in traditional China. Administrative mediation was, in fact, more similar to filing a lawsuit in the magistrate's office during the Ch'ing period because both of them involved the executive authority of the state.

158. Haley, p. 369.

159. Ritsurei No. 1 and No. 5 of 1899. See J. Ac., pp. 289–302, 307.

160. The number of civil cases in the courts of first instance per 100,000 people in Japan was 233 in 1920 and 390 in 1930; in contrast, this number in Taiwan was 206 in 1920 and 202 in 1930. See Haley, p. 369; table 3.7 herein.

161. Taiwan was divided into five *shū* and two *chō* in 1919; one *chō* was added in 1926. *Tōchi gaiyō*, p. 10. From 1919 to 1932, three district courts were established in Taipei, Taichung, and Tainan, and three branches of district courts were established in I-lan, Hsin-chu, and Chia-i. *KSEK*, p. 41. Consequently, one *shū* (Kaohsiung) and three *chō* (Hua-lien, T'ai-tung, and P'eng-hu) had no district courts or their branches.

162. See *TWTT*, p. 401. Those civil cases were tried in the court of first instance in Taiwan. The percentage is calculated by the author.

163. See Haley, p. 383.

NOTES

164. Judging from the civil cases in a Taiwanese country village under Japanese rule, litigation was divided fairly roughly between those suits involving only village residents and cases involving outsiders. Most of the former were disputes involving debt. The primary issues of the latter were also debt and contract; furthermore, the litigants in those cases were restricted to landlords, merchants, and other wealthy individuals. See Moser, pp. 29–32.

165. Barclay, pp. 103–4, 107, 115, 119–20, 125–26.

166. Ibid., p. 115.

167. For the initial period of colonial education, see Mukōyama, pp. 147–51.

168. Tsurumi, p. 144.

169. Ibid., pp. 79, 148. The percentage of Taiwanese school-age children enrolled in elementary school was 20.69 in 1919, 33.11 in 1930, 57.56 in 1940, and 71.31 in 1944.

170. See Ho, *Economic Development of Taiwan, 1860–1970*, pp. 91–100, tables 6.1–6.3.

171. Ting Yüeh-chien, ed., *Chih-T'ai pi-kao lu*, p. 55.

172. See TWTT, pp. 431–33.

173. Seirei No. 10, 1910 (in Korea); see Gaimushō Jōyakukyoku Hōkika (Japan), *Seirei*, pp. 260–62.

174. KSEK, pp. 325–35, 355–57.

175. The Enforcement of the Summary Judgment Law, art. 3. See KSEK, p. 355.

176. Summary Judgment Law, art. 5.

177. KSEK, p. 350.

178. Kamiuchi Tsusaburō, *Taiwan keiji shihō seisaku ron*, pp. 132 n., 136, table 6.

179. See infra table 3.9.

180. See KSEK, pp. 353–54.

181. See KSEK, pp. 328–29.

182. See ibid., pp. 350–52; Mochiji, pp. 94–95.

183. A Japanese procurator in 1916 criticized the police summary judgment, noting that it potentially created arbitrary decisions and therefore should be restricted in the future. His suggestion was never carried out. See Kamiuchi, p. 154.

4 / CRIMINAL JUSTICE AND CHANGING SOCIETY

1. See Niida Noboru, "Chūgoku kyūshakai no kōzō to keibatsuken," pp. 191–223.

2. TTK, vol. 1, pp. 104–5.

3. Nakamura Kichisaburō, "Keihō," pp. 15–16.

4. See Wu Mi-ch'a, *T'ai-wan chin-tai shih yen-chiu*, pp. 1–51.

5. Itō Hirobumi, ed., *Taiwan shiryō*, p. 10.

6. Ibid., pp. 16–19.

7. Ibid., pp. 463–66.

8. Mukōyama Hiroo, *Nihon tōchika ni okeru Taiwan minzoku undō shi*, p. 108.

9. Disposition for Taiwanese Military Criminals, art. 3; Inhabitants of Taiwan Criminal Instruction Order, art. 1.

10. See, e.g., Mukōyama, pp. 165, 168. These two cases both occurred in Taipei, which Japan controlled.

11. J. Ac., pp. 52, 75–77.

12. Mukōyama, p. 164.

13. See, e.g., Weng Chia-yin, T'ai-wan Han-jen wu-chuang k'ang-jih, pp. 95, 152, 161.

14. See, e.g., Mukōyama, pp. 164, 168.

15. Kō Se-kai, Nihon tōchika no Taiwan, pp. 80–84, 92.

16. They did not kill Taiwanese or loot Taiwanese property and therefore were not real bandits at all. See, e.g., Mukōyama, pp. 253, 280, 292; Weng, pp. 149–50. Kodama, the fourth governor-general of Taiwan, acknowledged that some "bandits" actually were political dissidents and tried to specifically dispose of them. See Mukōyama, pp. 204, 224.

17. See Weng, p. 108; Mukōyama, p. 110; Kō, p. 81.

18. Kō, pp. 94–96.

19. See, e.g., Mukōyama, pp. 257–58, 270–71.

20. See Weng, p. 157.

21. See Mukōyama, pp. 180, 207; Yamabe Kentarō, ed., Gendai shi shiryō: Taiwan, p. 19. Only in an exceptional situation could the decisions of this court be applied to the Higher Court. See the 1896 GGT Temporary Court Law, art. 6.

22. See, e.g., Tōgō Minoru, Taiwan shokumin hattatsu shi, p. 160. According to article 121 of the Japanese Criminal Code of 1880, punishments for such offenses were divided into many different catagories, and only the most serious was a capital offense.

23. Many judicial officials, including Chief Justice Takano, criticized the misrule of executive officials and the brutality of the army. See, e.g., Kō, p. 89, 121; J. Ac., p. 42. Takano was chief justice from May 1896 to October 1897. Hōmubu (GGT), Taiwan shihō seido enkaku shi, app. p. 41.

24. An internal report made by the procurator of the temporary court clearly pointed out this situation. See J. Ac., pp. 35–36, 39.

25. The 1896 GGT court Organization Law, art. 3.

26. See, e.g., Mukōyama, pp. 169–71, 181–82, 190–93.

27. Ibid., p. 226.

28. See, e.g., ibid., pp. 233, 239, 252, 267. See also C. Chen, "The Japanese Adaptation of the Pao-Chia System in Taiwan," pp. 394–95. As mentioned above, some armed resisters became real bandits. The Taiwanese militia therefore were willing to help the Japanese government to terminate them. See Mukōyama, p. 293; Kō, p. 117.

29. Arts. 1, 2, 7; see appendix D.

NOTES

30. Kō, p. 134. For instance, in November 1898, the army assembled all male villagers aged 17–60 and then killed 238 of them who were considered bandits on the basis of a report made by a Japanese spy. See Mukōyama, p. 203.

31. See Kō, p. 137.

32. See Yamabe, p. 17; Mukōyama, p. 250.

33. GGT vs. Huang, Hōinroku 1: 1 (criminal), 10 (Ct. App., Sept. 28, 1901).

34. Liu vs. GGT, Hōinroku 2: 1 (criminal), 4 (Ct. App., Dec. 10, 1903).

35. See, e.g., GGT vs. Chang, Hōinroku 1: 1 (criminal), 5 (Ct. App., Oct. 1, 1901); Shen vs. GGT, Hōinroku 1: 5 (criminal), 98 (Ct. App., June 24, 1902). In the latter case, the facts of decision revealed that the defendant had been pardoned before.

36. See Mukōyama, p. 271; Kō, pp. 139–40.

37. Mukōyama, pp. 266–67, 280, 286–87; Kō, pp. 143–51.

38. Yamabe, p. xxxi.

39. Huang Chao-t'ang, T'ai-wan tsung-tu-fu, p. 93.

40. Mukōyama, p. 288.

41. Ibid., p. 293.

42. According to other statistics, 1905 was the first year in which no Taiwanese were accused of being bandits and thus sentenced to death. KSEK, pp. 264–65.

43. See Yamabe, pp. 23–87.

44 Mukōyama, p. 396.

45. Ibid., pp. 401–2; Kō, p. 156.

46. Keimukyoku (GGT), Taiwan no keisatsu, p. 235.

47. See, e.g., Yamabe, pp. 31–32, 51–52, 81.

48. See Shih Ming, T'ai-wan-jen ssu-pai-nien shih, pp. 447–48.

49. See Yamabe, p. 81.

50. See, e.g., Mukōyama, pp. 400, 404, 410.

51. See ibid., p. 417. This case also illustrates that the procurator at times was willing to consider the weight of the evidence in prosecuting those Taiwanese who were arrested by the police as bandits.

52. Kō, pp. 168–78.

53. on those Taiwanese political movements, see E. Chen, "Formosan Political Movements under Japanese Colonial Rule, 1914–1937," pp. 477–97.

54. Chou Wan-yao, Jih-chü shih-tai te T'ai-wan i-hui, p. 8.

55. Kō, pp. 226, 228–29. Similar views were expressed by Lai Ho, a great Taiwanese writer in the 1920s. See Li Nan-heng, ed., Jih-chü hsia T'ai-wan hsin-wen-hsüeh, ming chi 1, p. 336.

56. It was said that Taiwan Communists had even prepared for armed revolution in 1932, but someone said that this incident was fabricated by a police officer. See Lu Hsiu-i, Jih-chü shih-tai T'ai-wan Kung-ch'an-tang shih, pp. 135–38.

57. The Chung-yu-hui Incident in 1934. See Kō, pp. 399–400.

58. See Kō, pp. 401, 409.

59. From 1898 to 1915, some 4,236 Taiwanese were sentenced to death in accordance with the Law. See KSEK, pp. 264–65.

60. Arts. 8, 10, 12. See Nagao Keitoku, *Taiwan keijihō taii*, pp. 183–89. See, e.g., Mukōyama, pp. 643–46, 664, 686, 708, 731, 787, 813, 837; Yamabe, p. 508. According to official statistics, the Cultural Association held 315 public lectures during the 1923–26 period. Nearly half of these public lectures were interrupted by the police and over 10 percent were forced to dissolve. See Mukōyama, p. 644.

61. Arts. 1–5. See Nagao, pp. 195–204. See, e.g., Mukōyama, pp. 882, 917, 932, 1064.

62. Arts. 1–3. See Nagao, pp. 227–29. See, e.g., Mukōyama, pp. 669, 807, 848.

63. See, e.g., Mukōyama, pp. 612, 824.

64. The 1908 Taiwan Criminal Law, according to the 1907 Japanese Criminal Code, art. 74. See Nagao, p. 51. See, e.g., Mukōyama, p. 1180; TWTT, p. 447.

65. The Japanese Criminal Code of 1907, arts. 95, 106, 204, 249. See Nagao, pp. 59–60, 65, 119, 142–43, 207–16, 217–18, 230–39. See, e.g., Mukōyama, pp. 664, 786–87, 791, 798, 807, 839, 849, 1062. The Executive Enforcement Law did not relate directly to political control, but the police valued it as a powerful weapon for the control of social movement. Tipton, *The Japanese Police State*, p. 60.

66. Haruyama Meitetsu, ed., *Taiwan tōnai jōhō*, pp. 52, 88.

67. Tipton, p. 24; Keimukyoku (GGT), *Taiwan Sōtokufu keisatsu enkaku shi, dai-ichi-hen: keisatsu kikan no kōsei*, pp. 194–95, 199, 657–58.

68. See, e.g., T'ai-wan-sheng wen-hsien wei-yüan-hui, comp., *T'ai-wan-sheng t'ung-chi, chuan chiu, ke-min chih, k'ang-jih p'ien*, p. 57 (hereafter cited as *T'ai-wan-sheng t'ung-chi*). See also Tipton, p. 25; Kim Kyu-sung, *Nihon no shokuminchi hōsei no kenkyū*, p. 100.

69. The severest penalty for violation of the Peace Preservation Law was penal servitude for life. The severest penalty for committing disrespectful acts against the imperial family was penal servitude of not more than five years.

70. The most severe penalty for violations of the Violence Punishment Law was penal servitude of not more than three years. The most severe penalty for violations of the Public Order Police Law was penal servitude of not more than six months

71. Tipton, pp. 23–30; Mitchell, *Thought Control in Prewar Japan*, p. 142, table 1.

72. See KSEK, p. 287. In 1935, the ratio of Taiwan's population to Japan's population was 1:13.3; the ratio of Taiwan's population to the Korean Peninsula's population was 1:4.4. NTTN, 1939, p. 6. If the frequency of application of the Peace Preservation Law in Taiwan had been the same as in Japan or Korea, the number of suspects arrested in Japan between 1931 and 1940 would have been 11,385, and in Korea 3,766. But, in fact, between 1931 and 1940 50,617 suspects were arrested under the law in Japan. See Mitchell, p. 142, table 1.

NOTES

73. See Mitchell, p. 142, table 1; Kim, p. 102.

74. See KSEK, p. 287; the 1922 Japanese Code of Criminal Procedure, arts. 362–65. In Japan, cases involving the Peace Preservation Law also had very high conviction rates and an extremely low ratio of prosecutions to suspects arrested. According to the statistics for the period 1928–41, only 8 percent of suspects arrested were prosecuted, whereas in colonial Taiwan the figure was 27.5 percent. See Mitchell, pp. 140–41. But, as mentioned above, there were far more suspects in metropolitan Japan than in colonial Taiwan.

75. Mitchell, pp. 127–47; Tipton, p. 73.

76. In practice, the special high police seemed to be more active than thought procurators. See, e.g., Mitchell, pp. 173–74.

77. Tipton, p. 26, 31, 56; Kim, p. 79.

78. See, e.g., T'ai-wan-sheng t'ung-chi, p. 53; Mukōyama, pp. 1137, 1191.

79. See Kō, p. 402; Mukōyama, pp. 1267–68.

80. As an exception, a former participator in the Hsi-lai-an Incident, Chiang Pao-ch'eng, prepared for armed resistance during the Sino-Japanese War but failed to carry out his plan. He finally was arrested by the police in 1940. See Mukōyama, pp. 1230–31.

81. See Takumudaijin kambō Bunshoka (Japan), Nai-gai-chi hōrei taishōhyō, p. 10; Tipton, pp. 29, 70; Kim, pp. 100–2.

82. See, e.g., Wu Cho-liu, Wu-hua-kuo, pp. 104–5.

83. See, e.g., Mukōyama, pp. 1232–34, 1269–71.

84. See, e.g., ibid., p. 1233; Wu Cho-liu, T'ai-wan lien-ch'iao, pp. 145–46.

85. See, e.g., Mukōyama, p. 1270.

86. Before 1937, the most severe punishment imposed under the Peace Preservation Law was fifteen years of penal servitude in the decisions against Taiwanese Communists. See, e.g., Mukōyama, p. 917.

87. From November 1895 to March 1896, the military tribunal received only 346 criminal cases. A hundred fifty-eight of these cases involved theft; only 3 involved gambling, which was prevalent in Taiwan. See J. Ac., pp. 76–77.

88. J. Ac., pp. 17, 21, 49.

89. See Mukōyama, p. 295.

90. See Washinosu Atsuya, Taiwan keisatsu shijunen shiwa, pp. 200–4.

91. See ibid., p. 205. The colonial compulsory labor systems in Africa were enacted to force the natives to supply labor to the colonial enterprises rather than to prevent crimes. See Yanaihara Tadao, Shokumin, pp. 432–37. On the provision of this regulation, see Mukōyama, pp. 295–96.

92. See Washinosu, p. 209.

93. See ibid., p. 210; Nagao Keitoku and Ōda Shūkichi, Taiwan gyōseihō taii, pp. 253–54.

94. See Washinosu, pp. 269–73; J. Ac., pp. 822–23.

95. Fine and Flogging Law, arts. 1–3. For instance, the court decided that a sentence of three months penal servitude would be replaced with ninety-one strokes of flogging. See Kamiuchi Tsusaburō, *Taiwan keiji shihō seisaku ron*, p. 146.

96. Fine and Flogging Law, art. 4.

97. Ibid., art. 5.

98. The offense of assault was added in 1909, after the Japanese new criminal code of 1907 was conformed to deal with criminal matters in Taiwan.

99. The Summary Judgment Law, arts. 1, 7–13. See KSEK, pp. 329–32. Those who were sentenced to penal servitude by the summary judgment officer were usually sent to prison. But penal servitude not exceeding one month could be executed in the police station. In some areas, anyone who was sentenced to penal servitude by the summary judgment officer could be executed in the police station. See TTK, vol. 2, pp. 359–60.

100. C. Chen, "Police and Community Control Systems in the Empire," pp. 225, 227–35.

101. See Kamiuchi, pp. 136–37; NTTN, 1921, pp. 654–55.

102. See Mukōyama, p. 296.

103. See Washinosu, pp. 205–7.

104. The majority of criminals convicted by the court were sentenced to penal servitude of not more than one year. See table 4.8.

105. Wu San-lien et al., *T'ai-wan min-tsu yün-tung shih*, p. 397.

106. See also Washinosu, p. 212.

107. See Mukōyama, pp. 1240–48; *Tōchi gaiyō*, pp. 1–2, 109–15.

108. T'ai-pei-shih wen-hsien wei-yüan-hui (ROC), *T'ai-pei-shih chi kao, chuan san, cheng-chih chi, ssu-fa p'ien pao-an p'ien*, pp. 54–55 (hereafter cited as *T'ai-pei-shih chi*).

109. See ibid., pp. 5, 53.

110. See ibid., p. 55.

111. Gambling was the most common of all offenses in Taiwan. In 1915, some 5,835 cases of gambling were prosecuted in the court and the summary judgment office. This number is more than twice that of the second most frequent cases, which involved theft (2,076 cases). The third most frequent were the cases involving assault (1,125 cases). See NTTN, 1917, p. 734. Meanwhile, during the 1909–14 period, the ratio of court decisions to police summary judgments for the offense of gambling was 1:7.2; the ratio for offenses of assault was 1:39.8. See Kamiuchi, pp. 201–2, table 37, 208 n., 249–52, tables 58 and 59. It should be added that the ratio of court decisions to police summary judgments during 1909–14 is the average one for the entire Japanese rule. See table 3.9.

112. The opium-related crimes belonged to special law violation in colonial Taiwan, unlike in metropolitan Japan. In 1914, the number of violations of the Taiwan Opium Law was second to the number of offenses of gambling in all the criminal cases comprising penal code offenses and special law violations. The average proportion of

court decisions to administrative summary judgments for this kind of violation during the 1909–14 period was 1:20.6. See Kamiuchi, pp. 258, table 60, 263.

113. During the Japanese period there were still some cases in which people imposing their private punishments were prosecuted. See Kamiuchi, pp. 118–19.

114. See ibid., p. 176. Any robbery conducted by a group was to be punished by the Bandit Punishment Law rather than the offense of robbery in the Japanese Criminal Code. See, e.g., Judgment Nos. 29, 30 of March 7, 1901, in *Fukuinshū* 374 (Ct. App.).

115. On the average, there were only 15 convictions of robbery out of 4,402 penal code convictions between 1915 and 1919. See NTTN, 1921, pp. 666–67, table 655. There was a similar situation between 1932 and 1937. See *T'ai-pei-shih chi,* p. 66.

116. On communal strife in the early Japanese period, see, e.g., Weng, p. 160.

117. See Washinosu, p. 211; Mukōyama, p. 1264.

118. After Japan lost its authority in 1945, some Taiwanese vagrants became active again. See Wu Cho-liu, *Wu-fa-kuo,* p. 147.

119. According to Kamiuchi, a great number of cases of theft in Taiwan were attributed to the Taiwanese tendency to steal. However, during the 1909–14 period, on average 8.96 persons per 10,000 resident Japanese committed theft, while an average 6.35 persons per 10,000 Taiwanese committed the same offense. He thought the high rate among the resident Japanese was due to their hard living conditions. Why was the same reason not used to explain the cases of theft among the Taiwanese? See Kamiuchi, pp. 158–59, table 12; 161, table 13; 162.

120. See also TWTT, pp. 1362–63.

121. Gambling cases brought to court declined somewhat in the late period of Japanese rule (see table 4.5). But during the same period the administrative summary judgment process was more broadly employed than before (see table 3.9). Therefore the actual number of gambling offenses probably did not drop. On the gambling cases dealt with by the summary judgment office, see TWTT, pp. 1360–61.

122. See Kamiuchi, p. 269; Wu San-lien, pp. 399–415. On the number of cases involving this violation, see, e.g., TWTT, p. 450.

123. Shiga Shūzō, *Shindai Chūgoku no hō to saiban,* pp. 74–79.

124. See appendix D.

125. Li Nan-heng, p. 333.

126. See, e.g., Taiwan Vagrant Discipline Regulation, art. 1; Peace Order Police Law, arts. 10, 16.

127. Li Nan-heng, p. 335.

128. Shiga, pp. 71–72, 78–79; Alford, "Of Arsenic and Old Laws: Looking Anew at Criminal Justice in Late Imperial China," pp. 1192, 1196.

129. See Alford, pp. 1194–95. The appellate system in traditional Chinese law was different from that in modern Western-style law. Under Ch'ing law, those "civil" decisions or criminal decisions with punishment of flogging that had been made by the

magistrates in the district level were reviewed by the superiors only upon the request of the people concerned. Other criminal decisions made by the district magistrates had to be reviewed by the superior levels (prefecture, province, and sometimes central government) of magistrates, regardless of the will of the people concerned. In addition, an individual who felt that he had received less than a fair hearing at the district, prefectural, or provincial level could send a special petition to the Censorate, the Board of Punishments, or the Commandant of Gendarmerie in Peking (the capital) requesting a reexamination of his case. However, even though such capital petitions were accepted, appeals were ordinarily sent back to the officials who had previously tried the case. Imperial Chinese law seemed not to consider it necessary in criminal process to avoid the prejudice of the previous adjudicators. In addition, as the case examined by William Alford shows, although the defendant's capital petition indicated the failure of the prefect (judge) to provide him with an opportunity to confront an important witness (the druggist Ch'ien) so that the superiors could know that the prefect actually did not speak directly with this witness (which was contrary to statutory procedure), the superiors did not remedy this flaw in the process. See ibid., pp. 1207–11, 1230–33.

130. See Ritsurei No. 8 of 1899; Taiwan Criminal Law, arts. 1, 7; Exceptions of Applied Statutes (revised by Ordinance No. 514, 1923), arts. 28–41.

131. Judgment No. 80 of Sept. 15, 1905, in *Fukuinshū* 356 (Ct. App.); Judgment No. 63 of Aug. 15, 1905, in *Fukuinshū* 360 (Ct. App.).

132. The Temporary Court, which tried plenty of political criminals before 1919, was composed of qualified judges in the ordinary court.

133. Judgment No. 127 of Dec. 23, 1905, in *Fukuinshū* 359 (Ct. App.).

134. For instance, a defendant was prosecuted for intimidation, but the judge, after looking at the facts presented, convicted the defendant of illegal detention. Judgment No. 119 of April 15, 1899, in *Fukuinshū* 356 (Ct. App.).

135. *Lin vs. GGT,* in *Kōinshū* 239 (Re-app Div., Higher Ct., Nov. 8, 1923).

136. Taiwan-inhabitants Criminal Instruction Order, arts. 2–8.

137. Ritsurei No. 4 of 1901; Ritsurei No. 10 of 1905; Taiwan Criminal Law, art. 7; Exceptions of Applied Statutes (revised by Ordinance No. 514, 1923), arts. 28, 32. See, e.g., *Chen vs. GGT,* in *Kōinshū* 229 (Re-app. Div., Higher Ct., Sept. 13, 1923). In metropolitan Japan, procurators and the police had only the authority to summon suspects for questioning. In practice, however, preliminary judges generally granted the request of procurators to search houses and so on, and the police and procurators developed many ways to hold suspects for interrogation for months. See Shirai Masaaki, "Senzen no shihō," p. 34; Foote, "Confessions and the Right to Silence in Japan," pp. 423–24. In colonial Taiwan, the Japanese government did not need to pay attention to Western response to Japan's criminal justice system or to popular reaction and thus

it explicitly granted procurators and the police the authority of preliminary judges.

138. *Huang vs. GGT*, in *Kōinshū* 455 (Re-app. Div., Higher Ct., Aug. 8, 1924).

139. Ritsurei No. 25 of 1898, rescinded in 1919. See Tōgō, p. 85.

140. The same situation happened in metropolitan Japan. Torture was by no means rare in prewar Japan. See Foote, p. 424.

141. In the process of investigation the only power that the police did not have but the procurator did was the power to issue a writ of detention.

142. See Kō, p. 89.

143. Kamiuchi, p. 182. See, e.g., *Kadaoka vs. GGT*, *Hōinroku* 1: 3 (criminal), 67 (Ct. App., March 24, 1903).

144. *Liao vs. GGT*, in *Hōinroku* 1: 2 (criminal), 40 (Ct. App., March 3, 1900).

145. Cheng Sung-yü, "Keisatsu gyōsei to keikan no taido," p. 19.

146. Mukōyama, p. 651.

147. See ibid., pp. 1178–79; Taiwan Bengoshi Kyōkai, *Hōsei kōron*, no. 8, pp. 2, 9–10, 19–23, 26–27; no. 9, pp. 6–9, 27.

148. Some people were arrested and detained even without any interrogation in advance. See, e.g., Wu Cho-liu, *T'ai-wan lien-ch'iao*, p. 75; *Lai Ho* case, see Li Nan-heng, p. 268.

149. See Mukōyama, pp. 692, 718, 720, 732.

150. Lai Ho wrote, "The police came . . . without presenting the warrant of arrest issued by the procurator." Li Nan-heng, p. 336. But when he had been arrested during the wartime period, he had not questioned the lack of due process (p. 268). The practice of extralegal "notice" of the police was prevalent in prewar Japan. See Tipton, p. 67.

151. Those demands were made after the February 28 Incident of 1947, which will be discussed in chapter 6. See Wu Cho-liu, *T'ai-wan lien-ch'iao*, p. 215.

152. On imperial Chinese law, see Bodde and Morris, *Law in Imperial China*, pp. 33–35.

153. C. Chen, "The Japanese Adaptation of the Pao-Chia System in Taiwan," p. 396.

154. The 1908 Taiwan Criminal Law, art. 4.

155. Kamiuchi, pp. 542–44.

156. KSEK, pp. 155–56.

157. Kamiuchi, p. 205.

158. See TWTT, p. 447; Kamiuchi, p. 322.

159. See Tsurumi, *Japanese Colonial Education in Taiwan, 1895–1945*, p. 159.

160. See, e.g., Kuo Chia-hsiung, "Jih-chü shih-ch'i T'ai-wan fa-chih chih yen-pien li-ch'eng chi ch'i hsing-chih," p. 1162.

161. See Kamiuchi, p. 357.

162. Between 1915 and 1920, the number of criminal cases in the court rose (see table 3.9), but the number of convicts sentenced to penal servitude by the court dropped. These convicts were sentenced to the fine or the police fine.

163. See Kamiuchi, p. 533, table 117.

164. On the effects of this disposition, see the 1890 Japanese Code of Criminal Procedure, art. 175; the 1922 Japanese Code of Criminal Procedure, art. 317.

165. Chinese "five punishments" (*wu-hsing*) included (1) beating with light stick, (2) beating with heavy stick, (3) penal servitude, (4) life exile, and (5) death. See Bodde and Morris, pp. 76–95. The jail in Ch'ing Taiwan was legally used for detention. See TTK, vol. 1, pp. 128–40.

166. Taiwan-inhabitants Punishment Order, art. 4.

167. See Taiwan Sōtokufu, *Taiwan Sōtokufu tōkeishu*, no. 8 p. 785, table 391; data for 1904. In 1900, the expenditure for the court was 283,038,863 yen; in contrast, the expenditure for constructing prisons was 164,503,610 yen. See also Takekoshi, *Japanese Rule in Formosa*, pp. 194–95.

168. See Washinosu, p. 275.

169. See *Tōchi gaiyō*, p. 28.

170. See Bodde and Morris, p. 99.

171. See TTK, vol. 2, pp. 213–44.

172. Ibid., pp. 216, 218.

173. See J. Ac., pp. 823, 833–37.

174. *Tochi gaiyō*, pp. 84–85.

174. Ibid., pp. 84–85.

175. See Mukōyama, pp. 1254, 1264.

176. For Western scholars, see, e.g., Tsurumi, p. 156; Gold, p. 44. On the native scholars who are Chinese-mainlanders, see, e.g., Chan Heng-chü, *Chung-kuo chin-tai fa-chih shih*, p. 477. On the native scholars who are original Taiwanese, see, e.g., Huang Chao-t'ang, p. 247; P'eng, *A Taste of Freedom*, pp. 61–62. On the Chinese Nationalist government, see, e.g., Ssu-fa hsing-cheng pu (ROC), ed., *Chan-shih ssu-fa chi-yao*, chap. 26, p. 3. On the anti-Nationalist side, see, e.g., Liao, "Formosa Speaks" app., p. 191.

177. E. Chen, "Japan: Oppressor or Modernizer?" pp. 252–55.

178. See also Wu Cho-liu, *T'ai-wan lien-ch'iao*, p. 226.

5 / WESTERNIZATION OF CIVIL JUSTICE

1. Taiwan-inhabitants Civil Litigation Order, art. 2.

2. Ritsurei No. 8, 1898, art. 1.

3. Ritsurei No. 8, 1899; the 1908 Taiwan Civil Law, art. 3.

4. On civil customs in Ch'ing Taiwan, see, e.g., Brockman, "Commercial Contract Law in Late Nineteenth-Century Taiwan," p. 81

5. *Koseki hō,* April 4, 1871. See Hosokawa Kameichi, *Nihon kindai hōseishi,* pp. 69, 169, 238–39.

6. See Aneha Shōhei, *Hontōjin nomi ni kansuru shinzokuhō oyobi sōzokuhō no taiyō,* pp. 7, 22 (hereafter cited as *Taiyō*). Not until 1933 was intermarriage and adoption between Taiwanese and Japanese recognized by law in Taiwan. See GGT Ac., 1931, permanent vol. 4, pt. 6, the first category, no. 4; GGT Ac., 1933, permanent vol. 12, pt. 6, the first category, no. 2. Based on intermarriage or adoption, a Taiwanese could enter a Japanese household and thus was regarded as a Japanese mainlander. But once such relation of marriage or adoption ended and the Taiwanese left the Japanese household, he was restored to his original status as a Taiwanese. Therefore, a Taiwanese in law could not permanently become a Japanese mainlander.

7. A Japanese scholar once argued that old customs should not be compulsorily applied to Taiwanese matters concerning property law. Okamatsu Santarō, "Taiwan genji no hōritsu," p. 6. But there was no example to show that the colonial court followed this opinion.

8. Jones, "Studying the Ch'ing Code," pp. 338–39, 348. The term "civil" law did not exist in imperial China.

9. "Charging interest at forbidden rates," Statute 149. See Yao Yu-hsiang and Hu Yang-shan comps., *Ta-Ch'inq lü-li hui-t'ung hsin-ts'uan,* vol. 4, p. 1338; Brockman, pp. 85–88.

10. See Brockman, pp. 106–127.

11. See Huang, "Between Informal Mediation and Formal Adjudication," pp. 269, 287.

12. See, e.g., TTK, vol. 1, p. 99.

13. Haley, *Authority without Power,* pp. 20–21.

14. Ibid., p. 21.

15. Tōgō Minoru, *Taiwan shokumin hattatsu shi,* p. 95.

16. Okamatsu, "Taiwan genji no hōritsu," pp. 7–8.

17. Okamatsu Santarō, "Dai-so-ken no hōritsu jō no seishitsu," p. 6.

18. TWSH, 3 vols. (every volume included 2 parts). For the works in English, see Okamatsu, comp., *Provisional Report on Investigation of Laws and Customs in the Island of Formosa* (hereafter cited as *Report*). The special terms concerning Taiwanese customs and usages in this report were pronounced in the dialect of the majority of Taiwanese, i.e., Southern Fukienese.

19. See Haley, pp. 5–9.

20. Aneha Shōhei, *Chi-ssu-kung-yeh yü T'ai-wan t'e-shu fa-lü chih yen-chiu,* p. 380 n. (hereafter cited as *T'e-shu fa-lü*).

21. Yamada Tokiyuki, "Kokuhō jō kyūkan no chi-i," p. 30.

22. See also TTK, vol. 1, p. 262.

23. See Ishizaka Otoshirō, "Taiwan ni okeru dojinhō seitei no hitsuyō," pp. 40–41.

24. Aneha, *T'e-shu fa-lü*, pp. 142–43.

25. If there was no custom to deal with specific issues involved, a colonial judge had to make his decision based on legal theory. See, e.g., ibid., pp. 65–66.

26. GGT's Court Organization Law of 1919, art. 8-5. See also KSEK, pp. 29, 31.

27. Ishi Tsunehide, "Hontō sōshō no tokushoku," p. 28; Aneha, *T'e-shu fa-lü*, p. 379.

28. Kempin, *Historical Introduction to Anglo-American Law*, pp. 12–14.

29. On the judgment applying customary law in which a judge did not cite precedents but interpreted customary law by himself, see, e.g., *Pai Huang vs. Huang*, in *Kōinshū* 5 (Re-app. Div., Higher Ct., Feb. 10, 1921). On the judgment involving the issue of distinguishing cited precedents on customary law, see, e.g., *Lin vs. Lin*, in *Kōinshū* 11 (Re-app. Div., Higher Ct., Feb. 17, 1921). On the judgment referring the reports of the Survey Commission, see, e.g., *Chang vs. Chang*, in *Kōinshū* 57 (Re-app. Div., Higher Ct., June 30, 1921).

30. GGT Ac., 1910, permanent vol. 49, pt. 6, no. 6.

31. Okamatsu, "Taiwan no rippō," pp. 1–7.

32. Tōgō, pp. 96–97.

33. Rinji Taiwan Kyūkan Chōsakai, *Hōan Shinsakai kaigi giji-roku*, vol. 1, pp. 5–6.

34. Okamatsu, "Taiwan no rippō," p. 3.

35. See, e.g., Rinji Taiwan Kyūkan Chōsakai, *Hōan Shinsakai kaigi giji-roku*, vol. 1, pp. 8–9, 25, 70–78.

36. Ordinance No. 406, 1922.

37. Ordinance No. 407, 1922, art. 5.

38. Ordinance No. 407, 1922, arts. 6–19.

39. Kondō Masami, "'Sōshi kaimei' kenkyū no kentō to 'kaiseimei,'" pp. 10–11; Aneha, *T'e-shu fa-lü*, p. 136.

40. Mukōyama Hiroo, *Nihon tōchika ni okeru Taiwan minzoku undō shi*, p. 1264.

41. In terms of the shares of the employment in colonial Taiwan, there were approximately 70 percent in the agricultural sector and 30 percent in the nonagricultural sector. See Ho, *Economic Development of Taiwan*, p. 28.

42. TWSH, vol. 1, pts. 1 and 2.

43. In terms of Continental European law, the legal rights relating to real estate can be categorized as the right over things or the right of claim (e.g., the right concerning lease of real estate).

44. Okamatsu, *Report*, pp. 29–30.

45. TWSH, vol. 1, pt. 1, pp. 474–77.

46. Ibid. pp. 577–86.

47. Ibid, pp. 595–96.

48. Okamatsu, *Report*, pp. 143–50. Under the Ch'ing Code, when the *tien* pledge seller failed to pay back the money for *tien* pledge at the stipulated time, the *tien* pledge buyer could buy the transferred objects or rights or have others buy them

to terminate *tien* pledge relations. However, those statutory provisions were seldom enforced in Ch'ing Taiwan. In Taiwanese custom, the *tien* pledge relations were ordinarily maintained under such a circumstance. See TWSH, vol. 1, pt. 1, pp. 663, 673–74.

49. Ibid., pp. 710–14.

50. Ibid., pp. 558–68. The *ekiken* of a person, another kind of *ekiken*, meant that a piece of land should be run for the interests of a certain person.

51. Ritsurei No. 14, 1898.

52. *Wu vs. Wu*, in *Kōinshū* 71 (Re-app. Div., Higher Ct., Aug. 25, 1921).

53. *Chen vs. Kao*, in *Kōinshū* 45 (Re-app. Div., Higher Ct., March 5, 1932).

54. The opinion concerning the ownership of unreported land in the 1932 case is merely a dictum because the key issue therein was whether a permanent tenant on the unreported land could advocate his rights against a third party who bought this unreported land from the owner later; the court mentioned the ownership of land only to confirm that this tenant legally acquired his rights from an owner.

55. *Chou vs. Yang*, in *Kōinshū* 312 (Re-app. Div., Higher Ct., March 13, 1924). In this case the unreported land had already been registered as another's; the original real owner therefore lost his ownership of the land and could only enjoy the right of superficies for his building on this land.

56. Aneha, *T'e-shu fa-lü*, pp. 326–27.

57. According to article 270 of the Japanese Civil Code, an emphyteuticary is one who possesses the right on payment of rent as a farmer to cultivate the land of another person or to rear upon it his horses and cattle.

58. Ritsurei No. 2, 1900; Tanino Tadasu, *Taiwan shin minjihō*, p. 15; Aneha, *T'e-shu fa-lü*, pp. 143, 177.

59. Ritsurei No. 9, 1903, arts. 1, 3, 12.

60. Ritsurei No. 6, 1904.

61. The registration system for the civil law rights on Taiwanese buildings took effect on January 1, 1923. See Tanino, p. 66.

62. Aneha, *T'e-shu fa-lü*, pp. 144–46, 150, 154–55, 171–72.

63. E.g., Judgment No. 190 of May 24, 1906, in *Fukuinshū* 83 (Ct. App.).

64. TWSH, vol. 1, pt. 1, p. 580.

65. Ritsurei No. 3, 1905, art. 2.

66. Ibid., art. 5.

67. Ordinance No. 407, 1922, art. 6 and app.

68. Ibid., art. 7; Aneha, *T'e-shu fa-lü*, pp. 181–82; Tanino, p. 126.

69. Aneha, *T'e-shu fa-lü*, pp. 181–82.

70. Ibid., p. 181.

71. Ibid., p. 180.

72. See TWSH, vol. 1, pt. 1, pp. 224–27.

73. Brockman, pp. 83, 129.

74. GGT Ac., 1922, permanent vol. 140, pt. 6, no. 4, the reasons for enacting Ordinance No. 407, 1922, art. 19.

75. Ishii, ed., *Japanese Legislation in the Meiji Era*, p. 596.

76. Judgment No. 326 of Sept. 26, 1918, in *Fukuinshū* 292 (Ct. App.).

77. TWSH, vol. 3, pt. 2, pp. 255–56.

78. Aneha, *T'e-shu fa-lü*, pp. 339–41.

79. Judgment No. 230 of June 25, 1918, in *Fukuinshū* 292 (Ct. App.).

80. Judgment No. 247 of June 14, 1911, in *Fukuinshū* 290 (Ct. App.).

81. Japanese Civil Code of 1896, art. 675; Japanese Commercial Code of 1899, art. 273.

82. See also Tanino, p. 144.

83. For interpretation of the Court of Appeal in 1911, see *Fukuinshū*, p. 299.

84. See Furei No. 15, 1912; Japanese Commercial Code of 1899, art. 18.

85. See also Yanaihara Tadao, *Jih-pen ti-kuo-chu-i hsia chih T'ai-wan*, pp. 49–50, n. 9.

86. See Yanaihara, p. 50, n. 10. For example, the banks controlled by GGT forced those who subscribed the shares of the company to return loans unless they canceled such subscriptions.

87. Wu Mi-ch'a, *T'ai-wan chin-tai shih yen-chiu*, p. 214. See also GGT Ac., 1936, permanent vol. 9, pt. 2, the second category, no. 2. Some resident Japanese considered that Japanese medium and small enterprises suffered great pressure from Taiwanese businessmen.

88. Yūgengaisha hō (Law No. 74, 1938), effective in Taiwan from January 1, 1940.

89. Ordinance No. 520, Aug. 14, 1940; No. 521, Aug. 14, 1940.

90. According to statistics of 1929, the Japanese share in all modern companies in Taiwan was 76.5 percent (Ho, p. 87). But these data are from 1929, only six years after the Taiwanese by law were allowed to incorporate modern companies in 1923. The precise proportion of Japanese capital to Taiwanese capital in Taiwan's modern companies in the 1930s and mid-1940s is unknown.

91. Between 1933 and 1942, the number of Taiwan's modern companies increased from 444 to 1,131. Taiwan Sōtokufu, *Taiwan tōchi gaiyō*, p. 335.

92. According to my observation when practicing in Taiwan. Some Taiwanese businessmen have no idea that a company is a juristic person. When a "shareholder" wanted to leave the company, he often demanded the partition of the assets of the company, as a partner did to a partnership property, rather than the sale of his shares (stock).

93. See TWSH, vol. 3, pt. 2, pp. 305–75; Japanese Commercial Code of 1922, arts. 435, 440, 455, 464, 486.

94. Ordinance No. 406, 1922. Later the law of negotiable instruments and the law of checks were separated from the Japanese Commercial Code and each enacted by a single statute in 1932 and 1933, respectively. *Tegata hō* (Law No. 20, 1932); *kogitte hō* (Law No. 57, 1933). These two statutes extended to Taiwan in 1933. Ordinance No. 331, Dec. 28, 1933.

95. Li Nan-heng, ed., *Jih-chü hsia T'ai-wan hsin-wen-hsüeh, ming chi 1*, p. 115.

96. TWSH, vol. 3, pt. 2, pp. 431–50.

97. Ordinance No. 522, 1922.

98. I have been unable to find information about the cases involving bankruptcy proceedings in the GGT's statistics of judicial affairs.

99. According to my experience as an attorney in Taiwan.

100. Tai Yen-hui, "Jih-pen t'ung-chih shih-ch'i te T'ai-wan fa-chih," p. 82.

101. Huang Ching-chia, *Jih-chü shih-ch'i chih T'ai-wan chih-min-ti fa-chih*, p. 112.

102. TWSH, vol. 2, pt. 2, pp. 179–82, 211–27.

103. Judgment No. 172 (1903) of May 24, 1904 (Ct. App.) and Judgment No. 139 of June 13, 1904 (Ct. App.); Judgment No. 200 of June 24, 1911 (Ct. App.). See Tai Yen-hui, "Taiwan no kazoku seido to sosen saishi dantai," p. 202–3 (hereafter cited as *Kazoku*).

104. Toguchi kisoku (Furei No. 93, 1906).

105. Mannen Norishige, comp., *Minpō taishō Taiwan jinji kōgyō kanshū kenkyū*, p. 104; see the 1898 Japanese Civil Code, arts. 735–37, 741, 743.

106. See also Aneha, *Taiyō*, p. 43.

107. TWSH, vol. 2, pt. 2, pp. 220–21.

108. Judgment No. 202 of May 23, 1911, in *Fukuinshū* 242 (Ct. App.).

109. *Su vs. Su*, in *Kōinshū* 116 (Re-app. Div., Higher Ct., Dec. 11, 1920).

110. See also Tai, *Kazoku*, p. 212.

111. Judgment No. 125 of June 25, 1920, in *Kōinshū* 211 (App. Div., Higher Ct.). I suspect that this decision was to some extent influenced by the new colonial policy adopted in 1919 (i.e., the extension of Japanese law).

112. Aneha, *Taiyō*, pp. 43, 359.

113. Ibid., pp. 43–44; the 1898 Japanese Civil Code, art. 752 (2). Under Taiwanese customary law as interpreted by the Japanese, only the eldest son could become head of house, but all the sons were to share in the family property.

114. See e.g., Mannen, pp. 105–6. This book contrasts provisions regarding family in the Japanese Civil Code with Taiwanese customary family law article by article.

115. TWSH, vol. 2, pt. 2, pp. 201–5. For recent research on Taiwanese families and their division, see, e.g., Wolf and Huang, *Marriage and Adoption in China, 1895–1945*, pp. 58–59, 66–67; M. Cohen, *House United, House Divided*, pp. 57–69, 193–225.

116. See, e.g., Judgment No. 294 of Oct. 6, 1905, in *Fukuinshū* 276 (Ct. App.); Judgment No. 544 of Dec. 26, 1908, in *Fukuinshū* 277 (Ct. App.).

117. Judgment No. 371 of Aug. 4, 1909, in *Fukuinshū* 232 (Ct. App.).

118. See, e.g., Judgment No. 577 of Dec. 6, 1915, in *Fukuinshū* 242 (Ct. App.).

119. *Liao vs. Liao*, in *Kōinshū* 341 (Re-app. Div., Higher Ct., May 23, 1924).

120. See, e.g., Judgment No. 56 of May 13, 1911, in *Fukuinshū* 233 (Ct. App.).

121. See, e.g., Judgment No. 563 of Nov. 2, 1910, in *Fukuinshū* 232 (Ct. App.).

122. Judgment No. 69 of May 24, 1930 (Re-app. Div., Higher Ct.), in Aneha, *T'e-shu fa-lü*, p. 355.

123. *Lin vs. Lin*, in *Kōinshū* 144 (Re-app. Div., Higher Ct., May 6, 1936).

124. *Ch'en vs. Ch'en*, in *Kōinshū* 210 (Re-app. Div., Higher Ct., Sept. 31, 1936).

125. According to the opinion of the head of the GGT Higher Court. See Aneha, *Taiyō*, p. 50, n. 3. When a married son moved to live in town, he probably established a new household therein, but he was still a member of the joint family in the country.

126. Influential Japanese judge Aneha interpreted the family as those on whom the head of house could exercise his powers. Aneha, *Taiyō*, p. 44.

127. Judgment No. 288 (1907) of April 29, 1908, in *Fukuinshū* 243 (Ct. App.).

128. Judgment No. 332 of Aug. 9, 1919 (Ct. App.), in Tanino, p. 80.

129. Okamatsu, *Report*, app., p. v.

130. Judgment No. 356 of June 27, 1924 (App. Div., Higher Ct.), in Mannen, p. 39.

131. See Judgment No. 473 of Oct. 14, 1920 (App. Div., Higher Ct.), in Mannen, p. 42.

132. Judgment No. 767 of Dec. 18, 1909 (Ct. App.); Judgment No. 30 of May 11, 1910 (Ct. App.), in Tanino, p. 105.

133. Judgment No. 720 (1916) of Jan. 23, 1917, in *Fukuinshū* 244 (Ct. App.).

134. But their children had rights to inherit the estate of the wife's family.

135. Aneha, *T'e-shu fa-lü*, pp. 391–92.

136. Judgment No. 504 of Sept. 24, 1920 (App. Div., Higher Ct.), in Mannen, p. 57.

137. Judgment No. 765 of Dec. 24, 1913, in *Fukuinshū* 259 (Ct. App.); Judgment No. 354 of July 8, 1915, in *Fukuinshū* 259 (Ct. App.).

138. *Hsu Wu vs. Hsu Wu*, in *Kōinshū* 354 (Re-app. Div., Higher Ct., March 11, 1931).

139. Judgment No. 294 of Aug. 31, 1906, in *Fukuinshū* 250 (Ct. App.).

140. Judgment No. 774 of Jan. 18, 1922 (App. Div., Higher Ct.), Judgment No. 123 of Feb. 1, 1923 (Re-app. Div., Higher Ct.), in Mannen, p. 64.

141. See Okamatsu, *Report*, app. p. x.

142. Judgment No. 288 (1907) of April 29, 1908, in *Fukuinshū* 243 (Ct. App.).

143. See Judgment No. 233 of May 27, 1912, in *Fukuinshū* 235 (Ct. App.).

144. Judgment No. 654 (1908) of March 1, 1909, in *Fukuinshū* 246 (Ct. App.).

145. Judgment No. 90 of April 14, 1917, in *Fukuinshū* 249 (Ct. App.).

146. Judgment No. 677 (1915) of Jan. 26, 1916, in *Fukuinshū* 248 (Ct. App.).

147. Judgment No. 132 (1923) of Feb. 14, 1924 (Re-app. Div., Higher Ct.), Judgment

No. 27 of April 22, 1922 (App. Div., Higher Ct.), Judgment No. 61 of Aug. 24, 1922 (Re-app. Div., Higher Ct.), Judgment No. 816 of Nov. 20, 1922 (App. Div., Higher Ct.), in Mannen, pp. 50–51.

148. See Aneha, *Taiyō*, pp. 121–25.

149. See TWTT, p. 199.

150. See Okamatsu, *Report*, app. pp. x–xiii.

151. Judgment No. 315 of Aug. 7, 1908, in *Fukuinshū* 257 (Ct. App.).

152. Judgment No. 473 of Oct. 4, 1920, in *Kōinshū* 241–42 (App. Div., Higher Ct., 1920).

153. *Chen vs. Su*, in *Kōinshū* 322 (Re-app. Div., Higher Ct., Sept. 25, 1929).

154. Kondō Masami, p. 230.

155. As mentioned before, ordinarily after the eldest male in a family died, the family estate would be divided by the *fang*. Only a son could constitute a *fang*, a new family. As a result, only a son had the right to inherit the family estate owned by his parents (especially the father). But a daughter also made contributions on the family estate before she got married and left her parents' family; therefore, when a daughter married, she was usually rewarded with a dowry. Further, a daughter could inherit her deceased parents' (especially her mother's) "private estate," which was separate from the family estate and belonged to an individual member in a family.

156. Aneha, *Taiyō*, pp. 424–25.

157. Judgment No. 557 of Nov. 7, 1917, in *Fukuinshū* 261 (Ct. App.). Under old Taiwanese custom, a female indentured servant was attached to the master family and had to obey the orders of the head of this family.

158. Mannen, p. 128.

159. See TWTT, p. 199. In 1930, only 53 divorces were ordered by judicial decision; in contrast, 4,237 divorces were effected by agreement. In 1940, only 61 divorces were ordered by judicial decision; 3,186 divorces were effected by agreement.

160. There are no figures directly relating to the number of concubines in Taiwan. But looking at statistics relating to the children born to concubines, we can make certain inferences regarding the number of concubines. The percentage of the children born to concubines in all children is 1.0 percent in 1910, 1.0 percent in 1920, 1.0 percent in 1930, 1.7 percent in 1940, and 2.1 percent in 1943. See TWTT, p. 216, table 79. Because concubines bore more children in 1940 and 1943, it can be inferred that the number of marriages to concubines grew in the 1930s.

6 / APPRAISAL AND LEGACY

1. Peattie, "Introduction," in *The Japanese Colonial Empire, 1895–1945*, ed. Myers and Peattie, p. 36.

2. Osborne, *The French Presence in Cochinchina and Cambodia*, pp. 75–76, 82.

NOTES

3. D. Henderson, "Law and Political Modernization in Japan," pp. 415–16.

4. W. Cohen, *Rulers of Empire*, p. 140.

5. Yanaihara Tadao, *Shokumin*, pp. 340–41.

6. Unlike the gentry class on the Chinese mainland or the Korean *yangban* class, the literati on Taiwan could not dominate Taiwanese settler society. As of 1810, the total literati on Taiwan comprised less than 0.5 percent of the population, a ratio much smaller than on the Chinese mainland. Myers, "Taiwan under Ch'ing Imperial Rule, 1684–1895," p. 509. In traditional Korea, only the *yangban* class could take the government examination on Confucianism and become bureaucrats. Hahm, *The Korean Political Tradition and Law*, p. 62.

7. See Cumings, "The Legacy of Japanese Colonialism in Korea," p. 490.

8. Hahm, "Korea's Initial Encounter with the Western Law," p. 183.

9. Huang Chao-t'ang, *T'ai-wan tsung-tu-fu*, pp. 239–46.

10. See, e.g., P'eng Ming-min and Huang Chao-t'ang, *Taiwan no hōteki chi-i*.

11. D. Henderson, "Japanese Influence on Communist Chinese Legal Language," 159–63, 173, 177–78.

12. See ibid., pp. 179–80; Yang Hung-lieh, *Chung-kuo fa-lü fa-ta shih*, pp. 893–916.

13. See Yang Hung-lieh, pp. 1032, 1054–56; Igeda, Yamanaka, and Ishikawa, *Nihon kindaihō shi*, pp. 119–24, 240–43.

14. Chan Heng-chü, *Chung-kuo chin-tai fa-chih shih*, pp. 169–70, 175–76, 178, 182–83, 191, 195, 202.

15. See also Lockenour, "The Chinese Court System," p. 256.

16. Declaration of November 3, 1945, Taiwan Provincial Administrative Executive Office. See T'ai-wan-sheng hsing-cheng chang-kuan kung-shu (ROC), *T'ai-wan-sheng hsing-cheng chang-kuan kung-shu kung-pao* (hereafter cited as *Kung-pao*), 1: 6 (Dec. 1945), p. 1.

17. T'ai-wan-sheng hsing-cheng chang-kuan kung-shu (ROC), comp., *T'ai-wan-sheng hsing-cheng chang-kuan kung-shu shih-cheng pao-kao*, p. 285.

18. In Korea, for the fifteen years from 1945 to the enforcement of the new codes, Japanese codes were still in effect, a situation recognized by the contemporaneous constitution of the Republic of Korea. See Lee, "The Legal Status of Korean Women," p. 95.

19. Lai, Myers, and Wei, *A Tragic Beginning*, pp. 56–57.

20. Article 12 of the Summary Plan for Taking over Taiwan, which was enacted in Chungking (China). See T'ai-wan-sheng hsing-cheng chang-kuan kung-shu Min-cheng ch'u (ROC), comp., *T'ai-wan min-cheng ti-i-chi*, p. 93.

21. Lai, Myers, and Wei, p. 57.

22. Chiang Mu-yün, *Wei T'ai-wan shuo-hua*, p. 173. But after the military massacre of Taiwanese people in 1947, which will be discussed later, the 1947 ROC

Constitution (which became effective on December 25, 1947) was also enforced in Taiwan, probably to placate the Taiwanese people.

23. *T'ai-wan-sheng hsing-cheng chang-kuan kung-shu tsu-chih t'iao-li* (Sept. 20, 1945, the Nationalist government; hereafter cited as "ROC Organic Regulations"). For the entire provisions, see *Kung-pao*, 1: 1 (Dec. 1945), pp. 1–2. Cf. *Taiwan Sōtokufu kansei* (Ordinance No. 209, 1945, the Empire of Japan; hereafter cited as "GGT Organic Regulations"). The original regulation was promulgated by Ordinance No. 88, 1896, and then revised several times until 1945. See Gaimushō Jōyakukyoku Hōkika (Japan), *Nihon tōchika gojunen no Taiwan*, pp. 148–77 (hereafter cited as *Gojunen no Taiwan*).

24. ROC Organic Regulations, art. 1; Orders of Appointment, in *Kung-pao*, 1: 1 (Dec. 1945), p. 1. Cf. GGT Organic Regulations, arts. 1–4.

25. ROC Organic Regulations, art. 3 (2). Cf. GGT Organic Regulations, art. 11.

26. ROC Organic Regulations, arts. 4, 6. Cf. GGT Organic Regulations, arts. 17, 20.

27. See *Kung-pao*, 1: 1 (Dec. 1945), pp. 2–3; *Gojunen no Taiwan*, pp. 184–85; Huang Chao-t'ang, p. 140.

28. ROC Organic Regulations, art. 2. Cf. GGT Organic Regulations, art. 4. Like the Japanese governor-general, who had the power to issue *furei*, the ROC's governor-general was granted the power to promulgate executive ordinances (*shu-lin*) and enact special regulations for Taiwan (*T'ai-wan-sheng tan-hsing kuei-chang*). But only the central government could regulate certain matters; the Administrative Executive Office would draft a bill based on Taiwan's special circumstances and then have it promulgated by the central government. See T'ai-wan-sheng hsing-cheng chang-kuan kung-shu (ROC), comp., *T'ai-wan-sheng hsing-cheng chang-kuan kung-shu san-yüeh lai kung-tso kai-yao*, p. 108.

29. Wu Cho-liu, *T'ai-wan lien-ch'iao*, pp. 174–77.

30. See, e.g., ibid., pp. 174, 239–40.

31. This incident is under serious research in Taiwan now, after half a century. On the political demands of the original Taiwanese in this incident, see Lai, Myers, and Wei, p. 120, app. A.

32. See Wu Cho-lu, p. 226.

33. Especially in the 1950s and 1960s, this interpretation served a political purpose: the Chinese mainland minority dominated the original Taiwanese majority.

34. See also Fairbank, Reischauer, and Craig, *East Asia*, pp. 900–7.

35. In the late 1980s the idea of the reelection of the entire congress was generally accepted in Taiwan. Recently, many Taiwanese people have advocated a Taiwan constitution. Similar approaches occurred in the Japanese period. The movement for the establishment of a Taiwan parliament began in 1921 and burgeoned after the mid- 1920s. In the late 1920s, some Taiwanese intellectuals further demanded a Taiwan constitution.

NOTES

36. As in the Japanese period, the Taiwanese people have more recently sought to establish a Taiwanese parliament at least in part to preserve Taiwanese culture and identity.

37. Ssu-fa hsing-cheng pu (ROC), *Chan-shih ssu-fa chi-yao*, no. 2, p. 1 (hereafter cited as *Chan-shih ssu-fa*).

38. Yang P'eng, *T'ai-wan ssu-fa chieh-shou pao-kao shu*, pp. 27–53. In 1944 the Ministry of Justice of the ROC recognized that the actual number of Taiwan's courts was unknown, but predicted that thirty-one district courts would be needed. See *Chan-shih ssu-fa*, no. 25, p. 12. This prediction indicates that they did not know the actual dimensions of Taiwan because in fact Taiwan is so small that it does not need thirty-one district courts.

39. *Chan-shih ssu-fa*, no. 25, p. 41; Yang P'eng, p. 27.

40. Yang P'eng, pp. 30–31, 43. The ROC regime recognized as qualified those who had been judges or lawyers in the Japanese period. Ibid., pp. 43, 49.

41. See, e.g., Mukōyama Hiroo, *Nihon tōchika ni okeru Taiwan minzoku undō shi*, pp. 1300–1; Lai, Myers, and Wei, pp. 162–63.

42. T'ai-wan kao-teng fa-yüan (ROC), *T'ai-wan ssu-fa erh-shih nien*, p. 68.

43. Chang Yu-chung, *Gaichijin*, p. 55.

44. Ibid., pp. 56–58. Under the ROC Code of Criminal Procedure, a procurator had power to issue a warrant of arrest.

45. Chang Yu-chung, *Gaichijin*, pp. 57–58. See, e.g., Yang Hung-lieh, p. 1032.

46. Pound, "Ssu-fa hsing-cheng pu ku-wen p'ang-te fa-lü chiao-yu ti-i-tz'u pao-kao shu," p. 74.

47. Yang Hui-ch'in, "Chung-Jih ts'ai-p'an feng-ke chih pi-chiao yen-chiu," pp. 93–94.

48. Chang Yu-chung, *Watashi no aisuru Taiwan*, pp. 201, 206–7. The author himself participated in some trials for the defendants involved in the February 28 Incident.

49. Yang Hung-lieh, p. 1056.

50. Interpretation No. 166 of the Council of Grand Justices of the Judicial Yuan (ROC), 1980.

51. In 1988, 66 defendants in the "serious crime cases" were sentenced to death by the ROC courts; in 1989, more than twice as many (138) were sentenced to death. The ROC Judicial Yuan explained that because serious crimes occurred more frequently than before, severe punishments had to be employed to as a deterrent. Ssu-fa-yüan (ROC), *Ssu-fa an-chien fen-hsi*, pp. 246–47, 350, table II-51. According to the 1989 figures, in Taiwan on average one person was sentenced to the death penalty every three days.

52. Gold, p. 20.

53. Buxbaum, p. 187.

NOTES

APPENDIX A

1. Some Western judicial institutions were enacted by the Japanese government in 1872, but they were not well enforced; similarly, in the case of China, the 1906 Court Organization Law was poorly implemented.

2. Taiwan's wartime legal period has been discussed in the preceding chapters. For the Chinese wartime legal period, see Li Sheng-p'o, *Chan-shih ssu-fa,* pp. 1–2, 4, 13–14, 16–17, 20–22. Starting from late 1937, many Chinese wartime special statutes were brought into effect.

3. Although the ROC's war against Japan ended in 1945, the ROC regime declared that its war against the PRC had not ended, and thus wartime special statutes had to continue in force.

Bibliography

CHINESE-LANGUAGE SOURCES

Aneha Shōhei. *Chi-ssu-kung-yeh yü T'ai-wan t'e-shu fa-lü chih yen-chiu* [Studies on ancestor worship and the special law in Taiwan]. Taihoku, 1937. Translated. Taipei: Chung-wen Publishing Co., 1991.

Chan Heng-chü. *Chung-kuo chin-tai fa-chih shih* [Legal institutions of modern China]. Taipei: Taiwan Commercial Press, 1973.

Chang Lung-chih. *Tsu-ch'ün kuan-hsi yü hsiang-ts'un T'ai-wan, i-ke Ch'ing-tai T'ai-wan P'ing-pu tsu-ch'ün shih te tsung-chien ho li-chien* [Ethnicity and rural Taiwan: An ethno-historical study of the Pazeh in Ch'ing Taiwan]. Taipei: National Taiwan University, 1991.

Chang Sheng-yen. *T'ai-wan shih yen-chiu* [Studies on the history of Taiwan]. Taipei: Hua-shih Publishing Co., 1981.

Chang Shih-hsien. "Ch'ing-tai chih-T'ai cheng-ts'e te hua-chan" [The development of ruling policies toward Taiwan during the Ch'ing period]. In *T'ai-wan shih lun ts'ung*, ed. Huang Fu-san and Ts'ao Yung-he.

Chang Tzu-hui. *T'ai-wan shih-jen chih* [A who's who of Taiwan]. Taipei: Kuo-kuang Publishing Co., 1947.

Chang Wei-jen. *Ch'ing-tai fa-chih yen-chiu* [Studies on Ch'ing legal institutions]. 3 vols. Taipei: Academia Sinica, Institute of History and Philology, 1983.

Chang Yen-hsien. "Tui T'ai-wan shih yen-chiu te ch'i-tai." [Expectations for the study of Taiwan's history]. *T'ai-wan shih t'ien-yeh yen-chiu t'ung-hsün*, no. 12 (Sept. 1989), pp. 4–5.

Chang Yu-chung. Letter to author, April 5, 1991.

Ch'en Ch'i-nan. "T'ai-wan pen-t'u i-shih te hsing-ch'eng chi ch'i han-i" [Formation and meaning of the Taiwanese native consciousness]. In *Chin-tai T'ai-wan te she-hui fa-chan yü min-tsu i-shih*, ed. Hong Kong University. Hong Kong: Hong Kong University, 1987.

Ch'en Ch'iu-k'un. "T'ai-wan t'u-ti te k'ai-hua (1700–1756)" [Reclamation of land in Taiwan]. In *T'ai-wan shih lun ts'ung*, ed. Huang Fu-san and Ts'ao Yung-he.

Ch'en K'ung-li. "Ch'ing-tai T'ai-wan she-hui fa-chan te mo-shih wen-t'i" [Issues concerning the development models of Ch'ing Taiwan]. *Tang-tai* (Taipei), no. 30 (Oct. 1988), pp. 61–75.

Ch'en Shao-hsiang. *T'ai-wan te jen-k'ou pien-ch'ien yü she-hui pien-ch'ien*. Taipei: Lien-ching Publishing Co., 1979.

Cheng Sung-yü (Hsüeh-ling). "Chiu min-shang-fa shih-hsing erh yen" [Concerning the application of civil and commercial law]. TWSN, 3: 4 (Oct. 1921), Chinese version, pp. 17–21.

Chiang Mu-yün. *Wei T'ai-wan shuo-hua* [Speaking for Taiwan]. Shanghai, 1948.

Chou Wan-yao. *Jih-chü shih-tai te T'ai-wan i-hui sheh-chih ch'ing-yüan yün-tung* [Petitional movement for the creation of a Taiwan parliament during the period of Japanese occupation]. Taipei: Tzu-li-pao-hsi Publishing Co., 1989.

Chuang Yung-ming. "T'ai-wan ti-i-wei fa-hsüeh po-shih: Yeh Ch'ing-yao" [The first Taiwanese Ph.D. in law]. In *T'ai-wan chin-tai ming-jen chih, ti-erh-ts'e* [A who's who of modern Taiwan, vol. 2], ed. Chang Yen-hsien et al. Taipei: Tzu-li Wan-pao Publishing Co., 1987.

Fix, Douglas. "Mei-kuo hsüeh-sui-chieh te T'ai-wan shih yen-chiu" [The study of Taiwan's history in the U.S. academic circles]. *Tang-tai* (Taipei), no. 30 (Oct. 1988), pp. 55–60.

Hsing-cheng-yüan Chu-chi-ch'u (ROC). *Chung-hua min-kuo t'ung-chi nien-chien* [Statistical yearbook of the Republic of China]. Taipei, 1990.

Hsü Hsüeh-chi et al., comps. *Hsien tsang T'ai-wan tsung-tu-fu tang an tsung mu lu* [General catalog of the presently stored archives of the Government-General of Taiwan]. Taipei: Academia Sinica, Institute of Modern History, 1988.

Huang Chao-t'ang (Ng Yuzin Chiautong). *T'ai-wan tsung-tu-fu* [Government-General of Taiwan]. Trans. Huang Ying-che. Taipei: Tzu-yu shih-tai Publishing Co., 1989.

Huang Ching-chia. *Jih-chü shih-ch'i chih T'ai-wan chih-min-ti fa-chih yü chih-min t'ung-chih* [Taiwan colonial legal institutions and colonial rule during the period of Japanese occupation]. Taipei: Huang Ching-chia, 1960.

Huang Fu-san. "Ch'ing-tai T'ai-wan Han-jen chih keng-ti ch'ü-te wen-ti" [The problems of the acquisition of fields by Han Chinese in Ch'ing Taiwan]. In *T'ai-wan shih lun ts'ung*, ed. Huang Fu-san and Ts'ao Yung-he.

——— and Ts'ao Yung-he. *T'ai-wan shih lun ts'ung* [Essays on Taiwan's history]. Taipei: Chung-wen Publishing Co, 1980.

Kuo Chia-hsiung. "Jih-chü shih-ch'i T'ai-wan fa-chih chih yen-pien li-ch'eng chi ch'i hsing-chih" [The development process and characteristics of the legal institutions on Taiwan during the period of Japanese occupation]. In *Jih-chü ch'u-chi ssu-fa chih-to tang-an*, ed. T'ai-wan-sheng wen-hsien wei-yüan-hui (ROC).

Li Nan-heng, ed. *Jih-chü hsia T'ai-wan hsin-wen-hsüeh, ming chi 1: Lai Ho hsien-sheng ch'üan-chi* [Taiwanese new literature under Japanese occupation, *ming* collection no. 1: The collection of Mr. Lai Ho]. Taipei: Ming-t'an Publishing Co, 1979.

———, ed. *Jih-chü hsia T'ai-wan hsin-wen-hsüeh, ming chi 2: Hsiao-shuo hsüan-chi, i* [Taiwanese new literature under Japanese occupation, *ming* collection: no. 2: Collections of novels, vol. 1]. Taipei: Ming-t'an Publishing Co., 1979.

Li Sheng-p'o. *Chan-shih ssu-fa* [Wartime judiciary]. Changsha (China): Commercial Press, 1939.

Lien Heng. *T'ai-wan t'ung-shih* [History of Taiwan]. 1918. Reprint. Taipei: Li-ming Publishing Co., 1985.

Lin Ch'eng-lu (Tz'u-chou). "Liu-san wen-ti chih yün-ming" [The fate of the issue of Title 63]. *TWSN*, 1: 5 (Dec. 1920), Chinese version, pp. 16–29.

———. "Kai-cheng T'ai-wan t'ung-chih chi-pen-fa yü chih-min-ti t'ung-chih fang-chen" [Correction for the fundamental law of Taiwan and the principles of colonial rule]. *TWSN*, 3:1 (July 1921), Chinese version, pp. 1–13.

———(?). "Shih-hsing min-fa shang-fa i chih ch'u-wai-li" [Exceptions for the application of civil law and commercial law]. *TWSN*, 3: 4 (Oct. 1921), Chinese version, pp. 21–26.

Lin Man-hung. "Mao-i yü Ch'ing-mo T'ai-wan te ching-chi she-hui pien-ch'ien (1960–1895)" [Trade and socioeconomic changes in late Ch'ing Taiwan]. In *T'ai-wan shih lun ts'ung*, ed. Huang Fu-san and Ts'ao Yung-he.

Lin Mei-jung. *Jen-lei-hsüeh yü T'ai-wan* [Anthropology and Taiwan]. Taipei: Lin Mei-jung, 1989.

Lu Hsiu-i. *Jih-chü shih-tai T'ai-wan Kung-ch'an-tang shih* [A history of the Taiwan Communist Party during the period of Japanese occupation]. Taipei: Ch'ien-wei Publishing Co., 1989.

Pound, Roscoe. "Ssu-fa hsing-cheng pu ku-wen p'ang-te fa-lü chiao-yu ti-i-tz'u pao-kao shu." [The first report on legal education by R. Pound, an adviser to the Ministry of Justice]. Trans. Chang Ch'i-tay. *Chung-hua fa-hsüeh tsa-chih*, 5: 8 (April 1947), pp. 67–92.

Shih Ming. *T'ai-wan-jen ssu-pai-nien shih* [Taiwan's four-hundred-year history]. San Jose, Calif.: Paradise Culture Associates, 1980.

Ssu-fa hsing-cheng pu (ROC). *Chan-shih ssu-fa chi-yao* [Summary of the wartime judiciary]. Nanking, 1948.

Ssu-fa-yüan (ROC). *Ssu-fa-yüan shih-shih chi-yao* [A summary of the history of the Judicial Yuan]. Taipei, 1982.

Sung Chin-hsiu. "Jih-pen chung-ching ta-hsüeh she-hui k'o-hsüeh yen-chiu-so, T'ai-wan shih-liao yen-chiu-hui" [The Society for the Study of Taiwan's Historical

Materials, Social Science Institute, Chūkyō University in Japan]. *T'ai-wan shih t'ien-yeh yen-chiu t'ung-hsün*, no. 13 (Dec. 1989), pp. 30–33.

Tai Yen-hui. *Ch'ing-tai T'ai-wan chih hsiang-chih* [Local governance in Ch'ing Taiwan]. Taipei: Lien-ching Publishing Co., 1979.

———. "Jih-pen t'ung-chih shih-ch'i te T'ai-wan fa-chih" [Taiwan legal institutions during the period of Japanese rule]. *Chin-tai chung-kuo*, no. 19 (Oct. 1980), pp. 79–86.

T'ai-pei-shih wen-hsien wei-yüan-hui (ROC). *T'ai-pei-shih chi kao, chuan san, cheng-chih chi, ssu-fa p'ien pao-an p'ien* [Draft gazetteer of Taipei City, vol. 3, on political institutions, with chapters on the judiciary and peace preservation]. Taipei, 1960.

T'ai-wan kao-teng fa-yüan (ROC). *T'ai-wan ssu-fa erh-shih nien* [Twenty-years of Taiwan's judiciary]. Taipei, 1965.

T'ai-wan-sheng hsing-cheng chang-kuan kung-shu (ROC). *T'ai-wan-sheng hsing-cheng chang-kuan kung-shu kung-pao* [Gazette of the Taiwan Provincial Administrative Executive Office]. Taipei, 1945–47.

———, comp. *T'ai-wan-sheng hsing-cheng chang-kuan kung-shu shih-cheng pao-kao* [Administrative report of the Taiwan Provincial Administrative Executive Office]. Taipei, 1946.

———, comp. *T'ai-wan-sheng hsing-cheng chang-kuan kung-shu san-yüeh lai kung-tso kai-yao (October 25, 1945–January 24, 1946)* [Summary of the work of the Taiwan Provincial Administrative Executive Office in a recent three-month period] Taipei, 1946.

T'ai-wan-sheng hsing-cheng chang-kuan kung-shu Min-cheng ch'u (ROC). *T'ai-wan min-cheng ti-i-chi* [The civilian administration in Taiwan, the first collection]. Taipei, 1946.

T'ai-wan-sheng hsing-cheng chang-kuan kung-shu T'ung-chi-shih (ROC), comp. *T'ai-wan-sheng wu-shih-i-nien-lai t'ung-chi t'i-yao* [A statistical summary of Taiwan Province for the past fifty-one years]. Taipei, 1946.

T'ai-wan-sheng wen-hsien wei-yüan-hui (ROC), comp. *T'ai-wan-sheng t'ung-chi kao, chuan san, cheng-shih chih, ssu-fa p'ien* [Draft gazetteer of Taiwan Province, vol. 3, on political affairs, with a chapter on the judiciary], by Tai Yen-hui, Ts'ai Chang-lin, Hung Sun-hsin, and Ch'en Shih-jung. 2 vols. Taipei, 1960.

———. *T'ai-wan-sheng t'ung-chi, chuan chiu, ke-min chih, k'ang-jih p'ien* [Gazetteer of Taiwan Province, vol. 9, on revolution, with a chapter on anti-Japan activities]. Taichung, 1971.

———, trans. and ed. *Jih-chü ch'u-ch'i ssu-fa chih-to tang-an* [Archives for the judicial system in the early period of Japanese occupation]. Taichung, 1982.

Ting Yüeh-chien, ed. *Chih-T'ai pi-kao lu* [Collected writings for governing Taiwan]. 1867. Reprint. Taipei: Taiwan Bank, 1959.

Ts'ai Shu-lin. "She-hui ti-wei ch'ü-te: shan-ti, min-k'e chi wai-sheng chih pi-chiao" [Acquisition of social status: Comparison of Aborigines, South Fukienese and Hakka, and Mainlanders]. In *Pien-chi'en chung te she-hui,* ed. Yang Kuo-shu and Chü Hai-yüan. Taipei: Academia Sinica, Institute of Ethnology, 1988.

Ts'ai Tun-ming. "Opening Remarks." In *Chan-hou Chung-jih fa-hsüeh chih pien-ch'ien yü chan-wang* [Changes in and prospects for jurisprudence in postwar China (ROC) and Japan], comp. Chang-kuo pi-chiao fa-hsüeh hui. Taipei: Chang-kuo pi-chìao fa-hsüeh hui, 1987.

Ts'ao Yung-he. "Ming-Cheng shih-ch'i i-ch'ien chih T'ai-wan" [Taiwan prior to the period of Cheng]. In *T'ai-wan shih lun ts'ung,* ed. Huang Fu-san and Ts'ao Yung-he.

Wang Shih-ch'ing. "Chieh-shao jih-chü shih-ch'i T'ai-wan tsung-tu-fu tang-an" [Introduction to the archives of the Government-General of Taiwan during the period of Japanese occupation]. *T'ai-wan wen-hsien,* 17: 4 (Dec. 1966), pp. 157–92.

Wang Tse-chien. "Min-fa wu-shih nien" [Fifty years of civil law]. In *Min-fa hsüeh-shuo yü p'an-li yen-chiu, ti-wu-ts'e,* ed. Wang Tse-chien. Taipei: Wang Tse-chien, 1990.

Wang Yu-te (Ong Ioktek). *T'ai-wan: K'u-men te li-shih* [Taiwan: A history of anguish and struggle]. Tokyo: Wang Yu-te, 1979.

Weng Chia-yin. *T'ai-wan Han-jen wu-chuang k'ang-jih shih yen-chiu (1895–1902)* [Study on the history of armed anti-Japanese resistance by Han Chinese on Taiwan]. Taipei: National Taiwan University, 1986.

Wu Cho-liu. *T'ai-wan lien-ch'iao* [Taiwan forsythia]. Trans. Chung Chao-cheng. Taipei, 1987.

———. *Wu-hua-kuo* [The fig]. 1970. Reprint. Monterey Park, Calif.: Taiwan Publishing Co., 1984.

Wu Mi-ch'a. *T'ai-wan chin-tai shih yen-chiu* [Studies on the modern history of Taiwan]. Taipei: Tao-hsiang Publishing Co, 1990.

Wu San-lien et al. *T'ai-wan min-tsu yün-tung shih* [A history of the Taiwanese national movement]. Taipei: Tzu-li Wan-pao, 1971.

Wu Wen-hsing. "Jih-chü shih-chi T'ai-wan te fang-tsu tuan-fa yün-tung" [The movements for anti-footbinding and cutting off the Manchu queue during the period of Japanese occupation]. In *T'ai-wan she-hui yü wen-hua pien-chi'en,* ed. Chü Hai-yüan and Chang Ying-hwa. Taipei: Academia Sinica, Institute of Ethnology, 1986.

———. "Jih-chü shih-ch'i T'ai-wan she-hui ling-tao chieh-ts'eng" [A study of the leading class in Taiwanese society during the period of Japanese occupation]. Ph.D. diss., National Taiwan Normal University, 1986.

Yanaihara Tadao. *Jih-pen ti-kuo-chu-i hsia chih T'ai-wan* [Taiwan under Japanese imperialism]. Trans. Chou Hsien-wen. Taipei: Taiwan Bank, 1956.

Yang Hui-ch'in. "Chung-Jih ts'ai-p'an feng-ke chih pi-chiao yen-chiu" [A comparative study on the fashion of judgments between China and Japan]. LL.M. thesis, National Cheng-chih University (Taipei), 1985.

Yang Hung-lieh. *Chung-kuo fa-lü fa-ta shih* [A history of Chinese legal development]. Shanghai: Commercial Press, 1930.

Yang P'eng. *T'ai-wan ssu-fa chien-shou pao-kao shu* [Report of judicial takeover in Taiwan]. N.p., 1946.

Yao Yu-hsiang and Hu Yang-shan, comps. *Ta-Ch'ing lü-li hui-t'ung hsin-ts'uan* [The new general compilation of the Ch'ing Code]. Vol. 8. Reprint. Taipei: Wen-hai Publishing Co., n.d.

JAPANESE-LANGUAGE SOURCES

Aoyagi Tsunatarō. *Sōtoku seiji shi ron* [Discussion of the history of the governor-general's politics]. Seoul: Keijō Shimbunsha, 1928.

Aneha Shōhei. *Hontōjin nomi ni kansuru shinzokuhō oyobi sōzokuhō no taiyō* [Summary on the family law and succession law for matters involving only Taiwanese]. Taihoku: Taihō Geppō Hakkōsho, 1938.

Chang Yu-chung. *Gaichijin, Gaikokujin, to Nihonjin* [Outer-area people, foreigners, and Japanese]. Osaka: Chang Yu-chung, 1985.

——. *Watashi no aisuru Taiwan to Chūgoku to Nihon* [My beloved Taiwan, China, and Japan]. Osaka: Chang Yu-chung, 1987.

Chōsen Sōtokufu. *Shisei nijūgonen shi* [A history of twenty-five-year administration]. Seoul: Chōsen Sōtokufu, 1935.

Chōsen Sōtokufu Hōmukyoku. *Kōtō hōin Daishin'in ishushi hanrei yōshi* [Precedents differently interpretated by the Higher Court and the Great Court of Cassation]. Seoul: Chōsen Sōtokufu Hōmukyoku, 1943.

Chōsen Sōtokufu Hōmukyoku Hōmuka. *Chōsen no shihō seido* [The Korean judicial system]. Seoul: Chōsen Sōtokufu Hōmukyoku Hōmuka, 1935.

Fukushima Masao. "Hō no keiju to shakai=keizai no kindaika (I), (III)" [The reception of law and the modernization of society and the economy]. *Hikaku hōgaku*, 4: 1 (Feb. 1967), pp. 1–27; 6: 1 (May 1970), pp. 1–50.

——, ed. *Nihon kindaihō taisei no keisei, jōkan, gekan* [The formation of Japan's modern legal institutions, the first volume and the last volume]. Tokyo: Nihon Hyōronsha, 1981–82.

Fukushin hōin (GGT), comp. *Fukushin hūin hanrei zenshū* [Collection of the precedents of the Court of Appeal]. Taihoku, 1920.

Gaijibu (GGT), *Nan-Shi hōmen shihō jimu shisatsu hōkokusho* [Report on the inspection of judicial affairs in South China]. Taihoku, 1944.

Gaimushō Jōyakukyoku Hōkika (Japan). *Taiwan no inin rippō seido* ("*Gaichi hōsei shi" dai-san-bu no ichi*) [The delegated legislation system of Taiwan, "Records for outer-area legal institutions," volume 3-1]. Tokyo, 1959.

———. *Seirei ("Gaichi hōsei shi" dai-shi-bu no ichi) zempen* [*Seirei*, "Records for outer-area legal institutions," volume 4-1, part one]. Tokyo, 1960.

———. *Nihon tōchika gojunen no Taiwan ("Gaichi hōsei shi" dai-san-bu no san)* [Taiwan under fifty-year Japanese rule, "Records for outer-area legal institutions," volume 3-3]. Tokyo, 1964.

Girault, Arthur. *Shokumin oyobi shokumin hōsei genron* [On the principles of colonization and colonial legal institutions]. Trans. Wakabayashi Ējirō. Taihoku: Rinji Taiwan kyūkan chōsakai, 1918.

Gotō Shimpei. *Taiwan keiei jō kyūkan seido no chōsa o hitsuyō to suru iken* [Opinion about the necessity of investigation of old customary institutions for the management of Taiwan]. 1901. Reprint. Tokyo: Tōa Kenkyūsho, 1940.

Haruyama Meitetsu. "Kindai Nihon no shokuminchi tōchi to Hara Kei" [Modern Japan's colonial rule and Hara Kei]. In *Nihon shokuminchi-shugi no seijiteki tenkai, 1895–1934* [Political evolution of Japanese colonialism], ed. Haruyama Meitetsu and Wakabayashi Masahiro. Tokyo: Azia Seiken Gakukai, 1980.

———, ed. *Taiwan tōnai jōhō. Hontōjin no dōkō* [The situation on the island of Taiwan, and attitudes of the Taiwanese]. Reproduction of confidential documents issued 1937–39. Tokyo: Fuji Shuppan, 1990.

Higashi Yoshio. *Taiwan kenzaishi kenkyū* [Studies on the history of Taiwan's economy]. Tokyo: Tōto Shoseki Co., 1944.

Hōmubu (GGT), ed. *Taiwan shihō seido enkaku shi* [Records for the development of a judicial system in Taiwan]. Taihoku, 1917.

Hōmukyoku (GGT), ed. *Taiwan shihō ichiran* [Summary of justice in Taiwan]. Taihoku, 1941.

Hosokawa Kameichi. *Nihon kindai hōseishi* [Legal history of modern Japan]. Tokyo: Yūhikaku, 1961.

Hozumi Nobushiga. *Goningumi seido ron* [Discussion of the system of "five-man group"]. Tokyo: Yūhikaku, 1921.

Hozumi Yatsuka. *Kempō teiyō, jōkan* [Summary of constitutional law, the first volume]. Tokyo: Yūhikaku, 1911.

Hsiu Hu-sheng. "Taiwan gikai to musan kaikyū kaihō" [The Taiwan parliament and the emancipation of proletarians]. TWSN, 4: 7 (July 1923), Japanese version, pp. 43–48.

Ichimura Mitsue. *Teikoku kempō ron* [A treatise on the Imperial Constitution]. Tokyo: Yūhikaku, 1927.

Igeda Kōjin. "Taiwan shikō no hōritsu to ritsurei" [Statutes applied to Taiwan and ritsurei]. THGP, 4: 10 (Oct. 1910), pp. 15–26.

Igeda Ryōji, Yamanaka Ēnosuke, and Ishikawa Hikio. *Nihon kindaihō shi* [A history of modern Japanese law]. Kyoto: Hōritsu Bunkashisha, 1982.

Inoue Masahiro. "Taiwan minji chōtei zakkō" [Miscellaneous research on civil mediation in Taiwan]. THGP, 37: 4 (April 1943), pp. 1–10.

Ishi Tsunehide. "Hontō sōshō no tokushoku" [Characteristics of lawsuits in Taiwan]. THGP, 2: 10 (Oct. 1908), pp. 21–28.

Ishida Hiroshi. "Taiwan-kenkyū to Chūkoku-kenkyū: Taiwan-kenkyū no genjō to kadai" [Recent trends and problems in Taiwan Studies]. *Taiwanshi-kenkyū* (Kensei University), no. 8 (March 1990), pp. 1–11.

Ishizaka Otoshirō. "Taiwan ni okeru dojinhō seitei no hitsuyō, ka" [The necessity of enacting native statutes in Taiwan, the last part]. THGP, 4: 2 (Feb. 1910), pp. 31–41.

Itō Hirobumi, ed. *Taiwan shiryō* [Sources related to Taiwan]. Tokyo: Hissho Ruisan Kankōkai, 1936.

Itō Masami, ed. *Gaikokuhō to Nihonhō* [Foreign law and Japanese law]. *Gendaihō*, no. 14. Tokyo: Iwanami Shoten, 1966.

Izumi Akira. *Shokuminchi tōchi ron* [A treatise on colonial governance]. Tokyo: Yūhikaku, 1924.

Kambō Shingishitsu (GGT). *Ritsurei seido no enkaku* [The development of the *ritsurei* system]. Taihoku, 1940.

Kamiuchi Tsusaburō. *Taiwan keiji shihō seisaku ron* [Discussion on criminological policies in Taiwan]. Taihoku: Taiwan Nichi-nichi Shimpōsha, 1916.

Keimukyoku (GGT). *Taiwan no keisatsu* [Taiwan's police]. Taihoku, 1932.

———. *Taiwan Sōtokufu keisatsu enkaku shi, dai-ichi-hen: keisatsu kikan no kōsei* [A history of the GGT police, part 1: The organization of the police agency]. Taihoku, 1933.

———. *Taiwan Sōtokufu keisatsu enkaku shi, dai-ni-hen: Ryō-Tai igo no chian jōkyō, (gekan)* [A history of the GGT police, part 2: Public peace after the possession of Taiwan, the last volume]. Taihoku, 1942.

Kim Kyu-sung. *Nihon no shokuminchi hōsei no kenkyū* [Studies on the Japanese colonial legal system]. Tokyo: Shakai Hyōronsha, 1987.

Kim Tetsu. *Kankoku no jinkō to keizai* [Korean population and economy]. Tokyo: Iwanami Shoten, 1965.

Kō Se-kai. *Nihon tōchika no Taiwan* [Taiwan under Japanese rule]. Tokyo: Tōkyō Daigaku Shuppankai, 1972.

Kobayashi Masahito. *Taiwan keiei ron* [Discussion on the management of Taiwan]. Tokyo: Kobayashi Masahito, 1902.

Kōnan Shimbunsha. *Taiwan jinshi kan* [A who's who of Taiwan]. Taihoku: Kōnan Shimbunsha, 1943.

Kondō Ken'ichi, ed. *Taiheiyō senka no Chōsen oyobi Taiwan* [Korea and Taiwan during the Pacific War]. Tokyo: Gannandō Shoten, 1961.

Kondō Masami. "'Sōshi kaimei' kenkyū no kentō to 'kaiseimei'" [An examination of the studies on "the creation of surnames" and "change of names"]. In *International Symposium on the History of Taiwan during Japanese Rule, 1895–1945*, ed. Depart-

ment of History, National Taiwan University. Taipei: National Taiwan University, 1993.
Kōtō hōin (GGT), comp. *Kōtō hōin hanrei zenshū* (*Kōtō hōin hanreishū*, or *Taiwan Sōtokufu Kōtō hōin Jōkoku-bu hanreishū*) [Collection of the precedents of the Higher Court]. Taihoku, 1921–41.
Kusunoki Seiichirō. *Meiji rikkensei to shihōkan* [Meiji constitutional system and judges]. Tokyo: Keiō tsūshin Co., 1989.
Lin Ch'eng-lu. "Minpō no shinzoku kitei o Taiwan-jin ni tekiyō suru hōan no gigi" [Doubts on the bill that family provisions in the Civil Code be applied to the Taiwanese], *TWSN*, 3: 6 (Sept. 1922), Japanese version, pp. 21–35.
Mannen Norishige, comp. *Minpō taishō Taiwan jinji kōgyō kanshū kenkyū* [Studies on Taiwanese customs concerning personal matters and common estate in contrast with the Japanese Civil Code]. Taihoku: Taihō Geppō Hakkōsho, 1931.
Matsui Yoshirō. "Jōyaku kaisei" [Treaty revision]. In *Nihon kindaihō taisei no keisei, gekan*, ed. Fukushima Masao.
Minobe Tatsukichi. *Chikujō kempō seigi* [Summary of the Constitution article by article]. Tokyo: Yūhikaku, 1927.
Mizuta Yohio. "Gaikokuhō no eikyō to wa nani ka" [The influence of foreign law in Japan]. *Hikaku hōgaku*, 6: 2 (March 1971), pp. 17–52.
Mochiji Rokusaburō. *Taiwan shokumin seisaku* [The colonial policy of Taiwan]. Tokyo: Fuzanbō, 1912.
Mukai Ken. "Mimpō-ten no hensan" [The compilation of the Civil Code]. In *Nihon kindaihō taisei no keisei, gekan*, ed. Fukushima Masao.
Mukōyama Hiroo. "Nihon tōchi ka ni okeru Taiwan no hō to seiji" [Law and politics of Taiwan under Japanese rule]. *Kokugakuin hōgaku*, 21: 2 (Sept. 1983), pp. 61–106.
———. *Nihon tōchika ni okeru Taiwan minzoku undō shi* [A history of the national movement in Taiwan under Japanese rule]. Tokyo: Chūō Keizai Kenkyūjo, 1987.
Nagao Keitoku. *Taiwan keijihō taii* [Summary of the criminal law in Taiwan]. Taihoku: Bummeidō Shoten, 1926.
Nagao Keitoku and Ōda Shūkichi. *Taiwan gyōseihō taii* [Summary of the administrative law in Taiwan]. Rev. ed. Taihoku: Sugita Shoten, 1934.
Naichi oyobi Taiwan shihō kyōtsū ni kansuru ikensho [Memorandum for the unified judiciary on the mainland and Taiwan]. N.p., 1909?
Naikaku Kirokuka (Japan), comp. *Taiwan ni shikō subeki hōrei ni kansuru hōritsu so no enkaku oyobi genkō ritsurei* [The law relating to laws and regulations to be enforced in Taiwan and its development as well as present *ritsurei*]. Tokyo, 1915.
Naikaku Tōkeikyoku (Japan), comp. *Nihon-teikoku tōkei nenkan* [Statistics of the Empire of Japan]. Tokyo, 1903–40.
Nakamura Akira. *Shokuminchi tōchihō no konpon mondai* [Fundamental legal issues on colonial governance]. Tokyo: Nihon Hyōronsha, 1943.

———. "Shokuminchi hō" [The colonial law]. In vol. 5 of *Kōza Nihon kindaihō hattatsu shi*, ed. Ukai Nobushige et al.

Nakamura Hideo. "Shihō seido to Nihon no kindaika" [The judicial system and Japan's modernization]. *Hikaku hōgaku*, 7: 1 (Sept. 1971), pp. 7–17.

Nakamura Kichisaburō. "Keihō" [Criminal law]. In vol. 9 of *Kōza Nihon kindaihō hattatsu shi*, ed. Ukai Nobushige et al.

Nakamura Yasutada, comp. *Taiwan Sōtokufu hōin hanketsuroku* [Collection of the precedents of the GGT court], 7 vols. Taihoku: Nakamura Yasutada, 1903–4.

Niida Noboru. "Chūgoku kyūshakai no kōzō to keibatsuken—Kokkateki, hikokkateki to wa nani ka" [The framework of old Chinese society and criminal penalty power—What is the so-called state's or non-state's?]. In *Keibatsu to kokka kenryoku* [National power and criminal penalties], comp. Hōseishi gakkai. Tokyo: Sōbunsha, 1960.

Noda Yoshiyuki et al. "Nihon ni okeru gaikokuhō no sesshu" [Adoption of foreign law in Japan]. In *Gaikokuhō to Nihonhō*, ed. Itō Masami.

Okamatsu Santarō. "Dai-so-ken no hōritsu jō seishitsu" [Legal nature of the large-lease right]. *TWKS*, 1: 1 (Jan. 1901), pp. 4–14.

———. "Taiwan genji no hōritsu" [Present law in Taiwan]. *TWKS*, 3: 2 (Feb. 1903), pp. 1–9.

P'eng Ming-min and Huang Chao-t'ang (Ng Yuzin Chiautong). *Taiwan no hōteki chi-i* [Legal status of Taiwan]. Tokyo: Tōkyō Daigaku Shuppankai, 1976.

Rinji Taiwan Kyūkan Chōsakai. *Taiwan shihō* [Taiwanese private law], 3 vols. (2 parts per vol.). Taihoku: Rinji Taiwan Kyūkan Chōsakai, 1910–11.

———. *Hōan Shinsakai kaigi giji-roku* [Records of hearings for bills]. 5 vols. Taihoku: Rinji Taiwan Kyūkan Chōsakai, n.d.

Sanka Shiho. "Taiwan kakyō, ni" [Overseas Chinese in Taiwan, II], *THGP*, 37: 6 (June 1943), pp. 54–76.

Sasaki Chūzō and Tagahashi Buichirō. *Taiwan gyōseihō ron* [Discussion of the administrative law in Taiwan]. Taihoku: Katsubunsha, 1915.

Sasaki Sōichi. *Nihon kempō yōron* [Outline treatise of the Japanese constitution]. Tokyo: Kinshi Hōryūdō, 1932.

Sawaki Takao. "Hō no keiju" [The reception of law]. In *Gaikokuhō to Nihonhō*, ed. Itō Masami.

Shiga Shūzō. *Shindai Chūgoku no hō to saiban* [Law and adjudication in Ch'ing China]. Tokyo: Sōbunsha, 1984.

Shimizu Chō. *Chikujō teikoku kempō kōgi* [Lectures on the Imperial Constitution article by article]. Tokyo: Shōkadō Shoten, 1940.

Shirai Masaaki. "Senzen no shihō" [Prewar justice]. In *Shihō kaikaku no tembō* [Prospect for judicial reform], ed. Tōkyō Bengoshikai. Tokyo: Yūhikaku, 1982.

Someno Yoshinopu. "Shihō seido" [Judicial system]. In vol. 2 of *Kōza Nihon kindaihō hattatsu shi*, ed. Ukai Nobushige et al.

Tai Yen-hui (Tai Teruo). "Taiwan no kazoku seido to sosen saishi dantai" [The Taiwanese family system and ancestor-worship associations]. In *Taiwan bunka ronsō, dai-ni-shū* [Essays on Taiwan's culture, the second collection]. Taihoku: Shimizu Shoten, 1945.

Taihō Geppō Hakkōsho. *Taihō geppō* (*Hōin geppō* before January 1911) [Monthly report of Taiwan's law]. Taihoku, 1907–43.

Taiwan Bengoshi Kyōkai. *Hōsei kōron* [Comments on law and politics] (journal of the Association of Taiwan's Lawyers). Nos. 8, 9 (March, April, 1935).

Taiwan Kanshū Kenkyūkai. *Taiwan kanshū kiji* [Records of Taiwanese custom], 7 vols. Taihoku, 1901–07. Reprint. Taipei: Ku-t'ing shu-chü, 1969.

Taiwan Kingendaishi Kenkyūkai, comp. "Sengo Nihon ni okeru Taiwan kingendaishi kenkyū bunken mokuroku" [A bibliography of literature of studies on Taiwan's modern history in postwar Japan]. *Taiwan Kingendaishi Kenkyū*, no. 3 (Jan. 1981), pp. 152–204.

Taiwan Seinen Zasshisha. *Taiwan seinen* (*Taiwan* after April 1922) [Taiwanese youth]. Tokyo, 1920–24. Reprint. Taipei: Tung-fang wen-hua shu-chü, 1973.

Taiwan Sōtokufu. *Taiwan Sōtokufu hōin hanketsuroku* [Collection of the decisions of the GGT court]. Taihoku, 1903–4.

———. *Taiwan Sōtokufu kōbun ruisan* [Archives of the GGT]. Comp. T'ai-wan-sheng wen-hsien wei-yüan-hui. Taihoku, 1895–1945.

———. *Taiwan Sōtokufu tōkeisho* [Statistical yearbooks of the GGT]. Taihoku, 1899–1944.

———. *Taiwan Sōtokufu hanzai tōkei* [Criminal statistics of the GGT]. Taihoku, 1911–44.

———. *Taiwan Sōtokufu oyobi shozoku kansho shokuinroku* [Register of officials in the Government-General and attached agencies]. Taihoku, 1943, 1945.

———. *Taiwan tōchi gaiyō* [A summary of the administration of Taiwan]. Taihoku, 1945.

Takumudaijin kambō Bunshoka (Japan). *Nai-gai-chi hōrei taishōhyō* [Table of comparison of laws and regulations for the Japanese mainland and outer areas]. Tokyo, 1941.

Tanino Tadasu. *Taiwan shin minjihō* [Taiwan's new civil law]. Taihoku: Taiwan Jihō Hakkōsho, 1923.

Teshima Heijirō. *Shokumin hōsei chosho mokuji shū* [Collection of the tables of contents in the literature concerning the colonial legal system]. Taihoku: Hōin Geppō Hakkosho, 1910.

To Shōgen. *Nihon teikokushugika no Taiwan* [Taiwan under Japanese imperialism]. Tokyo: Tōkyō Daigaku Shuppankai, 1975.

Tōgō Minoru. *Taiwan shokumin hattatsu shi* [A history of the colonization of Taiwan]. Taihoku: Kōbunkan, 1916.
Uesugi Shinkichi. *Teikoku kempō jutsugi* [Lectures on the Imperial Constitution]. Tokyo: Yūhikaku, 1923.
Ukai Nobushige et al., eds. *Kōza Nihon kindaihō hattatsu shi* [Series on the development of modern Japanese law]. 11 vols. Tokyo: Keisō Shobō, 1958–61.
Wakabayashi Masahiro. *Taiwan kōnichi undō shi kenkyū* [A study of the anti-Japanese movement in Taiwan]. Tokyo: Kenbun Shuppan, 1983.
Washinosu Atsuya. *Taiwan keisatsu shijūnen shiwa* [A forty-year history of the police in Taiwan]. Taihoku: Washinosu Atsuya, 1938.
Watanabe Yōzō. "Nihon fashizumu hō-taisei—sōron" [Japan's fascist legal system—general discussion]. In *Senji Nihon hō-taisei* [Wartime Japan's legal system], ed. Tōkyō Taigaku Shakai Kagaku Kenkyūsho, chap. 1. Tokyo: Tōkyō Daigaku Shuppankai, 1979.
Yamabe Kentarō, ed. *Gendai shi shiryō: Taiwan, I* [Modern historical documents: Taiwan, I]. Tokyo: Misuzu Shobō, 1971.
Yamada Tokiyuki. "Kokuhō jō kyūkan no chi-i" [The position of old customs in national law]. THGP, 9: 8 (Aug. 1915), pp. 23–30.
Yamazaki Tanshō. *Gaichi tōchi kikō no kenkyū* [A study of the strutures of outer-area administration]. Tokyo: Takayama Shoin, 1943.
Yanaihara Tadao. *Shokumin oyobi shokumin seisaku* [Colonization and colonial policy]. Tokyo: Yūhikaku, 1933.
Yokoyama Kōichirō. "Keibatsu chian kikō no seibi" [The completion of the mechanism for punishing criminals and maintaining public peace]. In *Nihon kindaihō taisei no keisei, jōkan*, ed. Fukushima Masao.

WESTERN-LANGUAGE SOURCES

Ahern, Emily. *The Cult of the Dead in a Chinese Village*. Stanford, Calif.: Stanford University Press, 1973.
Ahern, Emily, and Hill Gates, eds. *The Anthropology of Taiwanese Society*. Stanford, Calif.: Stanford University Press, 1981.
Allee, Mark Anton. *Law and Local Society in Late Imperial China in the Nineteenth Century*. Stanford, Calif.: Stanford University Press, 1994.
Alford, William P. "Of Arsenic and Old Laws: Looking Anew at Criminal Justice in Late Imperial China." *California Law Review*, 72 (1984), pp. 1180–1256.
Angelino, De Kat. *Colonial Policy*. 2 vols. Trans. G. J. Renier. The Hague: Martinus Nijhoff, 1931.
Baker, Edward J. "The Role of Legal Reforms in the Japanese Annexation and Rule of Korea, 1905–1919." In *Introduction to the Law and Legal System of Korea*, ed. Sang Hyun Song.

Barclay, George W. *Colonial Development and Population in Taiwan.* Princeton, N.J.: Princeton University Press, 1954.

Beckmann, George. "Brief Episodes—Dutch and Spanish Rule." In *Taiwan in Modern Times,* ed. Paul K. T. Sih.

Betts, Raymond F. *Assimilation and Association in French Colonial Theory, 1890–1914.* New York: Columbia University Press, 1961.

Bodde, Derk, and Clarence Morris. *Law in Imperial China.* Philadelphia: University of Pennsylvania Press, 1973.

Brockman, Rosser H. "Commercial Contract Law in Late Nineteenth-Century Taiwan." In *Essays on China's Legal Tradition,* ed. Jerome Alan Cohen, R. Randle Edwards, and Fu-mei Chang Chen. Princeton, N.J.: Princeton University Press, 1980.

Buxbaum, David C. "Some Aspects of Substantive Family Law and Society Change in Rural China (1896–1967): With a Case Study of a North Taiwan Village." Ph.D. diss., University of Washington, 1968.

Campbell, William, ed. *Formosa under the Dutch.* London: Kegan, Paul, Trench, Trubner, 1903.

Chang, Han-yu, and Ramon H. Myers. "Japanese Colonial Development Policy in Taiwan, 1895–1906: A Case of Bureaucratic Entrepreneurship." *Journal of Asian Studies,* 22: 4 (Aug. 1963), pp. 433–49.

Chen, Ch'ing-chih. "Japanese Socio-political Control in Taiwan: 1895–1945." Ph.D. diss., Harvard University, 1973.

———. "The Japanese Adaptation of the Pao-Chia System in Taiwan, 1895–1945." *Journal of Asian Studies,* 34: 2 (Feb. 1975), pp. 391–416.

———. "Police and Community Control Systems in the Empire." In *The Japanese Colonial Empire, 1895–1945,* ed. Ramon H. Myers and Mark R. Peattie.

Chen, Edward I-te. "Japanese Colonialism in Korea and Formosa: A Comparison of Its Effects upon the Development of Nationalism." Ph.D. diss., University of Pennsylvania, 1968.

———. "Japanese Colonialism in Korea and Formosa: A Comparison of the Systems of Political Control." *Harvard Journal of Asiatic Studies,* no. 30 (1970), pp. 126–58.

———. "Formosa Political Movements under Japanese Colonial Rule, 1914–1937." *Journal of Asian Studies,* 31: 3 (May 1972), pp. 477–97.

———. "Japan: Oppressor or Modernizer?" In *Korea under Japanese Colonial Rule: Studies of the Policy and Techniques of Japanese Colonialism,* ed. Andrew C. Nahm. Kalamazoo: Center for Korean Studies, Institute of International and Area Studies, Western Michigan University, 1973.

———. "Japan's Decision to Annex Taiwan: A Study of Itō-Mutsu Diplomacy, 1894–95." *Journal of Asian Studies,* 37: 1 (Nov. 1977), pp. 61–72.

———. "The Attempt to Integrate the Empire: Legal Perspectives." In *The Japanese Colonial Empire, 1895–1945*, ed. Ramon H. Myers and Mark R. Peattie.

Chiba, Masaji. *Legal Pluralism: Toward a General Theory through Japanese Legal Culture*. Tokyo: Tokai University Press, 1989.

Cohen, Myron L. *House United, House Divided: The Chinese Family in Taiwan*. New York: Columbia University Press, 1976.

Cohen, William B. *Rulers of Empire: The French Colonial Service in Africa*. Stanford, Calif.: Stanford University Press, 1971.

Chu, Samuel C. "Liu Ming-ch'uan and the Modernization of Taiwan." *Journal of Asian Studies*, 23: 1 (Nov. 1963), pp. 37–53.

Ch'ü, T'ung-tsu. *Local Government in China under the Ch'ing*. Cambridge, Mass.: Harvard University Press, 1988.

Cumings, Bruce. "The Legacy of Japanese Colonialism in Korea." In *The Japanese Colonial Empire, 1895–1945*, ed. Ramon H. Myers and Mark R. Peattie.

Epp, Robert Charles. "Threat to Tradition: The Reaction to Japan's 1890 Civil Code." Ph.D. diss., Harvard University, 1964.

Fairbank, John K., Edwin O. Reischauer, and Albert M. Craig. *East Asia: Tradition and Transformation*. Rev. ed. Boston: Houghton Mifflin, 1989.

Foote, Daniel H. "Confessions and the Rights to Silence in Japan." *Georgia Journal of International and Comparative Law*, 21 (1991), pp. 415–88.

Freedman, Maurice, ed. *Family and Kinship in Chinese Society*. Stanford, Calif.: Stanford University Press, 1970.

Gallin, Bernard. *Hsin Hsing, Taiwan: A Chinese Village in Change*. Berkeley: University of California Press, 1966.

Gann, Levis. H. "Western and Japanese Colonialism: Some Preliminary Comparisons." In *The Japanese Colonial Empire*, ed. Ramon H. Myers and Mark R. Peattie.

Gates, Hill. "Introduction" In *The Anthropology of Taiwanese Society*, ed. Emily Martin Ahern and Hill Gates.

Goddard, W. G. *The Makers of Taiwan*. Taipei: China Publishing Co., 1963.

Gold, Thomas B. *State and Society in the Taiwan Miracle*. Armonk, N.Y.: M. E. Sharpe, 1986.

Gordon, Leonard H. D., ed. *Taiwan: Studies in Chinese Local History*. New York: Columbia University Press, 1970.

Grajdanzev, A. J. "Formosa (Taiwan) under Japanese Rule." *Pacific Affairs* (1942), pp. 311–24.

Hahm, Pyong-Choon. *The Korean Political Tradition and Law*. 2d ed. Seoul: Seoul Computer Press, 1971.

———. "Korea's Initial Encounter with the Western Law: 1866–1910 A.D." In *Introduction to the Law and Legal System of Korea*, ed. Sang Hyun Song.

Haley, John Owen. "The Myth of the Reluctant Litigation." *Journal of Japanese Studies*, 4: 2 (1978), pp. 359–89.

———. *Authority without Power: Law and the Japanese Paradox*. New York: Oxford University Press, 1991.

Harrell, Stevan. "From Xiedou to Yijun, the Decline of Ethnicity in Northern Taiwan, 1885–1895." *Late Imperial China*, 11: 1 (June 1990), pp. 99–127.

Hattori, Takaaki. "The Legal Profession in Japan: Its Historical Development and Present State." In *Law in Japan: The Legal Order in a Changing Society*, ed. Arthur Taylor von Mehren.

Henderson, Dan Fenno. "Law and Political Modernization in Japan." In *Political Development in Modern Japan*, ed. Robert E. Ward. Princeton, N.J.: Princeton University Press. 1968.

———. "Japanese Influence on Communist Chinese Legal Language." In *Contemporary Chinese Law: Research Problems and Perspectives*, ed. Jerome Alan Cohen. Cambridge, Mass.: Harvard University Press, 1970.

Henderson, George. "Human Rights in South Korea, 1945–1953." In *Human Rights in Korea: Historical and Political Perspective*, ed. William Shaw.

Ho, Samuel P. S. "Economic Development of Colonial Taiwan: Evidence and Interpretation." *Journal of Asian Studies*, 34: 2 (Feb. 1975), pp. 417–39.

———. *Economic Development of Taiwan, 1860–1970*. New Haven, Conn.: Yale University Press, 1978.

Hsieh, Chiao-min. "The Physical Setting of Taiwan." In *Taiwan in Modern Times*, ed. Paul K. T. Sih.

Hsu, Wen-hsiung. "Chinese Colonization of Taiwan." Ph.D. diss., University of Chicago, 1975.

Huang, Philip C. C. "Between Informal Mediation and Formal Adjudication: The Third Realm of Qing Civil Justice." *Modern China*, 19: 3 (July 1993), pp. 251–98.

———. "Codified Law and Magisterial Adjudication in the Qing." In *Civil Law in Qing and Republic China*, ed. Kathryn Bernhardt and Philip C. C. Huang. Stanford, Calif.: Stanford University Press, 1994.

Hung, Chien-chao. "Taiwan under the Cheng Family 1662–1683: Sinicization after Dutch Rule." Ph.D. diss., Georgetown University, 1981.

Ishii, Ryosuke, ed. *Japanese Legislation in the Meiji Era*. Trans. William J. Chambliss. Tokyo: Kasai Publishing and Printing Co., 1958.

Jansen, Marius B. "Japanese Imperialism: Late Meiji Perspectives." In *The Japanese Colonial Empire, 1895–1945*, ed. Ramon H. Myers and Mark R. Peattie.

Jones, William C. "Studying the Ch'ing Code—The Ta Ch'ing Lü." *American Journal of Comparative Law*, 22: 2 (Spring 1974), pp. 330–64.

Kempin, Frederick G., Jr. *Historical Introduction to Anglo-American Law*. 2d ed. St. Paul, Minn.: West Publishing Co., 1973.

Kerr, George H. *Formosa, Licensed Revolution, and the Home Rule Movement, 1895–1945.* Honolulu: University Press of Hawaii, 1974.
Kirk, William. "Social Change in Formosa." *Sociology and Social Research,* 24: 1 (Sept. 1941), pp. 10–26.
Kodansha, comp. *Kodansha Encyclopedia of Japan.* Tokyo: Kodansha, 1983.
Kuo, Ting-yee. "Early Stages of the Sinicization of Taiwan, 230–1683." In *Taiwan in Modern Time,* ed. Paul K. T. Sih.
Kuroki, Saburo. "Modernization on the Law." *Hikaku hōgaku,* 6: 2 (March 1971), English version, pp. 4–5.
Lai, Tse-han; Ramon H. Myers, and Wou Wei. *A Tragic Beginning: The Taiwan Uprising of February 28, 1947.* Stanford, Calif.: Stanford University Press, 1991.
Lee, Tai-Yung. "The Legal Status of Korean Women." In *Legal System of Korea,* ed. Chun Shin-Yong. Seoul: International Cultural Foundation, 1975.
Liao, Joshua. "Formosa Speaks." In the appendix of *Formosa under Chinese Nationalist Rule,* by Fred W. Riggs. New York: Macmillan, 1952.
Liu, Chang Bin. "Chinese Commercial Law in the Late Ch'ing (1842–1911): Jurisprudence and the Disputes Resolution Process in Taiwan." Ph.D. diss., University of Washington, 1983.
Lockenour, Roy M. "The Chinese Court System." *Temple Law Quarterly,* 5 (1931), pp. 253–59.
Mitchell, Richard H. *Thought Control in Prewar Japan.* Ithaca, N.Y.: Cornell University Press, 1976.
Moser, Michael J. *Law and Social Change in a Chinese Community: A Case Study from Rural Taiwan.* Dobbs Ferry, N.Y.: Oceana Publications, 1982.
Mukai, Ken, and Nobuyoshi Toshitani. "The Progress and Problems of Compiling the Civil Code in the Early Meiji Era." Trans. Dan Fenno Henderson. *Law in Japan,* 1 (1967), pp. 25–59.
Myers, Ramon H. "Taiwan under Ch'ing Imperial Rule, 1684–1895: The Traditional Order." *Journal of the Institute of Chinese Studies of the Chinese University of Hong Kong,* 4: 2 (Dec. 1971), pp. 495–522.
———. "Taiwan under Ch'ing Imperial Rule, 1684–1895: The Traditional Economy." *Journal of the Institute of Chinese Studies of the Chinese University of Hong Kong,* 5: 2 (Dec. 1972), pp. 373–411.
Myers, Ramon H., and Mark R. Peattie, eds. *The Japanese Colonial Empire, 1895–1945.* Princeton, N.J.: Princeton University Press, 1984.
Nakano, Tomio. *The Ordinance Power of the Japanese Emperor.* Baltimore, Md.: John Hopkins Press, 1923.
Noda, Yosiyuki. *Introduction to Japanese Law.* Trans. Anthony H. Angelo. Tokyo: University of Tokyo Press, 1976.

Okamatsu, Santaro, comp. *Provisional Report on Investigation of Laws and Customs in the Island of Formosa*. Kobe, 1900. Reprint. Taipei: Ch'eng-wen Publishing Co., 1971.

Osborne, Milton E. *The French Presence in Cochinchina and Cambodia: Rule and Response (1859–1905)*. Ithaca, N.Y.: Cornell University Press, 1969.

Pasternak, Burton. *Kinship and Community in Two Chinese Villages*. Stanford Calif.: Stanford University Press, 1972.

Peattie, Mark R. "Japanese Attitudes toward Colonialism, 1895–1945." In *The Japanese Colonial Empire, 1895–1945*, ed. Ramon H. Myers and Mark R. Peattie.

———. "Introduction." In *The Japanese Colonial Empire, 1895–1945*, ed. Ramon H. Myers and Mark R. Peattie.

P'eng, Ming-min. *A Taste of Freedom: Memoirs of a Formosan Independence Leader*. New York: Holt, Rinehart and Winston, 1972.

Rice, Joseph W. "Notes on International Law." *American Law Review*, 42 (1908), pp. 891–96.

Robinson, Michael E. "Nationalism and Human-Rights Thought in Korea under Colonial Rule." In *Human Rights in Korea: Historical and Political Perspective*, ed. William Shaw.

Shaw, William, ed. *Human Rights in Korea: Historical and Political Perspective*. Cambridge, Mass.: Harvard University Press, 1991.

Sih, Paul K. T., ed. *Taiwan in Modern Times*. New York: St. John's University Press, 1973.

Song, Sang Hyun, ed. *Introduction to the Law and Legal System of Korea*. Seoul: Kyung Mun Sa Publishing Co, 1983.

Stead, Alfred, ed. *Japan by the Japanese: A Survey by Its Highest Authorities*. New York: Dodd, Mead, 1904.

Takayanagi, Kenzo. "A Century of Innovation: The Development of Japanese Law, 1868–1961." In *Law in Japan: The Legal Order in a Changing Society*, ed. Arthur Taylor von Mehren.

Takekoshi, Yosaburo. *Japanese Rule in Formosa*. Trans. George Braithwaite. London: Longmans, Green, 1907.

———. "Japan's Colonial Policy." In *Japan to America*, ed. Naoichi Masaoka. New York: G. P. Putnam's Sons, 1914.

Tipton, Elise K. *The Japanese Police State: The Tokkō in Interwar Japan*. Honolulu: University of Hawaii Press, 1990.

Tsurumi, E. Patricia. *Japanese Colonial Education in Taiwan, 1895–1945*. Cambridge, Mass.: Harvard University Press, 1977.

U.S. Department of the Navy, Office of the Chief of Naval Operations. *Civil Affairs Handbook: Taiwan (Formosa), Taichu Province, OPNAV 13-26*. Washington, D.C.: U.S. Government Printing Office, 1944.

———. *Civil Affairs Handbook: Taiwan (Formosa), Taihoku Province, OPNAV 13-27*. Washington, D.C.: U.S. Government Printing Office, 1944.

———. *Civil Affairs Handbook: Taiwan (Formosa), OPNAV 50E-12*. Washington, D.C.: U.S. Government Printing Office, 1944.

von Mehren, Arthur Taylor, ed. *Law in Japan: The Legal Order in a Changing Society*. Cambridge, Mass.: Harvard University Press, 1963.

Walz, W. E. "A Constitutional Struggle in Japan." *American Law Review*, 32 (1898), pp. 31–33.

Wang, Tay-sheng. "Chapter 4: Taiwan." In *Asian Legal Systems: Law, Society, and Pluralism in East Asia*, ed. Tan Poh-Ling. Sydney: Butterworths, 1997.

Wichberg, Edgar. "Continuities in Land Tenure, 1900–1940." In *The Anthropology of Taiwanese Society*, ed. Emily Martin Ahern and Hill Gates.

Wolf, Arthur P., and Chieh-shan Huang. *Marriage and Adoption in China, 1895–1945*. Stanford, Calif.: Stanford University Press, 1980.

Wolf, Margery. *Women and the Family in Rural Taiwan*. Stanford, Calif.: Stanford University Press, 1972.

Index

Aborigines: history of, 5; defined, 9, 211*n*46; population of, 10; race and culture, 13; and Dutch education, 15; segregation of, 18, 20–21. *See also* Ethnic relations

Administrative mediation: reduction of judicial expenditure, 50–51; reasons for enactment of, 89; contents of, 90–91; use of, 91, 95, 235*n*142; importance of, 94; and hortatory proceeding in courts, 98

Adoption: of daughters, 59, 167, 168; requirements for, 161, 167; between Taiwanese and Japanese, 247*n*6. *See also* Family and succession law

Alien rulers. *See* Outside rulers

Amended Criminal Regulations (1873), 27

Application of Civil Statutes Order (1922), 53, 145

Appraisals for regimes, 26–27, 170–74, 176–79, 181

Armed resistance: and legislative institutions, 38; initial, 38, 45–46, 105–6, 118; political ideas for, 107, 112; in 1907–16 period, 112–13; as exception, 114

Arms regulations, 19, 21

Arrangement for Large-lease (1904), 50, 151

Assault, 99, 120–22, 124, 242*n*111

Assimilation Society, 113–14

Bandit Punishment Law (1898): provisions of, 47, 128 196–97, 224*n*90; enactment of, 50, 54, 56, 110; application of, 115, 125, 243*n*114. *See also* Banditry

Banditry: in Ch'ing period, 22, 124; legislation for, 50; bandit cases in temporary court, 51, 107–8, 110–11, 112–13; and number of judicial officials, 75; bandits killed without trial, 106, 108, 111; political "bandits" and real bandits, 106–7, 238*n*16; bandit cases in ordinary courts, 108–9, 112; pardon for, 110–11, 239*n*35; cases not prosecuted or acquitted, 111, 113, 239*n*51; annihilation of, 119. *See also* Colonial courts; Political criminals

Banjin. See Aborigines

Bankruptcy law, 156, 160

Barbarian areas, 9

Boissonade, Gustave, 31

Burglary Prevention Law, 54

Capitalism: in Japan, 27–28, 33; in Taiwan, 51, 59, 227*n*163, 250*n*90

277

Central government: supervision of, 39, 44, 221*n*52; and determination of colonial law, 42, 43, 145, 146, 221*n*46; minister of justice in, 64, 70, 81; of China, 177

Chang-chou people, 22, 23

Checks, 159

Cheng band. *See* Cheng regime

Cheng Ch'eng-kung, 16, 212*n*10, 213*n*40

Cheng Ching, 16, 213*nn*30,32

Cheng regime, 16–18, 25, 173, 212*n*10

Cheng Sung-yü, 58, 59

Chia-i, 74

Chien-tan, 159

China: relations with Taiwan, 13, 18, 37, 105; Westernization of law in, 175–76. *See also* Taiwan; Western law, reception of

Chinese imperial law. *See* Traditional Chinese law

Chinese legal traditions. *See* Traditional Chinese law

Chinese mainlanders: defined, 9, 175, 211*n*46; compared to Japanese mainlanders, 177–78

Chinese people: defined, 9; population of, 10; civil and commercial matters involving, 49; criminals, 126–27

Ch'ing Code, 19, 141, 142, 248*n*48. *See also* Traditional Chinese law

Ch'ing regime: officials of, 19, 21; rule of, 20, 26, 173; magistrates of, 86, 124, 127–28, 141, 216*n*85, 235*n*144. *See also* Government policy

Ch'üan-chou people, 22, 23

Chūkaminkokujin. *See* Chinese people

Civil administrators, 47, 71

Civil Code: of 1890, 31, 33; of 1896 and 1898, 31, 49–56 *passim*, 144, 145–46, 152–54, 162, 167

Civil Code Enforcement Order, 53

Civil, Commercial, and Criminal Law (1898), 47, 48, 49, 195, 224*n*101

Civil Disputes Mediation Law, 50, 55, 56, 90. *See also* Administrative mediation

Civil law: Westernization of, 7, 140, 146, 168–69; in Meiji reform, 30–31; in experimental period, 45–46; in 1898–1922 period, 49–50; in 1923–45 period, 53, 55; under common law system, 144–45. *See also* Civil lawsuits; Family and succession law; Taiwanese customs

Civil lawsuits: in Ch'ing period, 24; in military administration period, 45; impartiality of, 87; civil trials represented by lawyers, 88, 235*n*131; numbers of civil trials and hortatory suits in, 91–93, 236*n*160; reasons for increase, 94–99; rate of success in civil trials, 96–99; parties in, 234*n*124. *See also* Civil law; Colonial courts

Civil Litigation Order for Inhabitants of Taiwan, 45

Code of Civil Procedure: of 1890, 30, 50, 53, 91; of 1926, 53, 91, 236*n*156

Code of Criminal Instruction (1880), 30, 48

Code of Criminal Procedure (1922), 55, 227*n*157

Colonial courts: and old customs, 4, 142–44; reported decisions, 8, 210*n*39; military tribunals, 45, 63, 106, 129, 241*n*87; establishment of, 46, 63; Temporary Court, 46, 65, 107; District Court, 46, 63–67 *passim*, 95, 108–9; punishment of Japanese, 52, 131–32; administrative court, 60, 66, 172; jury system in, 60,

INDEX

130; Court of Appeal, 63, 65, 67, 110, 112, 144; Higher Court, 63–67 *passim*, 144, 168, 238*n*21; two or three instances in lawsuits, 63–67; caseload of, 64, 95; rejection of old disputes in, 64, 89, 94, 229*n*10; with supreme court in Taiwan, 64, 65, 144, 229*n*13; Appellate Division, 65–67; Re-appeal Division, 65–67, 144; Branch or Detached Office of District Court, 66–67; Collegiate Division, 66–67; Single Division, 66–67; relations between judges and procurators, 70–71; court building, 74, 179, 183; number of, 74–75, 95, 135, 236*n*161; number of personnel in, 75–76, 95; population per judge in, 76–78; language problem in, 84–85, 234*n*107; interpretation of *jishu* in, 110; Council of Judges in, 144; General Meeting of Judges in, 168; legacy of, 179–81, 183. *See also* Judicial independence; Judicial officials; Procuracy

Colonial education, 57, 81, 96, 237*n*169

Colonialism: and reception of law, 5; French, 37, 69, 171, 172; for assimilation, 37, 226*n*140; British, 37, 38, 69; and constitutional law, 40; of the United States, 172. *See also* Dutch rule in Taiwan; Japanese colonialism; Spanish rule in Taiwan

Commercial Code, 53, 146, 157, 251*n*94

Commercial Code Enforcement Order, 53

Commission for the Investigation of Old Laws and Customs in Taiwan, 142–43, 146

Communal strife. *See Fen-lei-hsieh-tou*

Company law, 156–59, 225*n*130

Conciliation, 24, 30, 91

Constitutional law. *See* Meiji Constitution

Consultative Council, 42–43, 177, 222*n*53

Council of Grand Justices, 181

Court Organization Law (1890), 29, 64, 69

Court system: in crime control structure, 121–22. *See also* Colonial courts; Japanese courts

Crime: in Ch'ing period, 124; and police summary judgment, 124–25; serious and minor, 124–25; number of criminals, 125–27; and social order, 137. *See also* Criminal cases

Criminal cases: impartiality of, 87; adjudication by court system (judicial officials) or police summary judgment (police officers) for, 100–103; rate of acquittal, 107–9, 111, 117, 134; rate of nonprosecution, 107–9, 117, 134, 182. *See also* Criminal law; Colonial courts; Police summary judgment

Criminal Code: of 1880, 30–31, 32, 45–46, 110, 223*n*87; of 1907, 47, 54, 115, 144

Criminal Indemnity Law (1933), 123, 130

Criminal Instruction Order for Inhabitants of Taiwan, 45

Criminal law: Westernization of, 7, 128–29, 131, 135; in Meiji reform, 29–31, 32–33; special law violations in, 31, 47, 50, 54, 121–22; for authoritarian control, 32, 50, 54–55, 115; in experimental period, 45–46; in 1898–1922 period, 47–49; on confession, 49, 113, 119; in 1923–45 period, 54–55, 123; on the scope of trial, 129; on separation of procurators and judges in criminal proceedings, 129; Japanese legacy in, 181–82

279

Criminal punishments: death penalty, 106–13 *passim*, 132, 181, 256*n*51; equality of, 131–32; assurance of, 132–34; severity of, 132–33; Western-style, 135; traditional Chinese, 246*n*165. *See also* Flogging

Customary law: defined, 142–43; Westernization of, 143; and statutory regulation, 143–44; codification of, 144–45; for family and succession matters, 145. *See also* Civil law; Family and succession law; Land rights; Taiwanese customs

Debt, 141, 159, 160, 168, 237*n*164
Defense council. *See* Lawyers
Delegated legislation. *See* Law Relating to Laws and Ordinances to Be Enforced in Taiwan
Den Kenjirō, 53
Deposit for appeal, 64–65, 130, 229*n*10
Dispositions for Taiwanese Military Criminals, 45, 106, 222*nn*59,62
Dispute resolution: in Ch'ing period, 24; numbers of civil lawsuits and administrative mediation cases for, 91–93; and urbanization, 95. *See also* Administrative mediation; Civil lawsuits; Conciliation; Mediation
Disrespectful acts, 32, 115–16
Divorce, 166–68, 253*n*159. *See also* Family and succession law
Due process, 128–31, 245*n*150
Dutch East India Company, 14
Dutch rule in Taiwan, 14–16, 173; colonial judiciary, 69

Emperor: status of, 27, 33; legislative prerogative for the colony, 37
Ethnic relations, 7, 22–23, 57

Exceptions of Applied Statutes, 53, 55
Executive Enforcement Law, 115, 240*n*65
Extraterritoriality, 28–29, 208*n*17, 223*n*78

Family: institutions, 4; elders, 161–62; estates, 161, 163, 164, 167; head of, 161–62; as economic body, 163–64; division of, 163–64; joint, 163; units (*fang*), 163, 167. *See also* Family and succession law
Family and succession law: courts and changes of, 4, 161; Japanese, 33; Taiwanese, 55–56, 59, 145–46, 227*n*164; Westernization of, 160–61, 164, 168. *See also* Taiwanese customs
Farmer Association, 114, 115
February 28 Incident, 131, 178–81 *passim*, 245*n*151
Fen-lei-hsieh-tou, 22–23, 125, 215*n*75
Fine and Flogging Law (1904), 48, 120
Flogging: punishment by, 48, 51, 120–21, 123, 135; abolition of, 54, 133, 135

Gambling: offenses of, 51, 99, 124–25, 226*n*134; number of cases, 119, 241*n*87, 242*n*111, 243*n*121
Gendarmerie, 46, 107–8
GGT Court Organization Law, 46
Gotō Shimpei, 47, 111
Government policy: Ch'ing, 18–20; Japanese, 36–38, 41, 46–47, 53; ROC, 176–77. *See also* Colonialism
Government-General of Taiwan (GGT) Court. *See* Colonial courts
Government-General of Taiwan (Taiwan Sōtokufu, GGT): archives of, 8, 43, 73, 209*n*36; military administration of, 38, 46; and colonial law, 44, 61; and judicial expenditure, 51,

INDEX

74, 77, 120, 231*n*59; and movement for a Taiwan parliament, 60; Department of Judicial Affairs in, 64, 67, 69. *See also* Central government

Governor-general of Taiwan: broad and arbitrary power of, 37; executive and military authority of, 38–39, 223*n*76; legislative authority of, 38–44, 128; judicial authority of, 39, 64, 69–72, 81, 230*n*33; military, 46, 47; civil, 53; counterpart of, 177

Hakka people, 9, 22, 215*n*77. *See also* Ethnic relations

Han Chinese people in Taiwan: as settlers, 4, 23, 34–35; immigration, 13–20 *passim*, population, 15, 17, 20, 214*n*41; compared to those in mainland China, 17, 24–26, 173, 254*n*6; leading class of, 25–26; culture of, 58; kingdom of, 112. *See also* Aborigines; Hakka people; Southern Fukienese people; Taiwanese society

Hara Kei (Takashi), 37–38, 53

Hokō Law (1898), 48

Hokō system: name of, 9; contents of, 48; and anti-Japanese activities, 50, 108, 118, 225*n*123; under police control, 51, 113, 122; abolition of, 54, 226*n*151; for mediation, 90; collective responsibility under, 131, 136

Ho-ku, 156–59

Hontōjin See Taiwanese people

Hōritsu. See Statutes

Hortatory proceeding, 91–94, 98

Household Registration Law, 141, 162

Households: system, 33, 162; heads of, 161–64, 165, 251*n*113; registry of, 163, 164. *See also* Family and succession law

Hsiao-tsu. *See* Land rights: *hsiao-tsu*

Hsi-lai-an (Tainan) Incident, 108, 112, 114, 115, 241*n*80

Hsin-chu, 74, 135

Hua-lien, 74

Hui-p'iao, 159–60

Human rights, 32, 39, 58, 88, 137, 172

Ie. *See* Household

I-lan, 74

Immigration regulations, 18, 20

Imperial Diet: and issue of Title 63, 38–40; and Taiwan parliament, 57, 61; discussion of Taiwan's judiciary, 68–69

Inheritance: of all sons, 163, 167, 253*n*155; limited, 167–68; waive of, 167–68. *See also* Family and succession law

Injury, 124, 125

Interests of the people: 11, 20, 27, 34, 51, 173; and modern Western law, 138, 179

Itō Hirobumi, 37

Japanese Army or Navy Criminal Code, 45

Japanese colonialism: legacy of, 4, 183; studies in Japan, 6; unlike Western colonialism, 7, 64, 69, 84; influenced by idea of "Central Kingdom," 34, 38; Taiwan as showcase of, 36, 47, 223*n*83; and Western powers, 36; policy of assimilation in, 41, 52–53, 85, 114, 145, 207*n*5; compared to Western colonialism, 45, 47–50, 56, 69, 86. *See also* Colonialism

Japanese courts: establishment of, 28–29, 228*n*3; Great Court of Cassation (Daishin'in), 29, 63, 64; Appellate Chamber (courts of appeal), 29, 65; administrative court, 32, 66; District Court, 65; Ward Court, 65

Japanese people: defined, 9, 141, 220*n*37; population, 10; first contact with Taiwan, 13; and hierarchical society, 33; and imperialism, 34; laws applied only to, 48; civil and commercial matters of, 49; treatment of, 51, 52, 131–32, 156, 227*n*163, 250*nn*87,90; anti-GGT, 52; in early days of Japanese rule, 52; criminals, 126–27. *See also* Japanese colonialism; Japanese regime

Japanese regime: with sinicized legal culture, 7, 170–71; experience in homeland of, 8, 27–35; and colonial rule, 37, 218*n*12; Meiji legal reform taught by, 46, 47, 50, 86, 137, 149, 171; criminal policy of, 119, 124, 132–33; as Westernized government, 137. *See also* Government policy

Joint-stock company, 158

Judges. *See* Judicial officials

Judicial examination, 80, 81, 232*nn*77,78

Judicial independence: in Japan, 29, 68, 69–70; in Taiwan, 46, 60, 67–74, 231*n*56

Judicial institutions. *See* Colonial courts; Japanese courts

Judicial officials: legal commentaries of, 8; in Japan, 28–30; security of tenure, 46, 68–71; authority of, 49, 50, 51, 71, 129–30, 244*n*137; abilities and virtue of, 69, 72, 73, 84–86; qualifications of, 69–70; appointment of, 70, 80–83; promotion and discipline of, 70, 73; executive officials' relations with, 71; number of, 76; names and number of Taiwanese, 79–82, 232*n*88; probationary legal officials, 80, 82; Japanese, 83; honesty of, 86–87; in lawmaking, 144.

See also Ch'ing regime: magistrates of; Colonial courts

Judicial protection, 135

Judicial Yuan, 179

Jurists: Japanese, 8, 28, 171; Taiwanese, 9, 58, 59, 172

Juvenile reformatory, 135

Kakyō. *See* Chinese people

Kaohsiung, 74

Keelung, 13, 16, 36

Kinship, 4

Kirkwood, William Montague Hammett, 37

Kodama Gentarō, 47, 64, 68, 69, 71, 107–8, 110–11

Kōminka, 53

Korea: similarities to Taiwan, 7, 41, 60, 65, 79, 83, 90, 99; size of, 12; differences from Taiwan, 42, 65, 66, 71, 77, 88; 117, 118, 173–76 *passim*, 234*n*112; March First Movement of, 52; legal professionals in, 79–80, 83, 88, 233*n*92; governor-general of, 221*n*40; colonial courts in, 229*nn*14, 21, 230*n*35, 230*n*50; administrative mediation in, 236*n*145

Koxinga. *See* Cheng Ch'eng-kung

Kuo Huai-i Incident, 15, 213*nn*22,40

Kuo-hu, 155

Kuomintang government. *See* Republic of China regime

Lai Ho, 128, 130, 239*n*55

Land rights: *hsiao-tsu*, 24, 25, 147–55 *passim*; *ta-tsu*, 24, 25, 147–54 *passim*; effect of registration of, 143, 150–54 *passim*, 182; *yeh-chu*, 146–55 *passim*; ownership, 147–55 *passim*, 249*nn*54, 55; *ti-chi*, 147, 151, 153–54; *po*, 148;

pledge, 148, 153–54; *po-keng*, 148, 151–54; *tien* lease, 148, 151–54; *tien* pledge, 148, 150, 152–54, 248*n*48; *yung-tien*, 148, 151, 153–54; *ekiken*, 149, 151, 154; *t'ai*, 149, 151–54, 155; duration of, 150–51, 153–54; emphyteusis, 150, 153–54, 249*n*57; lease, 150, 153–54; *ch'i-keng-t'ai*, 153; mortgage, 153–54, 155; servitude, 154; in continental European law, 248*n*43
Land Survey Regulations (1898), 50, 150, 151–52
Land system: crown fields, 15, 213*n*26; military colony system, 17; aboriginal land, 19, 20–21; concealed fields, 21; three-tiered system of multiple ownership, 24; land survey for, 50, 146, 149–50; "one land, one owner," 151. *See also* Land rights
Large-lease. *See* Land rights: *ta-tsu*
Law: disrespect for, 20, 137; abiding, 33, 136, 182; rule by, 172, 181; rule of, 172
Law for Prevention and Disposition of Banditry (1930), 123
Law for Protection and Observation of Thought Criminals, 118
Law of Bills of Exchange, 156, 159, 160
Law of Procedure in Non-contentious Litigation, 53
Law of Procedure in Personal Matters, 53
Law Relating to Laws and Ordinances to Be Enforced in Taiwan: constitutionality of, 39–40; duration of, 39, 41, 42; enactment of, 39; for policy of assimilation, 41, 53; revision of, 41–42; actual implementation of, 42–44, 177, 221*n*45; Taiwanese perspectives on, 57. *See also* Central government; Meiji Constitution

Lawyers: in Japan, 28; trial advocates, 46, 87, 235*n*126; in bandit cases, 51; as dissenters, 52, 88; number of, 76, 84; social status of, 80; Taiwanese, 81, 83–84, 87, 88, 235*n*133; Japanese, 83, 84, 87, 88, 233*n*101; service of, 87–88; population per lawyer, 88–89
League for Attainment of Local Autonomy, 61, 114
League for the Creation of a Taiwan Parliament, 115, 117
Legal dualism, 15
Legal education: in Japan, 28, 79; in Korea, 79; in Taihoku Imperial University, 79; Taiwanese students in, 79–81, 83, 232*n*84; in private or imperial universities, 81, 83
Legal professionals. *See* Judicial officials; Lawyers
Legal theory: decisions according to, 46, 140, 144, 166; Japanese civil law as, 55, 143, 162, 167, 168; in courts of Republican China, 189
Legislative Yuan, 178, 179
Limited Company Law, 158
Lin Ch'eng-lu, 58, 59
Lineage, 4
Lin-i-p'u Incident, 108, 112
Liu Ming-ch'uan, 26
Liu-chia Incident, 112, 113
Lo Fu-hsing, 112
Lo-han-chiao. *See* Vagrants

Mainland law: extension of, 41, 44, 53–54, 58, 61, 65, 71, 154; as a principle, 45, 52–56; defined, 211*n*45, 220*n*37. *See also* Ordinances; *Ritsurei*; Statutes

Marriage: between Han Chinese and aborigines, 18, 20; adopted daughters-in-law, 59, 165; concubines, 59, 166, 168, 253*n*160; requirements for, 161, 164–65; adopted sons-in-law, 165; bridewealth (as a sale), 165, 166; invited husbands, 165; invited sons-in-law, 165; Japanese uxorilocal, 165; selling, giving, pledging, or mortgaging wives, 165; between Taiwanese and Japanese, 247*n*6. *See also* Family and succession law
Martial law, 17, 190
Massacre: by Japanese regime, 106, 107, 113, 137, 239*n*30; by ROC regime, 178, 254*n*22
Mediation: in Ch'ing period, 24, 50; didactic, 50; unofficial, 90, 91. *See also* Administrative mediation
Medium and small enterprises, 158
Meiji Constitution: and judicial independence, 29; enactment of, 32; applied to Taiwan, 37, 39, 68, 179, 219*nn*19,20
Meiji government: establishment of, 27; leaders and nature of, 31–35, 40
Miao-li Incident, 108, 112, 113
Military orders, 38, 223*n*70
Misdemeanors, 100
Municipalities, 74, 95

Naichijin. See Japanese people
National Defense Security Law, 123
National Mobilization Law (1938), 55, 123, 176
Nationalism: Chinese, 5, 23; modern, 7, 53, 112; Taiwanese, 23, 57–58, 60, 114
Nationalist government. *See* Republic of China regime
Nationality, 211*n*44

Natural law, 32, 37
Negotiable instrument, 159, 160
Nichirei. See Military orders

Obligation: enforcement of, 141–42, 155; and courts, 142; right of, 153; in commercial transactions, 156
Official Regulations for the Justice Department (1872), 29
Okamatsu Santarō, 142, 145
Opium smoking, 51, 54, 119, 226*n*134
Ordinances: for application, 38–39, 53, 145; for exception, 41, 42, 53, 152–53; enacting process of, 44; as main source of law, 44, 54. *See also* Central government
Organic Regulation of Taiwan Provincial Administrative Executive Office, 177
Organic Regulation of the GGT, 39, 177
Otsu case (1891), 29, 68
Outer area, 218*n*12, 220*n*37
Outline of the New Criminal Code (1870), 27, 48
Outside rulers, 12–27 *passim*, 34, 35, 175

Pao-chia system. *See Hokō* system
Partnership law, 157
Peace Preservation Law: of 1887, 48; of 1925, 54, 115–19 *passim*, 240*nn*69,72, 241*nn* 74,86
Pei-p'u, 108, 112
Penalty Order for Inhabitants of Taiwan, 45, 47, 223*n*87
P'eng-hu. *See* Pescadores
People's Republic of China, 3, 175, 190
Pescadores, 12, 13, 14
P'ing-tan, 159
Police: function of procurator performed by, 46, 70, 76–77; authority

of, 49, 121, 129, 130, 245*n*141; and procurators, 81, 83; bribery of, 86, 131; for mediation, 90; inspectors, 99; as summary judgment officers, 99; superintendents, 99; and political criminals, 107–19 *passim*; and crime-control structure, 121–23; illegal means of investigation, 130, 131; spies, 130; ranks, 232*n*89. *See also* Hokō system; Police summary judgment

Police offenses, 99–100, 181

Police summary judgment: beginning of, 46; reasons for enactment of, 89, 101, 237*n*183; contents of, 99–100; review of courts for, 100, 101–3; and Fine and Flogging Law, 120; in crime-control structure, 121–22, 242*n*99; executive and judicial power in, 136

Political criminals: trials for, 65, 72; prosecution of, 73; in 1895–1902 period, 105–12; carrot-and-stick policy of Kodama, 110; in 1907–16 period, 112–13; in 1920s-mid-1930, 116–17; wartime, 118–19; postwar, 181

Political movements: Communists in, 54, 114, 115, 117, 239*n*56, 241*n*86; for home rule, 57, 228*n*171; liberalism and socialism in, 59–60; political parties in, 60, 114; lawyers in, 88; modern nonviolent, 113, 255*n*35; for farmers, 114, 115–16; for labor, 114; within legal establishment, 114; decline of, 118–19. *See also* Armed resistance; Political criminals; Taiwan parliament

Popular uprisings: in Ch'ing period, 19, 23; in Meiji Japan, 32. *See also* Armed resistance

Preliminary examination: power of examining magistrate in, 49, 129; cases of, 100, 130, 134

Preventive Prohibition Regulation (1892), 48

Prison, 135

Procuracy: in Japan, 64; Bureau of, 70; cases of, 100–103; and cases of political crimes, 107, 113, 119. *See also* Colonial courts; Judicial officials

Procurators. *See* Judicial officials

Promissory notes, 159

Public order: in Ch'ing period, 22, 124; punishment of unemployed persons for disturbing, 48; in Japanese period, 124–25, 132–33

Public Order Police Law; purpose of, 54, 115; in Taiwan Parliament case, 60, 72–73, 117; in farmer movement, 116; in law of Republican China, 175; punishment in, 240*n*70

Real estate, 146, 182. *See also* Land rights

Regulation regarding the Organization of the GGT Courts, 45

Republic of China (ROC) Civil Code, 182, 183

Republic of China (ROC) regime: and Cheng regime, 175; Japan and laws of, 175–76, 181–82, 189; nature of, 175; enforcement of laws of, 176; like Japanese regime, 177–79; judiciary of, 179–81

Republic of Formosa, 105–6, 173

Revon, Michel Joseph, 37

Righteous Army, 105–6

Ritsurei: definition and effect of, 38, 41, 42, 221*n*48; enacting process of, 42–43; and mainland law, 43, 44, 54, 55; as main source of law, 44, 54, 140; and Western law, 44–45

INDEX

Robbery, 124, 125, 243nn114,115
ROC. *See* Republic of China
Roman law, 37, 86, 142

Servants, female indentured, 59, 168
Shih Lang, 17
Shikō chokurei. *See* Ordinances: for application
Shinkokujin. *See* Chinese people
Sino-Japanese war: of 1894–95, 20, 36; of 1937–45, 55, 123, 189
Small-lease. *See* Land rights: *hsiao-tsu*
Sources of law. *See* Military orders; Ordinances; *Ritsurei*; Statutes
Southern Fukienese people, 9, 22. *See also* Ethnic relations
Spanish rule in Taiwan, 14–16, 173
Special colonial law, 45
Special Law for Civil Litigation (1905), 50, 55
Special Law for Criminal Litigation (1905), 49, 55
Special legal zone, in Japan, 39, 42, 44, 61, 143; in China, 177
Special Wartime Criminal Law, 55
Status law. *See* Family and succession law
Statutes: definition and effect of, 38, 41, 42, enforcement by ordinance or by *ritsurei*, 43
Suffrage, 172, 178
Summary Judgment Law (1904), 49, 56, 99, 100. *See also* Police summary judgment

Taichung, 74
Taihō geppō, 8, 210n40
Tainan, 14, 74
Taipei, 74, 179
Taishō liberalism, 52

T'ai-tung, 119–20
Taiwan: location and size of, 12, 34, 211n1; agriculture and commerce of, 15, 20, 25; as independent state, 16, 175; peace talks with China, 16, 213n32; as province of China, 19, 25, 174; as special district or ordinary administrative area, 37, 47, 177; sovereignty over, 106, 212n15; influences of Chinese and Japanese laws on, 189–91; and Western law, 190. *See also* Taiwan history; Western law, reception of
Taiwan Affairs Bureau, 37
Taiwan Civil Code (1909–14), 56, 145
Taiwan Civil Law (1908), 49, 50
Taiwan Criminal Law (1908), 47, 48, 49, 54
Taiwan Cultural Association, 58, 115, 240n60
Taiwan Forest Regulation, 115–16
Taiwan Forest Survey (1910), 50
Taiwan High Court, 179
Taiwan history: variant perspectives on, 3, 5, 10–11; in pre-1624 period, 13–14; in Dutch and Spanish period, 14–16; in Cheng period, 16–17; in Ch'ing period, 18–26
Taiwan kanshū kiji, 8, 210n40
Taiwan Land Registration Regulations (1905), 50, 151, 152
Taiwan Opium Law (1897), 48, 122, 125, 242n112. *See also* Opium smoking
Taiwan parliament: political movement for, 39, 57, 60–61, 114, 178, 179, 227n169; criminal cases relating to, 71–73, 79
Taiwan Peace Preservation Regulation (1900), 48, 52

Taiwan Police Offense Law, 115
Taiwan Popular Party, 60, 114, 115
Taiwan Press Law (1900), 48, 116
Taiwan Provincial Administration: governor-general of, 177, 255*n*28; Administrative Council in, 177. *See also* Governor-general of Taiwan
Taiwan seinen, 9
Taiwan shihō, 8, 210*n*40
Taiwan studies: and China studies, 3–5, 209*n*28; perspective of, 7, 184
Taiwan Vagrant Discipline Regulation (1906), 48, 119
Taiwanese Communist Party, 60, 114
Taiwanese customs: under Chinese legal tradition, 19, 163; transformed by modern Western law, 4, 86, 156, 168; dispute resolution in, 25, 45, 46, 49; maintenance or abolition of, 51, 58, 59; investigation of, 85; courts' application of, 85–86, 142, 156
Taiwanese people: defined, 9, 141, 210*n*43, 211*n*46, 247*n*6; population of, 10; as object of governance, 41; laws applied only to, 48, 49; civil and commercial matters of, 49, 140–46; demand for autonomous legal reform, 57–61, 178; discrimination against, 57, 79, 81, 83, 87, 131, 158; identity of, 57, 137; intellectuals, 57–62 *passim*, 114, 130–31, 254*n*6; criminals, 126–27, 136; indifference to politics, 137, 178; orphans in Asia, 137; submission to authority, 137, 182; shareholders, 158, 250*nn*90,91; as second-class citizens, 174; Japanese-speaking, 234*n*111
Taiwanese society: rulers of, 3, 8, 11, 12–27; uniqueness of, 4, 7, 34, 173; continuity of, 5, 6, 208*n*15; changes in, under Japanese rule, 6, 155; modern Western legal ideas in, 61, 139, 187; esteemed professionals in, 88, 234*n*119; economic development of, 96, 146; and modern state authority, 105, 111, 113, 118, 140, 168; different historical experience in, 209*n*26. *See also* Han Chinese people in Taiwan
Takano Takenori, 68, 69, 71, 107, 111, 238*n*23
Takasagozoku. *See* Aborigines
Tanshui, 16
Tao-hao, 160
Ta-tsu. *See* Land rights: *ta-tsu*
Taxation, 15, 17, 21
Tegata, 160
Tennō. *See* Emperor
Theft, 124, 125, 241*n*87, 242*n*111, 243*n*119
Thought control: by procurators, 73, 83, 116, 117; law for, 115, 118; by special high police, 116, 117, 118, 241*n*76
Title 3. *See* Law Relating to Laws and Ordinances to Be Enforced in Taiwan
Title 31. *See* Law Relating to Laws and Ordinances to Be Enforced in Taiwan
Title 63. *See* Law Relating to Laws and Ordinances to Be Enforced in Taiwan
Tokugawa period: shogunate, 13, 27; traditions, 29–30, 32, 48
Tokurei chokurei. *See* Ordinances: for exception
Torture: in Japan, 30, 245*n*140; in traditional China, 49; in Taiwan, 113, 118, 119, 130, 137. *See also* Police

Traditional Chinese law: in Ch'ing period, 4, 5, 19, 63; compared to modern Western law, 7, 34, 67–68, 105, 127–28, 131, 135, 142, 243n129; in Cheng period, 17; influence on Japanese law, 27–34 *passim*, 189; Legalism in, 34; in colonial laws, 47–56 *passim*, 90, 135, 136; regarding civil matters, 141
Treaty of Shimonoseki, 37, 105
T'u-k'u Incident, 112
T'ung-yang-hsi. *See* Marriage: adopted daughters-in-law

Urbanization, 4, 95–96, 207n12

Vagrant discipline system: and political oppression, 118, 123; establishment of, 119–20; in crime control structure, 121, 123, 137; in postwar law, 181–82
Vagrants: in Ch'ing period, 22; in Japanese period, 125; in postwar period, 243n118
Violence Punishment Law, 54, 115, 116–17, 240n70

Warrants, 130–31
Wartime Exceptions of Court Organization Law, 66
Wartime legal system, 54–55, 189–90
Wartime Special Civil Law, 55
Western law, reception of: in Korea, 5, 7; in Taiwan, 5, 6, 7, 54–56, 61–62, 174–76, 184–87; in China, 6, 7; 175–76, 189–90; theory of, 7, 208n18,

209n34; legislative, 8; societal, 8; in Asian societies, 26, 216n96; in Japan, 27–33, 172, 189; decisive factors of selection in, 28, 31–33, 56; and treaty revision (extraterritoriality), 28, 29, 31, 175; progovernment, 31, 50; "autonomous" adoption in, 33; comparison of Taiwan to Japan, 46, 55, 56, 62, 77–78, 88–89, 90, 104, 156, 171, 173, 227n163; Taiwanese attitudes toward, 58–61, 138; meaning of access to court in, 89, 104; in dispute resolution, 93, 94, 98; and obedience to law, 137; as core of Japan-led reform, 170; comparison of Taiwan to China, 171–72, 173, 208n25. *See also* Western-style law
Western nations: first contact with Taiwan, 14, merchants, 25; pressure on Japan, 27, 28
Western-style law: Japanized and colonialized, 5; in colonial legislation, 8; for capitalism, 27–28, 156, 227n163; French law as model of, 29, 30; and fundamental principles of European law, 31, 47; German law as model of, 32; for criminal matters, 47–48, 54–55, 138–39; for civil matters, 49–50, 55, 168–69; legal rights in, 141–42, 155;. *See also* Western law, reception of
World War II, 189
Worship, 4, 215n82

Yu Ch'ing-fang, 112
Yun-lin, 107

www.ingramcontent.com/pod-product-compliance
Lightning Source LLC
Chambersburg PA
CBHW021348300426
44114CB00012B/1129